Helping Students with Dyslexia and Dysgraphia Make Connections

Helping Students with Dyslexia and Dysgraphia Make Connections

Differentiated Instruction Lesson Plans in Reading and Writing

Virginia W. Berninger, Ph.D.

University of Washington
Seattle

and

Beverly J. Wolf, M.Ed.

Slingerland Institute
Bellevue, Washington

·P·A·U·L·H·
BROOKES
PUBLISHING Co.®

Baltimore • London • Sydney

Paul H. Brookes Publishing Co.
Post Office Box 10624
Baltimore, Maryland 21285-0624
USA

www.brookespublishing.com

Typeset by Integrated Publishing Solutions, Grand Rapids, Michigan.
Manufactured in the United States of America by Sheridan Books, Inc.,
Chelsea, Michigan.

Library of Congress Cataloging-in-Publication Data

Berninger, Virginia Wise.
    Helping students with dyslexia and dysgraphia make connections : differentiated
instruction lesson plans in reading and writing / Virginia W. Berninger, Beverly J. Wolf.
        p.   cm.
    Includes bibliographical references.
    ISBN-13: 978-1-59857-021-2 (spiral-bound)
    ISBN-10: 1-59857-021-8
    1. Dyslexic children—Education.   2. Students with disabilities.   3. Reading disability
4. Learning disabilities.   5. Agraphia.   I. Wolf, Beverly J.   II. Title.
    LC4708.B46   2009
    371.91'44–dc22
                                                                                2009024085

British Library Cataloguing in Publication data are available from the British Library.

2013   2012   2011   2010   2009
10   9   8   7   6   5   4   3   2   1

Contents

UNIT I   Word Detectives

UNIT II   Mark Twain Writers Workshop

UNIT III   John Muir Writing-Readers in Science

UNIT IV   Sequoyah Writing Reader Club

About the Authors

Virginia W. Berninger, Ph.D., Professor and Director, Multidisciplinary Learning Disabilities Center, University of Washington, 322 Miller Box 363600, Seattle, WA 98195

Virginia Berninger is a professor in the Educational Psychology Department at the University of Washington. She has been director and principal investigator of the Eunice Kennedy Shriver National Institute of Child Health and Human Development (NICHD)-funded Literacy Trek and Multidisciplinary Learning Disabilities Center at the university. A former general and special educator and reading specialist, Dr. Berninger is also a licensed clinical psychologist. Dr. Berninger's research focuses on nature–nurture interactions in learning to read and write. She studies the language and nonlanguage processes in children with dyslexia, dysgraphia, or language learning disability and in typically developing readers and writers. With a team of brain imagers, Berninger also studies related brain processes and how they change as a result of specific instructional treatments.

Beverly J. Wolf, M.Ed., Director, Slingerland Institute, 12729 Northup Way, Suite 1, Bellevue, WA 98005

Beverly Wolf is a trainer of teachers and President of the Board of Directors of the Slingerland Institute in Washington State. She has worked with children and adults with language learning disabilities for more than 30 years in her positions as Dean of Faculty at the Slingerland Institute and Director Emeritus of the Hamlin Robinson School for students with dyslexia, and through contributions to local and national organizations. She has served on both local and national boards of The International Dyslexia Association and is also author of independent activity and language materials for classroom use.

Introduction

Problems in written language acquisition of children whose development is otherwise in the normal range are considered specific kinds of learning disabilities and may affect 10%–15% of students. *Dyslexia* is a word of Greek origin. *Dys* is a prefix that means "impaired." *Lexia* is a base word that is derived from the word *lexicon* (the mental dictionary of word meanings, spellings, and pronunciations) and means "word." Thus, students with dyslexia are impaired in word-level skills such as decoding, word reading, and spelling. Both accuracy and rate may be impaired, or only rate.

Decoding problems are usually assessed by asking children to read pseudowords (i.e., pronounceable words that do not have conventional meaning but sound like English words, such as in the "Jabberwocky" poem in *Through the Looking-Glass*, by Lewis Carroll). Word reading problems may be assessed by asking a child to pronounce real words that do have meaning on a list or in a passage with context clues. Some children do better when context clues are available.

Dyslexia is not just a reading problem. Invariably, students with dyslexia also have problems spelling (Berninger, Nielsen, Abbott, Wijsman, & Raskind, 2008). However, except for impaired phonological awareness interfering with learning to decode, read, and spell words, their oral language listening comprehension and verbal reasoning are spared. Once children with dyslexia learn to recognize words at a grade-appropriate level, their reading comprehension tends to be grade-appropriate (Berninger, 2000).

Some children, however, do have significant oral language problems, including listening comprehension and reading comprehension problems, in addition to the word decoding, word reading, and spelling problems that affect their learning to read and write. These children have oral and written language learning disability (OWL LD) rather than dyslexia per se. Chapter 4 of *Teaching Students with Dyslexia and Dysgraphia* (Berninger & Wolf, 2009), the companion to this workbook, provides more information about the nature of these oral language problems (e.g., phonological awareness as well as other aspects of oral language).

Dysgraphia is also of Greek origin. As noted previously, *dys* is a prefix that means "impaired." *Graphia* is a base word that means "letter form," "hand," or "making letter forms by hand." Students with dysgraphia, therefore, are impaired in letter writing skills. Their handwriting may be impaired in 1) legibility—how easily others can recognize their letters out of word context, 2) automaticity—how many legible letters they can write in 15 seconds, and 3) speed—how much time it takes them to complete a writing task. Students with handwriting disabilities may also have more difficulty in learning to spell written words. In one form of dysgraphia, which does not occur as often as typical dysgraphia, the child's handwriting is adequate, but written spelling problems occur in the absence of reading problems. Fayol, Zorman, and Lété (2009) showed that about 4% of French-speaking children have significant spelling problems despite their being able to read at developmentally appropriate levels. Some English-speaking children also have spelling problems but adequate handwriting and reading skills.

Students with dyslexia or OWL LD always have spelling problems but may also have dysgraphia. The learning problems resulting from dyslexia, OWL LD, and/or dysgraphia are not related to lack of cognitive or thinking ability, which is always at least in the normal range.

Even though students with dyslexia, OWL LD, and/or dysgraphia have a biologically based disorder with a genetic and brain basis, research has shown that they do respond to reading and writing instruction tailored to their learning profiles (e.g., Berninger, 2000; Berninger, Winn, et al., 2008).

It is important to remember that not all reading and writing problems are the result of dyslexia, OWL LD, and/or dysgraphia. Other disorders also cause reading and writing problems. Cognitive or thinking ability may not be within the normal range in these disorders. Some children fall outside the normal range in all areas of development (i.e., cognitive, language, motor, attention and executive function, and social emotional) or in one or more of these areas of development; or they have a neurogenetic developmental disorder (e.g., fragile X) or a brain disease or injury that affects their learning of written language. These children also are likely to have reading and writing problems—but the biological bases for their written language problems are different from those of children with dyslexia, OWL LD, and/or dysgraphia.

The nature of effective instruction may also be different. Although all students may respond to some of the same reading and writing instructional components, overall instructional programs may need to be tailored for students with specific kinds of developmental or learning disorders other than the three specific learning disabilities discussed in this book's lesson plans. Also, children with even more severe developmental disabilities or neurogenetic disorders, whose thinking ability falls outside the normal range, cannot be expected to reach the same levels of reading and writing achievement that children with dyslexia, OWL LD, and/or dysgraphia might reach in response to instructional intervention.

Teachers should be able to refer all students with significant and persisting reading and writing problems, many of whom are from families with a history of significant reading and writing problems (Berninger, Abbott, Thomson, & Raskind, 2001; Pennington & Lefly, 2001), to the multidisciplinary team in the school for comprehensive assessment to make an accurate diagnosis of the nature of the reading or writing problem and design an appropriate individualized education program (IEP). These lesson plans focus only on teaching students with dyslexia, OWL LD, and/or dysgraphia whose cognitive ability is within the normal range.

An appropriate IEP for students with dyslexia, OWL LD, and/or dysgraphia can often be implemented in the general education program using the instructional approaches described in this book and the companion text. Many students may need differentiated instruction to meet their individual learning needs. Both Berninger and Wolf have had experience in differentiated instruction and offer many practical suggestions for adapting the nature of reading and writing instruction to individual differences in learners—and organizing the learning environment to do so. On the one hand, all children may benefit from common components of literacy instruction. In response to a presentation in April 2000 by Berninger at the Science and Technology Roundable, Ranier Club, Seattle, WA, former Washington State governor Dan Evans remarked about effective instruction for students with dyslexia: "That kind of instruction should be beneficial for all students—not just those with reading disabilities!" On the other hand, when students at the same grade level are at different stages of reading and writing development, instruction does have to be adapted in some ways to meet all students' instructional needs, including reasonable challenges and sufficient success in daily learning. General educational teachers can organize the learning environment to meet those needs for all students in the classroom through differentiated instruction that is explained in the accompanying textbook.

OVERVIEW OF THE BOOK

This practical companion to *Teaching Students with Dyslexia and Dysgraphia* (Berninger & Wolf, 2009) is a set of lesson plans for differentiated instruction of students with dysgraphia, dyslexia, and OWL LD. With a year's worth of specialized group instruction, teachers can improve the literacy skills of students who struggle with written language. Each lesson comes with teacher and student materials. The teacher materials give educators warm-up exercises that target key skills, simple activities with clear and detailed descriptions, and adaptable lesson plans that help them elicit student responses. The student materials are photocopiable worksheets that help children sharpen their skills in engaging ways.

The lesson plans are proven effective by brain research studies and use multiple learning mechanisms to keep children responsive to instruction. Although the interventions are detailed, they are flexible enough to encourage teachers to monitor each student's individual response to instruction and make adjustments as needed.

These lesson plans can be used on their own or in conjunction with *Teaching Students with Dyslexia and Dysgraphia*. Each unit features a specific hope story and focuses on improving reading and writing skills. Students with chronic school failure may lose faith that they can learn successfully. Thus, each lesson begins with a story created to instill hope that 1) they can learn and 2) teachers can teach them. This "hope story," which is told the first day of each unit, is repeated and elaborated in greater depth throughout the intervention. For Unit I, students are encouraged to become word detectives and seek phonological awareness, orthographic awareness, and morphological awareness clues, just like the famous detectives Sherlock Holmes and Dr. John Watson searched for clues to solve mysteries. In Unit II, students are introduced the writers workshop model through Mark Twain and are given explicit instruction in spelling words and composing. Unit III helps teachers make the listening, reading, and writing connection through the story of John Muir. Finally, Unit IV uses the story of Sequoyah to integrate the students' writing and reading skills.

Each unit in this book comes from a different instructional study conducted by the NICHD-funded University of Washington Multidisciplinary Learning Disability Center. Unit I is based on a study described in Berninger, Nagy, et al. (2003) for a readers workshop. Unit II is based on the first study in Berninger, Winn, et al. (2003) and Unit III is based on the second study in Berninger, Winn, et al. (2003). Unit II is a writers workshop and Unit III is a writing-readers workshop. Unit IV, a reading-writers workshop, is from a study in preparation (Berninger, Lee, Abbott, & Breznitz, 2009) for a special issue of the *Annals of Dyslexia*. Children in Grades 4–6 participated in the Unit I and Unit III studies. Children in Grades 4–9 participated in the Unit II and Unit IV studies. All children were recruited from the University of Washington family genetics study for dyslexia and met evidence-based criteria for dyslexia (oral word reading/decoding and spelling problems). Some children also had dysgraphia (handwriting problems). The lessons have also been adapted for students with OWL LD by adding more morphological and syntax awareness activities (Berninger & O'Malley, May 2009). Other students may also benefit from and enjoy the workshop format, which incorporates explicit instruction with authentic reading and/or writing activities and much student–student and teacher–student interaction.

REFERENCES

Berninger, V.W. (2000). Dyslexia an invisible, treatable disorder: The story of Einstein's ninja turtles. *Learning Disability Quarterly, 23*, 175–195.

Berninger, V.W., Abbott, R., Thomson, J., & Raskind, W. (2001). Language phenotype for reading and writing disability: A family approach. *Scientific Studies in Reading, 5*, 59–105.

Berninger, V.W., Lee, Y., Abbott, R., & Breznitz, Z. (2009). Implementing and monitoring response to intervention in Sequoyah reading-writers and writing-readers workshop for students diagnosed with dyslexia. Manuscript in preparation.

Berninger, V.W., Nielsen, K., Abbott, R., Wijsman, E., & Raskind, W. (2008). Gender differences in severity of writing and reading disabilities. *Journal of School Psychology, 46*, 151–172.

Berninger, V.W., & O'Malley May, M. (2009). *Adapting evidence-based interventions for students with reading disability to other specific learning disabilities involving writing and oral language.* Manuscript submitted for publication.

Berninger, V.W., Winn, W., Stock, P., Abbott, R., Eschen, K., Lin, C., et al. (2008). Tier 3 specialized writing instruction for students with dyslexia. *Reading and Writing: An Interdisciplinary Journal, 21*, 95–129.

Berninger, V.W., & Wolf, B. (2009). *Teaching students with dyslexia and dysgraphia make connections: Lessons from Teaching and Science.* Baltimore: Paul H. Brookes Publishing Co.

Fayol, M., Zorman, M., & Lété, B. (2009). Associations and dissociations in reading and spelling French: Unexpectedly poor and good spellers. In Stainthorp, R., & Tomlinson, P. (Eds.), *British Journal of Educational Psychology Monograph Series II, No. 6. Teaching and learning writing* (Vol. 1, No. 1, pp. 63–75). Leicester, England: The British Psychological Society.

Pennington, B., & Lefly, D. (2001). Early reading development in children at family risk for dyslexia. *Child Development, 72*, 816–833.

Materials List

You will need the following materials to implement the lesson plans in this workbook:

Unit I

- *Talking Letters* and *More Talking Letters* cards (http://pearsonassess.com) For background in using these:
    1. Berninger, V.W. (1998). *PAL Guides for Intervention.* San Antonio, TX: Pearson Assessment. See *Talking Letters.*
    2. Berninger, V., & Abbott, S. (2003). *PAL Research-Supported Reading and Writing Lessons.* San Antonio, TX: Pearson Assessment. Also PAL Reproducibles for the Lessons.
- Book with short stories about detectives solving mysteries (e.g., Doyle, A.C. [1986]. *The adventures of Sherlock Holmes.* New York: Penguin Group)
- *Read Naturally* (Ihnot C. [1997]. *Read naturally.* St. Paul, MN: Turman Publishing)
- *Jabberwocky* poem from *Through the Looking-Glass* (available at http://www.jabberwocky.com/carroll/jabber/jabberwocky.html)
- Magnifying glasses (optional)
- Folders for students
- Flashcards
- Envelopes
- Timer

Unit II

- *Talking Letters, More Talking Letters* cards (http://pearsonassess.com) For background in using these:
    1. Berninger, V.W. (1998). *PAL Guides for Intervention.* San Antonio, TX: Pearson Assessment. See *Talking Letters.*
    2. Berninger, V., & Abbott, S. (2003). *PAL Research-supported reading and writing lessons.* San Antonio, TX: Pearson Assessment. Also PAL Reproducibles for the Lessons. See also Substitutes that go with *Talking Letters.*
- Flashcards
- Folders
- Access to computers

Unit III

- *Talking Letters, More Talking Letters* cards (http://pearsonassess.com)
  For background in using these:
  1. Berninger, V.W. (1998). *PAL Guides for Intervention.* San Antonio, TX: Pearson Assessment. See *Talking Letters.*
  2. Berninger, V., & Abbott, S. (2003). *PAL Research-Supported Reading and Writing Lessons.* San Antonio, TX: Pearson Assessment. Also PAL Reproducibles for the Lessons. See Substitutes and Nicknames that go with *Talking Letters.*
- Access to computers with Kurzweil or comparable software
- PAL-II User Guide (Berninger, V.W. [1998] *PAL Guides for Reading and Writing intervention.* San Antonio: TX Pearson Assessment)
- CD of John Muir life and adventures (Gilchrist, G. [2000]. *John Muir: My life of adventures.* CD recording by storyteller Garth Gilchrist. Nevada City, CA: Dawn Publications)
- Bird calls (For the Birds. [2000]. *LLC Birdsong Identiflyer* [audio birdsong dictionary]. P.O. Box 1731; Seneca, SC 29679-1731)
- Folders

Unit IV

- *Talking Letters, More Talking Letters* cards (http://pearsonassess.com)
  For background in using these:
  1. Berninger, V.W. (1998). *PAL Guides for Intervention.* San Antonio, TX: Pearson Assessment. See *Talking Letters.*
  2. Berninger, V., & Abbott, S. (2003). *PAL Research-Supported Reading and Writing Lessons.* San Antonio, TX: Pearson Assessment. Also PAL Reproducibles for the Lessons. See also Substitutes and Nicknames that go with *Talking Letters.*
- Reading selections:
  - Ihnot C. (1997). *Read naturally.* St. Paul, MN: Turman Publishing.
  - Levine, E. (1999). *If you lived with the Iroquois.* New York: Scholastic Paperbacks.
  - Rumford, J. (2004). *Sequoyah: The Cherokee man who gave his people writing.* Boston: Houghton Mifflin's Children's Books. Translator: Anna Sixkiller Huckaby.

Word Detectives

Conceptual Framework and Background Information

The Word Detective lesson plans contain all the components of reading instruction recommended by the National Reading Panel for general education students (National Reading Panel, 2000). In addition, these lesson plans contain instructional components for students with dyslexia, who also require specialized training to

1. Automatize alphabetic principle

2. Transfer alphabetic principle learned in isolation to decoding in and out of word and sentence context

3. Develop orthographic and morphological as well as phonological awareness

4. Coordinate phonological, orthographic, and morphological word forms and their parts

5. Guide oral word decoding and fluency

6. Guide silent reading for meaning

7. Learn comprehension strategies for independent reading

Children with dyslexia received all these instructional components in the Word Detective lesson plans, except that half the children were randomly assigned to phonological awareness treatment and half to morphological awareness treatment. The good reader controls were imaged at the same times—before and

after the children with dyslexia received these Word Detective lessons. The complete lesson sets were shown to normalize the brains of children with dyslexia compared with good reader controls (Aylward et al., 2003). However, more refined analyses showed that the chemical activation in the brain normalized in children who received the morphological awareness treatment but not in those who received only the phonological awareness treatment (Richards et al., 2002). This result suggests that phonological awareness is necessary but not sufficient. Also, consistent with triple word form theory (Berninger & Richards, 2002), individual functional magnetic resonance imaging (fMRI) brain analyses showed that the children who received the phonological awareness treatment improved on the fMRI morphological task, and children who received the morphological awareness treatment improved on the fMRI phonological task. This finding shows that the brain appears to be computing the interrelationships between these word forms and their parts just as triple word form theory predicts (Richards et al., 2006b). Subsequent behavioral studies showed that typically developing readers' word decoding, word reading, reading comprehension, handwriting, spelling, and written composition draw on the interrelationships among phonological, orthographic, and morphological word forms and their parts; and children with dyslexia also draw on these interrelationships, but to a larger degree on morphological awareness, in coordinating these three word forms and their parts than do typically developing readers (Berninger, Raskind, Richards, Abbott, & Stock, 2008).

Both the group that received phonological–orthographic awareness treatment and the group that received morphological awareness treatment improved on behavioral measures of reading (normed for age or grade) during the 3-week summer intervention in the following:

- Accuracy of phonological decoding (*Woodcock Reading Mastery Test–Revised* [WRMT-R; Woodcock, 1987] Word Attack subtest)

- Rate of phonological decoding (*Test of Word Reading Efficiency* [TOWRE; Torgesen, Wagner, & Rashotte, 1999] phonemic reading),

- Morphological awareness (University of Washington [UW] *Comes From* test [now PAL-II Are They Related?])

- Accuracy of morphological decoding fluency (UW Morphological Decoding Test [now PAL-II Morphological Decoding Fluency]).

However, the morphological treatment group improved significantly more than the phonological treatment group on rate of phonological decoding on TOWRE phonemic reading; this finding shows the advantage of adding morphological awareness treatment to alphabetic principle and phonological awareness training for phonological decoding.

Collectively, a number of University of Washington Multidisciplinary Learning Disabilities Center (UWLDC) treatment studies indicate that students benefit from initial phonological and orthographic awareness treatment, followed by morphological awareness treatment. That is why we recommend that phonological awareness–orthographic awareness activities (Lessons 1–14) be used first in Word Detectives, followed by morphological awareness activities (Lessons 15–28).

We always use a "hope story" that continues throughout the instructional sessions. Children who have struggled with learning to read may become sad or angry or feel hopeless. Teaching struggling readers involves more than instructional components. We use motivational themes to engage students in the treatment. In the Word Detective lessons, we begin with a story in which Albert Einstein's uncle urged him to become a word detective so he would do better in school, and when he did he became successful in school (from Reading Level 5.5 of *Read Naturally* [Ihnot, 1991]). We continually empha-

size how Sherlock Holmes and Dr. John Watson solved mysteries by being good detectives—the clues are there if you look and listen for them and think about them.

The theme of *Third Rocker's R-Files* is built upon the concept of aliens who come to Earth to observe and decipher Earth's culture (as in the TV series *Third Rock from the Sun*), and humans who try to decipher alien intelligence to find the truth that is out there (as in *The X-Files*). Our goal is to show the students the secrets to unlocking the code in written English words, which may seem like an alien language to them, but the key is out there. We emphasize that the strategies we are teaching them will help them unlock the code. Students are, therefore, encouraged to be Word Detectives, like Sherlock Holmes and Dr. Watson, using as many clues as possible to decipher the code and create their own R-Files in their mind. To explain the value of codes, we also discussed the Navajo code talkers and their contributions to winning World War II. We also discussed code writing in developing computer programs. Such themes help discouraged learners engage in the learning process despite struggles they encounter.

Structure of Lessons

Each lesson begins with a warm-up just as athletes and concert musicians do warm-ups before the performance. Each lesson contains seven activities to develop some aspect of linguistic awareness through reflective activities, first about the phonological structure of spoken words and the relationship of phonological to orthographic structure of written words (Lessons 1–14). Next, the reflective activities focus on the morphological structure of the word parts that signal meaning and grammar (Lessons 15–28).

These reflective activities are presented in such a way that students have constant opportunity to respond, their attention is monitored constantly, and they receive visible indicators of their progress. In each lesson, students time and graph 1-minute oral readings of short passages about real-world mysteries before and after practice in rereading them, summarizing them, and discussing them. Each lesson provides an opportunity to read a story or part of a story about Sherlock Holmes and Dr. Watson solving real-world mysteries.

Purpose of Each Activity in the Lessons

The purpose of the *alphabetic principle warm-up* is to develop

- Orthographic (letter) awareness of one- and two-letter spelling units

- Phonological (phoneme) awareness of corresponding phonemes in alphabetic principle for mainstream United States English dialect

- Automatic correspondences between these letter and sound units for the high-frequency grapheme–phoneme correspondences used in decoding and the high-frequency phoneme–grapheme correspondences used in spelling high-frequency written English words

Teachers who use these lessons with children who speak other dialects or are learning English may adapt them as necessary; preliminary evidence indicates that these children can also benefit from the structure of the lessons.

This warm-up is based on the work of Richard L. Venezky, who was the first consultant to the UWLDC. Venezky, a linguist, described how English represents the speech sounds in spoken words in written orthography (Venezky, 1970, 1999). He showed that English decoding and spelling are predictable, not irregular, but the alphabetic principle has alternations (alternative phonemes for the same one- or two-letter grapheme *and* alternative graphemes for the same phoneme).

A number of early intervention studies and three treatment studies with older students with dyslexia at the UWLDC, directed by Virginia (Ginger) Berninger, validated an approach to developing phonological and orthographic awareness along with automaticity of their connections and transfer of this knowledge to word decoding and spelling (Berninger & Abbott, 2003; Lesson Sets 1, 2, 4–7, 9–13, and 15). This approach to teaching awareness and automaticity of alphabetic principle is implemented with *Talking Letters* cards (Berninger, 1998); see Berninger and Abbott (2003) for instructions for introducing this approach to students. During the UWLDC studies, we found many students who could repeat phonics rules but not apply them. Teaching automaticity of phonics correspondences and modeling their transfer to decoding appeared to help them improve word decoding and reading.

The purpose of the *linguistic awareness activities* is to develop ability to attend to and reflect on the sound structure of *spoken* English words (phonological awareness), the orthographic (spelling) structure of *written* English words (orthographic awareness), and the morphological structure (morpheme units—base words and affixes) of *spoken and written* English words (morphological awareness) *and* the interrelationships among sound units, spelling units, and morpheme units. Venezky (1970, 1999) also called attention to the fact that English is a morphophonemic language. A number of recent studies are providing evidence for *triple word form theory* (Berninger et al., 2008). According to triple word form theory, because English is morphophonemic, children learn the interrelationships among these word forms and their parts (Nagy, Berninger, & Abbott, 2006; Nagy, Berninger, Abbott, Vaughan, & Vermeulen, 2003) *and* benefit from instruction that teaches the interrelationships among these word forms and their parts (Berninger et al., 2003; Berninger et al., in press):

- Phonological word forms (spoken words) and their parts

- Orthographic (written words) and their parts

- Morphological word forms (bases + affixes of spoken and written word forms) and their parts

The linguistic awareness part of the curriculum was developed in collaboration with William (Bill) Nagy, Seattle Pacific University; and Joanne Carlisle, University of Michigan. Nagy proposed the two categories of instructional activities for both phonological–orthographic and morphological awareness: *word learning* and *insight into the writing system.* Carlisle emphasized the importance of using *word sorts* (e.g., Bear, Invernizzi, Templeton, & Johnston, 2000) for practicing reflection in developing linguistic awareness rather than teaching morphological awareness as declarative knowledge by asking students to memorize the meaning of various morphemes. She also shared some of the clinical intervention materials she had piloted clinically.

Based on the recommendations of Nagy and Carlisle, Berninger developed four instructional activities for learning about words and three instructional activities for developing insight into the writing system that were as parallel as possible for the phonological and morphological awareness treatment. She also adapted the Carlisle materials for some of these activities.

The next activity in each lesson is devoted to transfer of alphabet principle and linguistic awareness to develop *fluent decoding, oral reading, and reading comprehension* in passages related in thematic content. Children with dyslexia often have had consider-

able instruction in phonics but have trouble applying it and because of their poor decoding do not have opportunities to read interesting texts that engage them intellectually. Thus, the Word Detectives lessons teach the transfer of automatic alphabetic principle and phonological, orthographic, and morphological awareness to word decoding and oral reading fluency in interesting text that is related to the theme of solving many different kinds of mysteries. Instructional treatment research for students with dyslexia showed that fluency training (repeated readings) alone is not sufficient if the student has not mastered decoding, in which case the student benefits from combined decoding and fluency (rereading) training (Berninger, Abbott, Abbott, Graham, & Richards, 2002). Thus, we combine decoding and fluency training with reading interesting texts for meaning.

The final activity in each lesson is devoted to reading for pleasure on the topic or theme of the unit; in this case, detectives. In the UWLDC study, a book about the mysteries that Sherlock Holmes and Dr. Watson solved was chosen; but any book with short stories about detectives solving mysteries could be selected. The guided reading of this story used the steps of the Directed Reading Activity (DRA; see Table 7.2 in Berninger, 1994). The DRA is an effective method of teaching reading that was developed in the 1950s and 1960s by teachers for teaching typically developing readers and students with reading disabilities. The steps are

1. Preparing the reader by discussing background knowledge and relevant vocabulary and posing purpose-setting questions to motivate silent reading of the passage

2. Silent reading of all or part of a passage

3. Answering explicit comprehension questions about vocabulary, sentence interpretation, and text comprehension at the discourse level and summarizing the story orally or in writing

4. Oral reading to develop fluency and also to find evidence in the passage for the answers to the comprehension questions

5. Providing explicit instruction for skill development

6. Practicing application of new skills (often through independent seatwork)

Word Detective Theme and Third Rocker's R-Files

As explained earlier, the lessons emphasize the secrets to unlocking the code in written English words. Students are told that reading may seem like an alien language to them, but it is not if they can decipher the code to create *reading (R-) Files* in their minds using the strategies they are taught. Students are encouraged to be Word Detectives (in the style of Holmes and Watson) in deciphering the code and creating their R-Files. In keeping with this theme, each student may receive a magnifying glass to use in the decoding process; these are available at most drug stores for a modest cost. Students also receive R-File award points in the special box on the last page of their Word Detectives work folder when they answer questions correctly.

Each student has a work folder to use during all the lessons. It has a cover page with a cartoon of Holmes and Watson using their magnifying glass to find clues and the title "Word Detectives." The cover also says "This R-File belongs to 3rd Rocker (name of child)." To build on the metaphor, on their last day, during the posttest an audio recording is made of each child transmitting a message to Dr. Lingo, the Grand Poobah of Linguists in the Universe, about the conclusion of their mission—what they learned about decoding Earth's English.

Approach to Instruction for Dealing with Brain Basis of Dyslexia

Teachers cannot program brains directly—only explicitly model, explain, and provide highly preplanned instructional cues and activities to help students self-program their own minds (Berninger & Richards, 2002). Therefore, the instruction for implementing Word Detectives lessons should meet both of these criteria:

- The teaching is highly preplanned. All instructional activities, teacher instruction, and student activities and response sheets have been prepared in advance for each moment of instruction (metaphor: sheet music as a guide but not a script implemented without adaptation).

- At the same time, good teaching is always highly responsive to the individual student: answering student questions even if these questions are not on the script, adapting instruction when students do not understand the task, and providing guidance to help students understand when they are not responding to the initial attempts to provide instructional cues.

The UWLDC research showed that students with dyslexia have difficulty paying attention to written language and benefit from instructional activities that are not only language based but also help them to *pay attention* to written language. The UWLDC research also showed that children and adults with dyslexia have impaired executive functions (Chenault, Thomson, Abbott, & Berninger, 2006; Thomson et al., 2005). They benefit from instructional strategies that help them self-regulate their learning and develop more effective executive functions for language processing. Finally, the UWLDC research showed that children with dyslexia need special help in automatizing some aspects of word decoding but also in reflecting on the structure of spoken and written words involving sound, spelling, and word parts signaling meaning and grammar. In implementing the Word Detectives lessons, teachers incorporate a number of strategies for helping children manage their attention, develop and use executive function strategies, and learn to automatize some language processes but also engage in reflective analysis of words and their word parts and interrelationships.

Some instructional approaches for the attentional system are

- Constant attention to monitoring and redirecting if necessary by the teacher

- Constant opportunities to respond (in writing, by talking, by walking around the room [e.g., to place a card in a category or bring a card up front to help construct a new word from word parts or to write a newly generated word on the chalk or white board or overhead transparency])

Some instructional approaches for the executive system are

- Daily monitoring and feedback about learning yoked to specific instructional goals (transfer words and fluency rate)

- Intermittent rewards (R-File points) for paying attention, staying on task, giving correct answers, and so forth

- Metalinguistic awareness—set of directions (talk story) for each linguistic awareness task kept in work folder and revisited periodically

Teach for both automaticity and reflection:

- Teach *automaticity of alphabetic principle* (mapping one- or two-letter units onto phonemes in a way that capitalizes on the synchronous timing of turn-taking in learning aural/oral language and makes both orthographic and phonological awareness explicit).

- Teach for *strategic transfer of alphabetic principle to word contexts* that vary in spelling–phoneme predictability (e.g., using the Jabberwocky words for the lessons).

- Teach for *self-regulated application of alphabetic principle* during independent reading.

The learning environment should provide instruction or learning activities directed to each of the subsystems contributing to the functional systems of the developing reading brain and writing brain (Berninger & Richards, 2002).

- To maintain arousal and attention, children are given R-File points for responding correctly and activities are designed for frequent responding in multiple modalities (e.g., oral, written, manipulating cards).

- To avoid habituation or off-task novelty seeking, activities are of brief duration, changed frequently, and varied in nature.

- To avoid overload in working memory, activities follow a predictable routine even though the content (items) of those activities changed.

- To develop automaticity, a small part of each lesson is aimed at creating automatic grapheme–phoneme correspondences.

- To optimize engagement and active, strategic thinking, the instructional activities, goals, and materials are highly preplanned in advance. However, during the sessions, teachers relinquish control and encourage children to respond freely to questions teachers pose, to question the teacher and each other, to debate, and to reflect about strategy application. However, instruction is not left to chance or incidental instruction during a "teachable moment." Each lesson has explicit instructional goals, and teachers use explicit, but flexible, means to achieve those goals.

- To provide feedback needed for executive management, the teacher provides other-regulation cues for goal-setting, self-monitoring, self-regulating, and staying on task. For example, the instructions provided by the teacher make the goals explicit; the R-File points children earn and the daily graphs during transferring and fluency activities provide immediate feedback about performance; and teacher prompts redirect off-task behaviors to the task at hand.

The lessons contain instructional components aimed at both automatization and strategy application because functional brain systems draw on both (Berninger & Richards, 2002). Automatizing low-level skills frees up limited resources of working memory for high-level reflection and problem solving. Strategizing is an effective way to self-regulate components of the brain system in meeting goals. The feedback component is important because children whose performance is continually assessed and who are given feedback learn more (Fuchs & Fuchs, 1999; Fuchs, Fuchs, Hamlet, Phillips, & Bertz, 1994). Overall, this learning environment implements a *direct explanation* approach rather than a *direct instruction* (scripted) approach (Duffy, 2002). Direct explanations often take the form of leading children to generalizations they articulate for themselves on the basis of the teacher's preplanned activities and clear instructional goals.

Implementing Lessons

Lessons can be implemented in an integrated unit that is applied daily across 6 weeks in twenty-eight 1- to 1.5-hour daily lessons plus one session for pretesting and one session for posttesting (total 30 sessions, five per week, over 6 weeks). We recommend that the Word Detectives lessons be implemented at the beginning of the school year to enhance the chance for reading success for the rest of the school year. Other lesson plans in this book can be used later in the school year to improve writing and writing-reading skills in the content areas.

PRETEST AND POSTTEST

School psychologists and speech and language specialists can partner with classroom teachers to provide assessment of response to instructional intervention. We recommend standardized, norm-referenced measures (e.g., *Woodcock-Johnson III* [WJ III; Woodcock, McGrew, & Mather, 2000]; *Wechsler Individual Achievement Test–Second Edition* (WIAT-II; Wechsler, 2001); *Kaufman Test of Educational Achievement, Second Edition* [KTEA-II; Kaufman & Kaufman, 2004]) of accuracy and rate of orally reading real words on a list without context clues, pseudowords, and grade-level passages with context clues, and of reading comprehension. Measures of phonological, orthographic, and morphological awareness are also desirable (e.g., PAL-II; Berninger, 2007).

All the introductions to the activities are reproduced in the Student Response Booklet for each lesson in the work folder so they can read along as teachers introduce each activity. Teachers read the general introduction and introduction to each of the seven activities each time during the first week and periodically thereafter to develop metalinguistic awareness for each activity.

PROCEDURAL INFORMATION

From this list of 30 Jabberwocky words, 10 are presented in each lesson (1 through 12) and each is presented three times all together; but these are randomized across the three presentations to avoid list-learning effects. For the last two lessons (13 and 14), half of the list (15 words) is presented in each lesson for a final review of the whole set (see Student Response Booklet in each lesson). Each session contains a mix of monosyllabic and polysyllabic words. These contain all the spelling unit–phoneme correspondences trained in *Talking Letters* (Berninger, 1998; Berninger & Abbott, 2003). In this first activity, the teacher presents the words orally without any visual input except for the six colored discs children keep in an envelope and use to count the phonemes in syllables.

Total set of Jabberwocky words:

chunglewums	swejeety	blesp	jeksie	haifraff
whulls	smewbry	grax	lutkaw	vopfow
thermb	quoopdro	pluce	soatyaz	cimdaut
knelph	wraltway	glofe	sognoy	yigfrue
sligursheck	zullcrusk	prite	hebtou	sceanruz
fladorudge	clostrills	trabe	nidmoin	snubarth

Table 1. Grapheme–phoneme correspondences from other word origins

	Spelling unit	Phoneme
Latin layer		
si	/sh/ as in discussion	or /zh/ as in vision
ti	/sh/ as in invention	
ci	/sh/ as in ancient	
tu	/sh/ as in picture	or /ch/ as in virtual
su	/zh/ as in pleasure	or /sh/ as in sugar
Greek layer		
ch	/k/ as in chorus	
ph	/f/ as in phone	
gh	/f/ as in laugh	
x	/z/ as in first x as in xerox	or in example
y	/ĭ/ as in first y in mystery	short i

Source: Berninger & Abbott, 2003, Reproducibles, page 15.

APPLICATION OF ALPHABETIC PRINCIPLE, LINGUISTIC AWARENESS, AND COMPREHENSION STRATEGIES TO READING WORDS IN TEXT FLUENTLY

For each lesson, the teacher not only models alphabetic principle (*Talking Letters* and grapheme–phoneme correspondences [Table 1]) and linguistic awareness activities but also shows children how to apply alphabetic principle linguistic awareness to reading words in text fluently and with comprehension. Individual children read orally to the teacher or paraprofessional or parent or grandparent aid who graphs their pre-practice "cold" accuracy for a 1-minute oral reading of a short passage of high interest about mysteries that were selected from *Read Naturally* (see the selections in Table 2). While the children are waiting for their turn for their 1-minute oral reading, they draw a picture about what they think the story will be about based on the title. After their "cold" reading, they read the whole short passage silently and use highlighters over a transparency overlay, which they keep in their Word Detectives work folder, to flag the words they cannot figure out while reading on their own. Children share up to two of these words, which the teacher writes on the board.

Table 2. List of passages from *Read Naturally* (Ihnot, 1997)

From 4.0 Book	15. Scorpion
1. The Tarantula	16. Flying Fox
2. Basilisk Lizard	17. Beatrix Potter
3. Portuguese Man-of-War	18. Charles Schulz
4. Thomas Edison	**From 5.5. Book**
5. Hank Aaron	19. The Case of Plant Killer
6. The Lost Fliers (about the Bermuda Triangle)	20. A Living Fossil
7. Amelia Earhart	21. Yeti
8. Space Base—Planet Earth	22. Lost Time in the Bermuda Triangle
9. Is There Life on Other Planets?	23. Vince Lombardi
10. A UFO Leaves Tracks.	**From 6.0 Book**
11. Bees at the Burial	24. Chameleon
12. The Floating Wonder	25. The Stone Fish
From 4.5 Book	26. A UFO Comes to a Picnic
13. Piranha Fish	27. A UFO in New Jersey
14. Black Widow Spider	28. Lost in the Bermuda Triangle

Then, based on activities with *Talking Letters* and linguistic awareness completed to date, children take turns offering strategies for decoding those words; for example, using the alphabetic principle and word parts for meaning. Teachers should teach them Carlisle's *Find the Fix* strategy for using word parts for meaning: Find the base and think about its meaning. Is there a prefix? If so, think about its meaning. Is there a postfix? If so, think about its meaning. Now say the word and figure out what it might mean in this context. The message the teacher conveys is that everyone can share and there is no stigma in not being able to decode the word instantly. Children share decoding strategies until everyone agrees that each word has been correctly identified.

Next, children practice reading the passage orally at least once to a buddy (partner they are assigned to for the rereading practice). Then, children summarize in writing what they read and share their written summarizations of the passage with the group. The teacher uses these as the basis for guiding the children in a reflective discussion of vocabulary meaning, sentence interpretation, and main idea and important details in the paragraph that was selected for its mystery theme—solving science or other kinds of mysteries.

Finally, children complete a second "hot" 1-minute oral reading of the passage after practice. The "cold" pretest and "hot" posttest accuracies for the constant 1-minute interval are graphed to provide a visible record of whether fluency (accuracy for a 1-minute interval) changes within and across lessons. While they wait their turn for the 1-minute oral reading, children illustrate the passage just read with colored pencils or markers. They can discuss how their expectations based on the title may have changed once they read the passage.

See Table 2 for the list of passages from *Read Naturally* (Ihnot, 1997). Books 4.0, 4.5, 5.5, and 6.0 are needed from *Read Naturally* in the Word Detectives work folder, along with a clear transparency and highlighter marker. The numbers refer to Unit 1, Lessons 1–28.

GUIDED SILENT AND ORAL READING FOR ENJOYMENT OF THEMED SHORT STORIES

Short stories about Sherlock Holmes and Dr. Watson may be selected from Doyle (1995). The teacher guides the silent and oral reading of each part of selected stories in each of the 28 lessons using the DRA, which was discussed previously (see p. 5).

During step 5 (providing explicit instruction for skill development), children summarize in writing what they read. After that, the group engages in a teacher-led reflective discussion in which children are encouraged to summarize accurately the content, including the main idea and supporting details (text-based comprehension; Kintsch, 1998), and to go beyond what was stated and engage in inferential thinking (situation-based comprehension; Kintsch, 1998). During step 6 (practicing application of new skills [often through independent seatwork]), individual children read orally to the teacher or teaching assistant who records on a graph the number of words read correctly in 1 minute.

LESSON 1 Words and Word Parts for Sound, Spelling, and Meaning

Paying Attention to Sound Units and Their Relationships to Spelling Units

Teacher Material

The following grapheme–phoneme correspondences are taught using *Talking Letters:* • Single-letter consonants • Short vowels in closed syllables • Long vowels in open syllables	Materials needed: • *Talking Letters* for automatic alphabetic principle • Work folders

WARM-UP (FOR THE TEACHER)

For the warm-up, name the letter or letter group on the *Talking Letters* card, say the pictured word containing a target phoneme, and then produce the target phoneme. Next, the students take a turn and repeat what is named or said by you. This approach develops orthographic awareness of spelling units; phonological awareness of corresponding phonemes in and out of word context; and, through close timing, the automaticity of spelling–phoneme correspondence. Monitor whether children are coordinating looking at the relevant letters and pictured words with naming of the letters and words and producing phonemes.

LESSON OVERVIEW (READ TO STUDENTS)

It is normal to come across words you do not know. One way to figure out an unknown word is to find the spelling units and think about their associated sounds. We will call these spelling–sound correspondences the *alphabetic principle.* Sometimes in English, more than one sound is associated with the same spelling unit. We will do seven different kinds of activities in each session to teach you to be a Word Detective who uses alphabetic principle and sound patterns in words to decode unknown words. These activities are *Word Building, Word Generating, Unit Finding, Word Transferring, Are They Relatives? Sorting by Sound Features,* and *Sorting by Word Context.* These activities should give you lots of strategies for using spelling units and their relationships to sounds to figure out words. We will use our electronic timer for the second through fourth activities but not the others. Let's begin.

ACTIVITIES

Word Building

Instructions: We always start by saying and analyzing the sounds in each word. We will not use real words but rather "Jabberwocky" words, like from *Alice in Wonderland* [read *Jabberwocky* poem from *Alice in Wonderland*]. First close your eyes and listen as I say a word. Then hold up the number of fingers for the number of syllables you hear in it. If we disagree, then we will discuss it. Then you will open your eyes and use these colored discs to count out the number of phonemes in each syllable. Together we will practice 10 words in each lesson.

Key:
S = syllable(s);
P = phoneme(s);
1st, 2nd, 3rd =
order of syllables

smewbry
(2 S: 3 P, 1st; 3 P, 2nd)

pluce
(1 S: 4 P)

prite
(1 S: 4 P)

knelph
(1 S: 4 P)

trabe
(1 S: 4 P)

hebtou
(2 S: 3 P, 1st; 2 P, 2nd)

blesp
(1 S: 5 P)

nimoin
(2 S: 3 P, 1st; 2 P, 2nd)

haifraff
(2 S: 3 P, 1st; 3 P, 2nd)

soatyaz
(2 S: 3 P, 1st; 3 P, 2nd)

Word Generating

Explain that R-Files have a double meaning. Not only are they the files in our work folders where we record our points for correct answers but they are also the "files in OUR minds" in which we store the words we learn. Teachers provide a sound unit (phoneme) and ask children to generate real words or Jabberwocky words that have in them that sound unit. The students write these words in their Response Booklets. Then after time is called after 5 minutes (30 seconds per phoneme), each child shares one word with the group. The teacher records on chalk or white board the word each child shares, providing feedback if necessary. Each child who contributes a word receives R-File points in his or her Response Booklet.

Instructions: Word Detectives sometimes get their clues from generating and reasoning about similar cases. Now I would like you to think of words that have the same sounds as the ones I say and are spelled this way (write on board). Write the words you think of in your Response Booklets. When you are done, we will share with the others. I will write the words on the board.

ch, u, ng, le, w, m, s (sound at end of *bees*), wh, ul, er

Note: After saying each sound, wait 30 seconds for the student to write the word, then say the next sound.

Unit Finding

The same 10 words practiced under Word Building are presented visually in the Student Response Booklet. Children are asked to underline (using two fine-point colored markers) each of the spelling units in a word using alternating colors for adjacent spelling units. (If this proves too difficult they can rewrite the word, spelling unit by spelling unit, with each adjacent spelling unit in a different color.) Remember, a spelling unit can be 1 or 2 letters and corresponds to a sound or blended sounds on *Talking Letters.* Children are given 2 minutes for 10 words, and their accuracy and time are recorded in work folders. Children who complete the activity correctly within the time limits receive R-File points. Initially some may not finish within the time limits, but eventually they will. Any discrepancies

among children or obvious errors are pointed out to them and discussed. Once everyone agrees on how to parse the words into spelling units, the group makes the sound that goes with each spelling unit and then synthesizes the sounds into a recognizable whole word.

Instructions: Word Detectives solve their mysteries by paying attention to details. The details you need to pay attention to in decoding are the spelling units and the sounds to which they correspond. See how many of these spelling units you can find in 2 minutes. Either underline the spelling units in alternating colors or rewrite the words in alternating colors with the fine-tip markers. After time is called, we will share with each other these word clues we found and then say the sound that goes with each of them (see *Talking Letters* card), moving from left to right, and then blend the sounds to say the whole word.

> smewbry, pluce, prite, knelph, trabe, hebtou, blesp, nimoin, haifraff, soatyaz

Word Transferring

Children are given 10 new words that were not practiced but contain target spelling units in the practiced words to evaluate whether they can pronounce them correctly in a different word context. The transfer words were constructed by altering one consonant- or one vowel-spelling unit in Jabberwocky words used in Word Building. Teachers record accuracy for whole words and spelling units, note whether children refer to the student *Talking Letters* card with spelling–phoneme correspondences, and time how long it takes to pronounce all the words on the transfer list. These results can be graphed on Reading Rockets or a teacher-designed chart so that both students and teacher have a visual record of student response to alphabetic principle instruction.

Instructions: Once Word Detectives figure out the code they can apply it to new words or cases. Here are 10 words that have the same spelling units that we have practiced but in different made-up words. How accurately and how fast can you use those spelling units to say these words? Record your accuracy and time on the Reading Rockets in your R-File. Refer to *Talking Letters* if that helps you.

> snewbry, plute, stite, chelph, blabe, rebtou, stesp, ridmoin, saifraff, loatyaz

Are They Relatives?

Does the underlined spelling unit in the first word correspond to the same phoneme as the underlined spelling unit in the second word? Children are asked to circle YES or NO on the worksheet in the Student Response Booklet if they think the spelling units underlined in the pair of pseudowords do or do not stand for the same sound (phonemes); that is, do they match? If there are differences of opinion, those items are discussed in reference to prior activities with *Talking Letters*. In contrast to the purpose of the warm-up that was to put this knowledge of grapheme–phoneme correspondences on automatic pilot, the purpose of this activity is to reflect consciously on the system of spelling–sound correspondences. Children receive R-File points for completing the activity within the time limits.

Instructions: Look carefully at each pair of words and circle YES on your worksheet if you think the underlined spelling units in each word stand for the same sound; circle NO if you think they don't. Remember that sometimes the same spelling unit stands for different sounds and that sometimes the same sound is spelled in different ways. Let's see how many you can do in 2 minutes. After time is called we will discuss any of your answers for which not everyone agreed.

ma<u>g</u>ic	ma<u>g</u>net
<u>c</u>ircus	cir<u>c</u>le
<u>wr</u>ong	<u>r</u>ight
plu<u>mb</u>er	<u>m</u>onkey
<u>s</u>uper	partie<u>s</u>
kno<u>cks</u>	fo<u>x</u>es
<u>ph</u>oto	enou<u>gh</u>
b<u>oo</u>kends	n<u>oo</u>ntime
<u>y</u>elling	fr<u>y</u>
ju<u>gg</u>le	fu<u>dge</u>

Sorting by Sound Features

The teacher points to one word at a time on a list in the Student Response Booklet. As you point to the word, name the word and point to the underlined spelling unit and produce the associated phoneme; then ask the children to choose the letter of the category at the top with the correct nickname sound for that spelling unit. Continue this procedure until all words are sorted into categories at the top of the list. Then help the children articulate the generalization that a specific spelling unit may stand for a small set of sounds. Children receive R-File points for each correct categorization of a spelling unit by its associated phoneme.

Although most of these alternations to be sorted are from the Anglo-Saxon layer of the language, a few (e.g., /zh/ for *s*, /short i/ for *y*, and /k/ for *ch*) are from the Romance or Greek layers of the language (see Table 1, p. 9).

Instructions: In this activity, categories for sorting words are listed at the top of the page. Each category has a capital letter. Sort each of the words in the list into one category by writing a capital letter beside it. At the end we will discuss what rule you applied to the sorting and what conclusion we can draw from the group sorting we just did.

Nicknames are /k/A and /s/B (labeled on card headings).

<u>c</u>ity	<u>c</u>ent	pen<u>c</u>il
<u>c</u>andle	be<u>c</u>ause	dan<u>c</u>e
<u>c</u>eiling	be<u>c</u>ome	<u>c</u>older
<u>c</u>ake		

Rule to discuss after sorting: *Hard c* is followed by *a* or *o*, and *soft c* is followed by *e* or *i*.

Sorting by Word Context

Children are given words with a blank and a box with choices of spelling units in the Student Response Booklet. The task is to choose the spelling unit that could fit into the blank in the word because in this word context adding that spelling unit spells a real word. These items contain spelling units that stand for the same sound but only one of the spelling units in a word-specific context spells a real word with meaning.

Instructions: Another way that Word Detectives have to make sense of their clues is by examining them for the context, that is the place in which they occur and all the surrounding clues. Each of the words you will see has a blank. Then you will see spellings but only one

spelling fits sensibly into the blank. To figure out which spellings would or would not fit into the blank—that is, into the context of the word—you need to pay close attention to all the spelling, sound, and meaning clues of the word. You have to fully analyze all the evidence you have at hand! As soon as you think you know a spelling that would fit into the word, circle it. As a Word Detective, it is important that you examine all the evidence—consider all the spelling units—before you make your decision about which spelling fits in the word.

spid _ (ar, er, ir, or, ur)   unle _ (s, ss, z)   an _ ent (sh, ci, si, ti)

larg _ st (a, e, i, o, u)   liz _ d (ar, er, ir, ur)   helm _ t (e, i, u)

bec _ se (a, au, aw)   br _ the (ea, ee, ei)   r _ sing (a, ai, ay)

p _ son (o, oi, oo, oy)

LESSON **1** ## Words and Word Parts for Sound, Spelling, and Meaning
Paying Attention to Sound Units and Their Relationships to Spelling Units

Student Response Booklet

Note: All lessons start with a warm-up, just as athletes warm up before a sports game. (See *Talking Letters* card.)

ACTIVITIES

Word Building

We always start by saying and analyzing the sounds in each word. We will not use real words but rather "Jabberwocky" words, like from *Alice in Wonderland* [read *Jabberwocky* poem from *Alice in Wonderland*]. First close your eyes and listen as I say a word. Then hold up the number of fingers for the number of syllables you hear in it. If we disagree, then we will discuss it. Then you will open your eyes and use these colored discs to count out the number of phonemes in each syllable. Together we will practice 10 words in each lesson.

Word Generating

Instructions: Word Detectives sometimes get their clues from generating and reasoning about similar cases. Now I would like you to think of words that have the same sounds as the ones I say. Write the words you think of in your Response Booklets. When you are done, we will share with the others. I will write the words on the board.

1. _____
2. _____
3. _____
4. _____
5. _____
6. _____
7. _____
8. _____
9. _____
10. _____

Unit Finding

Spelling units are one- or two-letter units that correspond to a sound. You may look at your *Talking Letters* card.

Instructions: Word Detectives solve their mysteries by paying attention to details. The details you need to pay attention to in decoding are the spelling units and the sounds to which they correspond. See how many of these spelling units you can find in 2 minutes. Either underline the spelling units in alternating colors or rewrite the words in alternating colors with the fine-tip markers. After time is called, we will share with each other these word clues we found and then say the sound that goes with each of them (see *Talking Letters* card), moving from left to right, and then blend the sounds to say the whole word.

smewbry	knelph	blesp	soatyaz
pluce	trabe	nimoin	
prite	hebtou	haifraff	

Word Transferring

Instructions: Once Word Detectives figure out the code they can apply it to new words or cases. Here are 10 words that have the same spelling units that we have practiced but in different made-up words. How accurately and how fast can you use those spelling units to say these words? Record your accuracy and time on the Reading Rockets in your R-File. Refer to *Talking Letters* if that helps you.

snewbry	chelph	stesp	loatyaz
plute	blabe	ridmoin	
stite	rebtou	saifraff	

Are They Relatives?

Instructions: Look carefully at each pair of words and circle YES on your worksheet if you think the underlined spelling units in each word stand for the same sound; circle NO if you think they don't. Remember that sometimes the same spelling unit stands for different sounds and that sometimes the same sound is spelled in different ways. Let's see how many you can do in 2 minutes. After time is called we will discuss any of your answers for which not everyone agreed.

ma<u>g</u>ic	ma<u>g</u>net	YES	NO
<u>c</u>ircus	cir<u>c</u>le	YES	NO
<u>wr</u>ong	<u>r</u>ight	YES	NO
plu<u>mb</u>er	<u>m</u>onkey	YES	NO

super	partie<u>s</u>	YES	NO
kno<u>cks</u>	fo<u>x</u>es	YES	NO
<u>ph</u>oto	enou<u>gh</u>	YES	NO
b<u>oo</u>kends	n<u>oo</u>ntime	YES	NO
<u>y</u>elling	fr<u>y</u>	YES	NO
<u>j</u>uggle	fu<u>dge</u>	YES	NO

Sorting by Sound Features

Instructions: In this activity, categories for sorting words are listed at the top of the page. Each category has a capital letter. Sort each of the words in the list into one category by writing a capital letter beside it. At the end we will discuss what rule you applied to the sorting and what conclusion we can draw from the group sorting we just did.

Nicknames are /k/ A and /s/ B.

<u>c</u>ity	<u>c</u>ake	be<u>c</u>ome	<u>c</u>older
<u>c</u>andle	<u>c</u>ent	pen<u>c</u>il	
<u>c</u>eiling	be<u>c</u>ause	dan<u>c</u>e	

Sorting by Word Context

Instructions: Another way that Word Detectives have to make sense of their clues is by examining them for the context, that is the place in which they occur and all the surrounding clues. Each of the words you will see has a blank. Then you will see spellings but only one spelling fits sensibly into the blank. To figure out which spellings would or would not fit into the blank—that is, into the context of the word—you need to pay close attention to all the spelling, sound, and meaning clues of the word. You have to fully analyze all the evidence you have at hand! As soon as you think you know a spelling that would fit into the word, circle it. As a Word Detective, it is important that you examine all the evidence—consider all the spelling units—before you make your decision about which spelling fits in the word.

spid __	p __ son	br __ the	r __ sing
(ar, er, ir, or, ur)	(o, oi, oo, oy)	(ea, ee, ei)	(a, ai, ay)
larg __ st	unle __	an __ ent	
(a, e, i, o, u)	(s, ss, z)	(sh, ci, si, ti)	
bec __ se	liz __ d	helm __ t	
(a, au, aw)	(ar, er, ir, ur)	(e, i, u)	

LESSON 2 Words and Word Parts for Sound, Spelling, and Meaning

Paying Attention to Sound Units and Their Relationships to Spelling Units

Teacher Material

The following grapheme–phoneme correspondences are taught using *Talking Letters:* • Consonant blends and vowel teams	Materials needed: • *Talking Letters* for automatic alphabetic principle • Work folders

WARM-UP (FOR THE TEACHER)

For the warm-up, name the letter or letter group on the *Talking Letters* card, say the pictured word containing a target phoneme, and then produce the target phoneme. Next, the students take a turn and repeat what is named or said by you. This approach develops orthographic awareness of spelling units; phonological awareness of corresponding phonemes in and out of word context; and, through close timing, the automaticity of spelling–phoneme correspondence. Monitor whether children are coordinating looking at the relevant letters and pictured words with naming of the letters and words and producing phonemes.

LESSON OVERVIEW (READ TO STUDENTS)

It is normal to come across words you do not know. One way to figure out an unknown word is to find the spelling units and think about their associated sounds. We will call these spelling–sound correspondences the *alphabetic principle.* Sometimes in English, more than one sound is associated with the same spelling unit. We will do seven different kinds of activities in each session to teach you to be a Word Detective who uses alphabetic principle and sound patterns in words to decode unknown words. These activities are *Word Building, Word Generating, Unit Finding, Word Transferring, Are They Relatives? Sorting by Sound Features,* and *Sorting by Word Context.* These activities should give you lots of strategies for using spelling units and their relationships to sounds to figure out words. We will use our electronic timer for the second through fourth activities but not the others. Let's begin.

ACTIVITIES

Word Building

Instructions: We always start by saying and analyzing the sounds in each word. We will not use real words but rather "Jabberwocky" words, like from Alice in Wonderland [read *Jabberwocky* poem from *Alice in Wonderland*]. First close your eyes and listen as I say a word. Then hold up the number of fingers for the number of syllables you hear in it. If we disagree, then we will discuss it. Then you will open your eyes and use these colored discs to count out the number of phonemes in each syllable. Together we will practice 10 words in each lesson.

Key:
S = syllable(s);
P = phoneme(s);
1st, 2nd, 3rd =
order of syllables

yigfrue
(2 S: 3 P, 1st; 3 P, 2nd)

lutkaw
(2 S: 3 P, 1st; 2 P, 2nd)

clostrills
(2 S: 5 P, 1st; 4 P, 2nd
[or 2 S: 4 P, 1st; 5 P, 2nd])

zullcrusk
(2 S: 3 P, 1st; 5 P, 2nd)

quoopdro
(2 S: 4 P, 1st; 3 P, 2nd)

glofe
(1 S: 4 P)

vopfow
(2 S: 3 P, 1st; 2 P, 2nd)

grax
(1 S: 5 P)

jeksie
(2 S: 3 P, 1st; 2 P, 2nd)

swejeety
(3 S: 3 P, 1st; 3 P, 2nd; 1 P, 3rd [or 2 P, 2nd; 2 P, 3rd])

Word Generating

Explain to the students that R-files have a double meaning. Not only are they the files in our work folders where we record our points for correct answers but they are also the "files in OUR minds" in which we store the words we learn. Provide a sound unit (phoneme) and ask children to generate real words or Jabberwocky words orally that have in them that sound unit. The teacher records on chalk or white board the words the *group* generates in 5 minutes (30 seconds per phoneme). The teacher encourages fast responding and a sense of excitement in word generation and accepts alternative, plausible spellings. Children who contribute a word receive R-file points.

Instructions: Word Detectives sometimes get their clues from generating and reasoning about similar cases. Now I would like you to think of words that have the same sounds as the ones I say and are spelled this way (write on board). Write the words you think of in your Response Booklets. When you are done, we will share with the others. I will write the words on the board.

mb, kn, r, ph, sl, i, g, ur, sh, short e

Note: After saying each sound, wait 30 seconds for the student to write the word, then say the next sound.

Unit Finding

The same 10 words practiced under Word Building are presented visually in the Student Response Booklet. Children are asked to underline (using two fine-point colored markers) each of the spelling units in a word, using alternating colors for adjacent spelling units. (If this proves too difficult they can rewrite the word, spelling unit by spelling unit, with each adjacent spelling unit in a different color.) Remember, a spelling unit can be 1 or 2 letters and corresponds to a sound or blended sounds on *Talking Letters.* Children are given 2 minutes for 10 words, and their accuracy and time are recorded in work folders. Children who complete the activity correctly within the time limits receive *R-File points.* Initially some may not finish within the time limits, but eventually they will. Any discrepancies among children or obvious errors are pointed out to them and discussed. Once everyone agrees on how to parse the words into spelling units, the group makes the sound that goes with each spelling unit and then synthesizes the sounds into a recognizable whole word.

Instructions: Word Detectives solve their mysteries by paying attention to details. The details you need to pay attention to in decoding are the spelling units and the sounds to which they correspond. I want to see how many of these spelling units you can find in 2 minutes. Either underline the spelling units in alternating colors or rewrite the words in alternating colors with the fine-tip markers. After time is called, we will share with each other these word clues we found and then say the sound that goes with each of them (see *Talking Letters* card), moving from left to right, and then blend the sounds to say the whole word.

> yigfrue, lutkaw, clostrills, zullcrusk, quoopdro, glofe, vopfow, grax, jeksie, swejeety

Word Transferring

Children are given 10 new words that were not practiced but contain target spelling units in the practiced words, in order to evaluate whether they can pronounce them correctly in a different word context. The transfer words were constructed by altering one consonant or one vowel spelling unit in the Jabberwocky words used in Word Building. Record accuracy for whole words and spelling units, note whether children refer to the student *Talking Letters* card with spelling–phoneme correspondences, and record the time taken to pronounce all the words on the transfer list.

Instructions: Once Word Detectives figure out the code they can apply it to new words or cases. Here are 10 words that have the same spelling units that we have practiced but in different made-up words. How accurately and how fast can you use those spelling units to say these words? Record your accuracy and time on the Reading Rockets in your R-File. Refer to *Talking Letters* if that helps you.

> sigfrue, mutkaw, chostrills, tullcrusk, choopdro, glome, dopfow, brax, meksie, hejeety

Are They Relatives?

Does the underlined spelling unit in the first word correspond to the same phoneme as the underlined spelling unit in the second word? Children are asked to circle YES or NO on the worksheet in the Student Response Booklet if they think the underlined spelling units in the pair of pseudowords could stand for the same sound (phonemes); that is, do they match? If there are differences of opinion, those items are discussed in reference to prior activities with *Talking Letters*. In contrast to the purpose of the warm-up, which was to put this knowledge of grapheme–phoneme correspondences on automatic pilot, the purpose of this activity is to reflect consciously on the system of spelling–sound correspondences. Children receive R-File points for completing the activity within the time limits.

Instructions: To solve puzzles, Word Detectives need to pay attention not only to clues in a single word but also to how the clues in a word are related to other words they know. I want you to look carefully at each pair of words and circle YES on your worksheet if you think the underlined spelling units in each word stand for the same sound; circle NO if you think they don't. Remember that sometimes the same spelling unit stands for different sounds and that sometimes the same sound is spelled in different ways. Let's see how many you can do in 2 minutes. After time is called we will discuss any of your answers for which not everyone agreed.

beagle   beeper
x-ray   boxes
word   letter
water   claw
blue   music
shine   riches
awful   salt
this   thin
hurts   dirtier
oyster   coins

Sorting by Sound Features

Point to one word at a time on a list in the Student Response Booklet. As you point to the word, name the word and point to the underlined spelling unit and produce the associated phoneme; then ask the children to choose the letter of the category at the top with the correct nickname sound for that spelling unit. Continue this procedure until all words are sorted into categories at the top of the list. Then help the children articulate the generalization that a specific spelling unit may stand for a small set of sounds. Children receive R-File points for each correct categorization of a spelling unit by its associated phoneme.

Although most of these alternations to be sorted are from the Anglo-Saxon layer of the language, a few (e.g., /zh/ for *s*, /short i/ for *y*, and /k/ for *ch*) are from the Romance or Greek layers of the language (see Table 1, p. 9).

Instructions: Once Word Detectives get clues, they have to make sense of them. They have to do a special kind of thinking in which they draw conclusions from the evidence, just like Sherlock Holmes and Dr. Watson did. In this activity, categories for sorting words are listed at the top of the page. Each category has a capital letter. You will sort each of the words in the list into one category by writing a capital letter beside it. At the end we will discuss what rule you applied to the sorting and what conclusion we can draw from the group sorting we just did.

Nicknames are /hard g as in *gate*/A and /soft g as in *giraffe*/B (labeled on card headings).

garden   again   begin
giant   large   giraffe
cage   change
getting   give

Rule to discuss after sorting: *Hard g* precedes *a, e, i, o, u,* but *soft g* may also precede *i,* and *soft g* occurs at end of syllables before *e.*

Sorting by Word Context

Children are given words with a blank and a box with choices of spelling units in the Student Response Booklet. The task is to choose the spelling unit that could fit into the blank in the word because in this word context adding that spelling unit spells a real word. These items contain spelling units that stand for the same sound, but only one of the spelling units in a word-specific context spells a real word with meaning.

Instructions: Another way that Word Detectives have to make sense of their clues is by examining them for the context, that is the place in which they occur and all the surrounding clues. Each of the words you will see has a blank. Then you will see spellings but only one spelling fits sensibly into the blank. To figure out which spellings would or would not fit into the blank—that is, into the context of the word—you need to pay close attention to all the spelling, sound, and meaning clues of the word. You have to fully analyze all the evidence you have at hand! As soon as you think you know a spelling that would fit into the word, circle it. As a Word Detective, it is important that you examine all the evidence—consider all the spelling units—before you make your decision about which spelling fits in the word.

jell _ fish
(e, i, y)

w _ dn't
(o, oo, oul)

stran _
(g, ge, j, je)

col _ ny
(a, i, e, o)

purp _
(el, le, ul)

__ lectric
(a, e, i, u)

c _ dn't
(o, oo, oul)

exper _ menting
(a, e, i, u)

n _ spapers
(ew, oo, o)

hundr _ d
(a, e, i, o, u)

LESSON **2** Words and Word Parts for
Sound, Spelling, and Meaning

Paying Attention to Sound Units
and Their Relationships to Spelling Units

Student Response Booklet

Note: All lessons start with a warm-up, just as athletes warm up before a
sports game. (See *Talking Letters* card.)

ACTIVITIES

Word Building

We always start by saying and analyzing the sounds in each word. We will not
use real words but rather "Jabberwocky" words, like from *Alice in Wonderland* [read *Jabberwocky* poem from *Alice in Wonderland*]. First close your eyes
and listen as I say a word. Then hold up the number of fingers for the number
of syllables you hear in it. If we disagree, then we will discuss it. Then you will
open your eyes and use these colored discs to count out the number of
phonemes in each syllable. Together we will practice 10 words in each lesson.

Word Generating

Instructions: Word Detectives sometimes get their clues from generating and
reasoning about similar cases. Now I would like you to think of words that
have the same sounds as the ones I say. Write the words you think of in your
Response Booklets. When you are done, we will share with the others. I will
write the words on the board.

1. _____
2. _____
3. _____
4. _____
5. _____
6. _____
7. _____
8. _____
9. _____
10. _____

Unit Finding

Spelling units are one- or two-letter units that correspond to a sound. You may look at your *Talking Letters* card.

Instructions: Word Detectives solve their mysteries by paying attention to details. The details you need to pay attention to in decoding are the spelling units and the sounds to which they correspond. See how many of these spelling units you can find in 2 minutes. Either underline the spelling units in alternating colors or rewrite the words in alternating colors with the fine-tip markers. After time is called, we will share with each other these word clues we found and then say the sound that goes with each of them (see *Talking Letters* card), moving from left to right, and then blend the sounds to say the whole word.

yigfrue	zullcrusk	vopfow	swejeety
lutkaw	quoopdro	grax	
clostrills	glofe	jeksie	

Word Transferring

Instructions: Once Word Detectives figure out the code they can apply it to new words or cases. Here are 10 words that have the same spelling units that we have practiced but in different made-up words. How accurately and how fast can you use those spelling units to say these words? Record your accuracy and time on the Reading Rockets in your R-File. Refer to *Talking Letters* if that helps you.

sigfrue	tullcrusk	dopfow	hejeety
mutkaw	choopdro	brax	
chostrills	glome	meksie	

Are They Relatives?

Instructions: Look carefully at each pair of words and circle YES on your worksheet if you think the underlined spelling units in each word stand for the same sound; circle NO if you think they don't. Remember that sometimes the same spelling unit stands for different sounds and that sometimes the same sound is spelled in different ways. Let's see how many you can do in 2 minutes. After time is called we will discuss any of your answers for which not everyone agreed.

b<u>ea</u>gle	b<u>ee</u>per	YES	NO
<u>x</u>-ray	bo<u>x</u>es	YES	NO

word	letter	YES	NO
water	claw	YES	NO
blue	music	YES	NO
shine	riches	YES	NO
awful	salt	YES	NO
this	thin	YES	NO
hurts	dirtier	YES	NO
oyster	coins	YES	NO

Sorting by Sound Features

Instructions: In this activity, categories for sorting words are listed at the top of the page. Each category has a capital letter. Sort each of the words in the list into one category by writing a capital letter beside it. At the end we will discuss what rule you applied to the sorting and what conclusion we can draw from the group sorting we just did.

Nicknames are /hard g as in *gate*/ (A) and /soft g as in *giraffe*/ (B).

garden	getting	change	giraffe
giant	again	give	
cage	large	begin	

Sorting by Word Context

Instructions: Another way that Word Detectives have to make sense of their clues is by examining them for the context, that is the place in which they occur and all the surrounding clues. Each of the words you will see has a blank. Then you will see spellings but only one spelling fits sensibly into the blank. To figure out which spellings would or would not fit into the blank—that is, into the context of the word—you need to pay close attention to all the spelling, sound, and meaning clues of the word. You have to fully analyze all the evidence you have at hand! As soon as you think you know a spelling that would fit into the word, circle it. As a Word Detective, it is important that you examine all the evidence—consider all the spelling units—before you make your decision about which spelling fits in the word.

jell __ fish	col __ ny	c __ dn't	n __ spapers
(e, i, y)	(a, i, e, o)	(o, oo, oul)	(ew, oo, o)
w __ dn't	purp __	exper __-menting	hundr __ d
(o, oo, oul)	(el, le, ul)	(a, e, i, u)	(a, e, i, o, u)
stran __	__ lectric		
(g, ge, j, je)	(a, e, i, u)		

LESSON 3 Words and Word Parts for Sound, Spelling, and Meaning

Paying Attention to Sound Units and Their Relationships to Spelling Units

Teacher Material

The following grapheme–phoneme correspondences are taught using *Talking Letters:* • Other consonant combinations • r- and l-controlled vowels	Materials needed: • *Talking Letters* for automatic alphabetic principle • Work folders

WARM-UP (FOR THE TEACHER)

For the warm-up, name the letter or letter group on the *Talking Letters* card, say the pictured word containing a target phoneme, and then produce the target phoneme. Next, the students take a turn and repeat what is named or said by you. This approach develops orthographic awareness of spelling units; phonological awareness of corresponding phonemes in and out of word context; and, through close timing, the automaticity of spelling–phoneme correspondence. Monitor whether children are coordinating looking at the relevant letters and pictured words with naming of the letters and words and producing phonemes.

LESSON OVERVIEW (READ TO STUDENTS)

It is normal to come across words you do not know. One way to figure out an unknown word is to find the spelling units and think about their associated sounds. We will call these spelling–sound correspondences the *alphabetic principle.* Sometimes in English, more than one sound is associated with the same spelling unit. We will do seven different kinds of activities in each session to teach you to be a Word Detective who uses alphabetic principle and sound patterns in words to decode unknown words. These activities are *Word Building, Word Generating, Unit Finding, Word Transferring, Are They Relatives? Sorting by Sound Features,* and *Sorting by Word Context.* These activities should give you lots of strategies for using spelling units and their relationships to sounds to figure out words. We will use our electronic timer for the second through fourth activities but not the others. Let's begin.

ACTIVITIES

Word Building

Instructions: We always start by saying and analyzing the sounds in each word. We will not use real words but rather "Jabberwocky" words, like from *Alice in Wonderland* [read *Jabberwocky* poem from *Alice in Wonderland*]. First close your eyes and listen as I say a word. Then hold up the number of fingers for the number of syllables you hear in it. If we disagree, then we will discuss it. Then you will open your eyes and use these colored discs to count out the number of phonemes in each syllable. Together we will practice 10 words in each lesson.

Key:
S = syllable(s);
P = phoneme(s);
1st, 2nd, 3rd = order of syllables

chunglewums
(3 S: 3 P, 1st; 2 P, 2nd; 4 P, 3rd)
whulls
(1 S: 4 P)
thermb
(1 S: 3 P)
sligursheck
(3 S: 4 P, 1st; 1 P, 2nd; 3 P, 3rd)

fladorudge
(3 S: 4 P, 1st; 1 P, 2nd; 3 or 4 P, 3rd)
wraltway
(2 S: 4 P, 1st; 2 P, 2nd)
cimdaut
(2 S: 3 P, 1st; 3 P, 2nd)

sognoy
(2 S: 3 P, 1st; 2 P, 2nd)
sceanruz
(2 S: 4 P, 1st; 3 P, 2nd)
snubarth
(2 S: 3 P, 1st; 3 P, 2nd)

Word Generating

Explain that R-Files have a double meaning. Not only are they the files in our work folders where we record our points for correct answers but they are also the "files in OUR minds" in which we store the words we learn. Provide a sound unit (phoneme) and ask children to generate real words or Jabberwocky words that have in them that sound unit. The students write these words in their Response Booklets. Then after time is called after 5 minutes (30 seconds per phoneme), each child shares one word with the group. Record on chalk or white board the word each child shares, providing feedback if necessary. Each child who contributes a word receives R-File points in his or her Response Booklet.

Instructions: Word Detectives sometimes get their clues from generating and reasoning about similar cases. Now I would like you to think of words that have the same sounds as the ones I say and are spelled this way (write on board). Write the words you think of in your Response Booklets. When you are done, we will share with the others. I will write the words on the board.

th, fl, a, d, or, r, u, dge, sw, ee

Note: After saying each sound, wait 30 seconds for the student to write the word, then say the next sound.

Unit Finding

The same 10 words practiced under Word Building are presented visually in the Student Response Booklet. Children are asked to underline (using two fine-point colored markers) each of the spelling units in a word using alternating colors for adjacent spelling units. (If this proves too difficult they can rewrite the word, spelling unit by spelling unit, with each adjacent spelling unit in a different color.) Remember, a spelling unit can be 1 or 2 letters and corresponds to a sound or blended sounds on *Talking Letters*. Children are given 2 minutes for 10 words, and their accuracy and time are recorded in work folders. Children who complete the activity correctly within the time limits receive R-File points. Initially some may not finish within the time limits, but eventually they will. Any discrepancies among children or obvious errors are pointed out to them and discussed. Once everyone agrees on how to parse the words into spelling units, the group makes the sound that goes with each spelling unit and then synthesizes the sounds into a recognizable whole word.

Instructions: Word Detectives solve their mysteries by paying attention to details. The details you need to pay attention to in decoding are the spelling units and the sounds to which they correspond. I want to see how many of these spelling units you can find in 2 minutes. Either underline the spelling units in alternating colors or rewrite the words in alternating colors with the fine-tip markers. After time is called, we will share with each other these word clues we found and then say the sound that goes with each of them (see *Talking Letters* card), moving from left to right, and then blend the sounds to say the whole word.

> chunglewums, whulls, thermb, sligursheck, fladorudge, wraltway, cimdaut, sognoy, sceanruz, snubarth

Word Transferring

Children are given 10 new words that were not practiced but contain target spelling units in the practiced words to evaluate whether they can pronounce them correctly in a different word context. The transfer words were constructed by altering one consonant or one vowel spelling unit in Jabberwocky words used in Word Building. Record accuracy for whole words and spelling units, note whether children refer to the student *Talking Letters* card with spelling–phoneme correspondences, and time how long it takes to pronounce all the words on the transfer list. These results can be graphed on Reading Rockets or a teacher-designed chart so that both students and teacher have a visual record of student response to alphabetic principle instruction.

Instructions: Once Word Detectives figure out the code they can apply it to new words or cases. Here are 10 words that have the same spelling units that we have practiced but in different made-up words. How accurately and how fast can you use those spelling units to say these words? Record your accuracy and time on the Reading Rockets in your R-File. Refer to *Talking Letters* if that helps you.

> dunglewums, brulls, shermb, bligursheck, gladorudge, baltway, dimdaut, tognoy, treanruz, shubarth

Are They Relatives?

Does the underlined spelling unit in the first word correspond to the same phoneme as the underlined spelling unit in the second word? Children are asked to circle YES or NO on the worksheet in the Student Response Booklet if they think the spelling units underlined in the pair of pseudowords do or do not stand for the same sound (phonemes); that is, do they match? If there are differences of opinion, those items are discussed in reference to prior activities with *Talking Letters*. In contrast to the purpose of the warm-up that was to put this knowledge of grapheme–phoneme correspondences on automatic pilot, the purpose of this activity is to reflect consciously on the system of spelling–sound correspondences. Children receive R-File points for completing the activity within the time limits.

Instructions: Look carefully at each pair of words and circle YES on your worksheet if you think the underlined spelling units in each word stand for the same sound; circle NO if you think they don't. Remember that sometimes the same spelling unit stands for different

sounds and that sometimes the same sound is spelled in different ways. Let's see how many you can do in 2 minutes. After time is called we will discuss any of your answers for which not everyone agreed.

m<u>oo</u>n	g<u>lue</u>
ch<u>ar</u>t	sc<u>ary</u>
st<u>ay</u>	sh<u>ape</u>
v<u>a</u>lentine	<u>a</u>lways
sl<u>ow</u>	h<u>ose</u>
s<u>ea</u>son	b<u>ear</u>
sh<u>oo</u>k	cr<u>oo</u>k
<u>r</u>unning	swimm<u>er</u>
s<u>ai</u>d	p<u>ai</u>n
ab<u>ou</u>t	cr<u>ow</u>d

Sorting by Sound Features

Point to one word at a time on a list in the Student Response Booklet. As you point to the word, name the word and point to the underlined spelling unit and produce the associated phoneme; then ask the children to choose the letter of the category at the top with the correct nickname sound for that spelling unit. Continue this procedure until all words are sorted into categories at the top of the list. Then help the children articulate the generalization that a specific spelling unit may stand for a small set of sounds. Children receive R-File points for each correct categorization of a spelling unit by its associated phoneme.

Although most of these alternations to be sorted are from the Anglo-Saxon layer of the language, a few (e.g., /zh/ for *s,* /short i/ for *y,* and /k/ for *ch*) are from the Romance or Greek layers of the language (see Table 1, p. 9).

Instructions: In this activity, categories for sorting words are listed at the top of the page. Each category has a capital letter. Sort each of the words in the list into one category by writing a capital letter beside it. At the end we will discuss what rule you applied to the sorting and what conclusion we can draw from the group sorting we just did.

Nicknames are /s/A, /z/B, and /zh/C (labeled on card headings).

<u>s</u>unny	<u>s</u>itting	doe<u>s</u>
eye<u>s</u>	alway<u>s</u>	<u>s</u>ickest
trea<u>s</u>ure	<u>s</u>everal	
new<u>s</u>	plea<u>s</u>ure	

Rule to discuss after sorting: *s* can stand for the /s/ sound, the /z/ sound, or the /zh/ sound.

Sorting by Word Context

Children are given words with a blank and a box with choices of spelling units in the Student Response Booklet. The task is to choose the spelling unit that could fit into the blank in the word because in this word context adding that spelling unit spells a real word. These items contain spelling units that stand for the same sound but only one of the spelling units in a word-specific context spells a real word with meaning.

Instructions: Another way that Word Detectives have to make sense of their clues is by examining them for the context, that is the place in which they occur and all the surrounding clues. Each of the words you will see has a blank. Then you will see spellings but only one spelling fits sensibly into the blank. To figure out which spellings would or would not fit into the blank—that is, into the context of the word—you need to pay close attention to all the spelling, sound, and meaning clues of the word. You have to fully analyze all the evidence you have at hand! As soon as you think you know a spelling that would fit into the word, circle it. As a Word Detective, it is important that you examine all the evidence—consider all the spelling units—before you make your decision about which spelling fits in the word.

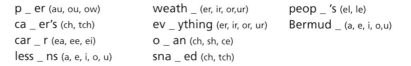

p _ er (au, ou, ow)   weath _ (er, ir, or, ur)   peop _ 's (el, le)

ca _ er's (ch, tch)   ev _ ything (er, ir, or, ur)   Bermud _ (a, e, i, o, u)

car _ r (ea, ee, ei)   o _ an (ch, sh, ce)

less _ ns (a, e, i, o, u)   sna _ ed (ch, tch)

LESSON **3** Words and Word Parts for
Sound, Spelling, and Meaning

Paying Attention to Sound Units and Their Relationships to Spelling Units

Student Response Booklet

Note: All lessons start with a warm-up, just as athletes warm up before a sports game. (See *Talking Letters* card.)

ACTIVITIES

Word Building

We always start by saying and analyzing the sounds in each word. We will not use real words but rather "Jabberwocky" words, like from *Alice in Wonderland* [read *Jabberwocky* poem from *Alice in Wonderland*]. First close your eyes and listen as I say a word. Then hold up the number of fingers for the number of syllables you hear in it. If we disagree, then we will discuss it. Then you will open your eyes and use these colored discs to count out the number of phonemes in each syllable. Together we will practice 10 words in each lesson.

Word Generating

Instructions: Word Detectives sometimes get their clues from generating and reasoning about similar cases. Now I would like you to think of words that have the same sounds as the ones I say. Write the words you think of in your Response Booklets. When you are done, we will share with the others. I will write the words on the board.

1. _____
2. _____
3. _____
4. _____
5. _____
6. _____
7. _____
8. _____
9. _____
10. _____

Unit Finding

Spelling units are one- or two-letter units that correspond to a sound. You may look at your *Talking Letters* card.

Instructions: Word Detectives solve their mysteries by paying attention to details. The details you need to pay attention to in decoding are the spelling units and the sounds to which they correspond. See how many of these spelling units you can find in 2 minutes. Either underline the spelling units in alternating colors or rewrite the words in alternating colors with the fine-tip markers. After time is called, we will share with each other these word clues we found and then say the sound that goes with each of them (see *Talking Letters* card), moving from left to right, and then blend the sounds to say the whole word.

chunglewums	sligursheck	cimdaut	snubarth
whulls	fladorudge	sognoy	
thermb	wraltway	sceanruz	

Word Transferring

Instructions: Once Word Detectives figure out the code they can apply it to new words or cases. Here are 10 words that have the same spelling units that we have practiced but in different made-up words. How accurately and how fast can you use those spelling units to say these words? Record your accuracy and time on the Reading Rockets in your R-File. Refer to *Talking Letters* if that helps you.

dunglewums	bligursheck	dimdaut	shubarth
brulls	gladorudge	tognoy	
shermb	baltway	treanruz	

Are They Relatives?

Instructions: Look carefully at each pair of words and circle YES on your worksheet if you think the underlined spelling units in each word stand for the same sound; circle NO if you think they don't. Remember that sometimes the same spelling unit stands for different sounds and that sometimes the same sound is spelled in different ways. Let's see how many you can do in 2 minutes. After time is called we will discuss any of your answers for which not everyone agreed.

m<u>oo</u>n	gl<u>ue</u>	YES	NO
ch<u>ar</u>t	sc<u>ary</u>	YES	NO

s<u>tay</u>	sh<u>a</u>pe	YES	NO
v<u>a</u>lentine	<u>a</u>lways	YES	NO
sl<u>ow</u>	h<u>o</u>se	YES	NO
season	b<u>ea</u>r	YES	NO
sh<u>oo</u>k	cr<u>oo</u>k	YES	NO
<u>r</u>unning	swimm<u>er</u>	YES	NO
s<u>ai</u>d	p<u>ai</u>n	YES	NO
ab<u>ou</u>t	cr<u>ow</u>d	YES	NO

Sorting by Sound Features

Instructions: In this activity, categories for sorting words are listed at the top of the page. Each category has a capital letter. Sort each of the words in the list into one category by writing a capital letter beside it. At the end we will discuss what rule you applied to the sorting and what conclusion we can draw from the group sorting we just did.

Nicknames are /s/ A, /z/ B, and /zh/ C.

<u>s</u>unny	new<u>s</u>	<u>s</u>everal	<u>s</u>ickest
eye<u>s</u>	<u>s</u>itting	plea<u>s</u>ure	
trea<u>s</u>ure	alway<u>s</u>	doe<u>s</u>	

Sorting by Word Context

Instructions: Another way that Word Detectives have to make sense of their clues is by examining them for the context, that is the place in which they occur and all the surrounding clues. Each of the words you will see has a blank. Then you will see spellings but only one spelling fits sensibly into the blank. To figure out which spellings would or would not fit into the blank—that is, into the context of the word—you need to pay close attention to all the spelling, sound, and meaning clues of the word. You have to fully analyze all the evidence you have at hand! As soon as you think you know a spelling that would fit into the word, circle it. As a Word Detective, it is important that you examine all the evidence—consider all the spelling units—before you make your decision about which spelling fits in the word.

p __ er	less __ ns	o __ ean	Bermud __
(au, ou, ow)	(a, e, i, o, u)	(ch, sh, ce)	(a, e, i, o,u)
ca __ er's	weath __	sna __ ed	
(ch, tch)	(er, ir, or,ur)	(ch, tch)	
car __ r	ev __ ything	peop __ 's	
(ea, ee, ei)	(er, ir, or, ur)	(el, le)	

LESSON 4 Words and Word Parts for
Sound, Spelling, and Meaning

Paying Attention to Sound Units
and Their Relationships to Spelling Units

Teacher Material

The following grapheme–phoneme correspondences are taught using *More Talking Letters:* • Latinate and Greek	Materials needed: • *More Talking Letters* (see Table 1) for automatic alphabetic principle • Work folders

WARM-UP (FOR THE TEACHER)

For the warm-up, name the letter or letter group on *More Talking Letters* (see Table 1), say the word containing a target phoneme, and then produce the target phoneme. Next, the students take a turn and repeat what is named or said by you. This approach develops orthographic awareness of spelling units; phonological awareness of corresponding phonemes in and out of word context; and, through close timing, the automaticity of spelling–phoneme correspondence. Monitor whether children are coordinating looking at the relevant letters and pictured words with naming of the letters and words and producing phonemes.

LESSON OVERVIEW (READ TO STUDENTS)

It is normal to come across words you do not know. One way to figure out an unknown word is to find the spelling units and think about their associated sounds. We will call these spelling–sound correspondences the *alphabetic principle.* Sometimes in English, more than one sound is associated with the same spelling unit. We will do seven different kinds of activities in each session to teach you to be a Word Detective who uses alphabetic principle and sound patterns in words to decode unknown words. These activities are *Word Building, Word Generating, Unit Finding, Word Transferring, Are They Relatives? Sorting by Sound Features,* and *Sorting by Word Context.* These activities should give you lots of strategies for using spelling units and their relationships to sounds to figure out words. We will use our electronic timer for the second through fourth activities but not the others. Let's begin.

ACTIVITIES

Word Building

Instructions: We always start by saying and analyzing the sounds in each word. We will not use real words but rather "Jabberwocky" words, like from *Alice in Wonderland* [read *Jabberwocky* poem from *Alice in Wonderland*]. First close your eyes and listen as I say a word. Then hold up the number of fingers for the number of syllables you hear in it. If we disagree, then we will discuss it. Then you will open your eyes and use these colored discs to count out the number of phonemes in each syllable. Together we will practice 10 words in each lesson.

Key:
S = syllable(s);
P = phoneme(s);
1st, 2nd, 3rd =
order of syllables

knelph
(1 S: 4 P)

quoopdro
(2 S: 4 P, 1st; 3 P, 2nd)

sognoy
(2 S: 3 P, 1st; 2 P, 2nd)

vopfow
(2 S: 3 P, 1st; 2 P, 2nd)

blesp
(1 S: 5 P)

clostrills
(2 S: 5 P, 1st; 4 P, 2nd
[or 2 S: 4 P, 1st; 5 P, 2nd])

whulls
(1 S: 4 P)

chunglewums
(3 S: 3 P, 1st; 2 P, 2nd;
4 P, 3rd)

swejeety
(3 S: 3 P, 1st; 3 P, 2nd; 1 P,
3rd [or 2 P, 2nd; 2 P, 3rd])

prite
(1 S: 4 P)

Word Generating

The teacher explains that R-Files have a double meaning. Not only are they the files in our work folders where we record our points for correct answers but they are also the "files in OUR minds" in which we store the words we learn. Teachers provide a sound unit (phoneme) and ask children to generate real words or Jabberwocky words that have in them that sound unit. The students write these words in their Response Booklets. Then after time is called after 5 minutes (30 seconds per phoneme), each child shares one word with the group. The teacher records on chalk or white board the word each child shares, providing feedback if necessary. Each child who contributes a word receives R-File points in his or her Response Booklet.

Instructions: Word Detectives sometimes get their clues from generating and reasoning about similar cases. Now I would like you to think of words that have the same sounds and are spelled this way (write on board). Write the words you think of in your Response Booklets. When you are done, we will share with the others. I will write the words on the board.

j, long e, t, sm, ew, br, y, sm, ew, br

Note: After saying each sound, wait 30 seconds for the student to write the word, then say the next sound.

Unit Finding

The same 10 words practiced under Word Building are presented visually in the Student Response Booklet. Children are asked to underline (using two fine-point colored markers) each of the spelling units in a word using alternating colors for adjacent spelling units. (If this proves too difficult they can rewrite the word, spelling unit by spelling unit, with each adjacent spelling unit in a different color.) Remember, a spelling unit can be 1 or 2 letters and corresponds to a sound or blended sounds on *Talking Letters*. Children are given 2 minutes for 10 words, and their accuracy and time are recorded in work folders. Children who complete the activity correctly within the time limits receive R-File points. Initially

some may not finish within the time limits, but eventually they will. Any discrepancies among children or obvious errors are pointed out to them and discussed. Once everyone agrees on how to parse the words into spelling units, the group makes the sound that goes with each spelling unit and then synthesizes the sounds into a recognizable whole word.

Instructions: Word Detectives solve their mysteries by paying attention to details. The details you need to pay attention to in decoding are the spelling units and the sounds to which they correspond. See how many of these spelling units you can find in 2 minutes. Either underline the spelling units in alternating colors or rewrite the words in alternating colors with the fine-tip markers. After time is called, we will share with each other these word clues we found and then say the sound that goes with each of them (see *Talking Letters* card), moving from left to right, and then blend the sounds to say the whole word.

> knelph, quoopdro, sognoy, vopfow, blesp, clostrills, whulls, chunglewums, swejeety, prite

Word Transferring

Children are given 10 new words that were not practiced but contain target spelling units in the practiced words to evaluate whether they can pronounce them correctly in a different word context. The transfer words were constructed by altering one consonant- or one vowel-spelling unit in Jabberwocky words used in Word Building. Teachers record accuracy for whole words and spelling units, note whether children refer to the student *Talking Letters* card with spelling–phoneme correspondences, and time how long it takes to pronounce all the words on the transfer list. These results can be graphed on Reading Rockets or a teacher-designed chart so that both students and teacher have a visual record of student response to alphabetic principle instruction.

Instructions: Once Word Detectives figure out the code they can apply it to new words or cases. Here are 10 words that have the same spelling units that we have practiced but in different made-up words. How accurately and how fast can you use those spelling units to say these words? Record your accuracy and time on the Reading Rockets in your R-File. Refer to *Talking Letters* if that helps you.

> knilph, shoopdro, sopnoy, smopfow, shesp, blostrills, whells, chunglebums, swepeety, pribe

Are They Relatives?

Does the underlined spelling unit in the first word correspond to the same phoneme as the underlined spelling unit in the second word? Children are asked to circle YES or NO on the worksheet in the Student Response Booklet if they think the spelling units underlined in the pair of pseudowords do or do not stand for the same sound (phonemes); that is, do they match? If there are differences of opinion, those items are discussed in reference to prior activities with *Talking Letters*. In contrast to the purpose of the warm-up that was to put this knowledge of grapheme–phoneme correspondences on automatic pilot, the purpose of this activity is to reflect consciously on the system of spelling–sound correspondences. Children receive R-File points for completing the activity within the time limits.

Instructions: Look carefully at each pair of words and circle YES on your worksheet if you think the underlined spelling units in each word stand for the same sound; circle NO if you think they don't. Remember that sometimes the same spelling unit stands for different sounds and that sometimes the same sound is spelled in different ways. Let's see how many

you can do in 2 minutes. After time is called we will discuss any of your answers for which not everyone agreed.

pr<u>e</u>fer	p<u>er</u>form
scr<u>ew</u>	n<u>oo</u>n
lad<u>y</u>	sk<u>y</u>
sailb<u>oa</u>t	t<u>oe</u>nail
sch<u>oo</u>l	f<u>oo</u>l
tr<u>ea</u>t	gr<u>ea</u>t
n<u>o</u>body	r<u>o</u>bber
b<u>e</u>fore	b<u>e</u>tter
pi<u>e</u>	m<u>i</u>ce
g<u>a</u>me	pl<u>ay</u>

Sorting by Sound Features

The teacher points to one word at a time on a list in the Student Response Booklet. As you point to the word, name the word and point to the underlined spelling unit and produce the associated phoneme; then ask the children to choose the letter of the category at the top with the correct nickname sound for that spelling unit. Continue this procedure until all words are sorted into categories at the top of the list. Then help the children articulate the generalization that a specific spelling unit may stand for a small set of sounds. Children receive R-File points for each correct categorization of a spelling unit by its associated phoneme.

Although most of these alternations to be sorted are from the Anglo-Saxon layer of the language, a few (e.g., /zh/ for *s,* /short i/ for *y,* and /k/ for *ch*) are from the Romance or Greek layers of the language (see Table 1, p. 9).

Instructions: In this activity, categories for sorting words are listed at the top of the page. Each category has a capital letter. Sort each of the words in the list into one category by writing a capital letter beside it. At the end we will discuss what rule you applied to the sorting and what conclusion we can draw from the group sorting we just did.

Nicknames are /ks/A and /z/B (labeled on card headings).

bo<u>x</u>	ta<u>x</u>	<u>X</u>erox
e<u>x</u>ample	<u>x</u>ylophone	si<u>x</u>
fo<u>x</u>	ne<u>x</u>t	
e<u>x</u>cept	bo<u>x</u>ing	

Rule to discuss after sorting: *x* at the end of a word can stand for two phonemes, /k/ or /s/; *x* at the beginning of a word can stand for /z/.

Sorting by Word Context

Children are given words with a blank and a box with choices of spelling units in the Student Response Booklet. The task is to choose the spelling unit that could fit into the blank in the word because in this word context adding that spelling unit spells a real word. These items contain spelling units that stand for the same sound but only one of the spelling units in a word-specific context spells a real word with meaning.

Instructions: Another way that Word Detectives have to make sense of their clues is by examining them for the context, that is the place in which they occur and all the surrounding clues. Each of the words you will see has a blank. Then you will see spellings but only one spelling fits sensibly into the blank. To figure out which spellings would or would not fit into the blank—that is, into the context of the word—you need to pay close attention to all the spelling, sound, and meaning clues of the word. You have to fully analyze all the evidence you have at hand! As soon as you think you know a spelling that would fit into the word, circle it. As a Word Detective, it is important that you examine all the evidence—consider all the spelling units—before you make your decision about which spelling fits in the word.

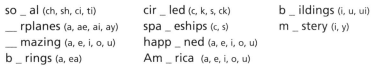

so _ al (ch, sh, ci, ti)   cir _ led (c, k, s, ck)   b _ ildings (i, u, ui)

__ rplanes (a, ae, ai, ay)   spa _ eships (c, s)   m _ stery (i, y)

__ mazing (a, e, i, o, u)   happ _ ned (a, e, i, o, u)

b _ rings (a, ea)   Am _ rica (a, e, i, o, u)

LESSON **4** Words and Word Parts for
Sound, Spelling, and Meaning

Paying Attention to Sound Units
and Their Relationships to Spelling Units

Student Response Booklet

Note: All lessons start with a warm-up, just as athletes warm up before a sports game. (See *Talking Letters* card.)

ACTIVITIES

Word Building

We always start by saying and analyzing the sounds in each word. We will not use real words but rather "Jabberwocky" words, like from *Alice in Wonderland* [read *Jabberwocky* poem from *Alice in Wonderland*]. First close your eyes and listen as I say a word. Then hold up the number of fingers for the number of syllables you hear in it. If we disagree, then we will discuss it. Then you will open your eyes and use these colored discs to count out the number of phonemes in each syllable. Together we will practice 10 words in each lesson.

Word Generating

Instructions: Word Detectives sometimes get their clues from generating and reasoning about similar cases. Now I would like you to think of words that have the same sounds as the ones I say. Write the words you think of in your Response Booklets. When you are done, we will share with the others. I will write the words on the board.

1. _____
2. _____
3. _____
4. _____
5. _____
6. _____
7. _____
8. _____
9. _____
10. _____

Unit Finding

Spelling units are one- or two-letter units that correspond to a sound. You may look at your *Talking Letters* card.

Instructions: Word Detectives solve their mysteries by paying attention to details. The details you need to pay attention to in decoding are the spelling units and the sounds to which they correspond. See how many of these spelling units you can find in 2 minutes. Either underline the spelling units in alternating colors or rewrite the words in alternating colors with the fine-tip markers. After time is called, we will share with each other these word clues we found and then say the sound that goes with each of them (see *Talking Letters* card), moving from left to right, and then blend the sounds to say the whole word.

knelph	vopfow	whulls	prite
quoopdro	blesp	chunglewums	
sognoy	clostrills	swejeety	

Word Transferring

Instructions: Once Word Detectives figure out the code they can apply it to new words or cases. Here are 10 words that have the same spelling units that we have practiced but in different made-up words. How accurately and how fast can you use those spelling units to say these words? Record your accuracy and time on the Reading Rockets in your R-File. Refer to *Talking Letters* if that helps you.

knilph	smopfow	whells	pribe
shoopdro	shesp	chunglebums	
sopnoy	blostrills	swepeety	

Are They Relatives?

Instructions: Look carefully at each pair of words and circle YES on your worksheet if you think the underlined spelling units in each word stand for the same sound; circle NO if you think they don't. Remember that sometimes the same spelling unit stands for different sounds and that sometimes the same sound is spelled in different ways. Let's see how many you can do in 2 minutes. After time is called we will discuss any of your answers for which not everyone agreed.

pr<u>e</u>fer	p<u>er</u>form	YES	NO
scr<u>ew</u>	n<u>oo</u>n	YES	NO

lady	sky	YES	NO
sailb**oa**t	t**oe**nail	YES	NO
sch**oo**l	f**oo**l	YES	NO
tr**ea**t	gr**ea**t	YES	NO
n**o**body	r**o**bber	YES	NO
b**e**fore	b**e**tter	YES	NO
p**ie**	m**i**c**e**	YES	NO
g**a**m**e**	pl**ay**	YES	NO

Sorting by Sound Features

Instructions: In this activity, categories for sorting words are listed at the top of the page. Each category has a capital letter. Sort each of the words in the list into one category by writing a capital letter beside it. At the end we will discuss what rule you applied to the sorting and what conclusion we can draw from the group sorting we just did.

Nicknames are /ks/ A and /z/ B.

bo**x**	e**x**cept	ne**x**t	si**x**
e**x**ample	ta**x**	bo**x**ing	
fo**x**	**x**ylophone	**X**erox	

Sorting by Word Context

Instructions: Another way that Word Detectives have to make sense of their clues is by examining them for the context, that is the place in which they occur and all the surrounding clues. Each of the words you will see has a blank. Then you will see spellings but only one spelling fits sensibly into the blank. To figure out which spellings would or would not fit into the blank—that is, into the context of the word—you need to pay close attention to all the spelling, sound, and meaning clues of the word. You have to fully analyze all the evidence you have at hand! As soon as you think you know a spelling that would fit into the word, circle it. As a Word Detective, it is important that you examine all the evidence—consider all the spelling units—before you make your decision about which spelling fits in the word.

so __ al	cir __ led	b __ ildings
(ch, sh, ci, ti)	(c, k, s, ck)	(i, u, ui)
__ rplanes	spa __ eships	m __ stery
(a, ae, ai, ay)	(c, s)	(i, y)
__ mazing	happ __ ned	
(a, e, i, o, u)	(a, e, i, o, u)	
b __ rings	Am __ rica	
(a, ea)	(a, e, i, o, u)	

LESSON 5 Words and Word Parts for Sound, Spelling, and Meaning

Paying Attention to Sound Units and Their Relationships to Spelling Units

Teacher Material

The following grapheme–phoneme correspondences are taught using *Talking Letters:* • Single-letter consonants • Short vowels in closed syllables • Long vowels in open syllables	Materials needed: • *Talking Letters* for automatic alphabetic principle • Work folders

WARM-UP (FOR THE TEACHER)

For the warm-up, name the letter or letter group on the *Talking Letters* card, say the pictured word containing a target phoneme, and then produce the target phoneme. Next, the students take a turn and repeat what is named or said by you. This approach develops orthographic awareness of spelling units; phonological awareness of corresponding phonemes in and out of word context; and, through close timing, the automaticity of spelling–phoneme correspondence. Monitor whether children are coordinating looking at the relevant letters and pictured words with naming of the letters and words and producing phonemes.

LESSON OVERVIEW (READ TO STUDENTS)

It is normal to come across words you do not know. One way to figure out an unknown word is to find the spelling units and think about their associated sounds. We will call these spelling–sound correspondences the *alphabetic principle.* Sometimes in English, more than one sound is associated with the same spelling unit. We will do seven different kinds of activities in each session to teach you to be a Word Detective who uses alphabetic principle and sound patterns in words to decode unknown words. These activities are *Word Building, Word Generating, Unit Finding, Word Transferring, Are They Relatives? Sorting by Sound Features,* and *Sorting by Word Context.* These activities should give you lots of strategies for using spelling units and their relationships to sounds to figure out words. We will use our electronic timer for the second through fourth activities but not the others. Let's begin.

ACTIVITIES

Word Building

Instructions: We always start by saying and analyzing the sounds in each word. We will not use real words but rather "Jabberwocky" words, like from *Alice in Wonderland* [read *Jabberwocky* poem from *Alice in Wonderland*]. First close your eyes and listen as I say a word. Then hold up the number of fingers for the number of syllables you hear in it. If we disagree, then we will discuss it. Then you will open your eyes and use these colored discs to count out the number of phonemes in each syllable. Together we will practice 10 words in each lesson.

Key:
S = syllable(s);
P = phoneme(s);
1st, 2nd, 3rd =
order of syllables

thermb
(1 S: 3 P)

haifraff
(2 S: 3 P, 1st; 3 P, 2nd)

jeksie
(2 S: 3 P, 1st; 2 P, 2nd)

soatyaz
(2 S: 3 P, 1st; 3 P, 2nd)

glofe
(1 S: 4 P)

trabe
(1 S: 4 P)

smewbry
(2 S: 3 P, 1st; 3 P, 2nd)

fladorudge
(3 S: 4 P, 1st; 1 P, 2nd;
3 or 4 P, 3rd)

pluce
(1 S: 4 P)

sligurshek
(3 S: 4 P, 1st; 1 P, 2nd;
3 P, 3rd)

Word Generating

The teacher explains that R-Files have a double meaning. Not only are they the files in our work folders where we record our points for correct answers but they are also the "files in OUR minds" in which we store the words we learn. Teachers provide a sound unit (phoneme) and ask children to generate real words or Jabberwocky words that have in them that sound unit. The students write these words in their Response Booklets. Then after time is called after 5 minutes (30 seconds per phoneme), each child shares one word with the group. The teacher records on chalk or white board the word each child shares, providing feedback if necessary. Each child who contributes a word receives R-File points in his or her Response Booklet.

Instructions: Word Detectives sometimes get their clues from generating and reasoning about similar cases. Now I would like you to think of words that have the same sounds as the ones I say and are spelled this way (write on board). Write the words you think of in your Response Booklets. When you are done, we will share with the others. I will write the words on the board.

ck, qu, oo, p, dr, long o, wr, al, t, el

Note: After saying each sound, wait 30 seconds for the student to write the word, then say the next sound.

Unit Finding

The same 10 words practiced under Word Building are presented visually in the Student Response Booklet. Children are asked to underline (using two fine-point colored markers) each of the spelling units in a word using alternating colors for adjacent spelling units. (If this proves too difficult they can rewrite the word, spelling unit by spelling unit, with each adjacent spelling unit in a different color.) Remember, a spelling unit can be 1 or 2 letters and corresponds to a sound or blended sounds on *Talking Letters*. Children are given 2 minutes for 10 words, and their accuracy and time are recorded in work folders. Children who complete the activity correctly within the time limits receive R-File points. Initially

some may not finish within the time limits, but eventually they will. Any discrepancies among children or obvious errors are pointed out to them and discussed. Once everyone agrees on how to parse the words into spelling units, the group makes the sound that goes with each spelling unit and then synthesizes the sounds into a recognizable whole word.

Instructions: Word Detectives solve their mysteries by paying attention to details. The details you need to pay attention to in decoding are the spelling units and the sounds to which they correspond. See how many of these spelling units you can find in 2 minutes. Either underline the spelling units in alternating colors or rewrite the words in alternating colors with the fine-tip markers. After time is called, we will share with each other these word clues we found and then say the sound that goes with each of them (see *Talking Letters* card), moving from left to right, and then blend the sounds to say the whole word.

> thermb, haifraff, jeksie, soatyaz, glofe, trabe, smewbry, fladorudge, pluce, sligurshek

Word Transferring

Children are given 10 new words that were not practiced but contain target spelling units in the practiced words to evaluate whether they can pronounce them correctly in a different word context. The transfer words were constructed by altering one consonant- or one vowel-spelling unit in Jabberwocky words used in Word Building. Teachers record accuracy for whole words and spelling units, note whether children refer to the student *Talking Letters* card with spelling–phoneme correspondences, and time how long it takes to pronounce all the words on the transfer list. These results can be graphed on Reading Rockets or a teacher-designed chart so that both students and teacher have a visual record of student response to alphabetic principle instruction.

Instructions: Once Word Detectives figure out the code they can apply it to new words or cases. Here are 10 words that have the same spelling units that we have practiced but in different made-up words. How accurately and how fast can you use those spelling units to say these words? Record your accuracy and time on the Reading Rockets in your R-File. Refer to *Talking Letters* if that helps you.

> flermb, haidraff, jekfie, soatraz, stofe, trube, smobry, flaporudge, pluze, firgurshek

Are They Relatives?

Does the underlined spelling unit in the first word correspond to the same phoneme as the underlined spelling unit in the second word? Children are asked to circle YES or NO on the worksheet in the Student Response Booklet if they think the spelling units underlined in the pair of pseudowords do or do not stand for the same sound (phonemes); that is, do they match? If there are differences of opinion, those items are discussed in reference to prior activities with *Talking Letters*. In contrast to the purpose of the warm-up that was to put this knowledge of grapheme–phoneme correspondences on automatic pilot, the purpose of this activity is to reflect consciously on the system of spelling–sound correspondences. Children receive R-File points for completing the activity within the time limits.

Instructions: Look carefully at each pair of words and circle YES on your worksheet if you think the underlined spelling units in each word stand for the same sound; circle NO if you think they don't. Remember that sometimes the same spelling unit stands for different sounds and that sometimes the same sound is spelled in different ways. Let's see how many you can do in 2 minutes. After time is called we will discuss any of your answers for which not everyone agreed.

fa<u>c</u>es	<u>s</u>avings
<u>ch</u>orus	<u>k</u>etchup
ra<u>d</u>ar	b<u>a</u>tter
<u>kn</u>ock	balloo<u>n</u>
c<u>u</u>t	s<u>u</u>per
st<u>u</u>dent	p<u>u</u>ppy
br<u>ai</u>n	pla<u>ce</u>
st<u>o</u>ve	h<u>o</u>t
gr<u>ow</u>	cl<u>ow</u>n
thi<u>rs</u>ty	show<u>er</u>

Sorting by Sound Features

The teacher points to one word at a time on a list in the Student Response Booklet. As you point to the word, name the word and point to the underlined spelling unit and produce the associated phoneme; then ask the children to choose the letter of the category at the top with the correct nickname sound for that spelling unit. Continue this procedure until all words are sorted into categories at the top of the list. Then help the children articulate the generalization that a specific spelling unit may stand for a small set of sounds. Children receive R-File points for each correct categorization of a spelling unit by its associated phoneme.

Although most of these alternations to be sorted are from the Anglo-Saxon layer of the language, a few (e.g., /zh/ for *s*, /short i/ for *y*, and /k/ for *ch*) are from the Romance or Greek layers of the language (see Table 1, p. 9).

Instructions: In this activity, categories for sorting words are listed at the top of the page. Each category has a capital letter. Sort each of the words in the list into one category by writing a capital letter beside it. At the end we will discuss what rule you applied to the sorting and what conclusion we can draw from the group sorting we just did.

Nicknames are /y consonant/A, /long i/B, /long e/, /short i/C (labeled on card headings).

<u>y</u>es	<u>y</u>ellow	wh<u>y</u>
fl<u>y</u>	cr<u>y</u>	h<u>y</u>mn
bab<u>y</u>	lad<u>y</u>	
g<u>y</u>m	<u>y</u>ard	

Rule to discuss after sorting: *y* at the beginning of a word stands for a consonant sound; *y* at the end of a word can stand for *long i* or *long e* vowel; *y* in the middle of a syllable may stand for a *short i* vowel sound.

Sorting by Word Context

Children are given words with a blank and a box with choices of spelling units in the Student Response Booklet. The task is to choose the spelling unit that could fit into the blank in the word because in this word context adding that spelling unit spells a real word. These items contain spelling units that stand for the same sound but only one of the spelling units in a word-specific context spells a real word with meaning.

Instructions: Another way that Word Detectives have to make sense of their clues is by examining them for the context, that is the place in which they occur and all the surrounding

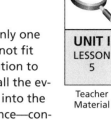

clues. Each of the words you will see has a blank. Then you will see spellings but only one spelling fits sensibly into the blank. To figure out which spellings would or would not fit into the blank—that is, into the context of the word—you need to pay close attention to all the spelling, sound, and meaning clues of the word. You have to fully analyze all the evidence you have at hand! As soon as you think you know a spelling that would fit into the word, circle it. As a Word Detective, it is important that you examine all the evidence—consider all the spelling units—before you make your decision about which spelling fits in the word.

_ ience	spa _ eship	fig _ res
(s, sc)	(c, s)	(y, u)
s _ ved	pol _ ceman	h _ ried
(al, ol, el)	(e, i)	(er, ir, ur)
e _ ample	invest _ gate	
(x, z)	(a, e, i, o, u)	
trav _	obs _ ved	
(el, le)	(er, ir, or, ur)	

47

LESSON **5** Words and Word Parts for
Sound, Spelling, and Meaning

Paying Attention to Sound Units
and Their Relationships to Spelling Units

Student Response Booklet

Note: All lessons start with a warm-up, just as athletes warm up before a sports game. (See *Talking Letters* card.)

ACTIVITIES

Word Building

We always start by saying and analyzing the sounds in each word. We will not use real words but rather "Jabberwocky" words, like from *Alice in Wonderland* [read *Jabberwocky* poem from *Alice in Wonderland*]. First close your eyes and listen as I say a word. Then hold up the number of fingers for the number of syllables you hear in it. If we disagree, then we will discuss it. Then you will open your eyes and use these colored discs to count out the number of phonemes in each syllable. Together we will practice 10 words in each lesson.

Word Generating

Instructions: Word Detectives sometimes get their clues from generating and reasoning about similar cases. Now I would like you to think of words that have the same sounds as the ones I say. Write the words you think of in your Response Booklets. When you are done, we will share with the others. I will write the words on the board.

1. _____
2. _____
3. _____
4. _____
5. _____
6. _____
7. _____
8. _____
9. _____
10. _____

Unit Finding

Spelling units are one- or two-letter units that correspond to a sound. You may look at your *Talking Letters* card.

Instructions: Word Detectives solve their mysteries by paying attention to details. The details you need to pay attention to in decoding are the spelling units and the sounds to which they correspond. See how many of these spelling units you can find in 2 minutes. Either underline the spelling units in alternating colors or rewrite the words in alternating colors with the fine-tip markers. After time is called, we will share with each other these word clues we found and then say the sound that goes with each of them (see *Talking Letters* card), moving from left to right, and then blend the sounds to say the whole word.

hermb	soatyaz	smewbry	sligurshek
haifraff	glofe	fladorudge	
jeksie	trabe	pluce	

Word Transferring

Instructions: Once Word Detectives figure out the code they can apply it to new words or cases. Here are 10 words that have the same spelling units that we have practiced but in different made-up words. How accurately and how fast can you use those spelling units to say these words? Record your accuracy and time on the Reading Rockets in your R-File. Refer to *Talking Letters* if that helps you.

flermb	soatraz	smobry	firgurshek
haidraff	stofe	flaporudge	
jekfie	trube	pluze	

Are They Relatives?

Instructions: Look carefully at each pair of words and circle YES on your worksheet if you think the underlined spelling units in each word stand for the same sound; circle NO if you think they don't. Remember that sometimes the same spelling unit stands for different sounds and that sometimes the same sound is spelled in different ways. Let's see how many you can do in 2 minutes. After time is called we will discuss any of your answers for which not everyone agreed.

fa<u>c</u>es	<u>s</u>avings	YES	NO
<u>ch</u>orus	<u>k</u>etchup	YES	NO

r<u>a</u>dar	<u>b</u>atter	YES	NO
<u>kn</u>ock	balloo<u>n</u>	YES	NO
c<u>u</u>t	s<u>u</u>per	YES	NO
st<u>u</u>dent	p<u>u</u>ppy	YES	NO
br<u>ai</u>n	pl<u>a</u>ce	YES	NO
st<u>o</u>ve	h<u>o</u>t	YES	NO
<u>gr</u>ow	cl<u>ow</u>n	YES	NO
thi<u>rs</u>ty	show<u>e</u>r	YES	NO

Sorting by Sound Features

Instructions: In this activity, categories for sorting words are listed at the top of the page. Each category has a capital letter. Sort each of the words in the list into one category by writing a capital letter beside it. At the end we will discuss what rule you applied to the sorting and what conclusion we can draw from the group sorting we just did.

Nicknames are /y consonant/ A, /long i/ B, /long e/ C, /short i/ D.

<u>y</u>es	g<u>y</u>m	lad<u>y</u>	h<u>y</u>mn
fl<u>y</u>	<u>y</u>ellow	<u>y</u>ard	
bab<u>y</u>	cr<u>y</u>	wh<u>y</u>	

Sorting by Word Context

Instructions: Another way that Word Detectives have to make sense of their clues is by examining them for the context, that is the place in which they occur and all the surrounding clues. Each of the words you will see has a blank. Then you will see spellings but only one spelling fits sensibly into the blank. To figure out which spellings would or would not fit into the blank—that is, into the context of the word—you need to pay close attention to all the spelling, sound, and meaning clues of the word. You have to fully analyze all the evidence you have at hand! As soon as you think you know a spelling that would fit into the word, circle it. As a Word Detective, it is important that you examine all the evidence—consider all the spelling units—before you make your decision about which spelling fits in the word.

__ ience	spa __ eship	fig __ res
(s, sc)	(c, s)	(y, u)
s __ ved	pol __ ceman	h __ ried
(al, ol, el)	(e, i)	(er, ir, ur)
e __ ample	invest __ gate	
(x, z)	(a, e, i, o, u)	
trav __	obs __ ved	
(el, le)	(er, ir, or, ur)	

LESSON **6** Words and Word Parts for Sound, Spelling, and Meaning

Paying Attention to Sound Units and Their Relationships to Spelling Units

Teacher Material

The following grapheme–phoneme correspondences are taught using *Talking Letters:* • Single-letter consonants • Short vowels in closed syllables • Long vowels in open syllables	Materials needed: • *Talking Letters* for automatic alphabetic principle • Work folders

WARM-UP (FOR THE TEACHER)

For the warm-up, name the letter or letter group on the *Talking Letters* card, say the pictured word containing a target phoneme, and then produce the target phoneme. Next, the students take a turn and repeat what is named or said by you. This approach develops orthographic awareness of spelling units; phonological awareness of corresponding phonemes in and out of word context; and, through close timing, the automaticity of spelling–phoneme correspondence. Monitor whether children are coordinating looking at the relevant letters and pictured words with naming of the letters and words and producing phonemes.

LESSON OVERVIEW (READ TO STUDENTS)

It is normal to come across words you do not know. One way to figure out an unknown word is to find the spelling units and think about their associated sounds. We will call these spelling–sound correspondences the *alphabetic principle.* Sometimes in English, more than one sound is associated with the same spelling unit. We will do seven different kinds of activities in each session to teach you to be a Word Detective who uses alphabetic principle and sound patterns in words to decode unknown words. These activities are *Word Building, Word Generating, Unit Finding, Word Transferring, Are They Relatives? Sorting by Sound Features,* and *Sorting by Word Context.* These activities should give you lots of strategies for using spelling units and their relationships to sounds to figure out words. We will use our electronic timer for the second through fourth activities but not the others. Let's begin.

ACTIVITIES

Word Building

Instructions: We always start by saying and analyzing the sounds in each word. We will not use real words but rather "Jabberwocky" words, like from *Alice in Wonderland* [read *Jabberwocky* poem from *Alice in Wonderland*]. First close your eyes and listen as I say a word. Then hold up the number of fingers for the number of syllables you hear in it. If we disagree, then we will discuss it. Then you will open your eyes and use these colored discs to count out the number of phonemes in each syllable. Together we will practice 10 words in each lesson.

Key:
S = syllable(s);
P = phoneme(s);
1st, 2nd, 3rd =
order of syllables

wraltway
(2 S: 4 P, 1st; 2 P, 2nd)

zullcrusk
(2 S: 3 P, 1st; 5 P, 2nd)

grax
(1 S: 5 P)

lutkaw
(2 S: 3 P, 1st; 2 P, 2nd)

hebtou
(2 S: 3 P, 1st; 2 P, 2nd)

nidmoin
(2 S: 3 P, 1st; 3 P, 2nd)

cimdaut
(2 S: 3 P, 1st; 3 P, 2nd)

yigfrue
(2 S: 3 P, 1st; 3 P, 2nd)

sceanruz
(2 S: 4 P, 1st; 3 P, 2nd)

snubarth
(2 S: 3 P, 1st; 3 P, 2nd)

Word Generating

The teacher explains that R-Files have a double meaning. Not only are they the files in our work folders where we record our points for correct answers but they are also the "files in OUR minds" in which we store the words we learn. Teachers provide a sound unit (phoneme) and ask children to generate real words or Jabberwocky words that have in them that sound unit. The students write these words in their Response Booklets. Then after time is called after 5 minutes (30 seconds per phoneme), each child shares one word with the group. The teacher records on chalk or white board the word each child shares, providing feedback if necessary. Each child who contributes a word receives R-File points in his or her Response Booklet.

Instructions: Word Detectives sometimes get their clues from generating and reasoning about similar cases. Now I would like you to think of words that have the same sounds as the ones I say and are spelled this way (write on board). Write the words you think of in your Response Booklets. When you are done, we will share with the others. I will write the words on the board.

w, ay, z, ul, cr, u, sk, d, short o, st

Note: After saying each sound, wait 30 seconds for the student to write the word, then say the next sound.

Unit Finding

The same 10 words practiced under Word Building are presented visually in the Student Response Booklet. Children are asked to underline (using two fine-point colored markers) each of the spelling units in a word using alternating colors for adjacent spelling units. (If this proves too difficult they can rewrite the word, spelling unit by spelling unit, with each adjacent spelling unit in a different color.) Remember, a spelling unit can be 1 or 2 letters and corresponds to a sound or blended sounds on *Talking Letters*. Children are given 2 minutes for 10 words, and their accuracy and time are recorded in work folders. Children who complete the activity correctly within the time limits receive R-File points. Initially some may not finish within the time limits, but eventually they will. Any discrepancies among children or obvious errors are pointed out to them and discussed. Once everyone agrees on how to parse the words into spelling units, the group makes the sound that goes with each spelling unit and then synthesizes the sounds into a recognizable whole word.

Instructions: Word Detectives solve their mysteries by paying attention to details. The details you need to pay attention to in decoding are the spelling units and the sounds to which they correspond. See how many of these spelling units you can find in 2 minutes. Either underline the spelling units in alternating colors or rewrite the words in alternating colors with the fine-tip markers. After time is called, we will share with each other these word clues we found and then say the sound that goes with each of them (see *Talking Letters* card), moving from left to right, and then blend the sounds to say the whole word.

> wraltway, zullcrusk, grax, lutkaw, hebtou, nidmoin, cimdaut, yigfrue, sceanruz, snubarth

Word Transferring

Children are given 10 new words that were not practiced but contain target spelling units in the practiced words to evaluate whether they can pronounce them correctly in a different word context. The transfer words were constructed by altering one consonant- or one vowel-spelling unit in Jabberwocky words used in Word Building. Teachers record accuracy for whole words and spelling units, note whether children refer to the student *Talking Letters* card with spelling–phoneme correspondences, and time how long it takes to pronounce all the words on the transfer list. These results can be graphed on Reading Rockets or a teacher-designed chart so that both students and teacher have a visual record of student response to alphabetic principle instruction.

Instructions: Once Word Detectives figure out the code they can apply it to new words or cases. Here are 10 words that have the same spelling units that we have practiced but in different made-up words. How accurately and how fast can you use those spelling units to say these words? Record your accuracy and time on the Reading Rockets in your R-File. Refer to *Talking Letters* if that helps you.

> saltway, tullcrusk, blax, lumkaw, hebsou, fidmoin, rimdaut, yogfrue, sheanruz, snudarth

Are They Relatives?

Does the underlined spelling unit in the first word correspond to the same phoneme as the underlined spelling unit in the second word? Children are asked to circle YES or NO on the worksheet in the Student Response Booklet if they think the spelling units underlined in the pair of pseudowords do or do not stand for the same sound (phonemes); that is, do they match? If there are differences of opinion, those items are discussed in reference to prior activities with *Talking Letters*. In contrast to the purpose of the warm-up that was to put this knowledge of grapheme–phoneme correspondences on automatic pilot, the purpose of this activity is to reflect consciously on the system of spelling–sound correspondences. Children receive R-File points for completing the activity within the time limits.

Instructions: Look carefully at each pair of words and circle YES on your worksheet if you think the underlined spelling units in each word stand for the same sound; circle NO if you think they don't. Remember that sometimes the same spelling unit stands for different sounds and that sometimes the same sound is spelled in different ways. Let's see how many you can do in 2 minutes. After time is called we will discuss any of your answers for which not everyone agreed.

engine	jet
plenty	breath
path	that
silver	child
education	ocean
whacks	wax
bunches	chorus
helping	laughing
evening	everyone
reflection	discussion

Sorting by Sound Features

The teacher points to one word at a time on a list in the Student Response Booklet. As you point to the word, name the word and point to the underlined spelling unit and produce the associated phoneme; then ask the children to choose the letter of the category at the top with the correct nickname sound for that spelling unit. Continue this procedure until all words are sorted into categories at the top of the list. Then help the children articulate the generalization that a specific spelling unit may stand for a small set of sounds. Children receive R-File points for each correct categorization of a spelling unit by its associated phoneme.

Although most of these alternations to be sorted are from the Anglo-Saxon layer of the language, a few (e.g., /zh/ for *s*, /short i/ for *y*, and /k/ for *ch*) are from the Romance or Greek layers of the language (see Table 1, p. 9).

Instructions: In this activity, categories for sorting words are listed at the top of the page. Each category has a capital letter. Sort each of the words in the list into one category by writing a capital letter beside it. At the end we will discuss what rule you applied to the sorting and what conclusion we can draw from the group sorting we just did.

Nicknames are /ch/A and /k/B (labeled on card headings).

chalk	chorus	beach
school	Chris	headache
chair	much	
watch	architect	

Rule to discuss after sorting: *ch* may stand for a single sound that does not correspond to c or h alone, as in *chair;* or it may stand for the /k/ sound, as in *chorus.*

Sorting by Word Context

Children are given words with a blank and a box with choices of spelling units in the Student Response Booklet. The task is to choose the spelling unit that could fit into the blank in the word because in this word context adding that spelling unit spells a real word. These items contain spelling units that stand for the same sound but only one of the spelling units in a word-specific context spells a real word with meaning.

Instructions: Another way that Word Detectives have to make sense of their clues is by examining them for the context, that is the place in which they occur and all the surrounding clues. Each of the words you will see has a blank. Then you will see spellings but only one

spelling fits sensibly into the blank. To figure out which spellings would or would not fit into the blank—that is, into the context of the word—you need to pay close attention to all the spelling, sound, and meaning clues of the word. You have to fully analyze all the evidence you have at hand! As soon as you think you know a spelling that would fit into the word, circle it. As a Word Detective, it is important that you examine all the evidence—consider all the spelling units—before you make your decision about which spelling fits in the word.

an _ mals
  (a, e, i, o, u)

occ _ red
  (er, ir, or, ur)

to _ stone
  (m, mb)

ba _ ground
  (c, k, ck)

flow _ s
  (ar, er, ir, or, ur)

c _ ling
  (e, ea, ee, ei, ie)

fl _ ting
  (o, oa, oo)

man _ ged
  (a, e, i, o, u)

_ larmed
  (a, e, i, o, u)

grav _ ty
  (a, e, i, o,u)

LESSON **6** Words and Word Parts for
Sound, Spelling, and Meaning

Paying Attention to Sound Units and Their Relationships to Spelling Units

Student Response Booklet

Note: All lessons start with a warm-up, just as athletes warm up before a sports game. (See *Talking Letters* card.)

ACTIVITIES

Word Building

We always start by saying and analyzing the sounds in each word. We will not use real words but rather "Jabberwocky" words, like from *Alice in Wonderland* [read *Jabberwocky* poem from *Alice in Wonderland*]. First close your eyes and listen as I say a word. Then hold up the number of fingers for the number of syllables you hear in it. If we disagree, then we will discuss it. Then you will open your eyes and use these colored discs to count out the number of phonemes in each syllable. Together we will practice 10 words in each lesson.

Word Generating

Instructions: Word Detectives sometimes get their clues from generating and reasoning about similar cases. Now I would like you to think of words that have the same sounds as the ones I say. Write the words you think of in your Response Booklets. When you are done, we will share with the others. I will write the words on the board.

1. _____
2. _____
3. _____
4. _____
5. _____
6. _____
7. _____
8. _____
9. _____
10. _____

Unit Finding

Spelling units are one- or two-letter units that correspond to a sound. You may look at your *Talking Letters* card.

Instructions: Word Detectives solve their mysteries by paying attention to details. The details you need to pay attention to in decoding are the spelling units and the sounds to which they correspond. See how many of these spelling units you can find in 2 minutes. Either underline the spelling units in alternating colors or rewrite the words in alternating colors with the fine-tip markers. After time is called, we will share with each other these word clues we found and then say the sound that goes with each of them (see *Talking Letters* card), moving from left to right, and then blend the sounds to say the whole word.

wraltway	lutkaw	cimdaut	snubarth
zullcrusk	hebtou	yigfrue	
grax	nidmoin	sceanruz	

Word Transferring

Instructions: Once Word Detectives figure out the code they can apply it to new words or cases. Here are 10 words that have the same spelling units that we have practiced but in different made-up words. How accurately and how fast can you use those spelling units to say these words? Record your accuracy and time on the Reading Rockets in your R-File. Refer to *Talking Letters* if that helps you.

saltway	lumkaw	rimdaut	snudarth
tullcrusk	hebsou	yogfrue	
blax	fidmoin	sheanruz	

Are They Relatives?

Instructions: Look carefully at each pair of words and circle YES on your worksheet if you think the underlined spelling units in each word stand for the same sound; circle NO if you think they don't. Remember that sometimes the same spelling unit stands for different sounds and that sometimes the same sound is spelled in different ways. Let's see how many you can do in 2 minutes. After time is called we will discuss any of your answers for which not everyone agreed.

en**g**ine	**j**et	YES	NO
pl**e**nty	br**ea**th	YES	NO
pa**th**	**th**at	YES	NO

silver	child	YES	NO
education	ocean	YES	NO
whacks	wax	YES	NO
bunches	chorus	YES	NO
helping	laughing	YES	NO
evening	everyone	YES	NO
reflection	discussion	YES	NO
thirsty	shower	YES	NO

Sorting by Sound Features

Instructions: In this activity, categories for sorting words are listed at the top of the page. Each category has a capital letter. Sort each of the words in the list into one category by writing a capital letter beside it. At the end we will discuss what rule you applied to the sorting and what conclusion we can draw from the group sorting we just did.

Nicknames are /ch/ A and /k/ B.

chalk	watch	much	headache
school	chorus	architect	
chair	Chris	beach	

Sorting by Word Context

Instructions: Another way that Word Detectives have to make sense of their clues is by examining them for the context, that is the place in which they occur and all the surrounding clues. Each of the words you will see has a blank. Then you will see spellings but only one spelling fits sensibly into the blank. To figure out which spellings would or would not fit into the blank—that is, into the context of the word—you need to pay close attention to all the spelling, sound, and meaning clues of the word. You have to fully analyze all the evidence you have at hand! As soon as you think you know a spelling that would fit into the word, circle it. As a Word Detective, it is important that you examine all the evidence—consider all the spelling units—before you make your decision about which spelling fits in the word.

an __ mals	flow __ s	__ larmed
(a, e, i, o, u)	(ar, er, ir, or, ur)	(a, e, i, o, u)
occ __ red	c __ ling	grav __ ty
(er, ir, or, ur)	(e, ea, ee, ei, ie)	(a, e, i, o,u)
to __ stone	fl __ ting	
(m, mb)	(o, oa, oo)	
ba __ ground	man __ ged	
(c, k, ck)	(a, e, i, o, u)	

LESSON 7 Words and Word Parts for Sound, Spelling, and Meaning

Paying Attention to Sound Units and Their Relationships to Spelling Units

Teacher Material

The following grapheme–phoneme correspondences are taught using *Talking Letters:* • Other consonant combinations • r- and l-controlled vowels	Materials needed: • *Talking Letters* for automatic alphabetic principle • Work folders

WARM-UP (FOR THE TEACHER)

For the warm-up, name the letter or letter group on the *Talking Letters* card, say the pictured word containing a target phoneme, and then produce the target phoneme. Next, the students take a turn and repeat what is named or said by you. This approach develops orthographic awareness of spelling units; phonological awareness of corresponding phonemes in and out of word context; and, through close timing, the automaticity of spelling–phoneme correspondence. Monitor whether children are coordinating looking at the relevant letters and pictured words with naming of the letters and words and producing phonemes.

LESSON OVERVIEW (READ TO STUDENTS)

It is normal to come across words you do not know. One way to figure out an unknown word is to find the spelling units and think about their associated sounds. We will call these spelling–sound correspondences the *alphabetic principle.* Sometimes in English, more than one sound is associated with the same spelling unit. We will do seven different kinds of activities in each session to teach you to be a Word Detective who uses alphabetic principle and sound patterns in words to decode unknown words. These activities are *Word Building, Word Generating, Unit Finding, Word Transferring, Are They Relatives? Sorting by Sound Features,* and *Sorting by Word Context.* These activities should give you lots of strategies for using spelling units and their relationships to sounds to figure out words. We will use our electronic timer for the second through fourth activities but not the others. Let's begin.

ACTIVITIES

Word Building

Instructions: We always start by saying and analyzing the sounds in each word. We will not use real words but rather "Jabberwocky" words, like from *Alice in Wonderland* [read *Jabberwocky* poem from *Alice in Wonderland*]. First close your eyes and listen as I say a word. Then hold up the number of fingers for the number of syllables you hear in it. If we disagree, then we will discuss it. Then you will open your eyes and use these colored discs to count out the number of phonemes in each syllable. Together we will practice 10 words in each lesson.

Key:
S = syllable(s);
P = phoneme(s);
1st, 2nd, 3rd =
order of syllables

sognoy
(2 S: 3 P, 1st; 2 P, 2nd)
sligursheck
(3 S: 4 P, 1st; 1 P, 2nd; 3 P, 3rd)
lutkaw
(2 S: 3 P, 1st; 2 P, 2nd)
haifraff
(2 S: 3 P, 1st; 3 P, 2nd)

hebtou
(2 S: 3 P, 1st; 2 P, 2nd)
smewbry
(2 S: 3 P, 1st; 3 P, 2nd)
cimdaut
(2 S: 3 P, 1st; 3 P, 2nd)
nidmoin
(2 S: 3 P, 1st; 3 P, 2nd)

vopfow
(2 S: 3 P, 1st; 2 P, 2nd)
soatyaz
(2 S: 3 P, 1st; 3 P, 2nd)

Word Generating

The teacher explains that R-Files have a double meaning. Not only are they the files in our work folders where we record our points for correct answers but they are also the "files in OUR minds" in which we store the words we learn. Teachers provide a sound unit (phoneme) and ask children to generate real words or Jabberwocky words that have in them that sound unit. The students write these words in their Response Booklets. Then after time is called after 5 minutes (30 seconds per phoneme), each child shares one word with the group. The teacher records on chalk or white board the word each child shares, providing feedback if necessary. Each child who contributes a word receives R-File points in his or her Response Booklet.

Instructions: Word Detectives sometimes get their clues from generating and reasoning about similar cases. Now I would like you to think of words that have the same sounds as the ones I say and are spelled this way (write on board). Write the words you think of in your Response Booklets. When you are done, we will share with the others. I will write the words on the board.

r, il, s, bl, e, sp, gr, a, x, pl

Note: After saying each sound, wait 30 seconds for the student to write the word, then say the next sound.

Unit Finding

The same 10 words practiced under Word Building are presented visually in the Student Response Booklet. Children are asked to underline (using two fine-point colored markers) each of the spelling units in a word using alternating colors for adjacent spelling units. (If this proves too difficult they can rewrite the word, spelling unit by spelling unit, with each adjacent spelling unit in a different color.) Remember, a spelling unit can be 1 or 2 letters and corresponds to a sound or blended sounds on *Talking Letters.* Children are given 2 minutes for 10 words, and their accuracy and time are recorded in work folders. Children

who complete the activity correctly within the time limits receive R-File points. Initially some may not finish within the time limits, but eventually they will. Any discrepancies among children or obvious errors are pointed out to them and discussed. Once everyone agrees on how to parse the words into spelling units, the group makes the sound that goes with each spelling unit and then synthesizes the sounds into a recognizable whole word.

Instructions: Word Detectives solve their mysteries by paying attention to details. The details you need to pay attention to in decoding are the spelling units and the sounds to which they correspond. See how many of these spelling units you can find in 2 minutes. Either underline the spelling units in alternating colors or rewrite the words in alternating colors with the fine-tip markers. After time is called, we will share with each other these word clues we found and then say the sound that goes with each of them (see *Talking Letters* card), moving from left to right, and then blend the sounds to say the whole word.

> sognoy, sligursheck, lutkaw, haifraff, hebtou, smewbry, cimdaut, nidmoin, vopfow, soatyaz

Word Transferring

Children are given 10 new words that were not practiced but contain target spelling units in the practiced words to evaluate whether they can pronounce them correctly in a different word context. The transfer words were constructed by altering one consonant- or one vowel-spelling unit in Jabberwocky words used in Word Building. Teachers record accuracy for whole words and spelling units, note whether children refer to the student *Talking Letters* card with spelling–phoneme correspondences, and time how long it takes to pronounce all the words on the transfer list. These results can be graphed on Reading Rockets or a teacher-designed chart so that both students and teacher have a visual record of student response to alphabetic principle instruction.

Instructions: Once Word Detectives figure out the code they can apply it to new words or cases. Here are 10 words that have the same spelling units that we have practiced but in different made-up words. How accurately and how fast can you use those spelling units to say these words? Record your accuracy and time on the Reading Rockets in your R-File. Refer to *Talking Letters* if that helps you.

> sognoo, slidursheck, lutbaw, haifrap, hebtoup, smewdry, camdaut, nidnoin, vapfow, croatyaz

Are They Relatives?

Does the underlined spelling unit in the first word correspond to the same phoneme as the underlined spelling unit in the second word? Children are asked to circle YES or NO on the worksheet in the Student Response Booklet if they think the spelling units underlined in the pair of pseudowords do or do not stand for the same sound (phonemes); that is, do they match? If there are differences of opinion, those items are discussed in reference to prior activities with *Talking Letters*. In contrast to the purpose of the warm-up that was to put this knowledge of grapheme–phoneme correspondences on automatic pilot, the purpose of this activity is to reflect consciously on the system of spelling–sound correspondences. Children receive R-File points for completing the activity within the time limits.

Instructions: Look carefully at each pair of words and circle YES on your worksheet if you think the underlined spelling units in each word stand for the same sound; circle NO if you think they don't. Remember that sometimes the same spelling unit stands for different

sounds and that sometimes the same sound is spelled in different ways. Let's see how many you can do in 2 minutes. After time is called we will discuss any of your answers for which not everyone agreed.

bea<u>g</u>le	bee<u>p</u>
ma<u>g</u>ic	ma<u>gn</u>et
<u>ph</u>oto	enou<u>gh</u>
<u>oy</u>ster	c<u>oi</u>ns
<u>c</u>ircus	cir<u>c</u>le
<u>x</u>-ray	bo<u>x</u>es
a<u>w</u>ful	sa<u>l</u>t
<u>w</u>ater	cla<u>w</u>
<u>sh</u>ine	ri<u>ch</u>es
kno<u>cks</u>	fo<u>x</u>es

Sorting by Sound Features

The teacher points to one word at a time on a list in the Student Response Booklet. As you point to the word, name the word and point to the underlined spelling unit and produce the associated phoneme; then ask the children to choose the letter of the category at the top with the correct nickname sound for that spelling unit. Continue this procedure until all words are sorted into categories at the top of the list. Then help the children articulate the generalization that a specific spelling unit may stand for a small set of sounds. Children receive R-File points for each correct categorization of a spelling unit by its associated phoneme.

Although most of these alternations to be sorted are from the Anglo-Saxon layer of the language, a few (e.g., /zh/ for *s*, /short i/ for *y*, and /k/ for *ch*) are from the Romance or Greek layers of the language (see Table 1, p. 9).

Instructions: In this activity, categories for sorting words are listed at the top of the page. Each category has a capital letter. Sort each of the words in the list into one category by writing a capital letter beside it. At the end we will discuss what rule you applied to the sorting and what conclusion we can draw from the group sorting we just did.

Nicknames are /th in thumb/A, /th in feather/B (labeled on card headings).

<u>th</u>is	<u>th</u>at	wea<u>th</u>er
<u>th</u>umb	<u>th</u>em	<u>th</u>in
<u>th</u>e	fea<u>th</u>er	
wi<u>th</u>	<u>th</u>ink	

Rule to discuss after sorting: *th* can stand for two sounds. One is voiced. Put the palm of your hand in front of your mouth as you say the sound. Do you feel your breath as you say the *th* sound? One is not voiced. When the palm of your hand is in front of your mouth, you do not feel your breath.

Sorting by Word Context

Children are given words with a blank and a box with choices of spelling units in the Student Response Booklet. The task is to choose the spelling unit that could fit into the blank in the word because in this word context adding that spelling unit spells a real word. These items contain spelling units that stand for the same sound but only one of the spelling units in a word-specific context spells a real word with meaning.

Instructions: Another way that Word Detectives have to make sense of their clues is by examining them for the context, that is the place in which they occur and all the surrounding clues. Each of the words you will see has a blank. Then you will see spellings but only one spelling fits sensibly into the blank. To figure out which spellings would or would not fit into the blank—that is, into the context of the word—you need to pay close attention to all the spelling, sound, and meaning clues of the word. You have to fully analyze all the evidence you have at hand! As soon as you think you know a spelling that would fit into the word, circle it. As a Word Detective, it is important that you examine all the evidence—consider all the spelling units—before you make your decision about which spelling fits in the word.

famil _ ar
(e, i, y)

carr _ ts
(i, e, o)

raz _ r
(a, e, i, o, u)

min _ tes
(e, i, u)

skel _ ton
(a, e, i, o, u)

husb _ nd
(a, e, i, o, u)

stom _ ch
(a, e, i, o, u)

hum _ n
(a, e, i, o, u)

wid _
(oa, oe, ow, oo)

comm _ n
(a, e, i, o, u)

LESSON **7** Words and Word Parts for
Sound, Spelling, and Meaning

Paying Attention to Sound Units and Their Relationships to Spelling Units

Student Response Booklet

Note: All lessons start with a warm-up, just as athletes warm up before a sports game. (See *Talking Letters* card.)

ACTIVITIES

Word Building

We always start by saying and analyzing the sounds in each word. We will not use real words but rather "Jabberwocky" words, like from *Alice in Wonderland* [read *Jabberwocky* poem from *Alice in Wonderland*]. First close your eyes and listen as I say a word. Then hold up the number of fingers for the number of syllables you hear in it. If we disagree, then we will discuss it. Then you will open your eyes and use these colored discs to count out the number of phonemes in each syllable. Together we will practice 10 words in each lesson.

Word Generating

Instructions: Word Detectives sometimes get their clues from generating and reasoning about similar cases. Now I would like you to think of words that have the same sounds as the ones I say. Write the words you think of in your Response Booklets. When you are done, we will share with the others. I will write the words on the board.

1. _____
2. _____
3. _____
4. _____
5. _____
6. _____
7. _____
8. _____
9. _____
10. _____

Unit Finding

Spelling units are one- or two-letter units that correspond to a sound. You may look at your *Talking Letters* card.

Instructions: Word Detectives solve their mysteries by paying attention to details. The details you need to pay attention to in decoding are the spelling units and the sounds to which they correspond. See how many of these spelling units you can find in 2 minutes. Either underline the spelling units in alternating colors or rewrite the words in alternating colors with the fine-tip markers. After time is called, we will share with each other these word clues we found and then say the sound that goes with each of them (see *Talking Letters* card), moving from left to right, and then blend the sounds to say the whole word.

sognoy	haifraff	cimdaut	soatyaz
sligursheck	hebtou	nidmoin	
lutkaw	smewbry	vopfow	

Word Transferring

Instructions: Once Word Detectives figure out the code they can apply it to new words or cases. Here are 10 words that have the same spelling units that we have practiced but in different made-up words. How accurately and how fast can you use those spelling units to say these words? Record your accuracy and time on the Reading Rockets in your R-File. Refer to *Talking Letters* if that helps you.

sognoo	haifrap	camdaut	croatyaz
slidursheck	hebtoup	nidnoin	
lutbaw	smewdry	vapfow	

Are They Relatives?

Instructions: Look carefully at each pair of words and circle YES on your worksheet if you think the underlined spelling units in each word stand for the same sound; circle NO if you think they don't. Remember that sometimes the same spelling unit stands for different sounds and that sometimes the same sound is spelled in different ways. Let's see how many you can do in 2 minutes. After time is called we will discuss any of your answers for which not everyone agreed.

be<u>a</u>gle	b<u>ee</u>p	YES	NO
ma<u>g</u>ic	ma<u>g</u>net	YES	NO
<u>ph</u>oto	enou<u>gh</u>	YES	NO
<u>oy</u>ster	c<u>oi</u>ns	YES	NO

circus	circle	YES	NO
x-ray	boxes	YES	NO
awful	salt	YES	NO
water	claw	YES	NO
shine	riches	YES	NO
knocks	foxes	YES	NO

Sorting by Sound Features

Instructions: In this activity, categories for sorting words are listed at the top of the page. Each category has a capital letter. Sort each of the words in the list into one category by writing a capital letter beside it. At the end we will discuss what rule you applied to the sorting and what conclusion we can draw from the group sorting we just did.

Nicknames are /th in *thumb*/ A, /th in *feather*/ B.

this	with	feather	thin
thumb	that	think	
the	them	feather	

Sorting by Word Context

Instructions: Another way that Word Detectives have to make sense of their clues is by examining them for the context, that is the place in which they occur and all the surrounding clues. Each of the words you will see has a blank. Then you will see spellings but only one spelling fits sensibly into the blank. To figure out which spellings would or would not fit into the blank—that is, into the context of the word—you need to pay close attention to all the spelling, sound, and meaning clues of the word. You have to fully analyze all the evidence you have at hand! As soon as you think you know a spelling that would fit into the word, circle it. As a Word Detective, it is important that you examine all the evidence—consider all the spelling units—before you make your decision about which spelling fits in the word.

famil __ ar	min __ tes	stom __ ch	comm __ n
(e, i, y)	(e, i, u)	(a, e, i, o, u)	(a, e, i, o, u)

carr __ ts	skel __ ton	hum __ n	
(i, e, o)	(a, e, i, o, u)	(a, e, i, o, u)	

raz __ r	husb __ nd	wid __	
(a, e, i, o, u)	(a, e, i, o, u)	(oa, oe, ow, oo)	

LESSON  Words and Word Parts for Sound, Spelling, and Meaning

Paying Attention to Sound Units and Their Relationships to Spelling Units

Teacher Material

The following grapheme–phoneme correspondences are taught using *Talking Letters:* • Latinate and Greek	Materials needed: • *More Talking Letters* (see Table 1) for automatic alphabetic principle • Work folders

WARM-UP (FOR THE TEACHER)

For the warm-up, name the letter or letter group in *More Talking Letters* (see Table 1), say the pictured word containing a target phoneme, and then produce the target phoneme. Next, the students take a turn and repeat what is named or said by you. This approach develops orthographic awareness of spelling units; phonological awareness of corresponding phonemes in and out of word context; and, through close timing, the automaticity of spelling–phoneme correspondence. Monitor whether children are coordinating looking at the relevant letters and pictured words with naming of the letters and words and producing phonemes.

LESSON OVERVIEW (READ TO STUDENTS)

It is normal to come across words you do not know. One way to figure out an unknown word is to find the spelling units and think about their associated sound. We will call these spelling–sound correspondences the *alphabetic principle.* Sometimes in English, more than one sound is associated with the same spelling unit. We will do seven different kinds of activities in each session to teach you to be a Word Detective who uses alphabetic principle and sound patterns in words to decode unknown words. These activities are *Word Building, Word Generating, Unit Finding, Word Transferring, Are They Relatives? Sorting by Sound Features,* and *Sorting by Word Context.* These activities should give you lots of strategies for using spelling units and their relationships to sounds to figure out words. We will use our electronic timer for the second through fourth activities but not the others. Let's begin.

ACTIVITIES

Word Building

Instructions: We always start by saying and analyzing the sounds in each word. We will not use real words but rather "Jabberwocky" words, like from *Alice in Wonderland* [read *Jabberwocky* poem from *Alice in Wonderland*]. First close your eyes and listen as I say a word. Then hold up the number of fingers for the number of syllables you hear in it. If we disagree, then we will discuss it. Then you will open your eyes and use these colored discs to count out the number of phonemes in each syllable. Together we will practice 10 words in each lesson.

Key:
S = syllable(s);
P = phoneme(s);
1st, 2nd, 3rd =
order of syllables

sceanruz
(2 S: 4 P, 1st; 3 P, 2nd)

trabe
(1 S: 4 P)

swejeety
(3 S: 3 P, 1st; 3 P, 2nd; 1 P,
3rd [or 2 P, 2nd; 2 P, 3rd])

zullcrusk
(2 S: 3 P, 1st; 5 P, 2nd)

yigfrue
(2 S: 3 P, 1st; 3 P, 2nd)

fladorudge
(3 S: 4 P, 1st; 1 P, 2nd;
3 or 4 P, 3rd)

pluce
(1 S: 4 P)

clostrills
(2 S: 5 P, 1st; 4 P, 2nd
[or 4 P, 1st; 5 P, 2nd])

prite
(1 S: 4 P)

glofe
(1 S: 4 P)

Word Generating

The teacher explains that R-Files have a double meaning. Not only are they the files in our work folders where we record our points for correct answers but they are also the "files in OUR minds" in which we store the words we learn. Teachers provide a sound unit (phoneme) and ask children to generate real words or Jabberwocky words that have in them that sound unit. The students write these words in their Response Booklets. Then after time is called after 5 minutes (30 seconds per phoneme), each child shares one word with the group. The teacher records on chalk or white board the word each child shares, providing feedback if necessary. Each child who contributes a word receives R-File points in his or her Response Booklet.

Instructions: Word Detectives sometimes get their clues from generating and reasoning about similar cases. Now I would like you to think of words that have the same sounds as the ones I say and are spelled this way (write on board). Write the words you think of in your Response Booklets. When you are done, we will share with the others. I will write the words on the board.

u.e, c/s, gl, o.e, f, pr, i.e, t, tr, a.e

Note: After saying each sound, wait 30 seconds for the student to write the word, then say the next sound.

Unit Finding

The same 10 words practiced under Word Building are presented visually in the Student Response Booklet. Children are asked to underline (using two fine-point colored markers) each of the spelling units in a word using alternating colors for adjacent spelling units. (If this proves too difficult they can rewrite the word, spelling unit by spelling unit, with each adjacent spelling unit in a different color.) Remember, a spelling unit can be 1 or 2 letters and corresponds to a sound or blended sounds on *Talking Letters*. Children are given 2 minutes for 10 words, and their accuracy and time are recorded in work folders. Children who complete the activity correctly within the time limits receive R-File points. Initially

some may not finish within the time limits, but eventually they will. Any discrepancies among children or obvious errors are pointed out to them and discussed. Once everyone agrees on how to parse the words into spelling units, the group makes the sound that goes with each spelling unit and then synthesizes the sounds into a recognizable whole word.

Instructions: Word Detectives solve their mysteries by paying attention to details. The details you need to pay attention to in decoding are the spelling units and the sounds to which they correspond. See how many of these spelling units you can find in 2 minutes. Either underline the spelling units in alternating colors or rewrite the words in alternating colors with the fine-tip markers. After time is called, we will share with each other these word clues we found and then say the sound that goes with each of them (see *Talking Letters* card), moving from left to right, and then blend the sounds to say the whole word.

> sceanruz, trabe, swejeety, zullcrusk, yigfrue, fladorudge, pluce, clostrills, prite, glofe

Word Transferring

Children are given 10 new words that were not practiced but contain target spelling units in the practiced words to evaluate whether they can pronounce them correctly in a different word context. The transfer words were constructed by altering one consonant- or one vowel-spelling unit in Jabberwocky words used in Word Building. Teachers record accuracy for whole words and spelling units, note whether children refer to the student *Talking Letters* card with spelling–phoneme correspondences, and time how long it takes to pronounce all the words on the transfer list. These results can be graphed on Reading Rockets or a teacher-designed chart so that both students and teacher have a visual record of student response to alphabetic principle instruction.

Instructions: Once Word Detectives figure out the code they can apply it to new words or cases. Here are 10 words that have the same spelling units that we have practiced but in different made-up words. How accurately and how fast can you use those spelling units to say these words? Record your accuracy and time on the Reading Rockets in your R-File. Refer to *Talking Letters* if that helps you.

> sceanfuz, shabe, swejeepy, mullcrusk, yigshue, fladofudge, stuce, chostrills, chike, glope

Are They Relatives?

Does the underlined spelling unit in the first word correspond to the same phoneme as the underlined spelling unit in the second word? Children are asked to circle YES or NO on the worksheet in the Student Response Booklet if they think the spelling units underlined in the pair of pseudowords do or do not stand for the same sound (phonemes); that is, do they match? If there are differences of opinion, those items are discussed in reference to prior activities with *Talking Letters*. In contrast to the purpose of the warm-up that was to put this knowledge of grapheme–phoneme correspondences on automatic pilot, the purpose of this activity is to reflect consciously on the system of spelling–sound correspondences. Children receive R-File points for completing the activity within the time limits.

Instructions: Look carefully at each pair of words and circle YES on your worksheet if you think the underlined spelling units in each word stand for the same sound; circle NO if you think they don't. Remember that sometimes the same spelling unit stands for different sounds and that sometimes the same sound is spelled in different ways. Let's see how many you can do in 2 minutes. After time is called we will discuss any of your answers for which not everyone agreed.

bl<u>ue</u>	m<u>u</u>sic
<u>j</u>uggle	fu<u>dge</u>
<u>s</u>uper	partie<u>s</u>
<u>aw</u>ful	s<u>a</u>lt
<u>boo</u>kends	n<u>oo</u>ntime
<u>wr</u>ong	<u>r</u>ight
<u>y</u>elling	fr<u>y</u>
<u>th</u>is	<u>th</u>in
plu<u>mb</u>er	<u>m</u>onkey
b<u>ea</u>gle	b<u>ee</u>per

Sorting by Sound Features

The teacher points to one word at a time on a list in the Student Response Booklet. As you point to the word, name the word and point to the underlined spelling unit and produce the associated phoneme; then ask the children to choose the letter of the category at the top with the correct nickname sound for that spelling unit. Continue this procedure until all words are sorted into categories at the top of the list. Then help the children articulate the generalization that a specific spelling unit may stand for a small set of sounds. Children receive R-File points for each correct categorization of a spelling unit by its associated phoneme.

Although most of these alternations to be sorted are from the Anglo-Saxon layer of the language, a few (e.g., /zh/ for *s*, /short i/ for *y*, and /k/ for *ch*) are from the Romance or Greek layers of the language (see Table 1, p. 9).

Instructions: In this activity, categories for sorting words are listed at the top of the page. Each category has a capital letter. Sort each of the words in the list into one category by writing a capital letter beside it. At the end we will discuss what rule you applied to the sorting and what conclusion we can draw from the group sorting we just did.

Nicknames are /long a/A, /short a/B, /schwa/C (as in *above*).

t<u>a</u>ble	<u>a</u>gain	r<u>a</u>ven
<u>a</u>pple	<u>a</u>fter	c<u>a</u>bin
<u>a</u>bove	m<u>a</u>ple	
p<u>a</u>per	<u>a</u>nything	

Rule to discuss after sorting: Sometimes, vowel sounds are pronounced fully as a long vowel sound or a short vowel sound. Sometimes the vowel is reduced (schwa) and does not make a sound that corresponds to a specific spelling. You have to learn its spelling for a specific word. It may be *e* or *i* or another vowel.

Sorting by Word Context

Children are given words with a blank and a box with choices of spelling units in the Student Response Booklet. The task is to choose the spelling unit that could fit into the blank in the word because in this word context adding that spelling unit spells a real word. These items contain spelling units that stand for the same sound but only one of the spelling units in a word-specific context spells a real word with meaning.

Instructions: Another way that Word Detectives have to make sense of their clues is by examining them for the context, that is the place in which they occur and all the surrounding clues. Each of the words you will see has a blank. Then you will see spellings but only one spelling fits sensibly into the blank. To figure out which spellings would or would not fit into the blank—that is, into the context of the word—you need to pay close attention to all the spelling, sound, and meaning clues of the word. You have to fully analyze all the evidence you have at hand! As soon as you think you know a spelling that would fit into the word, circle it. As a Word Detective, it is important that you examine all the evidence—consider all the spelling units—before you make your decision about which spelling fits in the word.

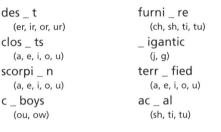

des _ t
(er, ir, or, ur)

clos _ ts
(a, e, i, o, u)

scorpi _ n
(a, e, i, o, u)

c _ boys
(ou, ow)

furni _ re
(ch, sh, ti, tu)

_ igantic
(j, g)

terr _ fied
(a, e, i, o, u)

ac _ al
(sh, ti, tu)

resemb _
(el, le)

rad _
(ar, er, ir, or, ur)

LESSON **8** Words and Word Parts for
Sound, Spelling, and Meaning

Paying Attention to Sound Units
and Their Relationships to Spelling Units

Student Response Booklet

Note: All lessons start with a warm-up, just as athletes warm up before a sports game. (See *Talking Letters* card.)

ACTIVITIES

Word Building

We always start by saying and analyzing the sounds in each word. We will not use real words but rather "Jabberwocky" words, like from *Alice in Wonderland* [read *Jabberwocky* poem from *Alice in Wonderland*]. First close your eyes and listen as I say a word. Then hold up the number of fingers for the number of syllables you hear in it. If we disagree, then we will discuss it. Then you will open your eyes and use these colored discs to count out the number of phonemes in each syllable. Together we will practice 10 words in each lesson.

Word Generating

Instructions: Word Detectives sometimes get their clues from generating and reasoning about similar cases. Now I would like you to think of words that have the same sounds as the ones I say. Write the words you think of in your Response Booklets. When you are done, we will share with the others. I will write the words on the board.

1. _____
2. _____
3. _____
4. _____
5. _____
6. _____
7. _____
8. _____
9. _____
10. _____

Unit Finding

Spelling units are one- or two-letter units that correspond to a sound. You may look at your *Talking Letters* card.

Instructions: Word Detectives solve their mysteries by paying attention to details. The details you need to pay attention to in decoding are the spelling units and the sounds to which they correspond. See how many of these spelling units you can find in 2 minutes. Either underline the spelling units in alternating colors or rewrite the words in alternating colors with the fine-tip markers. After time is called, we will share with each other these word clues we found and then say the sound that goes with each of them (see *Talking Letters* card), moving from left to right, and then blend the sounds to say the whole word.

sceanruz	zullcrusk	pluce	glofe
trabe	yigfrue	clostrills	
swejeety	fladorudge	prite	

Word Transferring

Instructions: Once Word Detectives figure out the code they can apply it to new words or cases. Here are 10 words that have the same spelling units that we have practiced but in different made-up words. How accurately and how fast can you use those spelling units to say these words? Record your accuracy and time on the Reading Rockets in your R-File. Refer to *Talking Letters* if that helps you.

sceanfuz	mullcrusk	stuce	glope
shabe	yigshue	chostrills	
swejeepy	fladofudge	chike	

Are They Relatives?

Instructions: Look carefully at each pair of words and circle YES on your worksheet if you think the underlined spelling units in each word stand for the same sound; circle NO if you think they don't. Remember that sometimes the same spelling unit stands for different sounds and that sometimes the same sound is spelled in different ways. Let's see how many you can do in 2 minutes. After time is called we will discuss any of your answers for which not everyone agreed.

blue	music	YES	NO
juggle	fudge	YES	NO

<u>su</u>per	par<u>ties</u>	YES	NO
<u>aw</u>ful	sa<u>l</u>t	YES	NO
b<u>oo</u>kends	n<u>oo</u>ntime	YES	NO
<u>wr</u>ong	<u>r</u>ight	YES	NO
<u>y</u>elling	fr<u>y</u>	YES	NO
<u>th</u>is	<u>th</u>in	YES	NO
plu<u>m</u>ber	<u>m</u>onkey	YES	NO
b<u>ea</u>gle	b<u>e</u>eper	YES	NO

Sorting by Sound Features

Instructions: In this activity, categories for sorting words are listed at the top of the page. Each category has a capital letter. Sort each of the words in the list into one category by writing a capital letter beside it. At the end we will discuss what rule you applied to the sorting and what conclusion we can draw from the group sorting we just did.

Nicknames are /long a/ A, /short a/ B, /schwa as in *above*/ C.

<u>t</u>able	p<u>a</u>per	m<u>a</u>ple	c<u>a</u>bin
<u>a</u>pple	<u>a</u>gain	<u>a</u>nything	
<u>a</u>bove	<u>a</u>fter	r<u>a</u>ven	

Sorting by Word Context

Instructions: Another way that Word Detectives have to make sense of their clues is by examining them for the context, that is the place in which they occur and all the surrounding clues. Each of the words you will see has a blank. Then you will see spellings but only one spelling fits sensibly into the blank. To figure out which spellings would or would not fit into the blank—that is, into the context of the word—you need to pay close attention to all the spelling, sound, and meaning clues of the word. You have to fully analyze all the evidence you have at hand! As soon as you think you know a spelling that would fit into the word, circle it. As a Word Detective, it is important that you examine all the evidence—consider all the spelling units—before you make your decision about which spelling fits in the word.

des __ t   c __ boys   terr __ fied   rad __
(er, ir, or, ur)   (ou, ow)   (a, e, i, o, u)   (ar, er, ir, or,
                                                            ur)
clos __ ts   furni __ re   ac __ al
(a, e, i, o, u)   (ch, sh, ti, tu)   (sh, ti, tu)

scorpi __ n   __ igantic   resemb __
(a, e, i, o, u)   (j, g)   (el, le)

LESSON **9** Words and Word Parts for
Sound, Spelling, and Meaning

Paying Attention to Sound Units
and Their Relationships to Spelling Units

Teacher Material

The following grapheme–phoneme correspondences are taught using *Talking Letters:* • Single-letter consonants • Short vowels in closed syllables • Long vowels in open syllables	Materials needed: • *Talking Letters* for automatic alphabetic principle • Work folders

WARM-UP (FOR THE TEACHER)

For the warm-up, name the letter or letter group on the *Talking Letters* card, say the pictured word containing a target phoneme, and then produce the target phoneme. Next, the students take a turn and repeat what is named or said by you. This approach develops orthographic awareness of spelling units; phonological awareness of corresponding phonemes in and out of word context; and, through close timing, the automaticity of spelling–phoneme correspondence. Monitor whether children are coordinating looking at the relevant letters and pictured words with naming of the letters and words and producing phonemes.

LESSON OVERVIEW (READ TO STUDENTS)

It is normal to come across words you do not know. One way to figure out an unknown word is to find the spelling units and think about their associated sounds. We will call these spelling–sound correspondences the *alphabetic principle.* Sometimes in English, more than one sound is associated with the same spelling unit. We will do seven different kinds of activities in each session to teach you to be a Word Detective who uses alphabetic principle and sound patterns in words to decode unknown words. These activities are *Word Building, Word Generating, Unit Finding, Word Transferring, Are They Relatives? Sorting by Sound Features,* and *Sorting by Word Context.* These activities should give you lots of strategies for using spelling units and their relationships to sounds to figure out words. We will use our electronic timer for the second through fourth activities but not the others. Let's begin.

ACTIVITIES

Word Building

Instructions: We always start by saying and analyzing the sounds in each word. We will not use real words but rather "Jabberwocky" words, like from *Alice in Wonderland* [read *Jabberwocky* poem from *Alice in Wonderland*]. First close your eyes and listen as I say a word. Then hold up the number of fingers for the number of syllables you hear in it. If we disagree, then we will discuss it. Then you will open your eyes and use these colored discs to count out the number of phonemes in each syllable. Together we will practice 10 words in each lesson.

Key:
S = syllable(s);
P = phoneme(s);
1st, 2nd, 3rd =
order of syllables

chunglewums
(3 S: 3 P, 1st; 2 P, 2nd;
4 P, 3rd)
whulls
(1 S: 4 P)
thermb
(1 S: 3 P)

knelph
(1 S: 4 P)
quoopdro
(2 S: 4 P, 1st; 3 P, 2nd)
wraltway
(2 S: 4 P, 1st; 2 P, 2nd)
blesp
(1 S: 5 P)

grax
(1 S: 5 P)
jeksie
(2 S: 3 P, 1st; 2 P, 2nd)
snubarth
(2 S: 3 P, 1st; 3 P, 2nd)

Word Generating

The teacher explains that R-Files have a double meaning. Not only are they the files in our work folders where we record our points for correct answers but they are also the "files in OUR minds" in which we store the words we learn. Teachers provide a sound unit (phoneme) and ask children to generate real words or Jabberwocky words that have in them that sound unit. The students write these words in their Response Booklets. Then after time is called after 5 minutes (30 seconds per phoneme), each child shares one word with the group. The teacher records on chalk or white board the word each child shares, providing feedback if necessary. Each child who contributes a word receives R-File points in his or her Response Booklet.

Instructions: Word Detectives sometimes get their clues from generating and reasoning about similar cases. Now I would like you to think of words that have the same sounds as the ones I say and are spelled this way (write on board). Write the words you think of in your Response Booklets. When you are done, we will share with the others. I will write the words on the board.

b, j, e, k, s, long e, l, u, t, k

Note: After saying each sound, wait 30 seconds for the student to write the word, then say the next sound.

Unit Finding

The same 10 words practiced under Word Building are presented visually in the Student Response Booklet. Children are asked to underline (using two fine-point colored markers) each of the spelling units in a word using alternating colors for adjacent spelling units. (If this proves too difficult they can rewrite the word, spelling unit by spelling unit, with each adjacent spelling unit in a different color.) Remember, a spelling unit can be 1 or 2 letters and corresponds to a sound or blended sounds on *Talking Letters.* Children are given 2 minutes for 10 words, and their accuracy and time are recorded in work folders. Children who complete the activity correctly within the time limits receive R-File points. Initially

some may not finish within the time limits, but eventually they will. Any discrepancies among children or obvious errors are pointed out to them and discussed. Once everyone agrees on how to parse the words into spelling units, the group makes the sound that goes with each spelling unit and then synthesizes the sounds into a recognizable whole word.

Instructions: Word Detectives solve their mysteries by paying attention to details. The details you need to pay attention to in decoding are the spelling units and the sounds to which they correspond. See how many of these spelling units you can find in 2 minutes. Either underline the spelling units in alternating colors or rewrite the words in alternating colors with the fine-tip markers. After time is called, we will share with each other these word clues we found and then say the sound that goes with each of them (see *Talking Letters* card), moving from left to right, and then blend the sounds to say the whole word.

> chunglewums, whulls, thermb, knelph, quoopdro, wraltway, blesp, grax, jeksie, snubarth

Word Transferring

Children are given 10 new words that were not practiced but contain target spelling units in the practiced words to evaluate whether they can pronounce them correctly in a different word context. The transfer words were constructed by altering one consonant- or one vowel-spelling unit in Jabberwocky words used in Word Building. Teachers record accuracy for whole words and spelling units, note whether children refer to the student *Talking Letters* card with spelling–phoneme correspondences, and time how long it takes to pronounce all the words on the transfer list. These results can be graphed on Reading Rockets or a teacher-designed chart so that both students and teacher have a visual record of student response to alphabetic principle instruction.

Instructions: Once Word Detectives figure out the code they can apply it to new words or cases. Here are 10 words that have the same spelling units that we have practiced but in different made-up words. How accurately and how fast can you use those spelling units to say these words? Record your accuracy and time on the Reading Rockets in your R-File. Refer to *Talking Letters* if that helps you.

> changlewums, whuds, therg, knelg, quoopbro, wraltbay, flest, glax, teksie, snuborth

Are They Relatives?

Does the underlined spelling unit in the first word correspond to the same phoneme as the underlined spelling unit in the second word? Children are asked to circle YES or NO on the worksheet in the Student Response Booklet if they think the spelling units underlined in the pair of pseudowords do or do not stand for the same sound (phonemes); that is, do they match? If there are differences of opinion, those items are discussed in reference to prior activities with *Talking Letters*. In contrast to the purpose of the warm-up that was to put this knowledge of grapheme–phoneme correspondences on automatic pilot, the purpose of this activity is to reflect consciously on the system of spelling–sound correspondences. Children receive R-File points for completing the activity within the time limits.

Instructions: Look carefully at each pair of words and circle YES on your worksheet if you think the underlined spelling units in each word stand for the same sound; circle NO if you think they don't. Remember that sometimes the same spelling unit stands for different sounds and that sometimes the same sound is spelled in different ways. Let's see how many you can do in 2 minutes. After time is called we will discuss any of your answers for which not everyone agreed.

m<u>oo</u>n	g<u>lue</u>
ch<u>art</u>	sc<u>ary</u>
sailb<u>oat</u>	t<u>oe</u>nail
v<u>a</u>lentine	<u>a</u>lways
st<u>ay</u>	sh<u>ape</u>
lad<u>y</u>	sk<u>y</u>
sl<u>ow</u>	h<u>ose</u>
n<u>o</u>body	r<u>o</u>bber
b<u>e</u>fore	b<u>e</u>tter
scr<u>ew</u>	n<u>oo</u>n

Sorting by Sound Features

The teacher points to one word at a time on a list in the Student Response Booklet. As you point to the word, name the word and point to the underlined spelling unit and produce the associated phoneme; then ask the children to choose the letter of the category at the top with the correct nickname sound for that spelling unit. Continue this procedure until all words are sorted into categories at the top of the list. Then help the children articulate the generalization that a specific spelling unit may stand for a small set of sounds. Children receive R-File points for each correct categorization of a spelling unit by its associated phoneme.

Although most of these alternations to be sorted are from the Anglo-Saxon layer of the language, a few (e.g., /zh/ for *s,* /short i/ for *y,* and /k/ for *ch*) are from the Romance or Greek layers of the language (see Table 1, p. 9).

Instructions: In this activity, categories for sorting words are listed at the top of the page. Each category has a capital letter. Sort each of the words in the list into one category by writing a capital letter beside it. At the end we will discuss what rule you applied to the sorting and what conclusion we can draw from the group sorting we just did.

Nicknames are /short e/A, /long e/B, and /schwa/C (labeled on card headings).

b<u>e</u>st	sl<u>e</u>d	st<u>e</u>p	z<u>e</u>ro
w<u>e</u>	sh<u>e</u>	b<u>e</u>came	
sev<u>e</u>n	wom<u>e</u>n	k<u>e</u>pt	

Rule to discuss after sorting: Sometimes, vowel sounds are pronounced fully as a long vowel sound or a short vowel sound. Sometimes the vowel is reduced (schwa) and does not make a sound that corresponds to a specific spelling. You have to learn its spelling for a specific word. It may be *e* or *i* or another vowel.

Sorting by Word Context

Children are given words with a blank and a box with choices of spelling units in the Student Response Booklet. The task is to choose the spelling unit that could fit into the blank in the word because in this word context adding that spelling unit spells a real word. These items contain spelling units that stand for the same sound but only one of the spelling units in a word-specific context spells a real word with meaning.

Instructions: Another way that Word Detectives have to make sense of their clues is by examining them for the context, that is the place in which they occur and all the surrounding clues. Each of the words you will see has a blank. Then you will see spellings but only one

spelling fits sensibly into the blank. To figure out which spellings would or would not fit into the blank—that is, into the context of the word—you need to pay close attention to all the spelling, sound, and meaning clues of the word. You have to fully analyze all the evidence you have at hand! As soon as you think you know a spelling that would fit into the word, circle it. As a Word Detective, it is important that you examine all the evidence—consider all the spelling units—before you make your decision about which spelling fits in the word.

fav _ rite
(ai, e, i, o, u)

childr _ n's
(a, e, i, o, u)

pers _ aded
(u, w)

publ _ shed
(e, i)

watercol _ r
(a, e, i, o, u)

p _ nuts
(e, ea, ee)

_ aracter
(c, k, ch, ck)

_ gnored
(a, e, i,o, u)

happ _ ned
(a, e, i, o, u)

gr _ f
(e, ee, ei, ie)

LESSON **9** Words and Word Parts for
Sound, Spelling, and Meaning

Paying Attention to Sound Units
and Their Relationships to Spelling Units

Student Response Booklet

Note: All lessons start with a warm-up, just as athletes warm up before a sports game. (See *Talking Letters* card.)

ACTIVITIES

Word Building

We always start by saying and analyzing the sounds in each word. We will not use real words but rather "Jabberwocky" words, like from *Alice in Wonderland* [read *Jabberwocky* poem from *Alice in Wonderland*]. First close your eyes and listen as I say a word. Then hold up the number of fingers for the number of syllables you hear in it. If we disagree, then we will discuss it. Then you will open your eyes and use these colored discs to count out the number of phonemes in each syllable. Together we will practice 10 words in each lesson.

Word Generating

Instructions: Word Detectives sometimes get their clues from generating and reasoning about similar cases. Now I would like you to think of words that have the same sounds as the ones I say. Write the words you think of in your Response Booklets. When you are done, we will share with the others. I will write the words on the board.

1. _____
2. _____
3. _____
4. _____
5. _____
6. _____
7. _____
8. _____
9. _____
10. _____

Unit Finding

Spelling units are one- or two-letter units that correspond to a sound. You may look at your *Talking Letters* card.

Instructions: Word Detectives solve their mysteries by paying attention to details. The details you need to pay attention to in decoding are the spelling units and the sounds to which they correspond. See how many of these spelling units you can find in 2 minutes. Either underline the spelling units in alternating colors or rewrite the words in alternating colors with the fine-tip markers. After time is called, we will share with each other these word clues we found and then say the sound that goes with each of them (see *Talking Letters* card), moving from left to right, and then blend the sounds to say the whole word.

chunglewums	knelph	blesp	snubarth
whulls	quoopdro	grax	
thermb	wraltway	jeksie	

Word Transferring

Instructions: Once Word Detectives figure out the code they can apply it to new words or cases. Here are 10 words that have the same spelling units that we have practiced but in different made-up words. How accurately and how fast can you use those spelling units to say these words? Record your accuracy and time on the Reading Rockets in your R-File. Refer to *Talking Letters* if that helps you.

changlewums	knelg	flest	snuborth
whuds	quoopbro	glax	
therg	wraltbay	teksie	

Are They Relatives?

Instructions: Look carefully at each pair of words and circle YES on your worksheet if you think the underlined spelling units in each word stand for the same sound; circle NO if you think they don't. Remember that sometimes the same spelling unit stands for different sounds and that sometimes the same sound is spelled in different ways. Let's see how many you can do in 2 minutes. After time is called we will discuss any of your answers for which not everyone agreed.

m<u>oo</u>n	gl<u>ue</u>	YES	NO
ch<u>ar</u>t	sc<u>ar</u>y	YES	NO

sailb<u>oa</u>t	t<u>oe</u>nail	YES	NO
v<u>a</u>lentine	<u>a</u>lways	YES	NO
st<u>ay</u>	shap<u>e</u>	YES	NO
lad<u>y</u>	sk<u>y</u>	YES	NO
sl<u>ow</u>	h<u>ose</u>	YES	NO
n<u>o</u>body	r<u>o</u>bber	YES	NO
b<u>e</u>fore	b<u>e</u>tter	YES	NO
scr<u>ew</u>	n<u>oo</u>n	YES	NO

Sorting by Sound Features

Instructions: In this activity, categories for sorting words are listed at the top of the page. Each category has a capital letter. Sort each of the words in the list into one category by writing a capital letter beside it. At the end we will discuss what rule you applied to the sorting and what conclusion we can draw from the group sorting we just did.

Nicknames are /short e/ A, /long e/ B, and /schwa/ C.

b<u>e</u>st	sl<u>e</u>d	st<u>e</u>p	z<u>e</u>ro
w<u>e</u>	sh<u>e</u>	b<u>e</u>came	
sev<u>e</u>n	wom<u>e</u>n	k<u>e</u>pt	

Sorting by Word Context

Instructions: Another way that Word Detectives have to make sense of their clues is by examining them for the context, that is the place in which they occur and all the surrounding clues. Each of the words you will see has a blank. Then you will see spellings but only one spelling fits sensibly into the blank. To figure out which spellings would or would not fit into the blank—that is, into the context of the word—you need to pay close attention to all the spelling, sound, and meaning clues of the word. You have to fully analyze all the evidence you have at hand! As soon as you think you know a spelling that would fit into the word, circle it. As a Word Detective, it is important that you examine all the evidence—consider all the spelling units—before you make your decision about which spelling fits in the word.

fav __ rite	watercol __ r	happ __ ned
(ai, e, i, o, u)	(a, e, i, o, u)	(a, e, i, o, u)
childr __ n's	p __ nuts	gr __ f
(a, e, i, o, u)	(e, ea, ee)	(e, ee, ei, ie)
pers __ aded	__ aracter	
(u, w)	(c, k, ch, ck)	
publ __ shed	__ gnored	
(e, i)	(a, e, i,o, u)	

LESSON **10** Words and Word Parts for Sound, Spelling, and Meaning

Paying Attention to Sound Units and Their Relationships to Spelling Units

Teacher Material

The following grapheme–phoneme correspondences are taught using *Talking Letters:* • Consonant blends and vowel teams	Materials needed: • *Talking Letters* for automatic alphabetic principle • Work folders

WARM-UP (FOR THE TEACHER)

For the warm-up, name the letter or letter group on the *Talking Letters* card, say the pictured word containing a target phoneme, and then produce the target phoneme. Next, the students take a turn and repeat what is named or said by you. This approach develops orthographic awareness of spelling units; phonological awareness of corresponding phonemes in and out of word context; and, through close timing, the automaticity of spelling–phoneme correspondence. Monitor whether children are coordinating looking at the relevant letters and pictured words with naming of the letters and words and producing phonemes.

LESSON OVERVIEW (READ TO STUDENTS)

It is normal to come across words you do not know. One way to figure out an unknown word is to find the spelling units and think about their associated sounds. We will call these spelling–sound correspondences the *alphabetic principle.* Sometimes in English, more than one sound is associated with the same spelling unit. We will do seven different kinds of activities in each session to teach you to be a Word Detective who uses alphabetic principle and sound patterns in words to decode unknown words. These activities are *Word Building, Word Generating, Unit Finding, Word Transferring, Are They Relatives? Sorting by Sound Features,* and *Sorting by Word Context.* These activities should give you lots of strategies for using spelling units and their relationships to sounds to figure out words. We will use our electronic timer for the second through fourth activities but not the others. Let's begin.

ACTIVITIES

Word Building

Instructions: We always start by saying and analyzing the sounds in each word. We will not use real words but rather "Jabberwocky" words, like from *Alice in Wonderland* [read *Jabberwocky* poem from *Alice in Wonderland*]. First close your eyes and listen as I say a word. Then hold up the number of fingers for the number of syllables you hear in it. If we disagree, then we will discuss it. Then you will open your eyes and use these colored discs to count out the number of phonemes in each syllable. Together we will practice 10 words in each lesson.

Key:
S = syllable(s);
P = phoneme(s);
1st, 2nd, 3rd =
order of syllables

quoopdro
(2 S: 4 P, 1st; 3 P, 2nd)

sognoy
(2 S: 3 P, 1st; 2 P, 2nd)

hebtou
(2 S: 3 P, 1st; 2 P, 2nd)

yigfrue
(2 S: 3 P, 1st; 3 P, 2nd)

pluce
(1 S: 4 P)

knelph
(1 S: 4 P)

soatyaz
(2 S: 3 P, 1st; 3 P, 2nd)

vopfow
(2 S: 3 P, 1st; 2 P, 2nd)

smewbry
(2 S: 3 P, 1st; 3 P, 2nd)

fladorudge
(3 S: 4 P, 1st; 1 P, 2nd;
3 or 4 P, 3rd)

Word Generating

The teacher explains that R-Files have a double meaning. Not only are they the files in our work folders where we record our points for correct answers but they are also the "files in OUR minds" in which we store the words we learn. Teachers provide a sound unit (phoneme) and ask children to generate real words or Jabberwocky words that have in them that sound unit. The students write these words in their Response Booklets. Then after time is called after 5 minutes (30 seconds per phoneme), each child shares one word with the group. The teacher records on chalk or white board the word each child shares, providing feedback if necessary. Each child who contributes a word receives R-File points in his or her Response Booklet.

Instructions: Word Detectives sometimes get their clues from generating and reasoning about similar cases. Now I would like you to think of words that have the same sounds as the ones I say and are spelled this way (write on board). Write the words you think of in your Response Booklets. When you are done, we will share with the others. I will write the words on the board.

aw, s, long o, t, y, a, z, s, short o, g

Note: After saying each sound, wait 30 seconds for the student to write the word, then say the next sound.

Unit Finding

The same 10 words practiced under Word Building are presented visually in the Student Response Booklet. Children are asked to underline (using two fine-point colored markers) each of the spelling units in a word using alternating colors for adjacent spelling units. (If this proves too difficult they can rewrite the word, spelling unit by spelling unit, with each adjacent spelling unit in a different color.) Remember, a spelling unit can be 1 or 2 letters and corresponds to a sound or blended sounds on *Talking Letters.* Children are given 2 minutes for 10 words, and their accuracy and time are recorded in work folders. Children who complete the activity correctly within the time limits receive R-File points. Initially

some may not finish within the time limits, but eventually they will. Any discrepancies among children or obvious errors are pointed out to them and discussed. Once everyone agrees on how to parse the words into spelling units, the group makes the sound that goes with each spelling unit and then synthesizes the sounds into a recognizable whole word.

Instructions: Word Detectives solve their mysteries by paying attention to details. The details you need to pay attention to in decoding are the spelling units and the sounds to which they correspond. See how many of these spelling units you can find in 2 minutes. Either underline the spelling units in alternating colors or rewrite the words in alternating colors with the fine-tip markers. After time is called, we will share with each other these word clues we found and then say the sound that goes with each of them (see *Talking Letters* card), moving from left to right, and then blend the sounds to say the whole word.

> quoopdro, sognoy, hebtou, yigfrue, pluce, knelph, soatyaz, vopfow, smewbry, fladorudge

Word Transferring

Children are given 10 new words that were not practiced but contain target spelling units in the practiced words to evaluate whether they can pronounce them correctly in a different word context. The transfer words were constructed by altering one consonant- or one vowel-spelling unit in Jabberwocky words used in Word Building. Teachers record accuracy for whole words and spelling units, note whether children refer to the student *Talking Letters* card with spelling–phoneme correspondences, and time how long it takes to pronounce all the words on the transfer list. These results can be graphed on Reading Rockets or a teacher-designed chart so that both students and teacher have a visual record of student response to alphabetic principle instruction.

Instructions: Once Word Detectives figure out the code they can apply it to new words or cases. Here are 10 words that have the same spelling units that we have practiced but in different made-up words. How accurately and how fast can you use those spelling units to say these words? Record your accuracy and time on the Reading Rockets in your R-File. Refer to *Talking Letters* if that helps you.

> quootdro, bognoy, shebtou, yigfray, shuce, knelp, soatbaz, vopfoo, shewbry, fladorup

Are They Relatives?

Does the underlined spelling unit in the first word correspond to the same phoneme as the underlined spelling unit in the second word? Children are asked to circle YES or NO on the worksheet in the Student Response Booklet if they think the spelling units underlined in the pair of pseudowords do or do not stand for the same sound (phonemes); that is, do they match? If there are differences of opinion, those items are discussed in reference to prior activities with *Talking Letters*. In contrast to the purpose of the warm-up that was to put this knowledge of grapheme–phoneme correspondences on automatic pilot, the purpose of this activity is to reflect consciously on the system of spelling–sound correspondences. Children receive R-File points for completing the activity within the time limits.

Instructions: Look carefully at each pair of words and circle YES on your worksheet if you think the underlined spelling units in each word stand for the same sound; circle NO if you think they don't. Remember that sometimes the same spelling unit stands for different sounds and that sometimes the same sound is spelled in different ways. Let's see how many you can do in 2 minutes. After time is called we will discuss any of your answers for which not everyone agreed.

s<u>ea</u>son   b<u>ea</u>r

<u>kn</u>ock   balloo<u>n</u>

<u>pr</u>efer   <u>pe</u>rform

<u>ch</u>orus   ketchup

tr<u>ea</u>t   gr<u>ea</u>t

sailb<u>oa</u>t   t<u>oe</u>nail

<u>r</u>unning   swimm<u>e</u>r

s<u>ai</u>d   p<u>ai</u>n

fa<u>c</u>es   <u>s</u>avings

scr<u>ew</u>   n<u>oo</u>n

Sorting by Sound Features

The teacher points to one word at a time on a list in the Student Response Booklet. As you point to the word, name the word and point to the underlined spelling unit and produce the associated phoneme; then ask the children to choose the letter of the category at the top with the correct nickname sound for that spelling unit. Continue this procedure until all words are sorted into categories at the top of the list. Then help the children articulate the generalization that a specific spelling unit may stand for a small set of sounds. Children receive R-File points for each correct categorization of a spelling unit by its associated phoneme.

Although most of these alternations to be sorted are from the Anglo-Saxon layer of the language, a few (e.g., /zh/ for *s*, /short i/ for *y*, and /k/ for *ch*) are from the Romance or Greek layers of the language (see Table 1, p. 9).

Instructions: In this activity, categories for sorting words are listed at the top of the page. Each category has a capital letter. Sort each of the words in the list into one category by writing a capital letter beside it. At the end we will discuss what rule you applied to the sorting and what conclusion we can draw from the group sorting we just did.

Nicknames are /short i/A, /long i/B, /schwa/C (labeled on card headings).

ri<u>c</u>h   lov<u>i</u>ng   s<u>i</u>ster

walk<u>i</u>ng   d<u>i</u>nosaur   p<u>i</u>lot

t<u>i</u>ger   h<u>i</u>mself

<u>i</u>nch   b<u>i</u>cycle

Rule to discuss after sorting: Sometimes, vowel sounds are pronounced fully as a long vowel sound or a short vowel sound. Sometimes the vowel is reduced (schwa) and does not make a sound that corresponds to a specific spelling. You have to learn its spelling for a specific word. It may be *e* or *i* or another vowel.

Sorting by Word Context

Children are given words with a blank and a box with choices of spelling units in the Student Response Booklet. The task is to choose the spelling unit that could fit into the blank in the word because in this word context adding that spelling unit spells a real word. These items contain spelling units that stand for the same sound but only one of the spelling units in a word-specific context spells a real word with meaning.

Instructions: Another way that Word Detectives have to make sense of their clues is by examining them for the context, that is the place in which they occur and all the surrounding clues. Each of the words you will see has a blank. Then you will see spellings but only one spelling fits sensibly into the blank. To figure out which spellings would or would not fit into the blank—that is, into the context of the word—you need to pay close attention to all the spelling, sound, and meaning clues of the word. You have to fully analyze all the evidence you have at hand! As soon as you think you know a spelling that would fit into the word, circle it. As a Word Detective, it is important that you examine all the evidence—consider all the spelling units—before you make your decision about which spelling fits in the word.

mach _ nes
(e, ei, ie, i)

bel _ ves
(e, ei, ie, i)

cont _ ning
(a, ai, ay)

_ ccused
(a, e, i, o, u)

pers _ n
(a, e, i, o, u)

thous _ nds
(a, e, i, o, u)

foss _ l
(a, e, i, o, u)

l _ mestone
(i, y)

acad _ my
(a, e, i, o, u)

an _ ers
(s, sw, sy)

LESSON **10** Words and Word Parts for
Sound, Spelling, and Meaning

Paying Attention to Sound Units
and Their Relationships to Spelling Units

Student Response Booklet

Note: All lessons start with a warm-up, just as athletes warm up before a sports game. (See *Talking Letters* card.)

ACTIVITIES

Word Building

We always start by saying and analyzing the sounds in each word. We will not use real words but rather "Jabberwocky" words, like from *Alice in Wonderland* [read *Jabberwocky* poem from *Alice in Wonderland*]. First close your eyes and listen as I say a word. Then hold up the number of fingers for the number of syllables you hear in it. If we disagree, then we will discuss it. Then you will open your eyes and use these colored discs to count out the number of phonemes in each syllable. Together we will practice 10 words in each lesson.

Word Generating

Instructions: Word Detectives sometimes get their clues from generating and reasoning about similar cases. Now I would like you to think of words that have the same sounds as the ones I say. Write the words you think of in your Response Booklets. When you are done, we will share with the others. I will write the words on the board.

1. _____
2. _____
3. _____
4. _____
5. _____
6. _____
7. _____
8. _____
9. _____
10. _____

Unit Finding

Spelling units are one- or two-letter units that correspond to a sound. You may look at your *Talking Letters* card.

Instructions: Word Detectives solve their mysteries by paying attention to details. The details you need to pay attention to in decoding are the spelling units and the sounds to which they correspond. See how many of these spelling units you can find in 2 minutes. Either underline the spelling units in alternating colors or rewrite the words in alternating colors with the fine-tip markers. After time is called, we will share with each other these word clues we found and then say the sound that goes with each of them (see *Talking Letters* card), moving from left to right, and then blend the sounds to say the whole word.

quoopdro	yigfrue	soatyaz	fladorudge
sognoy	pluce	vopfow	
hebtou	knelph	smewbry	

Word Transferring

Instructions: Once Word Detectives figure out the code they can apply it to new words or cases. Here are 10 words that have the same spelling units that we have practiced but in different made-up words. How accurately and how fast can you use those spelling units to say these words? Record your accuracy and time on the Reading Rockets in your R-File. Refer to *Talking Letters* if that helps you.

quootdro	yigfray	soatbaz	fladorup
bognoy	shuce	vopfoo	
shebtou	knelp	shewbry	

Are They Relatives?

Instructions: Look carefully at each pair of words and circle YES on your worksheet if you think the underlined spelling units in each word stand for the same sound, or circle NO if they don't. Remember that sometimes the same spelling unit stands for different sounds, and that sometimes the same sound is spelled in different ways. How many can you do in 2 minutes? After time is called we will discuss any of your answers for which not everyone agreed.

season	bear	YES	NO
knock	balloon	YES	NO
prefer	perform	YES	NO

<u>ch</u>orus	<u>k</u>etchup	YES	NO
tr<u>ea</u>t	gr<u>ea</u>t	YES	NO
sailb<u>oa</u>t	t<u>oe</u>nail	YES	NO
<u>r</u>unning	swimm<u>er</u>	YES	NO
s<u>ai</u>d	p<u>ai</u>n	YES	NO
fa<u>c</u>es	<u>s</u>avings	YES	NO
scr<u>ew</u>	n<u>oo</u>n	YES	NO

Sorting by Sound Features

Instructions: In this activity, categories for sorting words are listed at the top of the page. Each category has a capital letter. Sort each of the words in the list into one category by writing a capital letter beside it. At the end we will discuss what rule you applied to the sorting and what conclusion we can draw from the group sorting we just did.

Nicknames are /short i/ A, /long i/ B, /schwa/ C.

r<u>i</u>ch	<u>i</u>nch	h<u>i</u>mself	p<u>i</u>lot
walk<u>i</u>ng	lov<u>i</u>ng	b<u>i</u>cycle	
t<u>i</u>ger	d<u>i</u>nosaur	s<u>i</u>ster	

Sorting by Word Context

Instructions: Another way that Word Detectives have to make sense of their clues is by examining them for the context, that is the place in which they occur and all the surrounding clues. Each of the words you will see has a blank. Then you will see spellings but only one spelling fits sensibly into the blank. To figure out which spellings would or would not fit into the blank—that is, into the context of the word—you need to pay close attention to all the spelling, sound, and meaning clues of the word. You have to fully analyze all the evidence you have at hand! As soon as you think you know a spelling that would fit into the word, circle it. As a Word Detective, it is important that you examine all the evidence—consider all the spelling units—before you make your decision about which spelling fits in the word.

mach __ nes   __ ccused   foss __ l   an __ ers
(e, ei, ie, i)   (a, e, i, o, u)   (a, e, i, o, u)   (s, sw, sy)

bel __ ves   pers __ n   l __ mestone
(e, ei, ie, i)   (a, e, i, o, u)   (i, y)

cont __ ning   thous __ nds   acad __ my
(a, ai, ay)   (a, e, i, o, u)   (a, e, i, o, u)

LESSON  Words and Word Parts for Sound, Spelling, and Meaning

Paying Attention to Sound Units and Their Relationships to Spelling Units

Teacher Material

The following grapheme–phoneme correspondences are taught using *Talking Letters:*	Materials needed:
• Other consonant combinations • r- and l-controlled vowels	• *Talking Letters* for automatic alphabetic principle • Work folders

WARM-UP (FOR THE TEACHER)

For the warm-up, name the letter or letter group on the *Talking Letters* card, say the pictured word containing a target phoneme, and then produce the target phoneme. Next, the students take a turn and repeat what is named or said by you. This approach develops orthographic awareness of spelling units; phonological awareness of corresponding phonemes in and out of word context; and, through close timing, the automaticity of spelling–phoneme correspondence. Monitor whether children are coordinating looking at the relevant letters and pictured words with naming of the letters and words and producing phonemes.

LESSON OVERVIEW (READ TO STUDENTS)

It is normal to come across words you do not know. One way to figure out an unknown word is to find the spelling units and think about their associated sounds. We will call these spelling–sound correspondences the *alphabetic principle.* Sometimes in English, more than one sound is associated with the same spelling unit. We will do seven different kinds of activities in each session to teach you to be a Word Detective who uses alphabetic principle and sound patterns in words to decode unknown words. These activities are *Word Building, Word Generating, Unit Finding, Word Transferring, Are They Relatives? Sorting by Sound Features,* and *Sorting by Word Context.* These activities should give you lots of strategies for using spelling units and their relationships to sounds to figure out words. We will use our electronic timer for the second through fourth activities but not the others. Let's begin.

ACTIVITIES

Word Building

Instructions: We always start by saying and analyzing the sounds in each word. We will not use real words but rather "Jabberwocky" words, like from *Alice in Wonderland* [read *Jabberwocky* poem from *Alice in Wonderland*]. First close your eyes and listen as I say a word. Then hold up the number of fingers for the number of syllables you hear in it. If we disagree, then we will discuss it. Then you will open your eyes and use these colored discs to count out the number of phonemes in each syllable. Together we will practice 10 words in each lesson.

Key:
S = syllable(s);
P = phoneme(s);
1st, 2nd, 3rd =
order of syllables

nidmoin
(2 S: 3 P, 1st; 3 P, 2nd)

whulls
(1 S: 4 P)

chunglewums
(3 S: 3 P, 1st; 2 P, 2nd; 4 P, 3rd)

cimdaut
(2 S: 3 P, 1st; 3 P, 2nd)

thermb
(1 S: 3 P)

wraltway
(2 S: 4 P, 1st; 2 P, 2nd)

trabe
(1 S: 4 P)

prite
(1 S: 4 P)

zullcrusk
(2 S: 3 P, 1st; 5 P, 2nd)

sceanruz
(2 S: 4 P, 1st; 3 P, 2nd)

Word Generating

The teacher explains that R-Files have a double meaning. Not only are they the files in our work folders where we record our points for correct answers but they are also the "files in OUR minds" in which we store the words we learn. Teachers provide a sound unit (phoneme) and ask children to generate real words or Jabberwocky words that have in them that sound unit. The students write these words in their Response Booklets. Then after time is called after 5 minutes (30 seconds per phoneme), each child shares one word with the group. The teacher records on chalk or white board the word each child shares, providing feedback if necessary. Each child who contributes a word receives R-File points in his or her Response Booklet.

Instructions: Word Detectives sometimes get their clues from generating and reasoning about similar cases. Now I would like you to think of words that have the same sounds as the ones I say and are spelled this way (write on board). Write the words you think of in your Response Booklets. When you are done, we will share with the others. I will write the words on the board.

n, oy, h, e, b, t, ou, n, short i, d

Note: After saying each sound, wait 30 seconds for the student to write the word, then say the next sound.

Unit Finding

The same 10 words practiced under Word Building are presented visually in the Student Response Booklet. Children are asked to underline (using two fine-point colored markers) each of the spelling units in a word using alternating colors for adjacent spelling units. (If this proves too difficult they can rewrite the word, spelling unit by spelling unit, with each adjacent spelling unit in a different color.) Remember, a spelling unit can be 1 or 2 letters and corresponds to a sound or blended sounds on *Talking Letters.* Children are given 2 minutes for 10 words, and their accuracy and time are recorded in work folders. Children who complete the activity correctly within the time limits receive R-File points. Initially

some may not finish within the time limits, but eventually they will. Any discrepancies among children or obvious errors are pointed out to them and discussed. Once everyone agrees on how to parse the words into spelling units, the group makes the sound that goes with each spelling unit and then synthesizes the sounds into a recognizable whole word.

Instructions: Word Detectives solve their mysteries by paying attention to details. The details you need to pay attention to in decoding are the spelling units and the sounds to which they correspond. See how many of these spelling units you can find in 2 minutes. Either underline the spelling units in alternating colors or rewrite the words in alternating colors with the fine-tip markers. After time is called, we will share with each other these word clues we found and then say the sound that goes with each of them (see *Talking Letters* card), moving from left to right, and then blend the sounds to say the whole word.

> nidmoin, whulls, chunglewums, cimdaut, thermb, wraltway, trabe, prite, zullcrusk, sceanruz

Word Transferring

Children are given 10 new words that were not practiced but contain target spelling units in the practiced words to evaluate whether they can pronounce them correctly in a different word context. The transfer words were constructed by altering one consonant- or one vowel-spelling unit in Jabberwocky words used in Word Building. Teachers record accuracy for whole words and spelling units, note whether children refer to the student *Talking Letters* card with spelling–phoneme correspondences, and time how long it takes to pronounce all the words on the transfer list. These results can be graphed on Reading Rockets or a teacher-designed chart so that both students and teacher have a visual record of student response to alphabetic principle instruction.

Instructions: Once Word Detectives figure out the code they can apply it to new words or cases. Here are 10 words that have the same spelling units that we have practiced but in different made-up words. How accurately and how fast can you use those spelling units to say these words? Record your accuracy and time on the Reading Rockets in your R-File. Refer to *Talking Letters* if that helps you.

> nidmoip, shulls, bunglewums, cimbaut, themb, wraltee, trape, pripe, zullcrust, sceanriz

Are They Relatives?

Does the underlined spelling unit in the first word correspond to the same phoneme as the underlined spelling unit in the second word? Children are asked to circle YES or NO on the worksheet in the Student Response Booklet if they think the spelling units underlined in the pair of pseudowords do or do not stand for the same sound (phonemes); that is, do they match? If there are differences of opinion, those items are discussed in reference to prior activities with *Talking Letters*. In contrast to the purpose of the warm-up that was to put this knowledge of grapheme–phoneme correspondences on automatic pilot, the purpose of this activity is to reflect consciously on the system of spelling–sound correspondences. Children receive R-File points for completing the activity within the time limits.

Instructions: Look carefully at each pair of words and circle YES on your worksheet if you think the underlined spelling units in each word stand for the same sound; circle NO if you think they don't. Remember that sometimes the same spelling unit stands for different sounds and that sometimes the same sound is spelled in different ways. Let's see how many you can do in 2 minutes. After time is called we will discuss any of your answers for which not everyone agreed.

kn<u>o</u>ck	balloo<u>n</u>
pl<u>e</u>nty	br<u>ea</u>th
r<u>a</u>dar	b<u>a</u>tter
<u>ch</u>orus	<u>k</u>etchup
c<u>u</u>t	<u>s</u>uper
bun<u>ch</u>es	<u>ch</u>orus
hel<u>p</u>ing	lau<u>gh</u>ing
reflec<u>ti</u>on	discu<u>ssi</u>on
<u>e</u>vening	<u>e</u>veryone
en<u>g</u>ine	<u>j</u>et

Sorting by Sound Features

The teacher points to one word at a time on a list in the Student Response Booklet. As you point to the word, name the word and point to the underlined spelling unit and produce the associated phoneme; then ask the children to choose the letter of the category at the top with the correct nickname sound for that spelling unit. Continue this procedure until all words are sorted into categories at the top of the list. Then help the children articulate the generalization that a specific spelling unit may stand for a small set of sounds. Children receive R-File points for each correct categorization of a spelling unit by its associated phoneme.

Although most of these alternations to be sorted are from the Anglo-Saxon layer of the language, a few (e.g., /zh/ for *s,* /short i/ for *y,* and /k/ for *ch*) are from the Romance or Greek layers of the language (see Table 1, p. 9).

Instructions: In this activity, categories for sorting words are listed at the top of the page. Each category has a capital letter. Sort each of the words in the list into one category by writing a capital letter beside it. At the end we will discuss what rule you applied to the sorting and what conclusion we can draw from the group sorting we just did.

Nicknames are /short o/A, /long o/B, /schwa/C, /aw/D (labeled on card headings).

st<u>o</u>p	h<u>o</u>t	m<u>o</u>st
h<u>o</u>me	c<u>o</u>ld	cl<u>o</u>th
m<u>o</u>ther	l<u>o</u>st	
s<u>o</u>ng	r<u>o</u>ds	

Rule to discuss after sorting: Sometimes, vowel sounds are pronounced fully as a long vowel sound or a short vowel sound. Sometimes the vowel is reduced (schwa) and does not make a sound that corresponds to a specific spelling. You have to learn its spelling for a specific word. It may be *e* or *i* or another vowel. Sometimes, short vowel sounds can be pronounced two different ways; for example, *short o* in *hot* (/ah/) and *dog* (/aw/), but some regions of the United States do not make this distinction.

Sorting by Word Context

Children are given words with a blank and a box with choices of spelling units in the Student Response Booklet. The task is to choose the spelling unit that could fit into the blank in the word because in this word context adding that spelling unit spells a real word. These items contain spelling units that stand for the same sound but only one of the spelling units in a word-specific context spells a real word with meaning.

Instructions: Another way that Word Detectives have to make sense of their clues is by examining them for the context, that is the place in which they occur and all the surrounding clues. Each of the words you will see has a blank. Then you will see spellings but only one spelling fits sensibly into the blank. To figure out which spellings would or would not fit into the blank—that is, into the context of the word—you need to pay close attention to all the spelling, sound, and meaning clues of the word. You have to fully analyze all the evidence you have at hand! As soon as you think you know a spelling that would fit into the word, circle it. As a Word Detective, it is important that you examine all the evidence—consider all the spelling units—before you make your decision about which spelling fits in the word.

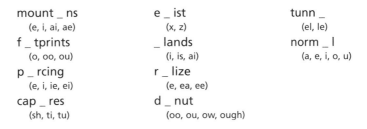

mount _ ns
(e, i, ai, ae)

f _ tprints
(o, oo, ou)

p _ rcing
(e, i, ie, ei)

cap _ res
(sh, ti, tu)

e _ ist
(x, z)

_ lands
(i, is, ai)

r _ lize
(e, ea, ee)

d _ nut
(oo, ou, ow, ough)

tunn _
(el, le)

norm _ l
(a, e, i, o, u)

LESSON **11** Words and Word Parts for
Sound, Spelling, and Meaning

Paying Attention to Sound Units
and Their Relationships to Spelling Units

Student Response Booklet

Note: All lessons start with a warm-up, just as athletes warm up before a
sports game. (See *Talking Letters* card.)

ACTIVITIES

Word Building

We always start by saying and analyzing the sounds in each word. We will not
use real words but rather "Jabberwocky" words, like from *Alice in Wonderland* [read *Jabberwocky* poem from *Alice in Wonderland*]. First close your eyes
and listen as I say a word. Then hold up the number of fingers for the number
of syllables you hear in it. If we disagree, then we will discuss it. Then you will
open your eyes and use these colored discs to count out the number of
phonemes in each syllable. Together we will practice 10 words in each lesson.

Word Generating

Instructions: Word Detectives sometimes get their clues from generating and
reasoning about similar cases. Now I would like you to think of words that
have the same sounds as the ones I say. Write the words you think of in your
Response Booklets. When you are done, we will share with the others. I will
write the words on the board.

1. _____
2. _____
3. _____
4. _____
5. _____
6. _____
7. _____
8. _____
9. _____
10. _____

Unit Finding

Spelling units are one- or two-letter units that correspond to a sound. You may look at your *Talking Letters* card.

Instructions: Word Detectives solve their mysteries by paying attention to details. The details you need to pay attention to in decoding are the spelling units and the sounds to which they correspond. See how many of these spelling units you can find in 2 minutes. Either underline the spelling units in alternating colors or rewrite the words in alternating colors with the fine-tip markers. After time is called, we will share with each other these word clues we found and then say the sound that goes with each of them (see *Talking Letters* card), moving from left to right, and then blend the sounds to say the whole word.

nidmoin	cimdaut	trabe	sceanruz
whulls	thermb	prite	
chunglewums	wraltway	zullcrusk	

Word Transferring

Instructions: Once Word Detectives figure out the code they can apply it to new words or cases. Here are 10 words that have the same spelling units that we have practiced but in different made-up words. How accurately and how fast can you use those spelling units to say these words? Record your accuracy and time on the Reading Rockets in your R-File. Refer to *Talking Letters* if that helps you.

nidmoip	cimbaut	trape	sceanriz
shulls	themb	pripe	
bunglewums	wraltee	zullcrust	

Are They Relatives?

Instructions: Look carefully at each pair of words and circle YES on your worksheet if you think the underlined spelling units in each word stand for the same sound; circle NO if you think they don't. Remember that sometimes the same spelling unit stands for different sounds and that sometimes the same sound is spelled in different ways. Let's see how many you can do in 2 minutes. After time is called we will discuss any of your answers for which not everyone agreed.

<u>kn</u>ock	balloo<u>n</u>	YES	NO
p<u>l</u>enty	br<u>ea</u>th	YES	NO

r<u>a</u>dar	<u>b</u>atter	YES	NO
<u>ch</u>orus	<u>k</u>etchup	YES	NO
c<u>u</u>t	s<u>u</u>per	YES	NO
bun<u>ch</u>e	<u>ch</u>orus	YES	NO
hel<u>p</u>ing	lau<u>gh</u>ing	YES	NO
reflec<u>ti</u>on	discus<u>si</u>on	YES	NO
<u>e</u>vening	<u>e</u>veryone	YES	NO
en<u>g</u>ine	<u>j</u>et	YES	NO

Sorting by Sound Features

Instructions: In this activity, categories for sorting words are listed at the top of the page. Each category has a capital letter. Sort each of the words in the list into one category by writing a capital letter beside it. At the end we will discuss what rule you applied to the sorting and what conclusion we can draw from the group sorting we just did.

Nicknames are /short o/ A, /long o/ B, /schwa/ C, /aw/ D.

st<u>o</u>p	s<u>o</u>ng	l<u>o</u>st	cl<u>o</u>th
h<u>o</u>me	h<u>o</u>t	r<u>o</u>ds	
m<u>o</u>ther	c<u>o</u>ld	m<u>o</u>st	

Sorting by Word Context

Instructions: Another way that Word Detectives have to make sense of their clues is by examining them for the context, that is the place in which they occur and all the surrounding clues. Each of the words you will see has a blank. Then you will see spellings but only one spelling fits sensibly into the blank. To figure out which spellings would or would not fit into the blank—that is, into the context of the word—you need to pay close attention to all the spelling, sound, and meaning clues of the word. You have to fully analyze all the evidence you have at hand! As soon as you think you know a spelling that would fit into the word, circle it. As a Word Detective, it is important that you examine all the evidence—consider all the spelling units—before you make your decision about which spelling fits in the word.

mount __ ns	cap __ res	r __ lize	tunn __
(e, i, ai, ae)	(sh, ti, tu)	(e, ea, ee)	(el, le)
f __ tprints	e __ ist	d __ nut	norm __ l
(o, oo, ou)	(x, z)	(oo, ou, ow, ough)	(a, e, i, o, u)
p __ rcing	__ lands		
(e, i, ie, ei)	(i, is, ai)		

LESSON 12 Words and Word Parts for Sound, Spelling, and Meaning

Paying Attention to Sound Units and Their Relationships to Spelling Units

Teacher Material

The following grapheme–phoneme correspondences are taught using *Talking Letters:* • Latinate and Greek	Materials needed: • *More Talking Letters* (see Table 1) for automatic alphabetic principle • Work folders

WARM-UP (FOR THE TEACHER)

For the warm-up, name the letter or letter group in *More Talking Letters* (see Table 1), say the pictured word containing a target phoneme, and then produce the target phoneme. Next, the students take a turn and repeat what is named or said by you. This approach develops orthographic awareness of spelling units; phonological awareness of corresponding phonemes in and out of word context; and, through close timing, the automaticity of spelling–phoneme correspondence. Monitor whether children are coordinating looking at the relevant letters and pictured words with naming of the letters and words and producing phonemes.

LESSON OVERVIEW (READ TO STUDENTS)

It is normal to come across words you do not know. One way to figure out an unknown word is to find the spelling units and think about their associated sounds. We will call these spelling–sound correspondences the *alphabetic principle.* Sometimes in English, more than one sound is associated with the same spelling unit. We will do seven different kinds of activities in each session to teach you to be a Word Detective who uses alphabetic principle and sound patterns in words to decode unknown words. These activities are *Word Building, Word Generating, Unit Finding, Word Transferring, Are They Relatives? Sorting by Sound Features,* and *Sorting by Word Context.* These activities should give you lots of strategies for using spelling units and their relationships to sounds to figure out words. We will use our electronic timer for the second through fourth activities but not the others. Let's begin.

ACTIVITIES

Word Building

Instructions: We always start by saying and analyzing the sounds in each word. We will not use real words but rather "Jabberwocky" words, like from *Alice in Wonderland* [read *Jabberwocky* poem from *Alice in Wonderland*]. First close your eyes and listen as I say a word. Then hold up the number of fingers for the number of syllables you hear in it. If we disagree, then we will discuss it. Then you will open your eyes and use these colored discs to count out the number of phonemes in each syllable. Together we will practice 10 words in each lesson.

Key:
S = syllable(s);
P = phoneme(s);
1st, 2nd, 3rd =
order of syllables

sligursheck
(3 S: 4 P, 1st; 1 P, 2nd;
3 P, 3rd)

swejeety
(3 S: 3 P, 1st; 3 P, 2nd; 1 P,
3rd [or 2 P, 2nd; 2 P, 3rd])

zullcrusk
(2 S: 3 P, 1st; 5 P, 2nd)

clostrills
(2 S: 5 P, 1st; 4 P, 2nd
[or 2 S: 4 P, 1st; 5 P, 2nd])

blesp
(1 S: 5 P)

grax
(1 S: 5 P)

jeksie
(2 S: 3 P, 1st; 2 P, 2nd)

lutkaw
(2 S: 3 P, 1st; 2 P, 2nd)

haifraff
(2 S: 3 P, 1st; 3 P, 2nd)

snubarth
(2 S: 3 P, 1st; 3 P, 2nd)

Word Generating

The teacher explains that R-Files have a double meaning. Not only are they the files in our work folders where we record our points for correct answers but they are also the "files in OUR minds" in which we store the words we learn. Teachers provide a sound unit (phoneme) and ask children to generate real words or Jabberwocky words that have in them that sound unit. The students write these words in their Response Booklets. Then after time is called after 5 minutes (30 seconds per phoneme), each child shares one word with the group. The teacher records on chalk or white board the word each child shares, providing feedback if necessary. Each child who contributes a word receives R-File points in his or her Response Booklet.

Instructions: Word Detectives sometimes get their clues from generating and reasoning about similar cases. Now I would like you to think of words that have the same sounds as the ones I say and are spelled this way (write on board). Write the words you think of in your Response Booklets. When you are done, we will share with the others. I will write the words on the board.

m, oi, n, h, ai, fr, a, f, v, o

Note: After saying each sound, wait 30 seconds for the student to write the word, then say the next sound.

Unit Finding

The same 10 words practiced under Word Building are presented visually in the Student Response Booklet. Children are asked to underline (using two fine-point colored markers) each of the spelling units in a word using alternating colors for adjacent spelling units. (If this proves too difficult they can rewrite the word, spelling unit by spelling unit, with each adjacent spelling unit in a different color.) Remember, a spelling unit can be 1 or 2 letters and corresponds to a sound or blended sounds on *Talking Letters.* Children are given 2 minutes for 10 words, and their accuracy and time are recorded in work folders. Children who complete the activity correctly within the time limits receive R-File points. Initially

some may not finish within the time limits, but eventually they will. Any discrepancies among children or obvious errors are pointed out to them and discussed. Once everyone agrees on how to parse the words into spelling units, the group makes the sound that goes with each spelling unit and then synthesizes the sounds into a recognizable whole word.

Instructions: Word Detectives solve their mysteries by paying attention to details. The details you need to pay attention to in decoding are the spelling units and the sounds to which they correspond. See how many of these spelling units you can find in 2 minutes. Either underline the spelling units in alternating colors or rewrite the words in alternating colors with the fine-tip markers. After time is called, we will share with each other these word clues we found and then say the sound that goes with each of them (see *Talking Letters* card), moving from left to right, and then blend the sounds to say the whole word.

> sligursheck, swejeety, zullcrusk, clostrills, blesp, grax, jeksie, lutkaw, haifraff, snubarth

Word Transferring

Children are given 10 new words that were not practiced but contain target spelling units in the practiced words to evaluate whether they can pronounce them correctly in a different word context. The transfer words were constructed by altering one consonant- or one vowel-spelling unit in Jabberwocky words used in Word Building. Teachers record accuracy for whole words and spelling units, note whether children refer to the student *Talking Letters* card with spelling–phoneme correspondences, and time how long it takes to pronounce all the words on the transfer list. These results can be graphed on Reading Rockets or a teacher-designed chart so that both students and teacher have a visual record of student response to alphabetic principle instruction.

Instructions: Once Word Detectives figure out the code they can apply it to new words or cases. Here are 10 words that have the same spelling units that we have practiced but in different made-up words. How accurately and how fast can you use those spelling units to say these words? Record your accuracy and time on the Reading Rockets in your R-File. Refer to *Talking Letters* if that helps you.

> sligurshep, swejoaty, zullbrusk, closprills, slesp, grat, joksie, lutkay, haifbraff, snubarm

Are They Relatives?

Does the underlined spelling unit in the first word correspond to the same phoneme as the underlined spelling unit in the second word? Children are asked to circle YES or NO on the worksheet in the Student Response Booklet if they think the spelling units underlined in the pair of pseudowords do or do not stand for the same sound (phonemes); that is, do they match? If there are differences of opinion, those items are discussed in reference to prior activities with *Talking Letters*. In contrast to the purpose of the warm-up that was to put this knowledge of grapheme–phoneme correspondences on automatic pilot, the purpose of this activity is to reflect consciously on the system of spelling–sound correspondences. Children receive R-File points for completing the activity within the time limits.

Instructions: Look carefully at each pair of words and circle YES on your worksheet if you think the underlined spelling units in each word stand for the same sound; circle NO if you think they don't. Remember that sometimes the same spelling unit stands for different sounds and that sometimes the same sound is spelled in different ways. Let's see how many you can do in 2 minutes. After time is called we will discuss any of your answers for which not everyone agreed.

fa<u>c</u>es	<u>s</u>avings
pa<u>th</u>	<u>th</u>at
pl<u>en</u>ty	br<u>ea</u>th
<u>s</u>ilver	chi<u>l</u>d
bun<u>ch</u>es	<u>ch</u>orus
br<u>ai</u>n	pla<u>c</u>e
he<u>l</u>ping	<u>l</u>aughing
<u>e</u>vening	<u>e</u>veryone
thi<u>r</u>sty	show<u>er</u>
en<u>g</u>ine	<u>j</u>et

Sorting by Sound Features

The teacher points to one word at a time on a list in the Student Response Booklet. As you point to the word, name the word and point to the underlined spelling unit and produce the associated phoneme; then ask the children to choose the letter of the category at the top with the correct nickname sound for that spelling unit. Continue this procedure until all words are sorted into categories at the top of the list. Then help the children articulate the generalization that a specific spelling unit may stand for a small set of sounds. Children receive R-File points for each correct categorization of a spelling unit by its associated phoneme.

Although most of these alternations to be sorted are from the Anglo-Saxon layer of the language, a few (e.g., /zh/ for *s,* /short i/ for *y,* and /k/ for *ch*) are from the Romance or Greek layers of the language (see Table 1, p. 9).

Instructions: In this activity, categories for sorting words are listed at the top of the page. Each category has a capital letter. Sort each of the words in the list into one category by writing a capital letter beside it. At the end we will discuss what rule you applied to the sorting and what conclusion we can draw from the group sorting we just did.

Nicknames are /short u/A, /long u/B, /short oo/C (labeled on card headings).

cl<u>u</u>b	n<u>u</u>mber	<u>u</u>nit	h<u>u</u>man
m<u>u</u>st	s<u>u</u>per	r<u>u</u>nning	
f<u>u</u>ll	p<u>u</u>ll	sh<u>u</u>t	

Rule to discuss after sorting: The letter u can stand for three different vowel sounds. Choose the one that results in a recognizable word.

Sorting by Word Context

Children are given words with a blank and a box with choices of spelling units in the Student Response Booklet. The task is to choose the spelling unit that could fit into the blank in the word because in this word context adding that spelling unit spells a real word. These items contain spelling units that stand for the same sound but only one of the spelling units in a word-specific context spells a real word with meaning.

Instructions: Another way that Word Detectives have to make sense of their clues is by examining them for the context, that is the place in which they occur and all the surrounding clues. Each of the words you will see has a blank. Then you will see spellings but only one spelling fits sensibly into the blank. To figure out which spellings would or would not fit into the blank—that is, into the context of the word—you need to pay close attention to all the spelling, sound, and meaning clues of the word. You have to fully analyze all the evidence you have at hand! As soon as you think you know a spelling that would fit into the word, circle it. As a Word Detective, it is important that you examine all the evidence—consider all the spelling units—before you make your decision about which spelling fits in the word.

coll _ ge
(a, e, i, o, u)

consid _ ed
(er, ir, or, ur)

chan _ es
(j, g)

convin _ ed
(c, s)

seas _ n
(a, e, i, o, u)

ridd _
(el, le)

accur _ te
(a, e, i, o, u)

cam _ flage
(a, o, u, ou, oa)

_ ttract
(a, e, i, o, u)

tong _ s
(e, ue)

LESSON **12** Words and Word Parts for
Sound, Spelling, and Meaning

Paying Attention to Sound Units
and Their Relationships to Spelling Units

Student Response Booklet

Note: All lessons start with a warm-up, just as athletes warm up before a
sports game. (See *Talking Letters* card.)

ACTIVITIES

Word Building

We always start by saying and analyzing the sounds in each word. We will not
use real words but rather "Jabberwocky" words, like from *Alice in Wonderland* [read *Jabberwocky* poem from *Alice in Wonderland*]. First close your eyes
and listen as I say a word. Then hold up the number of fingers for the number
of syllables you hear in it. If we disagree, then we will discuss it. Then you will
open your eyes and use these colored discs to count out the number of
phonemes in each syllable. Together we will practice 10 words in each lesson.

Word Generating

Instructions: Word Detectives sometimes get their clues from generating and
reasoning about similar cases. Now I would like you to think of words that
have the same sounds as the ones I say. Write the words you think of in your
Response Booklets. When you are done, we will share with the others. I will
write the words on the board.

1. _____
2. _____
3. _____
4. _____
5. _____
6. _____
7. _____
8. _____
9. _____
10. _____

Unit Finding

Spelling units are one- or two-letter units that correspond to a sound. You may look at your *Talking Letters* card.

Instructions: Word Detectives solve their mysteries by paying attention to details. The details you need to pay attention to in decoding are the spelling units and the sounds to which they correspond. See how many of these spelling units you can find in 2 minutes. Either underline the spelling units in alternating colors or rewrite the words in alternating colors with the fine-tip markers. After time is called, we will share with each other these word clues we found and then say the sound that goes with each of them (see *Talking Letters* card), moving from left to right, and then blend the sounds to say the whole word.

sligursheck	clostrills	jeksie	snubarth
swejeety	blesp	lutkaw	
zullcrusk	grax	haifraff	

Word Transferring

Instructions: Once Word Detectives figure out the code they can apply it to new words or cases. Here are 10 words that have the same spelling units that we have practiced but in different made-up words. How accurately and how fast can you use those spelling units to say these words? Record your accuracy and time on the Reading Rockets in your R-File. Refer to *Talking Letters* if that helps you.

sligurshep	closprills	joksie	snubarm
swejoaty	slesp	lutkay	
zullbrusk	grat	haifbraff	

Are They Relatives?

Instructions: Look carefully at each pair of words and circle YES on your worksheet if you think the underlined spelling units in each word stand for the same sound; circle NO if you think they don't. Remember that sometimes the same spelling unit stands for different sounds and that sometimes the same sound is spelled in different ways. Let's see how many you can do in 2 minutes. After time is called we will discuss any of your answers for which not everyone agreed.

fa<u>c</u>es	<u>s</u>avings	YES	NO
pa<u>th</u>	<u>th</u>at	YES	NO

plenty	breath	YES	NO
silver	child	YES	NO
bunches	chorus	YES	NO
brain	place	YES	NO
helping	laughing	YES	NO
evening	everyone	YES	NO
thirsty	shower	YES	NO
engine	jet	YES	NO

Sorting by Sound Features

Instructions: In this activity, categories for sorting words are listed at the top of the page. Each category has a capital letter. Sort each of the words in the list into one category by writing a capital letter beside it. At the end we will discuss what rule you applied to the sorting and what conclusion we can draw from the group sorting we just did.

Nicknames are /short u/ A, /long u/ B, /short oo/ C.

club	number	unit	human
must	super	running	
full	pull	shut	

Sorting by Word Context

Instructions: Another way that Word Detectives have to make sense of their clues is by examining them for the context, that is the place in which they occur and all the surrounding clues. Each of the words you will see has a blank. Then you will see spellings but only one spelling fits sensibly into the blank. To figure out which spellings would or would not fit into the blank—that is, into the context of the word—you need to pay close attention to all the spelling, sound, and meaning clues of the word. You have to fully analyze all the evidence you have at hand! As soon as you think you know a spelling that would fit into the word, circle it. As a Word Detective, it is important that you examine all the evidence—consider all the spelling units—before you make your decision about which spelling fits in the word.

coll __ ge   convin __ ed   accur __ te   __ ttract
(a, e, i, o, u)   (c, s)   (a,e, i, o, u)   (a, e, i, o, u)

consid __ ed   seas __ n   cam __ flage   tong __ s
(er, ir, or, ur) (a, e, i, o, u) (a, o, u, ou,   (e, ue)
                                   oa)

chan __ es   ridd __
(j, g)   (el, le)

LESSON 13 Words and Word Parts for Sound, Spelling, and Meaning

Paying Attention to Sound Units and Their Relationships to Spelling Units

Teacher Material

The following grapheme–phoneme correspondences are taught using *Talking Letters:* • Single-letter consonants • Short vowels in closed syllables • Long vowels in open syllables	Materials needed: • *Talking Letters* for automatic alphabetic principle • Work folders

WARM-UP (FOR THE TEACHER)

For the warm-up, name the letter or letter group on the *Talking Letters* card, say the pictured word containing a target phoneme, and then produce the target phoneme. Next, the students take a turn and repeat what is named or said by you. This approach develops orthographic awareness of spelling units; phonological awareness of corresponding phonemes in and out of word context; and, through close timing, the automaticity of spelling–phoneme correspondence. Monitor whether children are coordinating looking at the relevant letters and pictured words with naming of the letters and words and producing phonemes.

LESSON OVERVIEW (READ TO STUDENTS)

It is normal to come across words you do not know. One way to figure out an unknown word is to find the spelling units and think about their associated sound. We will call these spelling–sound correspondences the *alphabetic principle.* Sometimes in English, more than one sound is associated with the same spelling unit. We will do seven different kinds of activities in each session to teach you to be a Word Detective who uses alphabetic principle and sound patterns in words to decode unknown words. These activities are *Word Building, Word Generating, Unit Finding, Word Transferring, Are They Relatives? Sorting by Sound Features,* and *Sorting by Word Context.* These activities should give you lots of strategies for using spelling units and their relationships to sounds to figure out words. We will use our electronic timer for the second through fourth activities but not the others. Let's begin.

ACTIVITIES

Word Building

Instructions: We always start by saying and analyzing the sounds in each word. We will not use real words but rather "Jabberwocky" words, like from *Alice in Wonderland* [read *Jabberwocky* poem from *Alice in Wonderland*]. First close your eyes and listen as I say a word. Then hold up the number of fingers for the number of syllables you hear in it. If we disagree, then we will discuss it. Then you will open your eyes and use these colored discs to count out the number of phonemes in each syllable. Together we will practice 10 words in each lesson.

pluce
(1 S: 4 P)

cimdaut
(2 S: 3 P, 1st; 3 P, 2nd)

knelph
(1 S: 4 P)

quoopdro
(2 S: 4 P, 1st; 3 P, 2nd)

hebtou
(2 S: 3 P, 1st; 2 P, 2nd)

glofe
(1 S: 4 P)

clostrills
(2 S: 5 P, 1st; 4 P, 2nd
[or 2 S: 4 P, 1st; 5 P, 2nd])

grax
(1 S: 5 P)

sligursheck
(3 S: 4 P, 1st; 1 P, 2nd;
3 P, 3rd)

zullcrusk
(2 S: 3 P, 1st; 5 P, 2nd)

swejeety
(3 S: 3 P, 1st; 3 P, 2nd; 1 P,
3rd [or 2 P, 2nd; 2 P, 3rd])

yigfrue
(2 S: 3 P, 1st; 3 P, 2nd)

fladorudge
(3 S: 4 P, 1st; 1 P, 2nd;
3 or 4 P, 3rd)

prite
(1 S: 4 P)

lutkaw
(2 S: 3 P, 1st; 2 P, 2nd)

Word Generating

The teacher explains that R-Files have a double meaning. Not only are they the files in our work folders where we record our points for correct answers but they are also the "files in OUR minds" in which we store the words we learn. Teachers provide a sound unit (phoneme) and ask children to generate real words or Jabberwocky words that have in them that sound unit. The students write these words in their Response Booklets. Then after time is called after 5 minutes (30 seconds per phoneme), each child shares one word with the group. The teacher records on chalk or white board the word each child shares, providing feedback if necessary. Each child who contributes a word receives R-File points in his or her Response Booklet.

Instructions: Word Detectives sometimes get their clues from generating and reasoning about similar cases. Now I would like you to think of words that have the same sounds as the ones I say and are spelled this way (write on board). Write the words you think of in your Response Booklets. When you are done, we will share with the others. I will write the words on the board.

p, f, long o, ou, c/k, short i, m, d, au, t

Note: After saying each sound, wait 30 seconds for the student to write the word, then say the next sound.

Unit Finding

The same 10 words practiced under Word Building are presented visually in the Student Response Booklet. Children are asked to underline (using two fine-point colored markers) each of the spelling units in a word using alternating colors for adjacent spelling units. (If

this proves too difficult they can rewrite the word, spelling unit by spelling unit, with each adjacent spelling unit in a different color.) Remember, a spelling unit can be 1 or 2 letters and corresponds to a sound or blended sounds on *Talking Letters.* Children are given 2 minutes for 10 words, and their accuracy and time are recorded in work folders. Children who complete the activity correctly within the time limits receive R-File points. Initially some may not finish within the time limits, but eventually they will. Any discrepancies among children or obvious errors are pointed out to them and discussed. Once everyone agrees on how to parse the words into spelling units, the group makes the sound that goes with each spelling unit and then synthesizes the sounds into a recognizable whole word.

Instructions: Word Detectives solve their mysteries by paying attention to details. The details you need to pay attention to in decoding are the spelling units and the sounds to which they correspond. See how many of these spelling units you can find in 2 minutes. Either underline the spelling units in alternating colors or rewrite the words in alternating colors with the fine-tip markers. After time is called, we will share with each other these word clues we found and then say the sound that goes with each of them (see *Talking Letters* card), moving from left to right, and then blend the sounds to say the whole word.

> pluce, cimdaut, knelph, quoopdro, hebtou, glofe, clostrills, grax, sligursheck, zullcrusk, swejeety, yigfrue, fladorudge, prite, lutkaw

Word Transferring

Children are given 10 new words that were not practiced but contain target spelling units in the practiced words to evaluate whether they can pronounce them correctly in a different word context. The transfer words were constructed by altering one consonant- or one vowel-spelling unit in Jabberwocky words used in Word Building. Teachers record accuracy for whole words and spelling units, note whether children refer to the student *Talking Letters* card with spelling–phoneme correspondences, and time how long it takes to pronounce all the words on the transfer list. These results can be graphed on Reading Rockets or a teacher-designed chart so that both students and teacher have a visual record of student response to alphabetic principle instruction.

Instructions: Once Word Detectives figure out the code they can apply it to new words or cases. Here are 10 words that have the same spelling units that we have practiced but in different made-up words. How accurately and how fast can you use those spelling units to say these words? Record your accuracy and time on the Reading Rockets in your R-File. Refer to *Talking Letters* if that helps you.

> bunglewums, shulls, themb, knelp, sligurshep, fladorup, swejoaty, shewbry, quootdro, wraltwee, zullcrust, closprills, slesp, grat, shuce

Are They Relatives?

Does the underlined spelling unit in the first word correspond to the same phoneme as the underlined spelling unit in the second word? Children are asked to circle YES or NO on the worksheet in the Student Response Booklet if they think the spelling units underlined in the pair of pseudowords do or do not stand for the same sound (phonemes); that is, do they match? If there are differences of opinion, those items are discussed in reference to prior activities with *Talking Letters.* In contrast to the purpose of the warm-up that was to put this knowledge of grapheme–phoneme correspondences on automatic pilot, the purpose of this activity is to reflect consciously on the system of spelling–sound correspondences. Children receive R-File points for completing the activity within the time limits.

Instructions: Look carefully at each pair of words and circle YES on your worksheet if you think the underlined spelling units in each word stand for the same sound; circle NO if you think they don't. Remember that sometimes the same spelling unit stands for different sounds and that sometimes the same sound is spelled in different ways. Let's see how many you can do in 2 minutes. After time is called we will discuss any of your answers for which not everyone agreed.

cir<u>c</u>le	<u>c</u>ircus
<u>ph</u>oto	enou<u>gh</u>
<u>oy</u>ster	c<u>oi</u>ns
<u>x</u>-ray	bo<u>x</u>es
b<u>oo</u>kends	n<u>oo</u>ntime
plu<u>mb</u>er	<u>m</u>onkey
<u>y</u>elling	fr<u>y</u>
lad<u>y</u>	sk<u>y</u>
<u>wr</u>ong	<u>r</u>ight
sta<u>y</u>	sh<u>ape</u>

Sorting by Sound Features

The teacher points to one word at a time on a list in the Student Response Booklet. As you point to the word, name the word and point to the underlined spelling unit and produce the associated phoneme; then ask the children to choose the letter of the category at the top with the correct nickname sound for that spelling unit. Continue this procedure until all words are sorted into categories at the top of the list. Then help the children articulate the generalization that a specific spelling unit may stand for a small set of sounds. Children receive R-File points for each correct categorization of a spelling unit by its associated phoneme.

Although most of these alternations to be sorted are from the Anglo-Saxon layer of the language, a few (e.g., /zh/ for *s*, /short i/ for *y*, and /k/ for *ch*) are from the Romance or Greek layers of the language (see Table 1, p. 9).

Instructions: In this activity, categories for sorting words are listed at the top of the page. Each category has a capital letter. Sort each of the words in the list into one category by writing a capital letter beside it. At the end we will discuss what rule you applied to the sorting and what conclusion we can draw from the group sorting we just did.

Nicknames are /oo/A, /y + oo/B (labeled on card headings).

t<u>ube</u>	r<u>ule</u>	fl<u>ute</u>
m<u>ule</u>	pr<u>une</u>	am<u>use</u>
h<u>uge</u>	f<u>use</u>	
c<u>ube</u>	c<u>ute</u>	

Rule to discuss after sorting: Although all of the vowel sounds are spelled in consonant silent *e*, the *u* may be pronounced with two different sounds, only one of which says its name. So do not think that long vowels always say their own names!

Sorting by Word Context

Children are given words with a blank and a box with choices of spelling units in the Student Response Booklet. The task is to choose the spelling unit that could fit into the blank in the word because in this word context adding that spelling unit spells a real word. These

items contain spelling units that stand for the same sound but only one of the spelling units in a word-specific context spells a real word with meaning.

Instructions: Another way that Word Detectives have to make sense of their clues is by examining them for the context, that is the place in which they occur and all the surrounding clues. Each of the words you will see has a blank. Then you will see spellings but only one spelling fits sensibly into the blank. To figure out which spellings would or would not fit into the blank—that is, into the context of the word—you need to pay close attention to all the spelling, sound, and meaning clues of the word. You have to fully analyze all the evidence you have at hand! As soon as you think you know a spelling that would fit into the word, circle it. As a Word Detective, it is important that you examine all the evidence—consider all the spelling units—before you make your decision about which spelling fits in the word.

vict _ ms
(a, e, i, o, u)

t _ ched
(u, ou)

viol _ nt
(a, e, i, o, u)

r _ gh
(o, ou, u)

obt _ n
(ai, ay)

b _ lder
(o, u, ow)

c _ ple
(a, o, u, ou)

sec _ nds
(a, e, i, o, u)

rot _ ting
(a. silent e, ai)

s _ cer
(a, au, ow)

LESSON **13** Words and Word Parts for
Sound, Spelling, and Meaning

Paying Attention to Sound Units
and Their Relationships to Spelling Units

Student Response Booklet

Note: All lessons start with a warm-up, just as athletes warm up before a sports game. (See *Talking Letters* card.)

ACTIVITIES

Word Building

We always start by saying and analyzing the sounds in each word. We will not use real words but rather "Jabberwocky" words, like from *Alice in Wonderland* [read *Jabberwocky* poem from *Alice in Wonderland*]. First close your eyes and listen as I say a word. Then hold up the number of fingers for the number of syllables you hear in it. If we disagree, then we will discuss it. Then you will open your eyes and use these colored discs to count out the number of phonemes in each syllable. Together we will practice 10 words in each lesson.

Word Generating

Instructions: Word Detectives sometimes get their clues from generating and reasoning about similar cases. Now I would like you to think of words that have the same sounds as the ones I say. Write the words you think of in your Response Booklets. When you are done, we will share with the others. I will write the words on the board.

1. _____
2. _____
3. _____
4. _____
5. _____
6. _____
7. _____
8. _____
9. _____
10. _____

Unit Finding

Spelling units are one- or two-letter units that correspond to a sound. You may look at your *Talking Letters* card.

Instructions: Word Detectives solve their mysteries by paying attention to details. The details you need to pay attention to in decoding are the spelling units and the sounds to which they correspond. See how many of these spelling units you can find in 2 minutes. Either underline the spelling units in alternating colors or rewrite the words in alternating colors with the fine-tip markers. After time is called, we will share with each other these word clues we found and then say the sound that goes with each of them (see *Talking Letters* card), moving from left to right, and then blend the sounds to say the whole word.

pluce	hebtou	sligursheck	fladorudge
cimdaut	glofe	zullcrusk	prite
knelph	clostrills	swejeety	lutkaw
quoopdro	grax	yigfrue	

Word Transferring

Instructions: Once Word Detectives figure out the code they can apply it to new words or cases. Here are 10 words that have the same spelling units that we have practiced but in different made-up words. How accurately and how fast can you use those spelling units to say these words? Record your accuracy and time on the Reading Rockets in your R-File. Refer to *Talking Letters* if that helps you.

bunglewums	sligurshep	quootdro	slesp
shulls	fladorup	wraltwee	grat
themb	swejoaty	zullcrust	shuce
knelp	shewbry	closprills	

Are They Relatives?

Instructions: Look carefully at each pair of words and circle YES on your worksheet if you think the underlined spelling units in each word stand for the same sound; circle NO if you think they don't. Remember that sometimes the same spelling unit stands for different sounds and that sometimes the same sound is spelled in different ways. Let's see how many you can do in 2 minutes. After time is called we will discuss any of your answers for which not everyone agreed.

circus	circle	YES	NO
photo	enough	YES	NO
oyster	coins	YES	NO
x-ray	boxes	YES	NO
bookends	noontime	YES	NO
plumber	monkey	YES	NO
yelling	fry	YES	NO
lady	sky	YES	NO
wrong	right	YES	NO
stay	shape	YES	NO

Sorting by Sound Features

Instructions: In this activity, categories for sorting words are listed at the top of the page. Each category has a capital letter. Sort each of the words in the list into one category by writing a capital letter beside it. At the end we will discuss what rule you applied to the sorting and what conclusion we can draw from the group sorting we just did.

Nicknames are /oo/ A, /y + oo/ B.

tube	cube	fuse	amuse
mule	rule	cute	
huge	prune	flute	

Sorting by Word Context

Instructions: Another way that Word Detectives have to make sense of their clues is by examining them for the context, that is the place in which they occur and all the surrounding clues. Each of the words you will see has a blank. Then you will see spellings but only one spelling fits sensibly into the blank. To figure out which spellings would or would not fit into the blank—that is, into the context of the word—you need to pay close attention to all the spelling, sound, and meaning clues of the word. You have to fully analyze all the evidence you have at hand! As soon as you think you know a spelling that would fit into the word, circle it. As a Word Detective, it is important that you examine all the evidence—consider all the spelling units—before you make your decision about which spelling fits in the word.

vict __ ms	r __ gh	c __ ple	s __ cer
(a, e, i, o, u)	(o, ou, u)	(a, o, u, ou)	(a, au, ow)
t __ ched	obt __ n	sec __ nds	
(u, ou)	(ai, ay)	(a, e, i, o, u)	
viol __ nt	b __ lder	rot __ ting	
(a, e, i, o, u)	(o, u, ow)	(a. silent e, ai)	

LESSON **14** Words and Word Parts for Sound, Spelling, and Meaning

Paying Attention to Sound Units and Their Relationships to Spelling Units

Teacher Material

The following grapheme–phoneme correspondences are taught using *Talking Letters:* • Consonant blends and vowel teams	Materials needed: • *Talking Letters* for automatic alphabetic principle • Work folders

WARM-UP (FOR THE TEACHER)

For the warm-up, name the letter or letter group on the *Talking Letters* card, say the pictured word containing a target phoneme, and then produce the target phoneme. Next, the students take a turn and repeat what is named or said by you. This approach develops orthographic awareness of spelling units; phonological awareness of corresponding phonemes in and out of word context; and, through close timing, the automaticity of spelling–phoneme correspondence. Monitor whether children are coordinating looking at the relevant letters and pictured words with naming of the letters and words and producing phonemes.

LESSON OVERVIEW (READ TO STUDENTS)

It is normal to come across words you do not know. One way to figure out an unknown word is to find the spelling units and think about their associated sounds. We will call these spelling–sound correspondences the *alphabetic principle.* Sometimes in English, more than one sound is associated with the same spelling unit. We will do seven different kinds of activities in each session to teach you to be a Word Detective who uses alphabetic principle and sound patterns in words to decode unknown words. These activities are *Word Building, Word Generating, Unit Finding, Word Transferring, Are They Relatives? Sorting by Sound Features,* and *Sorting by Word Context.* These activities should give you lots of strategies for using spelling units and their relationships to sounds to figure out words. We will use our electronic timer for the second through fourth activities but not the others. Let's begin.

ACTIVITIES

Word Building

Instructions: We always start by saying and analyzing the sounds in each word. We will not use real words but rather "Jabberwocky" words, like from *Alice in Wonderland* [read *Jabberwocky* poem from *Alice in Wonderland*]. First close your eyes and listen as I say a word. Then hold up the number of fingers for the number of syllables you hear in it. If we disagree, then we will discuss it. Then you will open your eyes and use these colored discs to count out the number of phonemes in each syllable. Together we will practice 10 words in each lesson.

Key:
S = syllable(s);
P = phoneme(s);
1st, 2nd, 3rd =
order of syllables

chunglewums
(3 S: 3 P, 1st; 2 P, 2nd; 4 P, 3rd)

whulls
(1 S: 4 P)

thermb
(1 S: 3 P)

smewbry
(2 S: 3 P, 1st; 3 P, 2nd)

wraltway
(2 S: 4 P, 1st; 2 P, 2nd)

blesp
(1 S: 5 P)

trabe
(1 S: 4 P)

jeksie
(2 S: 3 P, 1st; 2 P, 2nd)

soatyaz
(2 S: 3 P, 1st; 3 P, 2nd)

sognoy
(2 S: 3 P, 1st; 2 P, 2nd)

snubarth
(2 S: 3 P, 1st; 3 P, 2nd)

nidmoin
(2 S: 3 P, 1st; 3 P, 2nd)

haifraff
(2 S: 3 P, 1st; 3 P, 2nd)

vopfow
(2 S: 3 P, 1st; 2 P, 2nd)

sceanruz
(2 S: 4 P, 1st; 3 P, 2nd)

Word Generating

The teacher explains that R-Files have a double meaning. Not only are they the files in our work folders where we record our points for correct answers but they are also the "files in OUR minds" in which we store the words we learn. Teachers provide a sound unit (phoneme) and ask children to generate real words or Jabberwocky words that have in them that sound unit. The students write these words in their Response Booklets. Then after time is called after 5 minutes (30 seconds per phoneme), each child shares one word with the group. The teacher records on chalk or white board the word each child shares, providing feedback if necessary. Each child who contributes a word receives R-File points in his or her Response Booklet.

Instructions: Word Detectives sometimes get their clues from generating and reasoning about similar cases. Now I would like you to think of words that have the same sounds as the ones I say and are spelled this way (write on board). Write the words you think of in your Response Booklets. When you are done, we will share with the others. I will write the words on the board.

y, short i, g, fr, u.e, sc, sn, ar, th, z

Note: After saying each sound, wait 30 seconds for the student to write the word, then say the next sound.

Unit Finding

The same 10 words practiced under Word Building are presented visually in the Student Response Booklet. Children are asked to underline (using two fine-point colored markers) each of the spelling units in a word using alternating colors for adjacent spelling units. (If this proves too difficult they can rewrite the word, spelling unit by spelling unit, with each adjacent spelling unit in a different color.) Remember, a spelling unit can be 1 or 2 letters and corresponds to a sound or blended sounds on *Talking Letters.* Children are given 2

minutes for 10 words, and their accuracy and time are recorded in work folders. Children who complete the activity correctly within the time limits receive R-File points. Initially some may not finish within the time limits, but eventually they will. Any discrepancies among children or obvious errors are pointed out to them and discussed. Once everyone agrees on how to parse the words into spelling units, the group makes the sound that goes with each spelling unit and then synthesizes the sounds into a recognizable whole word.

Instructions: Word Detectives solve their mysteries by paying attention to details. The details you need to pay attention to in decoding are the spelling units and the sounds to which they correspond. See how many of these spelling units you can find in 2 minutes. Either underline the spelling units in alternating colors or rewrite the words in alternating colors with the fine-tip markers. After time is called, we will share with each other these word clues we found and then say the sound that goes with each of them (see *Talking Letters* card), moving from left to right, and then blend the sounds to say the whole word.

> chunglewums, whulls, thermb, smewbry, wraltway, blesp, trabe, jeksie, soatyaz, sognoy, snubarth, nidmoin, haifraff, vopfow, sceanruz

Word Transferring

Children are given 10 new words that were not practiced but contain target spelling units in the practiced words to evaluate whether they can pronounce them correctly in a different word context. The transfer words were constructed by altering one consonant- or one vowel-spelling unit in Jabberwocky words used in Word Building. Teachers record accuracy for whole words and spelling units, note whether children refer to the student *Talking Letters* card with spelling–phoneme correspondences, and time how long it takes to pronounce all the words on the transfer list. These results can be graphed on Reading Rockets or a teacher-designed chart so that both students and teacher have a visual record of student response to alphabetic principle instruction.

Instructions: Once Word Detectives figure out the code they can apply it to new words or cases. Here are 10 words that have the same spelling units that we have practiced but in different made-up words. How accurately and how fast can you use those spelling units to say these words? Record your accuracy and time on the Reading Rockets in your R-File. Refer to *Talking Letters* if that helps you.

> glope, pripe, trape, joksie, lutkey, soatbaz, bognoy, shebtou, nidmoip, haifbraff, vopfoo, cimbaut, yigfray, sceanriz, snubarm

Are They Relatives?

Does the underlined spelling unit in the first word correspond to the same phoneme as the underlined spelling unit in the second word? Children are asked to circle YES or NO on the worksheet in the Student Response Booklet if they think the spelling units underlined in the pair of pseudowords do or do not stand for the same sound (phonemes); that is, do they match? If there are differences of opinion, those items are discussed in reference to prior activities with *Talking Letters*. In contrast to the purpose of the warm-up that was to put this knowledge of grapheme–phoneme correspondences on automatic pilot, the purpose of this activity is to reflect consciously on the system of spelling–sound correspondences. Children receive R-File points for completing the activity within the time limits.

Instructions: Look carefully at each pair of words and circle YES on your worksheet if you think the underlined spelling units in each word stand for the same sound; circle NO if you

think they don't. Remember that sometimes the same spelling unit stands for different sounds and that sometimes the same sound is spelled in different ways. Let's see how many you can do in 2 minutes. After time is called we will discuss any of your answers for which not everyone agreed.

<u>ch</u>orus	ketchup
fa<u>c</u>es	<u>s</u>avings
tr<u>ea</u>t	gr<u>ea</u>t
bun<u>ch</u>es	<u>ch</u>orus
<u>pr</u>efer	<u>p</u>erform
hel<u>p</u>ing	<u>l</u>aughing
reflec<u>ti</u>on	discu<u>ss</u>ion
pl<u>e</u>nty	br<u>ea</u>th
thi<u>rs</u>ty	show<u>er</u>
pa<u>th</u>	<u>th</u>at

Sorting by Sound Features

The teacher points to one word at a time on a list in the Student Response Booklet. As you point to the word, name the word and point to the underlined spelling unit and produce the associated phoneme; then ask the children to choose the letter of the category at the top with the correct nickname sound for that spelling unit. Continue this procedure until all words are sorted into categories at the top of the list. Then help the children articulate the generalization that a specific spelling unit may stand for a small set of sounds. Children receive R-File points for each correct categorization of a spelling unit by its associated phoneme.

Although most of these alternations to be sorted are from the Anglo-Saxon layer of the language, a few (e.g., /zh/ for *s*, /short i/ for *y*, and /k/ for *ch*) are from the Romance or Greek layers of the language (see Table 1, p. 9).

Instructions: In this activity, categories for sorting words are listed at the top of the page. Each category has a capital letter. Sort each of the words in the list into one category by writing a capital letter beside it. At the end we will discuss what rule you applied to the sorting and what conclusion we can draw from the group sorting we just did.

Nicknames are /ar/A, /air/B (labeled on card headings).

<u>car</u>	p<u>ar</u>rot	m<u>ar</u>ket	m<u>ar</u>ry
sc<u>are</u>	y<u>ar</u>d	c<u>ar</u>rot	
g<u>ar</u>den	ch<u>ar</u>ity	st<u>ars</u>	

Rule to discuss after sorting: *R*-controlled vowels are a single sound, but it is different from the sound that goes with the vowel (e.g., *a*) or *r* alone. The *r*-controlled vowel *a* has two nicknames (alternative sounds).

Sorting by Word Context

Children are given words with a blank and a box with choices of spelling units in the Student Response Booklet. The task is to choose the spelling unit that could fit into the blank in the word because in this word context adding that spelling unit spells a real word. These items contain spelling units that stand for the same sound but only one of the spelling units in a word-specific context spells a real word with meaning.

Instructions: Another way that Word Detectives have to make sense of their clues is by examining them for the context, that is the place in which they occur and all the surrounding clues. Each of the words you will see has a blank. Then you will see spellings but only one spelling fits sensibly into the blank. To figure out which spellings would or would not fit into the blank—that is, into the context of the word—you need to pay close attention to all the spelling, sound, and meaning clues of the word. You have to fully analyze all the evidence you have at hand! As soon as you think you know a spelling that would fit into the word, circle it. As a Word Detective, it is important that you examine all the evidence—consider all the spelling units—before you make your decision about which spelling fits in the word.

thr _
(o, ou, ough)

eyewitne _
(s, ss, z)

ag _ ny
(a, e, i, o, u)

ya _ tsmen
(h, ch)

int _ fering
(er, ir, or, ur)

compl _ cated
(a, e, i, o, u)

_ ene
(s, sc, sk)

sever _ l
(a, e, i, o, u)

ach _ ve
(e, ee, ie)

w _ ring
(e, ea)

LESSON 14 Words and Word Parts for Sound, Spelling, and Meaning

Paying Attention to Sound Units and Their Relationships to Spelling Units

Student Response Booklet

Note: All lessons start with a warm-up, just as athletes warm up before a sports game. (See *Talking Letters* card.)

ACTIVITIES

Word Building

We always start by saying and analyzing the sounds in each word. We will not use real words but rather "Jabberwocky" words, like from *Alice in Wonderland* [read *Jabberwocky* poem from *Alice in Wonderland*]. First close your eyes and listen as I say a word. Then hold up the number of fingers for the number of syllables you hear in it. If we disagree, then we will discuss it. Then you will open your eyes and use these colored discs to count out the number of phonemes in each syllable. Together we will practice 10 words in each lesson.

Word Generating

Instructions: Word Detectives sometimes get their clues from generating and reasoning about similar cases. Now I would like you to think of words that have the same sounds as the ones I say. Write the words you think of in your Response Booklets. When you are done, we will share with the others. I will write the words on the board.

1. _____
2. _____
3. _____
4. _____
5. _____
6. _____
7. _____
8. _____
9. _____
10. _____

Unit Finding

Spelling units are one- or two-letter units that correspond to a sound. You may look at your *Talking Letters* card.

Instructions: Word Detectives solve their mysteries by paying attention to details. The details you need to pay attention to in decoding are the spelling units and the sounds to which they correspond. See how many of these spelling units you can find in 2 minutes. Either underline the spelling units in alternating colors or rewrite the words in alternating colors with the fine-tip markers. After time is called, we will share with each other these word clues we found and then say the sound that goes with each of them (see *Talking Letters* card), moving from left to right, and then blend the sounds to say the whole word.

chunglewums	wraltway	soatyaz	haifraff
whulls	blesp	sognoy	vopfow
thermb	trabe	snubarth	sceanruz
smewbry	jeksie	nidmoin	

Word Transferring

Instructions: Once Word Detectives figure out the code they can apply it to new words or cases. Here are 10 words that have the same spelling units that we have practiced but in different made-up words. How accurately and how fast can you use those spelling units to say these words? Record your accuracy and time on the Reading Rockets in your R-File. Refer to *Talking Letters* if that helps you.

glope	lutkey	nidmoip	yigfray
pripe	soatbaz	haifbraff	sceanriz
trape	bognoy	vopfoo	snubarm
joksie	shebtou	cimbaut	

Are They Relatives?

Instructions: Look carefully at each pair of words and circle YES on your worksheet if you think the underlined spelling units in each word stand for the same sound; circle NO if you think they don't. Remember that sometimes the same spelling unit stands for different sounds and that sometimes the same sound is spelled in different ways. Let's see how many you can do in 2 minutes. After time is called we will discuss any of your answers for which not everyone agreed.

<u>ch</u>orus	<u>k</u>etchup	YES	NO
fa<u>c</u>es	<u>s</u>avings	YES	NO

tr<u>ea</u>t	gr<u>ea</u>t	YES	NO
bun<u>ch</u>es	<u>ch</u>orus	YES	NO
<u>pr</u>efer	<u>per</u>form	YES	NO
hel<u>p</u>ing	lau<u>gh</u>ing	YES	NO
reflec<u>tion</u>	discu<u>ss</u>ion	YES	NO
pl<u>e</u>nty	br<u>ea</u>th	YES	NO
thi<u>rs</u>ty	showe<u>r</u>	YES	NO
pa<u>th</u>	<u>th</u>at	YES	NO

Sorting by Sound Features

Instructions: In this activity, categories for sorting words are listed at the top of the page. Each category has a capital letter. Sort each of the words in the list into one category by writing a capital letter beside it. At the end we will discuss what rule you applied to the sorting and what conclusion we can draw from the group sorting we just did.

Nicknames are /ar/ A, /air/ B.

c<u>ar</u>	p<u>a</u>rrot	m<u>ar</u>ket	m<u>a</u>rry
sc<u>are</u>	y<u>ar</u>d	c<u>a</u>rrot	
g<u>ar</u>den	ch<u>ari</u>ty	st<u>ars</u>	

Sorting by Word Context

Instructions: Another way that Word Detectives have to make sense of their clues is by examining them for the context, that is the place in which they occur and all the surrounding clues. Each of the words you will see has a blank. Then you will see spellings but only one spelling fits sensibly into the blank. To figure out which spellings would or would not fit into the blank— that is, into the context of the word—you need to pay close attention to all the spelling, sound, and meaning clues of the word. You have to fully ana-lyze all the evidence you have at hand! As soon as you think you know a spelling that would fit into the word, circle it. As a Word Detective, it is im-portant that you examine all the evidence—consider all the spelling units— before you make your decision about which spelling fits in the word.

thr __
(o, ou, ough)

int __ fering
(er, ir, or, ur)

sever __ l
(a, e, i, o, u)

eyewitne __
(s, ss, z)

compl __ cated
(a, e, i, o, u)

ach __ ve
(e, ee, ie)

ag __ ny
(a, e, i, o, u)

__ ene
(s, sc, sk)

w __ ring
(e, ea)

ya __ tsmen
(h, ch)

LESSON **15** | Morphological Awareness Treatment

Teacher Material

The following grapheme–phoneme correspondences are taught using *Talking Letters:* • Single-letter consonants • Short vowels in closed syllables • Long vowels in open syllables	Materials needed: • *Talking Letters* for automatic alphabetic principle • Work folders

WARM-UP (FOR THE TEACHER)

For the warm-up, name the letter or letter group on the *Talking Letters* card, say the pictured word containing a target phoneme, and then produce the target phoneme. Next, the students take a turn and repeat what is named or said by you. This approach develops orthographic awareness of spelling units; phonological awareness of corresponding phonemes in and out of word context; and, through close timing, the automaticity of spelling–phoneme correspondence. If Lessons 1–14 have been completed, just name the letter or letter group and produce the target phoneme, and then the students take a turn and repeat what you have said. Monitor whether children are coordinating looking at the relevant letters and pictured words with naming of the letters and words and producing phonemes.

LESSON OVERVIEW (READ TO STUDENTS)

It is normal to come across words you do not know. One way to figure out unknown words is to use their word parts that signal or "fix" their meaning. We will call these parts at the beginning of words *prefixes* because they come before the rest of the word, and those parts at the end of the word *postfixes* because they come after the rest of the word. (Another term for the parts at the end of word is *suffixes.*) Words also have base parts that signal their meaning. Some words only have bases; some have prefixes and bases; some have bases and postfixes; and some have prefixes, bases, and postfixes. We will do seven different kinds of activities in each session to teach you to be Word Detectives who use these word parts to decode words: *Word Building, Word Generating, Unit Finding, Word Transferring, Are They Relatives? Sorting by Word Part Features,* and *Sorting by Sentence Context.* These activities should give you lots of strategies for using word parts to figure out words. We will use our electronic timer for the second through fourth activities but not for the others. Let's begin.

ACTIVITIES

Word Building

From this list of 30 words with highly frequent prefixes and derivational suffixes, 10 are presented in each lesson (1–14) and are presented three times altogether; but these will be randomized across the three presentations to avoid list learning effects. For the last two sessions (13 and 14), half of the list (15) is presented for a final review of the whole set. See the Student Response Booklet kept in your Word Detectives Work Folder. This set of affixes was generated by examining words in the McGraw-Hill Specific Skills *Working within Words Series* for Grades 3–6 and by reviewing morphological units in selected reading passages in *Read Naturally.* From these, Bill Nagy identified 30 suffixes that occur most frequently and thus are highly useful for struggling readers. Given limited instructional time, these are the ones on which to focus. Capital letters indicate these high-utility affixes, which were practiced in various lessons. The prefixes, bases, and postfixes are kept on 3 × 5 cards (or 5 × 8 cards or larger, depending on how large the word parts must be for all children in group to see them) in large envelopes—marked *prefixes, bases, and suffixes*—for the teacher to use in presenting the word parts and used as needed for a specific lesson (see Student Response Booklet for word parts). Then for each lesson, the teacher draws from the large envelopes the large cards with the word parts needed for each word in a lesson and holds them up high for all students to see. After one student correctly synthesizes the word parts to pronounce the word, each child writes the complete word built from its parts in the row on a worksheet.

Lessons 15–28 Complete Set of Words		
REmember	reportER	elementARY
UNclear	announceMENT	northERN
INvisible	mouthFUL	leaderSHIP
DISlike	sickNESS	differENT
IMpolite	washABLE	amazING
addiTION	nervOUS	projectOR
saltY	brownISH	magicAL
completeLY	scientIST	goldEN
importANT	expensIVE	creativITY
harmLESS	electrIC	toWARD

Instructions: Word Detectives solve cases by combining clues. We will start by building words from word part clues. I will show you word parts. As soon as you know the word that can be formed by these parts, raise your hand. When we agree, I will write it on the board and you can copy it in your Student Response Booklet. You will build the words from a base and fixes (*prefixes* before the base, or *suffixes* after the base).

completely, washable, brownish, dislike, scientist, leadership, mouthful, different, amazing, northern

Word Generating

Instructions: Word Detectives sometimes get their clues from generating and reasoning about similar cases. Readers can do the same—use what they know about words to generate new words in their minds. For 5 minutes, for each of the following word parts, think of a word that has that word part. Write the word in your Student Response Booklet. Go to the next word part and do the same, and so on. After 5 minutes, students share words generated for each word part. I will write one correct example for each word part on the board.

Note: Children do this independently for 5 minutes. Every 30 seconds, the teacher can prompt the children to try to think of a word for the next word part.

> ly, able, ish, dis, ist, ship, ful, ent, ing, ern

Unit Finding

Children are directed to the Student Response Booklet with lists of words and asked to underline the base word and circle the affixes. Children receive R-File points if all word part items are completed correctly within 2 minutes.

Instructions: Word Detectives solve mysteries by paying attention to details. The details you need to pay attention to in decoding are the base and the beginning and end "fixes" if there are any. Underline the base—the main meaning part of the word—and circle any fixes at the beginning or end that might modify or qualify that meaning. After 2 minutes, we will share with each other the word clues we found. I will write one shared correct example for each word part on the board.

> submarine, impersonate, irresponsible, imbalance, cooperation, previewed, unbecoming, unturned, misjudgment, unhappiness

Word Transferring

For each lesson, children read a list with 10 words containing the same affixes practiced under Word Building. They read the list to a teacher who times them, records the time on their R-File record, and indicates whether 1) the affix part was pronounced correctly and 2) the whole word was pronounced correctly.

Instructions: Once Word Detectives figure out the code, they can apply it to new words or cases. Here are some words that have the same parts that we have practiced. I will record how many you pronounce correctly and how long it took. We will graph your accuracy and time so you can see your progress.

> lonely, huggable, warmish, disable, druggist, friendship, helpful, movement, melting, western

Are They Relatives?

Does the first word come from the second word? The purpose of this task is to describe whether word parts at the end of a base word signal a semantic relationship with a base word. Children can record the total number they got correct.

Instructions: To solve puzzles, Word Detectives need to pay attention not only to clues in a single word but also to how the clues in a word may signal that words are related in meaning to other words they know. Just as a child comes from her or his parents, some words come from—that is, they are made from—meaning of other words and thus belong to the same family of word meanings, but other words are not from the same family of word meanings even though they may resemble other words in spelling or sound. I want you to

listen carefully and after I say each pair of words, circle YES on your worksheet if you think the first word comes from the second one and circle NO if you do not think it does. After that, we will discuss any of your answers on which not everyone has agreed.

reporter	report
respectfully	respect
mayor	may
transportation	transport
tenor	ten
orange	or
specifically	specific
injection	inject
onion	on
pillow	pill

Sorting by Word Part Features

The rules children write are discussed to make sure that all have grasped the underlying principle for sorting the words into categories.

Instructions: Once Word Detectives get clues they have to make sense of them. They have to do a special kind of thinking in which they draw conclusions from the evidence, just as Sherlock Holmes and Dr. Watson did. In this activity you will sort words into categories, each of which has a word label and capital letter. Write the capital letter that shows the category to which each word belongs. When you complete the sort, you will be asked to write the rule you used in sorting words into categories. Then we will discuss the rules to make sure that everyone agrees.

Generalization: A prefix cannot be identified just on the basis of spelling.

Labels for cards (i.e., categories for sorting): Prefix = A, No Prefix = B.

realize, rewind, recapture, ready, recall, renter, reach, redo, restaurant, retell, reorganize, reentry

Sorting by Sentence Context

The purpose of this activity is to help children see the importance of analyzing words fully. The words in the Word Pool from which a word is chosen for the blank in the sentence are in the Student Record Form. Record for each lesson the number correct.

Instructions: Another way that Word Detectives have to make sense of their clues is by examining them for *context*—the place in which they occur and all the surrounding clues. Each of the three sentences you will see has a blank. Each of the Word Pools you will see has one word in the box that fits sensibly into the blank but mostly words that would not fit into the blank. To figure out which words would or would not fit into the blank—that is, into the context of the sentence—you need to pay close attention to all the spelling, sound, and meaning clues of the words in the pool and in the words in the sentence. You have to fully analyze all the evidence you have at hand! As soon as you think you know a word that would fit into the sentence, raise your hand. As a Word Detective, it is important that you examine all the evidence—consider all the words—before you make your decision about which word fits. If someone disagrees with you, we will discuss why or why not that word might work in that sentence.

The melting popsicle turned into a _____ mess.
(former, formless, forming, helpless)

He could tell at a glance that the old apple was _____.
(worrisome, worm-like, wormy, icy)

He greeted his old friend _____.
(largely, happily, angrily, happiest)

He was fired from his job at the dog kennel because of his _____ toward the animals.
(quietness, meanness, loudness, meaning)

The boy didn't need to stay in bed but he certainly looked _____.
(sickness, carelessness, sickish, tallish)

LESSON **15** Morphological Awareness Treatment
Adding Word Parts for Meaning to Decoding

Student Response Booklet

Note: All lessons start with a warm-up, just as athletes warm up before a sports game. (See *Talking Letters* card.)

ACTIVITIES

Word Building

Instructions: Word Detectives solve cases by combining clues. We will start by building words from word part clues. I will show you word parts. As soon as you know the word that can be formed by these parts, raise your hand. When we agree, I will write it on the board and you can copy it in your Student Response Booklet. You will build the words from a base and fixes (*prefixes* before the base, or *suffixes* after the base).

complete + ly = _____

wash + able = _____

brown + ish = _____

dis + like = _____

science + ist = _____

leader + ship = _____

mouth + ful = _____

differ + ent = _____

amaze + ing = _____

north + ern = _____

Total correct = _____

Word Generating

Instructions: Word Detectives sometimes get their clues from generating and reasoning about similar cases. Readers can do the same—use what they know about words to generate new words in their minds. For 5 minutes, for each of the following word parts, think of a word that has that word part. Write the word in your Student Response Booklet. Go to the next word part and do the same, and so on. After 5 minutes, students share words generated for each word part. I will write one correct example for each word part on the board.

ly _____

able _____

ish _____

dis _____

ist _____

ship _____

ful _____

ent _____

ing _____

ern _____

Total new correct words generated in 5 minutes = _____

Unit Finding

Instructions: Word Detectives solve mysteries by paying attention to details. The details you need to pay attention to in decoding are the base and the beginning and end "fixes" if there are any. Underline the base—the main meaning part of the word—and circle any fixes at the beginning or end that might modify or qualify that meaning. After 2 minutes, we will share with each other the word clues we found. I will write one shared correct example for each word part on the board.

submarine	cooperation	misjudgment
impersonate	previewed	unhappiness
irresponsible	unbecoming	
imbalance	unturned	

Total number of words in which bases and fixes were correctly identified = _____

Word Transferring

Instructions: Once Word Detectives figure out the code, they can apply it to new words or cases. Here are some words that have the same parts that we have practiced. I will record how many you pronounce correctly and how long it took. We will graph your accuracy and time so you can see your progress.

lonely

huggable

warmish

disable

druggist

friendship

helpful

movement

melting

western

Correct words = _____   **Correct affixes** = _____

Total time = _____

Are They Relatives?

Instructions: To solve puzzles, Word Detectives need to pay attention not only to clues in a single word but also to how the clues in a word may signal that words are related in meaning to other words they know. Just as a child comes from her or his parents, some words come from—that is, they are made from—meaning of other words and thus belong to the same family of word meanings, but other words are not from the same family of word meanings even though they may resemble other words in spelling or sound. I want you to listen carefully and after I say each pair of words, circle YES on your worksheet if you think the first word comes from the second one and circle NO if you do not think it does. After that, we will discuss any of your answers on which not everyone has agreed.

Directions: Circle YES or NO beside the word pair.

reporter	report	YES	NO
respectfully	respect	YES	NO
mayor	may	YES	NO
transportation	transport	YES	NO
tenor	ten	YES	NO
orange	or	YES	NO

specifically	specific	YES	NO
injection	inject	YES	NO
onion	on	YES	NO
pillow	pill	YES	NO

Total correct in 2 minutes = _____

Sorting by Word Part Features

Instructions: Once Word Detectives get clues they have to make sense of them. They have to do a special kind of thinking in which they draw conclusions from the evidence, just as Sherlock Holmes and Dr. Watson did. In this activity you will sort words into categories, each of which has a word label and capital letter. Write the capital letter that shows the category to which each word belongs. When you complete the sort, you will be asked to write the rule you used in sorting words into categories. Then we will discuss the rules to make sure that everyone agrees.

Labels for categories: Prefix = A, No Prefix = B

realize

rewind

recapture

ready

recall

renter

reach

redo

restaurant

retell

reorganize

reentry

Explain the rule you used to sort: _____

_____

_____

_____

_____

Number sorted correctly = _____

Sorting by Sentence Context

Instructions: Another way that Word Detectives have to make sense of their clues is by examining them for *context*—the place in which they occur and all the surrounding clues. Each of the three sentences you will see has a blank. Each of the Word Pools you will see has one word that fits sensibly into the blank but mostly words that would not fit into the blank. To figure out which words would or would not fit into the blank—that is, into the context of the sentence—you need to pay close attention to all the spelling, sound, and meaning clues of the words in the pool and in the words in the sentence. You have to fully analyze all the evidence you have at hand! As soon as you think you know a word that would fit into the sentence, raise your hand. As a Word Detective, it is important that you examine all the evidence—consider all the words—before you make your decision about which word fits. If someone disagrees with you, we will discuss why or why not that word might work in that sentence.

The melting popsicle turned into a _____ mess.
(former, formless, forming, helpless)

He could tell at a glance that the old apple was _____.
(worrisome, worm-like, wormy, icy)

He greeted his old friend _____.
(largely, happily, angrily, happiest)

He was fired from his job at the dog kennel because of his

_____ toward the animals.
(quietness, meanness, loudness, meaning)

The boy didn't need to stay in bed but he certainly looked

_____.

(sickness, carelessness, sickish, tallish)

Total correct = _____

LESSON 16 Morphological Awareness Treatment

Teacher Material

The following grapheme–phoneme correspondences are taught using *Talking Letters:* • Consonant blends and vowel teams	Materials needed: • *Talking Letters* for automatic alphabetic principle • Work folders

WARM-UP (FOR THE TEACHER)

For the warm-up, name the letter or letter group on the *Talking Letters* card, say the pictured word containing a target phoneme, and then produce the target phoneme. Next, the students take a turn and repeat what is named or said by you. This approach develops orthographic awareness of spelling units; phonological awareness of corresponding phonemes in and out of word context; and, through close timing, the automaticity of spelling–phoneme correspondence. If Lessons 1–14 have been completed, just name the letter or letter group and produce the target phoneme, and then the students take a turn and repeat what you have said. Monitor whether children are coordinating looking at the relevant letters and pictured words with naming of the letters and words and producing phonemes.

LESSON OVERVIEW (READ TO STUDENTS)

It is normal to come across words you do not know. One way to figure out unknown words is to use their word parts that signal or "fix" their meaning. We will call these parts at the beginning of words *prefixes* because they come before the rest of the word, and those parts at the end of the word *postfixes* because they come after the rest of the word. (Another term for the parts at the end of word is *suffixes.*) Words also have base parts that signal their meaning. Some words only have bases; some have prefixes and bases; some have bases and postfixes; and some have prefixes, bases, and postfixes. We will do seven different kinds of activities in each session to teach you to be Word Detectives who use these word parts to decode words: *Word Building, Word Generating, Unit Finding, Word Transferring, Are They Relatives? Sorting by Word Part Features,* and *Sorting by Sentence Context.* These activities should give you lots of strategies for using word parts to figure out words. We will use our electronic timer for the second through fourth activities but not for the others. Let's begin.

ACTIVITIES

Word Building

From this list of 30 words with highly frequent prefixes and derivational suffixes, 10 are presented in each lesson (1–14) and are presented three times altogether; but these will be randomized across the three presentations to avoid list learning effects. For the last two sessions (13 and 14), half of the list (15) is presented for a final review of the whole set. See the Student Response Booklet kept in your Word Detectives Work Folder. This set of affixes was generated by examining words in the McGraw-Hill Specific Skills *Working within Words Series* for Grades 3–6 and by reviewing morphological units in selected reading passages in *Read Naturally*. From these, Bill Nagy identified 30 suffixes that occur most frequently and thus are highly useful for struggling readers. Given limited instructional time, these are the ones on which to focus. Capital letters indicate these high-utility affixes, which were practiced in various lessons. The prefixes, bases, and postfixes are kept on 3 × 5 cards (or 5 × 8 cards or larger, depending on how large the word parts must be for all children in group to see them) in large envelopes—marked *prefixes, bases, and suffixes*—for the teacher to use in presenting the word parts and used as needed for a specific lesson (see Student Response Booklet for word parts). Then for each lesson, the teacher draws from the large envelopes the large cards with the word parts needed for each word in a lesson and holds them up high for all students to see. After one student correctly synthesizes the word parts to pronounce the word, each child writes the complete word built from its parts in the row on a worksheet.

Instructions: Word Detectives solve cases by combining clues. We will start by building words from word part clues. I will show you word parts. As soon as you know the word that can be formed by these parts, raise your hand. When we agree, I will write it on the board and you can copy it in your Student Response Booklet. You will build the words from a base and fixes (*prefixes* before the base, or *suffixes* after the base).

golden, electricity, announcement, reporter, pleasant, nervous, projector, sickness, expensive, salty

Word Generating

Instructions: Word Detectives sometimes get their clues from generating and reasoning about similar cases. Readers can do the same—use what they know about words to generate new words in their minds. For 5 minutes, for each of the following word parts, think of a word that has that word part. Write the word in your Student Response Booklet. Go to the next word part and do the same, and so on. After 5 minutes, students share words generated for each word part. I will write one correct example for each word part on the board.

Note: Children do this independently for 5 minutes. Every 30 seconds, the teacher can prompt the children to try to think of a word for the next word part.

en, ic, ment, er, ant, ous, or, ness, ive, y

Unit Finding

Children are directed to the Student Response Booklet with lists of words and asked to underline the base word and circle the affixes. Children receive R-File points if all word part items are completed correctly within 2 minutes.

Instructions: Word Detectives solve mysteries by paying attention to details. The details you need to pay attention to in decoding are the base and the beginning and end "fixes" if there are any. Underline the base—the main meaning part of the word—and circle any fixes at the beginning or end that might modify or qualify that meaning. After 2 minutes, we will share with each other the word clues we found. I will write one shared correct example for each word part on the board.

> retraceable, forgetful, shamelessly, unfriendliness, librarian, abnormal, unhappiness, solidify, disappearance, misconduct

Word Transferring

For each lesson, children read a list with 10 words containing the same affixes practiced under Word Building. They read the list to a teacher who times them, records the time on their R-File record, and indicates whether 1) the affix part was pronounced correctly and 2) the whole word was pronounced correctly.

Instructions: Once Word Detectives figure out the code, they can apply it to new words or cases. Here are some words that have the same parts that we have practiced. I will record how many you pronounce correctly and how long it took. We will graph your accuracy and time so you can see your progress.

> darken, energetic, amazement, teacher, pleasant, dangerous, senator, quickness, active, rainy

Are They Relatives?

Does the first word come from the second word? The purpose of this task is to describe whether word parts at the end of a base word signal a semantic relationship with a base word. Children can record the total number they got correct.

Instructions: To solve puzzles, Word Detectives need to pay attention not only to clues in a single word but also to how the clues in a word may signal that words are related in meaning to other words they know. Just as a child comes from her or his parents, some words come from—that is, they are made from—meaning of other words and thus belong to the same family of word meanings, but other words are not from the same family of word meanings even though they may resemble other words in spelling or sound. I want you to listen carefully and after I say each pair of words, circle YES on your worksheet if you think the first word comes from the second one and circle NO if you do not think it does. After that, we will discuss any of your answers on which not everyone has agreed.

molecule	mole
projector	project
performance	perform
atoms	at
canyon	can
construction	construct
instructional	instruct
building	build
farmer	far
mustard	must

Sorting by Word Part Features

The rules children write are discussed to make sure that all have grasped the underlying principle for sorting the words into categories.

Instructions: Once Word Detectives get clues they have to make sense of them. They have to do a special kind of thinking in which they draw conclusions from the evidence, just as Sherlock Holmes and Dr. Watson did. In this activity you will sort words into categories, each of which has a word label and capital letter. Write the capital letter that shows the category to which each word belongs. When you complete the sort, you will be asked to write the rule you used in sorting words into categories. Then we will discuss the rules to make sure that everyone agrees.

Generalization: A prefix cannot be identified just on the basis of spelling. Some prefixes close in spelling have different meanings.

Labels for cards: Prefix Means *Not* = A, Prefix Means *One* = B, No Prefix = C

undemanding, unique, undress, unresponsive, unnecessary, universal, unity, unable, under, unwind, unfeeling, unit

Sorting by Sentence Context

The purpose of this activity is to help children see the importance of analyzing words fully. The words in the Word Pool from which a word is chosen for the blank in the sentence are in the Student Record Form. Record for each lesson the number correct.

Instructions: Another way that Word Detectives have to make sense of their clues is by examining them for *context*—the place in which they occur and all the surrounding clues. Each of the three sentences you will see has a blank. Each of the Word Pools you will see has one word in the box that fits sensibly into the blank but mostly words that would not fit into the blank. To figure out which words would or would not fit into the blank—that is, into the context of the sentence—you need to pay close attention to all the spelling, sound, and meaning clues of the words in the pool and in the words in the sentence. You have to fully analyze all the evidence you have at hand! As soon as you think you know a word that would fit into the sentence, raise your hand. As a Word Detective, it is important that you examine all the evidence—consider all the words—before you make your decision about which word fits. If someone disagrees with you, we will discuss why or why not that word might work in that sentence.

Because of concerns about everyone's health, the restaurant was a _____ place.
(smoky, dirty, smoke-free, cooking, peaceful)

The man had been to many different countries. He was a worldwide _____.
(teacher, rider, dangerous, traveler, traveling)

The machine was supposed to make ice cream, but it worked so poorly that Mrs. Smith thought it was _____.
(useful, playful, using, useless)

Mary turned out the light to _____ the room.
(brighter, darken, brighten, empty)

Mr. Jones was afraid of pulling his bandage off his _____ cut.
(painless, dangerous, painful, colorful)

LESSON **16** Morphological Awareness Treatment
Adding Word Parts for Meaning to Decoding

Student Response Booklet

Note: All lessons start with a warm-up, just as athletes warm up before a sports game. (See *Talking Letters* card.)

ACTIVITIES

Word Building

Instructions: Word Detectives solve cases by combining clues. We will start by building words from word part clues. I will show you word parts. As soon as you know the word that can be formed by these parts, raise your hand. When we agree, I will write it on the board and you can copy it in your Student Response Booklet. You will build the words from a base and fixes (*prefixes* before the base, or *suffixes* after the base).

gold + en = _____

electric + ity = _____

announce + ment = _____

report + er = _____

please + ant = _____

nerve + ous = _____

project + or = _____

sick + ness = _____

expense + ive = _____

salt + y = _____

Total correct = _____

Word Generating

Instructions: Word Detectives sometimes get their clues from generating and reasoning about similar cases. Readers can do the same—use what they know about words to generate new words in their minds. For 5 minutes, for each of the following word parts, think of a word that has that word part. Write the word in your Student Response Booklet. Go to the next word part and do the same, and so on. After 5 minutes, students share words generated for each word part. I will write one correct example for each word part on the board.

en _____

ic _____

ment _____

er _____

ant _____

ous _____

or _____

ness _____

ive _____

y _____

Total new correct words generated in 5 minutes = _____

Unit Finding

Instructions: Word Detectives solve mysteries by paying attention to details. The details you need to pay attention to in decoding are the base and the beginning and end "fixes" if there are any. Underline the base—the main meaning part of the word—and circle any fixes at the beginning or end that might modify or qualify that meaning. After 2 minutes, we will share with each other the word clues we found. I will write one shared correct example for each word part on the board.

retraceable	librarian	disappearance
forgetful	abnormal	misconduct
shamelessly	unhappiness	
unfriendliness	solidify	

Total number of words in which bases and fixes were correctly identified = _____

Word Transferring

Instructions: Once Word Detectives figure out the code, they can apply it to new words or cases. Here are some words that have the same parts that we have practiced. I will record how many you pronounce correctly and how long it took. We will graph your accuracy and time so you can see your progress.

darken

energetic

amazement

teacher

pleasant

dangerous

senator

quickness

active

rainy

Correct words = _____   **Correct affixes** = _____

Total time = _____

Are They Relatives?

Instructions: To solve puzzles, Word Detectives need to pay attention not only to clues in a single word but also to how the clues in a word may signal that words are related in meaning to other words they know. Just as a child comes from her or his parents, some words come from—that is, they are made from—meaning of other words and thus belong to the same family of word meanings, but other words are not from the same family of word meanings even though they may resemble other words in spelling or sound. I want you to listen carefully and after I say each pair of words, circle YES on your worksheet if you think the first word comes from the second one and circle NO if you do not think it does. After that, we will discuss any of your answers on which not everyone has agreed.

Directions: Circle YES or NO beside the word pair.

molecule	mole	YES	NO
projector	project	YES	NO
performance	perform	YES	NO
atoms	at	YES	NO
canyon	can	YES	NO
construction	construct	YES	NO
instructional	instruct	YES	NO

building	build	YES	NO
farmer	far	YES	NO
mustard	must	YES	NO

Total correct in 2 minutes = _____

Sorting by Word Part Features

Instructions: Once Word Detectives get clues they have to make sense of them. They have to do a special kind of thinking in which they draw conclusions from the evidence, just as Sherlock Holmes and Dr. Watson did. In this activity you will sort words into categories, each of which has a word label and capital letter. Write the capital letter that shows the category to which each word belongs. When you complete the sort, you will be asked to write the rule you used in sorting words into categories. Then we will discuss the rules to make sure that everyone agrees.

Labels for categories: Prefix Means *Not* = A, Prefix Means *One* = B, No Prefix = C

undemanding	universal	unfeeling
unique	unity	unit
undress	unable	
unresponsive	under	
unnecessary	unwind	

Explain the rule you used to sort: _____

_____

_____

_____

_____

Number sorted correctly = _____

Sorting by Sentence Context

Instructions: Another way that Word Detectives have to make sense of their clues is by examining them for *context*—the place in which they occur and all the surrounding clues. Each of the three sentences you will see has a blank. Each of the Word Pools you will see has one word that fits sensibly into the blank but mostly words that would not fit into the blank. To figure out which words would or would not fit into the blank—that is, into the context of the sentence—you need to pay close attention to all the spelling, sound,

and meaning clues of the words in the pool and in the words in the sentence. You have to fully analyze all the evidence you have at hand! As soon as you think you know a word that would fit into the sentence, raise your hand. As a Word Detective, it is important that you examine all the evidence—consider all the words—before you make your decision about which word fits. If someone disagrees with you, we will discuss why or why not that word might work in that sentence.

Mr. Jones was afraid of pulling his bandage off his _____ cut.
(painless, dangerous, painful, colorful)

Because of concerns about everyone's health, the restaurant was a
_____ place.
(smoky, dirty, smoke-free, cooking, peaceful)

The man had been to many different countries. He was a world-wide
_____.
(teacher, rider, dangerous, traveler, traveling)

The machine was supposed to make ice cream, but it worked so poorly that Mrs. Smith thought it was _____.
(useful, playful, using, useless)

Mary turned out the light to _____ the room.
(brighter, darken, brighten, empty)

LESSON **17** | Morphological Awareness Treatment

Teacher Material

The following grapheme–phoneme correspondences are taught using *Talking Letters:* • Other consonant combinations • r- and l-controlled vowels	Materials needed: • *Talking Letters* for automatic alphabetic principles • Work folders

WARM-UP (FOR THE TEACHER)

For the warm-up, name the letter or letter group on the *Talking Letters* card, say the pictured word containing a target phoneme, and then produce the target phoneme. Next, the students take a turn and repeat what is named or said by you. This approach develops orthographic awareness of spelling units; phonological awareness of corresponding phonemes in and out of word context; and, through close timing, the automaticity of spelling–phoneme correspondence. If Lessons 1–14 have been completed, just name the letter or letter group and produce the target phoneme, and then the students take a turn and repeat what you have said. Monitor whether children are coordinating looking at the relevant letters and pictured words with naming of the letters and words and producing phonemes.

LESSON OVERVIEW (READ TO STUDENTS)

It is normal to come across words you do not know. One way to figure out unknown words is to use their word parts that signal or "fix" their meaning. We will call these parts at the beginning of words *prefixes* because they come before the rest of the word, and those parts at the end of the word *postfixes* because they come after the rest of the word. (Another term for the parts at the end of word is *suffixes.*) Words also have base parts that signal their meaning. Some words only have bases; some have prefixes and bases; some have bases and postfixes; and some have prefixes, bases, and postfixes. We will do seven different kinds of activities in each session to teach you to be Word Detectives who use these word parts to decode words: *Word Building, Word Generating, Unit Finding, Word Transferring, Are They Relatives? Sorting by Word Part Features,* and *Sorting by Sentence Context.* These activities should give you lots of strategies for using word parts to figure out words. We will use our electronic timer for the second through fourth activities but not for the others. Let's begin.

ACTIVITIES

Word Building

From this list of 30 words with highly frequent prefixes and derivational suffixes, 10 are presented in each lesson (1–14) and are presented three times altogether; but these will be randomized across the three presentations to avoid list learning effects. For the last two sessions (13 and 14), half of the list (15) is presented for a final review of the whole set. See the Student Response Booklet kept in your Word Detectives Work Folder. This set of affixes was generated by examining words in the McGraw-Hill Specific Skills *Working within Words Series* for Grades 3–6 and by reviewing morphological units in selected reading passages in *Read Naturally.* From these, Bill Nagy identified 30 suffixes that occur most frequently and thus are highly useful for struggling readers. Given limited instructional time, these are the ones on which to focus. Capital letters indicate these high-utility affixes, which were practiced in various lessons. The prefixes, bases, and postfixes are kept on 3 × 5 cards (or 5 × 8 cards or larger, depending on how large the word parts must be for all children in group to see them) in large envelopes—marked *prefixes, bases, and suffixes*—for the teacher to use in presenting the word parts and used as needed for a specific lesson (see Student Response Booklet for word parts). Then for each lesson, the teacher draws from the large envelopes the large cards with the word parts needed for each word in a lesson and holds them up high for all students to see. After one student correctly synthesizes the word parts to pronounce the word, each child writes the complete word built from its parts in the row on a worksheet.

Instructions: Word Detectives solve cases by combining clues. We will start by building words from word part clues. I will show you word parts. As soon as you know the word that can be formed by these parts, raise your hand. When we agree, I will write it on the board and you can copy it in your Student Response Booklet. You will build the words from a base and fixes (*prefixes* before the base, or *suffixes* after the base).

> memorize, unclear, invisible, impolite, addition, harmless, magical,
> northern, creativity, forehead

Word Generating

Instructions: Word Detectives sometimes get their clues from generating and reasoning about similar cases. Readers can do the same—use what they know about words to generate new words in their minds. For 5 minutes, for each of the following word parts, think of a word that has that word part. Write the word in your Student Response Booklet. Go to the next word part and do the same, and so on. After 5 minutes, students share words generated for each word part. I will write one correct example for each word part on the board.

Note: Children do this independently for 5 minutes. Every 30 seconds, the teacher can prompt the children to try to think of a word for the next word part.

> er, un, in, im, tion, less, al, ern, ity, ward

Unit Finding

Children are directed to the Student Response Booklet with lists of words and asked to underline the base word and circle the affixes. Children receive R-File points if all word part items are completed correctly within 2 minutes.

Instructions: Word Detectives solve mysteries by paying attention to details. The details you need to pay attention to in decoding are the base and the beginning and end "fixes" if there are any. Underline the base—the main meaning part of the word—and circle any fixes at the beginning or end that might modify or qualify that meaning. After 2 minutes, we will share with each other the word clues we found. I will write one shared correct example for each word part on the board.

reappearance, returnable, uninvitingly, substandard, dissatisfaction, unwashable, profitable, predetermined, unsettled, rearrangement

Word Transferring

For each lesson, children read a list with 10 words containing the same affixes practiced under Word Building. They read the list to a teacher who times them, records the time on their R-File record, and indicates whether 1) the affix part was pronounced correctly and 2) the whole word was pronounced correctly.

Instructions: Once Word Detectives figure out the code, they can apply it to new words or cases. Here are some words that have the same parts that we have practiced. I will record how many you pronounce correctly and how long it took. We will graph your accuracy and time so you can see your progress.

helper, untie, indigestion, imagine, attention, helpless, removal, eastern, relativity, windward

Are They Relatives?

Does the first word come from the second word? The purpose of this task is to describe whether word parts at the end of a base word signal a semantic relationship with a base word. Children can record the total number they got correct.

Instructions: To solve puzzles, Word Detectives need to pay attention not only to clues in a single word but also to how the clues in a word may signal that words are related in meaning to other words they know. Just as a child comes from her or his parents, some words come from—that is, they are made from—meaning of other words and thus belong to the same family of word meanings, but other words are not from the same family of word meanings even though they may resemble other words in spelling or sound. I want you to listen carefully and after I say each pair of words, circle YES on your worksheet if you think the first word comes from the second one and circle NO if you do not think it does. After that, we will discuss any of your answers on which not everyone has agreed.

education	educate
introductory	introduce
hatchet	hat
production	product
candle	can
tongue	ton
Chinese	chin
reduction	reduce
carpet	car
reproduction	produce

Sorting by Word Part Features

The rules children write are discussed to make sure that all have grasped the underlying principle for sorting the words into categories.

Instructions: Once Word Detectives get clues they have to make sense of them. They have to do a special kind of thinking in which they draw conclusions from the evidence, just as Sherlock Holmes and Dr. Watson did. In this activity you will sort words into categories, each of which has a word label and capital letter. Write the capital letter that shows the category to which each word belongs. When you complete the sort, you will be asked to write the rule you used in sorting words into categories. Then we will discuss the rules to make sure that everyone agrees.

Generalization: A prefix meaning cannot be identified just on the basis of spelling or pronunciation.

Labels for cards: Prefix Means *Not* = A, Prefix Means *Separate* = B, No Prefix = C

discovery, Disneyland, distant, disbelief, diskette, disappoint, dishonest, dismal, dishes, dislike, discipline, disk jockey

Sorting by Sentence Context

The purpose of this activity is to help children see the importance of analyzing words fully. The words in the Word Pool from which a word is chosen for the blank in the sentence are in the Student Record Form. Record for each lesson the number correct.

Instructions: Another way that Word Detectives have to make sense of their clues is by examining them for *context*—the place in which they occur and all the surrounding clues. Each of the three sentences you will see has a blank. Each of the Word Pools you will see has one word in the box that fits sensibly into the blank but mostly words that would not fit into the blank. To figure out which words would or would not fit into the blank—that is, into the context of the sentence—you need to pay close attention to all the spelling, sound, and meaning clues of the words in the pool and in the words in the sentence. You have to fully analyze all the evidence you have at hand! As soon as you think you know a word that would fit into the sentence, raise your hand. As a Word Detective, it is important that you examine all the evidence—consider all the words—before you make your decision about which word fits. If someone disagrees with you, we will discuss why or why not that word might work in that sentence.

The woman who bought the running shoes is a _____.
(jogger, drummer, jogging, builder)

When the ice cube melted, it made a _____ puddle on the table.
(shadowy, shapely, shapeless, careless)

He liked the kind of music his son listened to but not its _____.
(sadness, loudly, dancer, loudness)

Joe laughed at the joke, but Sam didn't think it was _____.
(allowable, dangerous, humorous, humoring)

He would have bought the bike, but he thought it was _____.
(oldish, newish, older, shiny)

LESSON **17** | Morphological Awareness Treatment
Adding Word Parts for Meaning to Decoding

Student Response Booklet

Note: All lessons start with a warm-up, just as athletes warm up before a sports game. (See *Talking Letters* card.)

ACTIVITIES

Word Building

Instructions: Word Detectives solve cases by combining clues. We will start by building words from word part clues. I will show you word parts. As soon as you know the word that can be formed by these parts, raise your hand. When we agree, I will write it on the board and you can copy it in your Student Response Booklet. You will build the words from a base and fixes (*prefixes* before the base, or *suffixes* after the base).

memory + ize = _____

un + clear = _____

in + vision + able = _____

im + polite = _____

add + tion = _____

harm + less = _____

magic + al = _____

north + ern = _____

create + ive + y = _____

fore + head = _____

Total correct = _____

Word Generating

Instructions: Word Detectives sometimes get their clues from generating and reasoning about similar cases. Readers can do the same—use what they know about words to generate new words in their minds. For 5 minutes, for each of the following word parts, think of a word that has that word part. Write the word in your Student Response Booklet. Go to the next word part and do the same, and so on. After 5 minutes, students share words generated for each word part. I will write one correct example for each word part on the board.

er _____

un _____

in _____

im _____

tion _____

less _____

al _____

ern _____

ity _____

ward _____

Total new correct words generated in 5 minutes = _____

Unit Finding

Instructions: Word Detectives solve mysteries by paying attention to details. The details you need to pay attention to in decoding are the base and the beginning and end "fixes" if there are any. Underline the base—the main meaning part of the word—and circle any fixes at the beginning or end that might modify or qualify that meaning. After 2 minutes, we will share with each other the word clues we found. I will write one shared correct example for each word part on the board.

reappearance	dissatisfaction	predetermined
returnable	unwashable	unsettled
uninvitingly	profitable	rearrangement
substandard		

Total number of words in which bases and fixes were correctly identified = _____

Word Transferring

Instructions: Once Word Detectives figure out the code, they can apply it to new words or cases. Here are some words that have the same parts that we have practiced. I will record how many you pronounce correctly and how long it took. We will graph your accuracy and time so you can see your progress.

helper

untie

indigestion

imagine

attention

helpless

removal

eastern

relativity

windward

Correct words = _____   **Correct affixes** = _____

Total time = _____

Are They Relatives?

Instructions: To solve puzzles, Word Detectives need to pay attention not only to clues in a single word but also to how the clues in a word may signal that words are related in meaning to other words they know. Just as a child comes from her or his parents, some words come from—that is, they are made from—meaning of other words and thus belong to the same family of word meanings, but other words are not from the same family of word meanings even though they may resemble other words in spelling or sound. I want you to listen carefully and after I say each pair of words, circle YES on your worksheet if you think the first word comes from the second one and circle NO if you do not think it does. After that, we will discuss any of your answers on which not everyone has agreed.

Directions: Circle YES or NO beside the word pair.

education	educate	YES	NO
introductory	introduce	YES	NO
hatchet	hat	YES	NO
production	product	YES	NO
candle	can	YES	NO
tongue	ton	YES	NO

Chinese	chin	YES	NO
reduction	reduce	YES	NO
carpet	car	YES	NO
reproduction	produce	YES	NO

Total correct in 2 minutes = _____

Sorting by Word Part Features

Instructions: Once Word Detectives get clues they have to make sense of them. They have to do a special kind of thinking in which they draw conclusions from the evidence, just as Sherlock Holmes and Dr. Watson did. In this activity you will sort words into categories, each of which has a word label and capital letter. Write the capital letter that shows the category to which each word belongs. When you complete the sort, you will be asked to write the rule you used in sorting words into categories. Then we will discuss the rules to make sure that everyone agrees.

Labels for categories: Prefix Means *Not* = A, Prefix Means *Separate* = B, No Prefix = C

discovery

Disneyland

distant

disbelief

diskette

disappoint

dishonest

dismal

dishes

dislike

discipline

disk jockey

Explain the rule you used to sort: _____

_____

_____

_____

_____

Number sorted correctly = _____

Sorting by Sentence Context

Instructions: Another way that Word Detectives have to make sense of their clues is by examining them for *context*—the place in which they occur and all the surrounding clues. Each of the three sentences you will see has a blank. Each of the Word Pools you will see has one word that fits sensibly into the blank but mostly words that would not fit into the blank. To figure out which words would or would not fit into the blank—that is, into the context of the sentence—you need to pay close attention to all the spelling, sound, and meaning clues of the words in the pool and in the words in the sentence. You have to fully analyze all the evidence you have at hand! As soon as you think you know a word that would fit into the sentence, raise your hand. As a Word Detective, it is important that you examine all the evidence—consider all the words—before you make your decision about which word fits. If someone disagrees with you, we will discuss why or why not that word might work in that sentence.

The woman who bought the running shoes is a

_____.

(jogger, drummer, jogging, builder)

When the ice cube melted, it made a _____ puddle on the table.
(shadowy, shapely, shapeless, careless)

He liked the kind of music his son listened to but not its

_____.

(sadness, loudly, dancer, loudness)

Joe laughed at the joke, but Sam didn't think it was

_____.

(allowable, dangerous, humorous, humoring)

He would have bought the bike, but he thought it was

_____.

(oldish, newish, older, shiny)

LESSON **18** | Morphological Awareness Treatment

Teacher Material

The following grapheme–phoneme correspondences are taught using *More Talking Letters:* • Latinate and Greek	Materials needed: • *More Talking Letters* (see Table 1) for automatic alphabetic principles • Work folders

WARM-UP (FOR THE TEACHER)

For the warm-up, name the letter or letter group in *More Talking Letters* (see Table 1), say the pictured word containing a target phoneme, and then produce the target phoneme. Next, the students take a turn and repeat what is named or said by you. This approach develops orthographic awareness of spelling units; phonological awareness of corresponding phonemes in and out of word context; and, through close timing, the automaticity of spelling–phoneme correspondence. If Lessons 1–14 have been completed, just name the letter or letter group and produce the target phoneme, and then the students take a turn and repeat what you have said. Monitor whether children are coordinating looking at the relevant letters and pictured words with naming of the letters and words and producing phonemes.

LESSON OVERVIEW (READ TO STUDENTS)

It is normal to come across words you do not know. One way to figure out unknown words is to use their word parts that signal or "fix" their meaning. We will call these parts at the beginning of words *prefixes* because they come before the rest of the word, and those parts at the end of the word *postfixes* because they come after the rest of the word. (Another term for the parts at the end of word is *suffixes.*) Words also have base parts that signal their meaning. Some words only have bases; some have prefixes and bases; some have bases and postfixes; and some have prefixes, bases, and postfixes. We will do seven different kinds of activities in each session to teach you to be Word Detectives who use these word parts to decode words: *Word Building, Word Generating, Unit Finding, Word Transferring, Are They Relatives? Sorting by Word Part Features,* and *Sorting by Sentence Context.* These activities should give you lots of strategies for using word parts to figure out words. We will use our electronic timer for the second through fourth activities but not for the others. Let's begin.

ACTIVITIES

Word Building

From this list of 30 words with highly frequent prefixes and derivational suffixes, 10 are presented in each lesson (1–14) and are presented three times altogether; but these will be randomized across the three presentations to avoid list learning effects. For the last two sessions (13 and 14), half of the list (15) is presented for a final review of the whole set. See the Student Response Booklet kept in your Word Detectives Work Folder. This set of affixes was generated by examining words in the McGraw-Hill Specific Skills *Working within Words Series* for Grades 3–6 and by reviewing morphological units in selected reading passages in *Read Naturally.* From these, Bill Nagy identified 30 suffixes that occur most frequently and thus are highly useful for struggling readers. Given limited instructional time, these are the ones on which to focus. Capital letters indicate these high-utility affixes, which were practiced in various lessons. The prefixes, bases, and postfixes are kept on 3 × 5 cards (or 5 × 8 cards or larger, depending on how large the word parts must be for all children in group to see them) in large envelopes—marked *prefixes, bases, and suffixes*—for the teacher to use in presenting the word parts and used as needed for a specific lesson (see Student Response Booklet for word parts). Then for each lesson, the teacher draws from the large envelopes the large cards with the word parts needed for each word in a lesson and holds them up high for all students to see. After one student correctly synthesizes the word parts to pronounce the word, each child writes the complete word built from its parts in the row on a worksheet.

Instructions: Word Detectives solve cases by combining clues. We will start by building words from word part clues. I will show you word parts. As soon as you know the word that can be formed by these parts, raise your hand. When we agree, I will write it on the board and you can copy it in your Student Response Booklet. You will build the words from a base and fixes (*prefixes* before the base, or *suffixes* after the base).

elementary, sickness, leadership, willful, national, signal, beautiful, sensation, friendly, friendliness

Word Generating

Instructions: Word Detectives sometimes get their clues from generating and reasoning about similar cases. Readers can do the same—use what they know about words to generate new words in their minds. For 5 minutes, for each of the following word parts, think of a word that has that word part. Write the word in your Student Response Booklet. Go to the next word part and do the same, and so on. After 5 minutes, students share words generated for each word part. I will write one correct example for each word part on the board.

Note: Children do this independently for 5 minutes. Every 30 seconds, the teacher can prompt the children to try to think of a word for the next word part.

dis, im, ern, or, ful, ment, un, re, y, ish

Unit Finding

Children are directed to the Student Response Booklet with lists of words and asked to underline the base word and circle the affixes. Children receive R-File points if all word part items are completed correctly within 2 minutes.

Instructions: Word Detectives solve mysteries by paying attention to details. The details you need to pay attention to in decoding are the base and the beginning and end "fixes" if there are any. Underline the base—the main meaning part of the word—and circle any fixes at the beginning or end that might modify or qualify that meaning. After 2 minutes, we will share with each other the word clues we found. I will write one shared correct example for each word part on the board.

> unfairly, regrouping, previewing, inconsistent, distasteful, inactive, multimillionaire, unfortunate, supernatural, repayment

Word Transferring

For each lesson, children read a list with 10 words containing the same affixes practiced under Word Building. They read the list to a teacher who times them, records the time on their R-File record, and indicates whether 1) the affix part was pronounced correctly and 2) the whole word was pronounced correctly.

Instructions: Once Word Detectives figure out the code, they can apply it to new words or cases. Here are some words that have the same parts that we have practiced. I will record how many you pronounce correctly and how long it took. We will graph your accuracy and time so you can see your progress.

> disapprove, immovable, southern, elevator, harmful, enjoyment, unfair, refer, sunny, smallish

Are They Relatives?

Does the first word come from the second word? The purpose of this task is to describe whether word parts at the end of a base word signal a semantic relationship with a base word. Children can record the total number they got correct.

Instructions: To solve puzzles, Word Detectives need to pay attention not only to clues in a single word but also to how the clues in a word may signal that words are related in meaning to other words they know. Just as a child comes from her or his parents, some words come from—that is, they are made from—meaning of other words and thus belong to the same family of word meanings, but other words are not from the same family of word meanings even though they may resemble other words in spelling or sound. I want you to listen carefully and after I say each pair of words, circle YES on your worksheet if you think the first word comes from the second one and circle NO if you do not think it does. After that, we will discuss any of your answers on which not everyone has agreed.

jewelry	Jew
universally	universe
German	germ
advertisement	advertise
convertible	convert
social	so
knowledge	now
inch	in
attraction	attract
dictation	dictate

Sorting by Word Part Features

The rules children write are discussed to make sure that all have grasped the underlying principle for sorting the words into categories.

Instructions: Once Word Detectives get clues they have to make sense of them. They have to do a special kind of thinking in which they draw conclusions from the evidence, just as Sherlock Holmes and Dr. Watson did. In this activity you will sort words into categories, each of which has a word label and capital letter. Write the capital letter that shows the category to which each word belongs. When you complete the sort, you will be asked to write the rule you used in sorting words into categories. Then we will discuss the rules to make sure that everyone agrees.

Generalization: A prefix with the same spelling and pronunciation may have different meanings.

Labels for cards: Prefix Means *In* = A, Prefix Means *Not* = B, No Prefix = C

India, illegal, illusion, immature, immigrate, inch, I'm, inexpensive, incoming, interest, Illinois

Sorting by Sentence Context

The purpose of this activity is to help children see the importance of analyzing words fully. The words in the Word Pool from which a word is chosen for the blank in the sentence are in the Student Record Form. Record for each lesson the number correct.

Instructions: Another way that Word Detectives have to make sense of their clues is by examining them for *context*—the place in which they occur and all the surrounding clues. Each of the three sentences you will see has a blank. Each of the Word Pools you will see has one word in the box that fits sensibly into the blank but mostly words that would not fit into the blank. To figure out which words would or would not fit into the blank—that is, into the context of the sentence—you need to pay close attention to all the spelling, sound, and meaning clues of the words in the pool and in the words in the sentence. You have to fully analyze all the evidence you have at hand! As soon as you think you know a word that would fit into the sentence, raise your hand. As a Word Detective, it is important that you examine all the evidence—consider all the words—before you make your decision about which word fits. If someone disagrees with you, we will discuss why or why not that word might work in that sentence.

Gus was just learning how to type, and so he could not finish his paper _____.
(slowly, quickness, helpful, quickly)

He turned on the light in order to _____ the room.
(brightly, lasting, darken, brighten, trouble-free)

The father tried to make his son laugh in order to forget his _____.
(quietness, sadness, thirsty, sadly, selfish)

Pulling the splinter from his foot is going to be _____.
(painless, helpful, dangerous, painful, catlike)

Susie wishes her hair were straight. She doesn't like hair that is _____.
(colorful, childish, curly, windy, careless)

LESSON **18** Morphological Awareness Treatment
Adding Word Parts for Meaning to Decoding

Student Response Booklet

Note: All lessons start with a warm-up, just as athletes warm up before a sports game. (See *More Talking Letters.*)

ACTIVITIES

Word Building

Instructions: Word Detectives solve cases by combining clues. We will start by building words from word part clues. I will show you word parts. As soon as you know the word that can be formed by these parts, raise your hand. When we agree, I will write it on the board and you can copy it in your Student Response Booklet. You will build the words from a base and fixes (*prefixes* before the base, or *suffixes* after the base).

element + ary = _____

sick + ness = _____

lead + er + ship = _____

will + ful = _____

nation + al = _____

sign + al = _____

beauty + ful = _____

sense + tion = _____

friend + ly = _____

friend + ly + ness + _____

Total correct = _____

Word Generating

Instructions: Word Detectives sometimes get their clues from generating and reasoning about similar cases. Readers can do the same—use what they know about words to generate new words in their minds. For 5 minutes, for each of the following word parts, think of a word that has that word part. Write the word in your Student Response Booklet. Go to the next word part and do the same, and so on. After 5 minutes, students share words generated for each word part. I will write one correct example for each word part on the board.

dis _____

im _____

ern _____

or _____

ful _____

ment _____

un _____

re _____

y _____

ish _____

Total new correct words generated in 5 minutes = _____

Unit Finding

Instructions: Word Detectives solve mysteries by paying attention to details. The details you need to pay attention to in decoding are the base and the beginning and end "fixes" if there are any. Underline the base—the main meaning part of the word—and circle any fixes at the beginning or end that might modify or qualify that meaning. After 2 minutes, we will share with each other the word clues we found. I will write one shared correct example for each word part on the board.

unfairly	distasteful	unfortunate
regrouping	inactive	supernatural
previewing	multimillionaire	repayment
inconsistent		

Total number of words in which bases and fixes were correctly identified = _____

159

Word Transferring

Instructions: Once Word Detectives figure out the code, they can apply it to new words or cases. Here are some words that have the same parts that we have practiced. I will record how many you pronounce correctly and how long it took. We will graph your accuracy and time so you can see your progress.

disapprove

immovable

southern

elevator

harmful

enjoyment

unfair

refer

sunny

smallish

Correct words = _____   **Correct affixes** = _____

Total time = _____

Are They Relatives?

Instructions: To solve puzzles, Word Detectives need to pay attention not only to clues in a single word but also to how the clues in a word may signal that words are related in meaning to other words they know. Just as a child comes from her or his parents, some words come from—that is, they are made from—meaning of other words and thus belong to the same family of word meanings, but other words are not from the same family of word meanings even though they may resemble other words in spelling or sound. I want you to listen carefully and after I say each pair of words, circle YES on your worksheet if you think the first word comes from the second one and circle NO if you do not think it does. After that, we will discuss any of your answers on which not everyone has agreed.

Directions: Circle YES or NO beside the word pair.

jewelry	Jew	YES	NO
universally	universe	YES	NO
German	germ	YES	NO
advertisement	advertise	YES	NO
convertible	convert	YES	NO
social	so	YES	NO

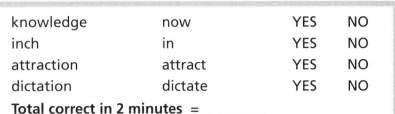

knowledge	now	YES	NO
inch	in	YES	NO
attraction	attract	YES	NO
dictation	dictate	YES	NO

Total correct in 2 minutes = _____

Sorting by Word Part Features

Instructions: Once Word Detectives get clues they have to make sense of them. They have to do a special kind of thinking in which they draw conclusions from the evidence, just as Sherlock Holmes and Dr. Watson did. In this activity you will sort words into categories, each of which has a word label and capital letter. Write the capital letter that shows the category to which each word belongs. When you complete the sort, you will be asked to write the rule you used in sorting words into categories. Then we will discuss the rules to make sure that everyone agrees.

Labels for categories: Prefix Means *In* = A, Prefix Means *Not* = B, No Prefix = C

India

illegal

illusion

immature

immigrate

inch

I'm

inexpensive

incoming

interest

Illinois

Explain the rule you used to sort: _____

_____

_____

_____

_____

Number sorted correctly = _____

Sorting by Sentence Context

Instructions: Another way that Word Detectives have to make sense of their clues is by examining them for *context*—the place in which they occur and all the surrounding clues. Each of the three sentences you will see has a blank. Each of the Word Pools you will see has one word that fits sensibly into the blank but mostly words that would not fit into the blank. To figure out which words would or would not fit into the blank—that is, into the context of the sentence—you need to pay close attention to all the spelling, sound, and meaning clues of the words in the pool and in the words in the sentence. You have to fully analyze all the evidence you have at hand! As soon as you think you know a word that would fit into the sentence, raise your hand. As a Word Detective, it is important that you examine all the evidence—consider all the words—before you make your decision about which word fits. If someone disagrees with you, we will discuss why or why not that word might work in that sentence.

Gus was just learning how to type, and so he could not finish his paper

_____.

(slowly, quickness, helpful, quickly)

He turned on the light in order to _____ the room.
(brightly, lasting, darken, brighten, trouble-free)

The father tried to make his son laugh in order to forget his

_____.

(quietness, sadness, thirsty, sadly, selfish)

Pulling the splinter from his foot is going to be _____.
(painless, helpful, dangerous, painful, catlike)

Susie wishes her hair was straight. She didn't like hair that is

_____.

(colorful, childish, curly, windy, careless)

LESSON 19 Morphological Awareness Treatment

Teacher Material

The following grapheme–phoneme correspondences are taught using *Talking Letters:* • Single-letter consonants • Short vowels in closed syllables • Long vowels in open syllables	Materials needed: • *Talking Letters* for automatic alphabetic principles • Work folders

WARM-UP (FOR THE TEACHER)

For the warm-up, name the letter or letter group on the *Talking Letters* card, say the pictured word containing a target phoneme, and then produce the target phoneme. Next, the students take a turn and repeat what is named or said by you. This approach develops orthographic awareness of spelling units; phonological awareness of corresponding phonemes in and out of word context; and, through close timing, the automaticity of spelling–phoneme correspondence. If Lessons 1–14 have been completed, just name the letter or letter group and produce the target phoneme, and then the students take a turn and repeat what you have said. Monitor whether children are coordinating looking at the relevant letters and pictured words with naming of the letters and words and producing phonemes.

LESSON OVERVIEW (READ TO STUDENTS)

It is normal to come across words you do not know. One way to figure out unknown words is to use their word parts that signal or "fix" their meaning. We will call these parts at the beginning of words *prefixes* because they come before the rest of the word, and those parts at the end of the word *postfixes* because they come after the rest of the word. (Another term for the parts at the end of word is *suffixes.*) Words also have base parts that signal their meaning. Some words only have bases; some have prefixes and bases; some have bases and postfixes; and some have prefixes, bases, and postfixes. We will do seven different kinds of activities in each session to teach you to be Word Detectives who use these word parts to decode words: *Word Building, Word Generating, Unit Finding, Word Transferring, Are They Relatives? Sorting by Word Part Features,* and *Sorting by Sentence Context.* These activities should give you lots of strategies for using word parts to figure out words. We will use our electronic timer for the second through fourth activities but not for the others. Let's begin.

ACTIVITIES

Word Building

From this list of 30 words with highly frequent prefixes and derivational suffixes, 10 are presented in each lesson (1–14) and are presented three times altogether; but these will be randomized across the three presentations to avoid list learning effects. For the last two sessions (13 and 14), half of the list (15) is presented for a final review of the whole set. See the Student Response Booklet kept in your Word Detectives Work Folder. This set of affixes was generated by examining words in the McGraw-Hill Specific Skills *Working within Words Series* for Grades 3–6 and by reviewing morphological units in selected reading passages in *Read Naturally.* From these, Bill Nagy identified 30 suffixes that occur most frequently and thus are highly useful for struggling readers. Given limited instructional time, these are the ones on which to focus. Capital letters indicate these high-utility affixes, which were practiced in various lessons. The prefixes, bases, and postfixes are kept on 3 × 5 cards (or 5 × 8 cards or larger, depending on how large the word parts must be for all children in group to see them) in large envelopes—marked *prefixes, bases, and suffixes*—for the teacher to use in presenting the word parts and used as needed for a specific lesson (see Student Response Booklet for word parts). Then for each lesson, the teacher draws from the large envelopes the large cards with the word parts needed for each word in a lesson and holds them up high for all students to see. After one student correctly synthesizes the word parts to pronounce the word, each child writes the complete word built from its parts in the row on a worksheet.

Instructions: Word Detectives solve cases by combining clues. We will start by building words from word part clues. I will show you word parts. As soon as you know the word that can be formed by these parts, raise your hand. When we agree, I will write it on the board and you can copy it in your Student Response Booklet. You will build the words from a base and fixes (*prefixes* before the base, or *suffixes* after the base).

> invisible, amazing, expensive, elementary, nervous, scientist, completely, addition, washable, impolite

Word Generating

Instructions: Word Detectives sometimes get their clues from generating and reasoning about similar cases. Readers can do the same—use what they know about words to generate new words in their minds. For 5 minutes, for each of the following word parts, think of a word that has that word part. Write the word in your Student Response Booklet. Go to the next word part and do the same, and so on. After 5 minutes, students share words generated for each word part. I will write one correct example for each word part on the board.

Note: Children do this independently for 5 minutes. Every 30 seconds, the teacher can prompt the children to try to think of a word for the next word part.

> in, ing, ive, ary, ous, ist, ly, tion, able, im

Unit Finding

Children are directed to the Student Response Booklet with lists of words and asked to underline the base word and circle the affixes. Children receive R-File points if all word part items are completed correctly within 2 minutes.

Instructions: Word Detectives solve mysteries by paying attention to details. The details you need to pay attention to in decoding are the base and the beginning and end "fixes" if there are any. Underline the base—the main meaning part of the word—and circle any fixes at the beginning or end that might modify or qualify that meaning. After 2 minutes, we will share with each other the word clues we found. I will write one shared correct example for each word part on the board.

> subzero, multicolored, hyperactive, immaturity, antislavery, overpriced, nonfiction, microphone, precautionary, unfriendliness

Word Transferring

For each lesson, children read a list with 10 words containing the same affixes practiced under Word Building. They read the list to a teacher who times them, records the time on their R-File record, and indicates whether 1) the affix part was pronounced correctly and 2) the whole word was pronounced correctly.

Instructions: Once Word Detectives figure out the code, they can apply it to new words or cases. Here are some words that have the same parts that we have practiced. I will record how many you pronounce correctly and how long it took. We will graph your accuracy and time so you can see your progress.

> inactive, steaming, hyperactive, cautionary, humorous, balloonist, sadly, attraction, squeezable, important

Are They Relatives?

Does the first word come from the second word? The purpose of this task is to describe whether word parts at the end of a base word signal a semantic relationship with a base word. Children can record the total number they got correct.

Instructions: To solve puzzles, Word Detectives need to pay attention not only to clues in a single word but also to how the clues in a word may signal that words are related in meaning to other words they know. Just as a child comes from her or his parents, some words come from—that is, they are made from—meaning of other words and thus belong to the same family of word meanings, but other words are not from the same family of word meanings even though they may resemble other words in spelling or sound. I want you to listen carefully and after I say each pair of words, circle YES on your worksheet if you think the first word comes from the second one and circle NO if you do not think it does. After that, we will discuss any of your answers on which not everyone has agreed.

butter	but
prediction	predict
dedication	dedicate
palace	pal
castle	cast
tennis	ten
unpredictable	predict
propeller	propel
admission	admit
camel	came

Sorting by Word Part Features

The rules children write are discussed to make sure that all have grasped the underlying principle for sorting the words into categories.

Instructions: Once Word Detectives get clues they have to make sense of them. They have to do a special kind of thinking in which they draw conclusions from the evidence, just as Sherlock Holmes and Dr. Watson did. In this activity you will sort words into categories, each of which has a word label and capital letter. Write the capital letter that shows the category to which each word belongs. When you complete the sort, you will be asked to write the rule you used in sorting words into categories. Then we will discuss the rules to make sure that everyone agrees.

Generalization: Suffixes can signal two kinds of comparison—between two items or among three or more items.

Labels for cards: Prefix Compares 2 Items   Prefix Compares 3+ Items

harder, strangest, biggest, tougher, smaller, happiest, straightest, cutest, darker, luckiest, slowest, faster

Sorting by Sentence Context

The purpose of this activity is to help children see the importance of analyzing words fully. The words in the Word Pool from which a word is chosen for the blank in the sentence are in the Student Record Form. Record for each lesson the number correct.

Instructions: Another way that Word Detectives have to make sense of their clues is by examining them for *context*—the place in which they occur and all the surrounding clues. Each of the three sentences you will see has a blank. Each of the Word Pools you will see has one word in the box that fits sensibly into the blank but mostly words that would not fit into the blank. To figure out which words would or would not fit into the blank—that is, into the context of the sentence—you need to pay close attention to all the spelling, sound, and meaning clues of the words in the pool and in the words in the sentence. You have to fully analyze all the evidence you have at hand! As soon as you think you know a word that would fit into the sentence, raise your hand. As a Word Detective, it is important that you examine all the evidence—consider all the words—before you make your decision about which word fits. If someone disagrees with you, we will discuss why or why not that word might work in that sentence.

With a broken wing, the plane was no longer _____.
(allowable, flier, flyable, grayish, distant)

The teacher looked at the uneven lines he made on his paper, and then told him to get a
ruler to _____ them.
(straighter, shorten, solidify, straighten, painter)

Even when the clown took off his mask, people thought that his face was
_____.
(famous, laughable, dangerous, eagerly)

He didn't like greasy food, so he ate popcorn that was _____.
(buttery, coldish, cookable, butterless, worthless)

The boat was tossing on the stormy sea, and the frightened man had a
_____ look to his face.
(doggish, sickish, humorous, child-like, angry)

LESSON **19** Morphological Awareness Treatment
Adding Word Parts for Meaning to Decoding

Student Response Booklet

Note: All lessons start with a warm-up, just as athletes warm up before a sports game. (See *Talking Letters* card.)

ACTIVITIES

Word Building

Instructions: Word Detectives solve cases by combining clues. We will start by building words from word part clues. I will show you word parts. As soon as you know the word that can be formed by these parts, raise your hand. When we agree, I will write it on the board and you can copy it in your Student Response Booklet. You will build the words from a base and fixes (*prefixes* before the base, or *suffixes* after the base).

in + vision + able = _____

amaze + ing = _____

explode + ive = _____

element + ary = _____

nerve + ous = _____

science + ist = _____

complete + ly = _____

add + ion = _____

wash + able = _____

im + polite = _____

Total correct = _____

Word Generating

Instructions: Word Detectives sometimes get their clues from generating and reasoning about similar cases. Readers can do the same—use what they know about words to generate new words in their minds. For 5 minutes, for each of the following word parts, think of a word that has that word part. Write the word in your Student Response Booklet. Go to the next word part and do the same, and so on. After 5 minutes, students share words generated for each word part. I will write one correct example for each word part on the board.

in _____

ing _____

ive _____

ary _____

ous _____

ist _____

ly _____

tion _____

able _____

im _____

Total new correct words generated in 5 minutes = _____

Unit Finding

Instructions: Word Detectives solve mysteries by paying attention to details. The details you need to pay attention to in decoding are the base and the beginning and end "fixes" if there are any. Underline the base—the main meaning part of the word—and circle any fixes at the beginning or end that might modify or qualify that meaning. After 2 minutes, we will share with each other the word clues we found. I will write one shared correct example for each word part on the board.

subzero	antislavery	precautionary
multicolored	overpriced	unfriendliness
hyperactive	nonfiction	
immaturity	microphone	

Total number of words in which bases and fixes were correctly identified = _____

Word Transferring

Instructions: Once Word Detectives figure out the code, they can apply it to new words or cases. Here are some words that have the same parts that we have practiced. I will record how many you pronounce correctly and how long it took. We will graph your accuracy and time so you can see your progress.

inactive

steaming

hyperactive

cautionary

humorous

balloonist

sadly

attraction

squeezable

important

Correct words = _____   **Correct affixes** = _____

Total time = _____

Are They Relatives?

Instructions: To solve puzzles, Word Detectives need to pay attention not only to clues in a single word but also to how the clues in a word may signal that words are related in meaning to other words they know. Just as a child comes from her or his parents, some words come from—that is, they are made from—meaning of other words and thus belong to the same family of word meanings, but other words are not from the same family of word meanings even though they may resemble other words in spelling or sound. I want you to listen carefully and after I say each pair of words, circle YES on your worksheet if you think the first word comes from the second one and circle NO if you do not think it does. After that, we will discuss any of your answers on which not everyone has agreed.

Directions: Circle YES or NO beside the word pair.

butter	but	YES	NO
prediction	predict	YES	NO
dedication	dedicate	YES	NO
palace	pal	YES	NO
castle	cast	YES	NO
tennis	ten	YES	NO

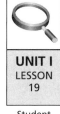

unpredictable	predict	YES	NO
propeller	propel	YES	NO
admission	admit	YES	NO
camel	came	YES	NO

Total correct in 2 minutes = _____

Sorting by Word Part Features

Instructions: Once Word Detectives get clues they have to make sense of them. They have to do a special kind of thinking in which they draw conclusions from the evidence, just as Sherlock Holmes and Dr. Watson did. In this activity you will sort words into categories, each of which has a word label and capital letter. Write the capital letter that shows the category to which each word belongs. When you complete the sort, you will be asked to write the rule you used in sorting words into categories. Then we will discuss the rules to make sure that everyone agrees.

Labels for categories: Suffix Compares 2 Items = A,
Suffix Compares 3+ Items = B

harder
strangest
biggest
tougher
smaller
happiest
straightest
cutest
darker
luckiest
slowest
faster

Explain the rule you used to sort: _____

_____

_____

_____

_____

Number sorted correctly = _____

Sorting by Sentence Context

Instructions: Another way that Word Detectives have to make sense of their clues is by examining them for *context*—the place in which they occur and all the surrounding clues. Each of the three sentences you will see has a blank. Each of the Word Pools you will see has one word that fits sensibly into the blank but mostly words that would not fit into the blank. To figure out which words would or would not fit into the blank—that is, into the context of the sentence—you need to pay close attention to all the spelling, sound, and meaning clues of the words in the pool and in the words in the sentence. You have to fully analyze all the evidence you have at hand! As soon as you think you know a word that would fit into the sentence, raise your hand. As a Word Detective, it is important that you examine all the evidence—consider all the words—before you make your decision about which word fits. If someone disagrees with you, we will discuss why or why not that word might work in that sentence.

With a broken wing, the plane was no longer _____.
(allowable, flier, flyable, grayish, distant)

The teacher looked at the uneven lines he made on his paper, and

then told him to get a ruler to _____ them.
(straighter, shorten, solidify, straighten, painter)

Even when the clown took off his mask, people thought that his face

was _____.
(famous, laughable, dangerous, eagerly)

He didn't like greasy food, so he ate popcorn that was

_____.
(buttery, coldish, cookable, butterless, worthless)

The boat was tossing on the stormy sea, and the frightened man had

a _____ look to his face.
(doggish, sickish, humorous, child-like, angry)

Teacher Material

The following grapheme–phoneme correspondences are taught using *Talking Letters:* • Single-letter consonants • Short vowels in closed syllables • Long vowels in open syllables	Materials needed: • *Talking Letters* for automatic alphabetic principles • Work folders

WARM-UP (FOR THE TEACHER)

For the warm-up, name the letter or letter group on the *Talking Letters* card, say the pictured word containing a target phoneme, and then produce the target phoneme. Next, the students take a turn and repeat what is named or said by you. This approach develops orthographic awareness of spelling units; phonological awareness of corresponding phonemes in and out of word context; and, through close timing, the automaticity of spelling–phoneme correspondence. If Lessons 1–14 have been completed, just name the letter or letter group and produce the target phoneme, and then the students take a turn and repeat what you have said. Monitor whether children are coordinating looking at the relevant letters and pictured words with naming of the letters and words and producing phonemes.

LESSON OVERVIEW (READ TO STUDENTS)

It is normal to come across words you do not know. One way to figure out unknown words is to use their word parts that signal or "fix" their meaning. We will call these parts at the beginning of words *prefixes* because they come before the rest of the word, and those parts at the end of the word *postfixes* because they come after the rest of the word. (Another term for the parts at the end of word is *suffixes*.) Words also have base parts that signal their meaning. Some words only have bases; some have prefixes and bases; some have bases and postfixes; and some have prefixes, bases, and postfixes. We will do seven different kinds of activities in each session to teach you to be Word Detectives who use these word parts to decode words: *Word Building, Word Generating, Unit Finding, Word Transferring, Are They Relatives? Sorting by Word Part Features,* and *Sorting by Sentence Context.* These activities should give you lots of strategies for using word parts to figure out words. We will use our electronic timer for the second through fourth activities but not for the others. Let's begin.

ACTIVITIES

Word Building

From this list of 30 words with highly frequent prefixes and derivational suffixes, 10 are presented in each lesson (1–14) and are presented three times altogether; but these will be randomized across the three presentations to avoid list learning effects. For the last two sessions (13 and 14), half of the list (15) is presented for a final review of the whole set. See the Student Response Booklet kept in your Word Detectives Work Folder. This set of affixes was generated by examining words in the McGraw-Hill Specific Skills *Working within Words Series* for Grades 3–6 and by reviewing morphological units in selected reading passages in *Read Naturally.* From these, Bill Nagy identified 30 suffixes that occur most frequently and thus are highly useful for struggling readers. Given limited instructional time, these are the ones on which to focus. Capital letters indicate these high-utility affixes, which were practiced in various lessons. The prefixes, bases, and postfixes are kept on 3 × 5 cards (or 5 × 8 cards or larger, depending on how large the word parts must be for all children in group to see them) in large envelopes—marked *prefixes, bases, and suffixes*—for the teacher to use in presenting the word parts and used as needed for a specific lesson (see Student Response Booklet for word parts). Then for each lesson, the teacher draws from the large envelopes the large cards with the word parts needed for each word in a lesson and holds them up high for all students to see. After one student correctly synthesizes the word parts to pronounce the word, each child writes the complete word built from its parts in the row on a worksheet.

Instructions: Word Detectives solve cases by combining clues. We will start by building words from word part clues. I will show you word parts. As soon as you know the word that can be formed by these parts, raise your hand. When we agree, I will write it on the board and you can copy it in your Student Response Booklet. You will build the words from a base and fixes (*prefixes* before the base, or *suffixes* after the base).

> harmless, reporter, sickness, electricity, leadership, different, magical, golden, creativity, salty

Word Generating

Instructions: Word Detectives sometimes get their clues from generating and reasoning about similar cases. Readers can do the same—use what they know about words to generate new words in their minds. For 5 minutes, for each of the following word parts, think of a word that has that word part. Write the word in your Student Response Booklet. Go to the next word part and do the same, and so on. After 5 minutes, students share words generated for each word part. I will write one correct example for each word part on the board.

Note: Children do this independently for 5 minutes. Every 30 seconds, the teacher can prompt the children to try to think of a word for the next word part.

> less, er, ness, ic, ship, ent, al, en, ity, ward

Unit Finding

Children are directed to the Student Response Booklet with lists of words and asked to underline the base word and circle the affixes. Children receive R-File points if all word part items are completed correctly within 2 minutes.

Instructions: Word Detectives solve mysteries by paying attention to details. The details you need to pay attention to in decoding are the base and the beginning and end "fixes" if there are any. Underline the base—the main meaning part of the word—and circle any fixes at the beginning or end that might modify or qualify that meaning. After 2 minutes, we will share with each other the word clues we found. I will write one shared correct example for each word part on the board.

> international, unexplained, supernatural, impossibility, carelessness, strengthen, unsatisfactory, infrequent, prenatal, midsummer

Word Transferring

For each lesson, children read a list with 10 words containing the same affixes practiced under Word Building. They read the list to a teacher who times them, records the time on their R-File record, and indicates whether 1) the affix part was pronounced correctly and 2) the whole word was pronounced correctly.

Instructions: Once Word Detectives figure out the code, they can apply it to new words or cases. Here are some words that have the same parts that we have practiced. I will record how many you pronounce correctly and how long it took. We will graph your accuracy and time so you can see your progress.

> useless, baker, quietness, historic, sportsmanship, payment, mechanical, brighten, maturity, forward

Are They Relatives?

Does the first word come from the second word? The purpose of this task is to describe whether word parts at the end of a base word signal a semantic relationship with a base word. Children can record the total number they got correct.

Instructions: To solve puzzles, Word Detectives need to pay attention not only to clues in a single word but also to how the clues in a word may signal that words are related in meaning to other words they know. Just as a child comes from her or his parents, some words come from—that is, they are made from—meaning of other words and thus belong to the same family of word meanings, but other words are not from the same family of word meanings even though they may resemble other words in spelling or sound. I want you to listen carefully and after I say each pair of words, circle YES on your worksheet if you think the first word comes from the second one and circle NO if you do not think it does. After that, we will discuss any of your answers on which not everyone has agreed.

missionary	mission
interruption	interrupt
badminton	mint
happiness	happy
differently	differ
begin	beg
market	mark
artichoke	choke
shuttle	shut
submission	submit

Sorting by Word Part Features

The rules children write are discussed to make sure that all have grasped the underlying principle for sorting the words into categories.

Instructions: Once Word Detectives get clues they have to make sense of them. They have to do a special kind of thinking in which they draw conclusions from the evidence, just as Sherlock Holmes and Dr. Watson did. In this activity you will sort words into categories, each of which has a word label and capital letter. Write the capital letter that shows the category to which each word belongs. When you complete the sort, you will be asked to write the rule you used in sorting words into categories. Then we will discuss the rules to make sure that everyone agrees.

Generalization: More than one suffix may signal the same meaning. Compounds are formed from two base words.

Labels for cards: Suffix Means Have Characteristic = A, Suffix Means Does Not Have Characteristic = B, No Suffix = C

helpless, helpful, warmish, harmful, harmless, reddish, settle, graceful, sparkle, formless, smallish, butterless, himself, someone

Sorting by Sentence Context

The purpose of this activity is to help children see the importance of analyzing words fully. The words in the Word Pool from which a word is chosen for the blank in the sentence are in the Student Record Form. Record for each lesson the number correct.

Instructions: Another way that Word Detectives have to make sense of their clues is by examining them for *context*—the place in which they occur and all the surrounding clues. Each of the three sentences you will see has a blank. Each of the Word Pools you will see has one word in the box that fits sensibly into the blank but mostly words that would not fit into the blank. To figure out which words would or would not fit into the blank—that is, into the context of the sentence—you need to pay close attention to all the spelling, sound, and meaning clues of the words in the pool and in the words in the sentence. You have to fully analyze all the evidence you have at hand! As soon as you think you know a word that would fit into the sentence, raise your hand. As a Word Detective, it is important that you examine all the evidence—consider all the words—before you make your decision about which word fits. If someone disagrees with you, we will discuss why or why not that word might work in that sentence.

When my little sister wants a cookie, she smiles _____ at me.
(sourly, sleepily, sweetly, cuter, guilty)

Cleaning out the garbage can was a _____ job.
(thankful, lifeless, thankless, friendly)

He didn't like to walk home at night because the _____ scared him.
(invention, usefulness, darkness, darker)

Don caught the man trying to steal his car, and the man had a _____ look
to his face.
(guilty, warmish, energetic, wormy)

When he moved to a new state, he had to take a test for _____ of his
driver's license.
(removal, renewal, movement, lengthen)

LESSON **20** Morphological Awareness Treatment
Adding Word Parts for Meaning to Decoding

Student Response Booklet

Note: All lessons start with a warm-up, just as athletes warm up before a sports game. (See *Talking Letters* card.)

ACTIVITIES

Word Building

Instructions: Word Detectives solve cases by combining clues. We will start by building words from word part clues. I will show you word parts. As soon as you know the word that can be formed by these parts, raise your hand. When we agree, I will write it on the board and you can copy it in your Student Response Booklet. You will build the words from a base and fixes (*prefixes* before the base, or *suffixes* after the base).

harm + less = _____

report + er = _____

sick + ness = _____

electric + ity = _____

lead + er + ship = _____

differ + ent = _____

magic + al = _____

gold + en = _____

create + ive + ity = _____

salt + y = _____

Total correct = _____

Word Generating

Instructions: Word Detectives sometimes get their clues from generating and reasoning about similar cases. Readers can do the same—use what they know about words to generate new words in their minds. For 5 minutes, for each of the following word parts, think of a word that has that word part. Write the word in your Student Response Booklet. Go to the next word part and do the same, and so on. After 5 minutes, students share words generated for each word part. I will write one correct example for each word part on the board.

less _____

er _____

ness _____

ic _____

ship _____

ent _____

al _____

en _____

ity _____

ward _____

Total new correct words generated in 5 minutes = _____

Unit Finding

Instructions: Word Detectives solve mysteries by paying attention to details. The details you need to pay attention to in decoding are the base and the beginning and end "fixes" if there are any. Underline the base—the main meaning part of the word—and circle any fixes at the beginning or end that might modify or qualify that meaning. After 2 minutes, we will share with each other the word clues we found. I will write one shared correct example for each word part on the board.

international	carelessness	prenatal
unexplained	strengthen	midsummer
supernatural	unsatisfactory	
impossibility	infrequent	

Total number of words in which bases and fixes were correctly identified = _____

Word Transferring

Instructions: Once Word Detectives figure out the code, they can apply it to new words or cases. Here are some words that have the same parts that we have practiced. I will record how many you pronounce correctly and how long it took. We will graph your accuracy and time so you can see your progress.

useless

baker

quietness

historic

sportsmanship

payment

mechanical

brighten

maturity

forward

Correct words = _____   **Correct affixes** = _____

Total time = _____

Are They Relatives?

Instructions: To solve puzzles, Word Detectives need to pay attention not only to clues in a single word but also to how the clues in a word may signal that words are related in meaning to other words they know. Just as a child comes from her or his parents, some words come from—that is, they are made from—meaning of other words and thus belong to the same family of word meanings, but other words are not from the same family of word meanings even though they may resemble other words in spelling or sound. I want you to listen carefully and after I say each pair of words, circle YES on your work-sheet if you think the first word comes from the second one and circle NO if you do not think it does. After that, we will discuss any of your answers on which not everyone has agreed.

Directions: Circle YES or NO beside the word pair.

missionary	mission	YES	NO
interruption	interrupt	YES	NO
badminton	mint	YES	NO
happiness	happy	YES	NO
differently	differ	YES	NO

begin	beg	YES	NO
market	mark	YES	NO
artichoke	choke	YES	NO
shuttle	shut	YES	NO
submission	submit	YES	NO

Total correct in 2 minutes = _____

Sorting by Word Part Features

Instructions: Once Word Detectives get clues they have to make sense of them. They have to do a special kind of thinking in which they draw conclusions from the evidence, just as Sherlock Holmes and Dr. Watson did. In this activity you will sort words into categories, each of which has a word label and capital letter. Write the capital letter that shows the category to which each word belongs. When you complete the sort, you will be asked to write the rule you used in sorting words into categories. Then we will discuss the rules to make sure that everyone agrees.

Labels for categories: Suffix Means Has Characteristic = A, Suffix Means Does Not Have Characteristic = B, Compound Word with 2 Bases = C, No Suffix = D

helpless

helpful

warmish

harmful

harmless

reddish

settle

graceful

sparkle

formless

smallish

butterless

himself

someone

Explain the rule you used to sort: _____

_____

_____

_____

Number sorted correctly = _____

Sorting by Sentence Context

Instructions: Another way that Word Detectives have to make sense of their clues is by examining them for *context*—the place in which they occur and all the surrounding clues. Each of the three sentences you will see has a blank. Each of the Word Pools you will see has one word that fits sensibly into the blank but mostly words that would not fit into the blank. To figure out which words would or would not fit into the blank—that is, into the context of the sentence—you need to pay close attention to all the spelling, sound, and meaning clues of the words in the pool and in the words in the sentence. You have to fully analyze all the evidence you have at hand! As soon as you think you know a word that would fit into the sentence, raise your hand. As a Word Detective, it is important that you examine all the evidence—consider all the words—before you make your decision about which word fits. If someone disagrees with you, we will discuss why or why not that word might work in that sentence.

When my little sister wants a cookie, she smiles _____ at me.
(sourly, sleepily, sweetly, cuter, guilty)

Cleaning out the garbage can was a _____ job.
(thankful, lifeless, thankless, friendly)

He didn't like to walk home at night because the _____ scared him.
(invention, usefulness, darkness, darker)

Don caught the man trying to steal his car, and the man had a

_____ look to his face.
(guilty, warmish, energetic, wormy)

When he moved to a new state, he had to take a test for

_____ of his driver's license.
(removal, renewal, movement, lengthen)

LESSON 21

Morphological Awareness Treatment

Teacher Material

The following grapheme–phoneme correspondences are taught using *Talking Letters:* • Other consonant combinations • r- and l-controlled vowels	Materials needed: • *Talking Letters* for automatic alphabetic principles • Work folders

WARM-UP (FOR THE TEACHER)

For the warm-up, name the letter or letter group on the *Talking Letters* card, say the pictured word containing a target phoneme, and then produce the target phoneme. Next, the students take a turn and repeat what is named or said by you. This approach develops orthographic awareness of spelling units; phonological awareness of corresponding phonemes in and out of word context; and, through close timing, the automaticity of spelling–phoneme correspondence. If Lessons 1–14 have been completed, just name the letter or letter group and produce the target phoneme, and then the students take a turn and repeat what you have said. Monitor whether children are coordinating looking at the relevant letters and pictured words with naming of the letters and words and producing phonemes.

LESSON OVERVIEW (READ TO STUDENTS)

It is normal to come across words you do not know. One way to figure out unknown words is to use their word parts that signal or "fix" their meaning. We will call these parts at the beginning of words *prefixes* because they come before the rest of the word, and those parts at the end of the word *postfixes* because they come after the rest of the word. (Another term for the parts at the end of word is *suffixes.*) Words also have base parts that signal their meaning. Some words only have bases; some have prefixes and bases; some have bases and postfixes; and some have prefixes, bases, and postfixes. We will do seven different kinds of activities in each session to teach you to be Word Detectives who use these word parts to decode words: *Word Building, Word Generating, Unit Finding, Word Transferring, Are They Relatives? Sorting by Word Part Features,* and *Sorting by Sentence Context.* These activities should give you lots of strategies for using word parts to figure out words. We will use our electronic timer for the second through fourth activities but not for the others. Let's begin.

ACTIVITIES

Word Building

From this list of 30 words with highly frequent prefixes and derivational suffixes, 10 are presented in each lesson (1–14) and are presented three times altogether; but these will be randomized across the three presentations to avoid list learning effects. For the last two sessions (13 and 14), half of the list (15) is presented for a final review of the whole set. See the Student Response Booklet kept in your Word Detectives Work Folder. This set of affixes was generated by examining words in the McGraw-Hill Specific Skills *Working within Words Series* for Grades 3–6 and by reviewing morphological units in selected reading passages in *Read Naturally.* From these, Bill Nagy identified 30 suffixes that occur most frequently and thus are highly useful for struggling readers. Given limited instructional time, these are the ones on which to focus. Capital letters indicate these high-utility affixes, which were practiced in various lessons. The prefixes, bases, and postfixes are kept on 3 × 5 cards (or 5 × 8 cards or larger, depending on how large the word parts must be for all children in group to see them) in large envelopes—marked *prefixes, bases, and suffixes*—for the teacher to use in presenting the word parts and used as needed for a specific lesson (see Student Response Booklet for word parts). Then for each lesson, the teacher draws from the large envelopes the large cards with the word parts needed for each word in a lesson and holds them up high for all students to see. After one student correctly synthesizes the word parts to pronounce the word, each child writes the complete word built from its parts in the row on a worksheet.

Instructions: Word Detectives solve cases by combining clues. We will start by building words from word part clues. I will show you word parts. As soon as you know the word that can be formed by these parts, raise your hand. When we agree, I will write it on the board and you can copy it in your Student Response Booklet. You will build the words from a base and fixes (*prefixes* before the base, or *suffixes* after the base).

> memorize, unclear, invisible, impolite, addition, harmless, magical, northern, creativity, forehead

Word Generating

Instructions: Word Detectives sometimes get their clues from generating and reasoning about similar cases. Readers can do the same—use what they know about words to generate new words in their minds. For 5 minutes, for each of the following word parts, think of a word that has that word part. Write the word in your Student Response Booklet. Go to the next word part and do the same, and so on. After 5 minutes, students share words generated for each word part. I will write one correct example for each word part on the board.

Note: Children do this independently for 5 minutes. Every 30 seconds, the teacher can prompt the children to try to think of a word for the next word part.

> ern, im, ic, ing, ship, ly, al, ent, or, ary

Unit Finding

Children are directed to the Student Response Booklet with lists of words and asked to underline the base word and circle the affixes. Children receive R-File points if all word part items are completed correctly within 2 minutes.

Instructions: Word Detectives solve mysteries by paying attention to details. The details you need to pay attention to in decoding are the base and the beginning and end "fixes" if there are any. Underline the base—the main meaning part of the word—and circle any fixes at the beginning or end that might modify or qualify that meaning. After 2 minutes, we will share with each other the word clues we found. I will write one shared correct example for each word part on the board.

> bimonthly, rewinding, disappointing, criticize, simplify, strengthen, luxurious, dependent, terrorist, geologist

Word Transferring

For each lesson, children read a list with 10 words containing the same affixes practiced under Word Building. They read the list to a teacher who times them, records the time on their R-File record, and indicates whether 1) the affix part was pronounced correctly and 2) the whole word was pronounced correctly.

Instructions: Once Word Detectives figure out the code, they can apply it to new words or cases. Here are some words that have the same parts that we have practiced. I will record how many you pronounce correctly and how long it took. We will graph your accuracy and time so you can see your progress.

> northwestern, imprison, athletic, dancing, craftsmanship, slowly, musical, frequent, escalator, dictionary

Are They Relatives?

Does the first word come from the second word? The purpose of this task is to describe whether word parts at the end of a base word signal a semantic relationship with a base word. Children can record the total number they got correct.

Instructions: To solve puzzles, Word Detectives need to pay attention not only to clues in a single word but also to how the clues in a word may signal that words are related in meaning to other words they know. Just as a child comes from her or his parents, some words come from—that is, they are made from—meaning of other words and thus belong to the same family of word meanings, but other words are not from the same family of word meanings even though they may resemble other words in spelling or sound. I want you to listen carefully and after I say each pair of words, circle YES on your worksheet if you think the first word comes from the second one and circle NO if you do not think it does. After that, we will discuss any of your answers on which not everyone has agreed.

needle	need
reflection	reflect
satisfaction	satisfy
blanket	blank
definition	define
surface	surf
factual	fact
fictitious	fiction
answer	an
human	hum

Sorting by Word Part Features

The rules children write are discussed to make sure that all have grasped the underlying principle for sorting the words into categories.

Instructions: Once Word Detectives get clues they have to make sense of them. They have to do a special kind of thinking in which they draw conclusions from the evidence, just as Sherlock Holmes and Dr. Watson did. In this activity you will sort words into categories, each of which has a word label and capital letter. Write the capital letter that shows the category to which each word belongs. When you complete the sort, you will be asked to write the rule you used in sorting words into categories. Then we will discuss the rules to make sure that everyone agrees.

Generalization: Suffixes spelled and pronounced the same may be used for different meanings. Different suffixes may be used for the same meaning.

Labels for cards: Suffix Means *One Who* = A, Suffix Means Compare 3+ Items = B, No Suffix = C

druggist, fist, painter, strangest, balloonist, hardest, artist, flier, mist, dentist, biggest, cyclist, list, toughest, jogger, hardest, happiest

Sorting by Sentence Context

The purpose of this activity is to help children see the importance of analyzing words fully. The words in the Word Pool from which a word is chosen for the blank in the sentence are in the Student Record Form. Record for each lesson the number correct.

Instructions: Another way that Word Detectives have to make sense of their clues is by examining them for *context*—the place in which they occur and all the surrounding clues. Each of the three sentences you will see has a blank. Each of the Word Pools you will see has one word in the box that fits sensibly into the blank but mostly words that would not fit into the blank. To figure out which words would or would not fit into the blank—that is, into the context of the sentence—you need to pay close attention to all the spelling, sound, and meaning clues of the words in the pool and in the words in the sentence. You have to fully analyze all the evidence you have at hand! As soon as you think you know a word that would fit into the sentence, raise your hand. As a Word Detective, it is important that you examine all the evidence—consider all the words—before you make your decision about which word fits. If someone disagrees with you, we will discuss why or why not that word might work in that sentence.

He signed up for lessons on the violin and he sang in the choir. He was a very

_____ boy.
(mechanical, musical, friendly, wonderful)

When he made the coin disappear and then suddenly show up on the table, his mother

was proud he had learned a _____ trick.
(damaging, circular, magical, accidental)

Before using his father's tools, Sam had to get his father's _____.
(looseness, amazement, reversal, approval)

He bought tickets to all of his son's _____ events.
(lateness, historic, athletic, angelic, respectful)

Sometimes he ate a big breakfast, but _____ he ate just a banana.
(usually, heavily, luckily, busily, playfully)

LESSON **21** Morphological Awareness Treatment

Adding Word Parts for Meaning to Decoding

Student Response Booklet

Note: All lessons start with a warm-up, just as athletes warm up before a sports game. (See *Talking Letters* card.)

ACTIVITIES

Word Building

Instructions: Word Detectives solve cases by combining clues. We will start by building words from word part clues. I will show you word parts. As soon as you know the word that can be formed by these parts, raise your hand. When we agree, I will write it on the board and you can copy it in your Student Response Booklet. You will build the words from a base and fixes (*prefixes* before the base, or *suffixes* after the base).

memory + ize = _____

un + clear = _____

in + vision + able = _____

im + polite = _____

add + tion = _____

harm + less = _____

magic + al = _____

north + ern = _____

create + ive + y = _____

fore + head = _____

Total correct = _____

Word Generating

Instructions: Word Detectives sometimes get their clues from generating and reasoning about similar cases. Readers can do the same—use what they know about words to generate new words in their minds. For 5 minutes, for each of the following word parts, think of a word that has that word part. Write the word in your Student Response Booklet. Go to the next word part and do the same, and so on. After 5 minutes, students share words generated for each word part. I will write one correct example for each word part on the board.

ern _____

im _____

ic _____

ing _____

ship _____

ly _____

al _____

ent _____

or _____

ary _____

Total new correct words generated in 5 minutes = _____

Unit Finding

Instructions: Word Detectives solve mysteries by paying attention to details. The details you need to pay attention to in decoding are the base and the beginning and end "fixes" if there are any. Underline the base—the main meaning part of the word—and circle any fixes at the beginning or end that might modify or qualify that meaning. After 2 minutes, we will share with each other the word clues we found. I will write one shared correct example for each word part on the board.

bimonthly	simplify	terrorist
rewinding	strengthen	geologist
disappointing	luxurious	
criticize	dependent	

Total number of words in which bases and fixes were correctly identified = _____

Word Transferring

Instructions: Once Word Detectives figure out the code, they can apply it to new words or cases. Here are some words that have the same parts that we have practiced. I will record how many you pronounce correctly and how long it took. We will graph your accuracy and time so you can see your progress.

northwestern

imprison

athletic

dancing

craftsmanship

slowly

musical

frequent

escalator

dictionary

Correct words = _____   **Correct affixes** = _____

Total time = _____

Are They Relatives?

Instructions: To solve puzzles, Word Detectives need to pay attention not only to clues in a single word but also to how the clues in a word may signal that words are related in meaning to other words they know. Just as a child comes from her or his parents, some words come from—that is, they are made from—meaning of other words and thus belong to the same family of word meanings, but other words are not from the same family of word meanings even though they may resemble other words in spelling or sound. I want you to listen carefully and after I say each pair of words, circle YES on your worksheet if you think the first word comes from the second one and circle NO if you do not think it does. After that, we will discuss any of your answers on which not everyone has agreed.

Directions: Circle YES or NO beside the word pair.

needle	need	YES	NO
reflection	reflect	YES	NO
satisfaction	satisfy	YES	NO
blanket	blank	YES	NO
definition	define	YES	NO
surface	surf	YES	NO
factual	fact	YES	NO

fictitious	fiction	YES	NO
answer	an	YES	NO
human	hum	YES	NO

Total correct in 2 minutes = _____

Sorting by Word Part Features

Instructions: Once Word Detectives get clues they have to make sense of them. They have to do a special kind of thinking in which they draw conclusions from the evidence, just as Sherlock Holmes and Dr. Watson did. In this activity you will sort words into categories, each of which has a word label and capital letter. Write the capital letter that shows the category to which each word belongs. When you complete the sort, you will be asked to write the rule you used in sorting words into categories. Then we will discuss the rules to make sure that everyone agrees.

Labels for categories: Suffix Means *One Who* = A, Suffix Means Compare 3 Items = B, No Suffix = C

druggist

fist

painter

strangest

balloonist

hardest

artist

flier

mist

dentist

biggest

cyclist

list

toughest

jogger

hardest

happiest

Explain the rule you used to sort: _____

_____

_____

Number sorted correctly = _____

Sorting by Sentence Context

Instructions: Another way that Word Detectives have to make sense of their clues is by examining them for *context*—the place in which they occur and all the surrounding clues. Each of the three sentences you will see has a blank. Each of the Word Pools you will see has one word that fits sensibly into the blank but mostly words that would not fit into the blank. To figure out which words would or would not fit into the blank—that is, into the context of the sentence—you need to pay close attention to all the spelling, sound, and meaning clues of the words in the pool and in the words in the sentence. You have to fully analyze all the evidence you have at hand! As soon as you think you know a word that would fit into the sentence, raise your hand. As a Word Detective, it is important that you examine all the evidence—consider all the words—before you make your decision about which word fits. If someone disagrees with you, we will discuss why or why not that word might work in that sentence.

He signed up for lessons on the violin and he sang in the choir. He was a very

_____ boy.
(mechanical, musical, friendly, wonderful)

When he made the coin disappear and then suddenly show up on the table,

his mother was proud he had learned a _____ trick.
(damaging, circular, magical, accidental)

Before using his father's tools, Sam had to get his father's

_____.
(looseness, amazement, reversal, approval)

He bought tickets to all of his son's _____ events.
(lateness, historic, athletic, angelic, respectful)

Sometimes he ate a big breakfast, but _____ he ate just a banana.
(usually, heavily, luckily, busily, playfully)

LESSON **22** | Morphological Awareness Treatment

Teacher Material

| The following grapheme–phoneme correspondences are taught using *More Talking Letters:*
 • Latinate and Greek | Materials needed:
 • *More Talking Letters* (see Table 1) for automatic alphabetic principles
 • Work folders |

WARM-UP (FOR THE TEACHER)

For the warm-up, name the letter or letter group in *More Talking Letters* (see Table 1), say the pictured word containing a target phoneme, and then produce the target phoneme. Next, the students take a turn and repeat what is named or said by you. This approach develops orthographic awareness of spelling units; phonological awareness of corresponding phonemes in and out of word context; and, through close timing, the automaticity of spelling–phoneme correspondence. If Lessons 1–14 have been completed, just name the letter or letter group and produce the target phoneme, and then the students take a turn and repeat what you have said. Monitor whether children are coordinating looking at the relevant letters and pictured words with naming of the letters and words and producing phonemes.

LESSON OVERVIEW (READ TO STUDENTS)

It is normal to come across words you do not know. One way to figure out unknown words is to use their word parts that signal or "fix" their meaning. We will call these parts at the beginning of words *prefixes* because they come before the rest of the word, and those parts at the end of the word *postfixes* because they come after the rest of the word. (Another term for the parts at the end of word is *suffixes.*) Words also have base parts that signal their meaning. Some words only have bases; some have prefixes and bases; some have bases and postfixes; and some have prefixes, bases, and postfixes. We will do seven different kinds of activities in each session to teach you to be Word Detectives who use these word parts to decode words: *Word Building, Word Generating, Unit Finding, Word Transferring, Are They Relatives? Sorting by Word Part Features,* and *Sorting by Sentence Context.* These activities should give you lots of strategies for using word parts to figure out words. We will use our electronic timer for the second through fourth activities but not for the others. Let's begin.

ACTIVITIES

Word Building

From this list of 30 words with highly frequent prefixes and derivational suffixes, 10 are presented in each lesson (1–14) and are presented three times altogether; but these will be randomized across the three presentations to avoid list learning effects. For the last two sessions (13 and 14), half of the list (15) is presented for a final review of the whole set. See the Student Response Booklet kept in your Word Detectives Work Folder. This set of affixes was generated by examining words in the McGraw-Hill Specific Skills *Working within Words Series* for Grades 3–6 and by reviewing morphological units in selected reading passages in *Read Naturally.* From these, Bill Nagy identified 30 suffixes that occur most frequently and thus are highly useful for struggling readers. Given limited instructional time, these are the ones on which to focus. Capital letters indicate these high-utility affixes, which were practiced in various lessons. The prefixes, bases, and postfixes are kept on 3 × 5 cards (or 5 × 8 cards or larger, depending on how large the word parts must be for all children in group to see them) in large envelopes—marked *prefixes, bases, and suffixes*—for the teacher to use in presenting the word parts and used as needed for a specific lesson (see Student Response Booklet for word parts). Then for each lesson, the teacher draws from the large envelopes the large cards with the word parts needed for each word in a lesson and holds them up high for all students to see. After one student correctly synthesizes the word parts to pronounce the word, each child writes the complete word built from its parts in the row on a worksheet.

Instructions: Word Detectives solve cases by combining clues. We will start by building words from word part clues. I will show you word parts. As soon as you know the word that can be formed by these parts, raise your hand. When we agree, I will write it on the board and you can copy it in your Student Response Booklet. You will build the words from a base and fixes (*prefixes* before the base, or *suffixes* after the base).

> elementary, sickness, leadership, helpful, national, signal, beautiful, sensation, friendly, friendliness

Word Generating

Instructions: Word Detectives sometimes get their clues from generating and reasoning about similar cases. Readers can do the same—use what they know about words to generate new words in their minds. For 5 minutes, for each of the following word parts, think of a word that has that word part. Write the word in your Student Response Booklet. Go to the next word part and do the same, and so on. After 5 minutes, students share words generated for each word part. I will write one correct example for each word part on the board.

Note: Children do this independently for 5 minutes. Every 30 seconds, the teacher can prompt the children to try to think of a word for the next word part.

> ity, ist, y, er, en, tion, able, ent, ish, ous

Unit Finding

Children are directed to the Student Response Booklet with lists of words and asked to underline the base word and circle the affixes. Children receive R-File points if all word part items are completed correctly within 2 minutes.

Instructions: Word Detectives solve mysteries by paying attention to details. The details you need to pay attention to in decoding are the base and the beginning and end "fixes" if there are any. Underline the base—the main meaning part of the word—and circle any fixes at the beginning or end that might modify or qualify that meaning. After 2 minutes, we will share with each other the word clues we found. I will write one shared correct example for each word part on the board.

> possibility, artist, foggy, runner, lengthen, affection, lovable, persistent, tallish, famous

Word Transferring

For each lesson, children read a list with 10 words containing the same affixes practiced under Word Building. They read the list to a teacher who times them, records the time on their R-File record, and indicates whether 1) the affix part was pronounced correctly and 2) the whole word was pronounced correctly.

Instructions: Once Word Detectives figure out the code, they can apply it to new words or cases. Here are some words that have the same parts that we have practiced. I will record how many you pronounce correctly and how long it took. We will graph your accuracy and time so you can see your progress.

> possibility, artist, foggy, runner, lengthen, affection, lovable, persistent, tallish, famous

Are They Relatives?

Does the first word come from the second word? The purpose of this task is to describe whether word parts at the end of a base word signal a semantic relationship with a base word. Children can record the total number they got correct.

Instructions: To solve puzzles, Word Detectives need to pay attention not only to clues in a single word but also to how the clues in a word may signal that words are related in meaning to other words they know. Just as a child comes from her or his parents, some words come from—that is, they are made from—meaning of other words and thus belong to the same family of word meanings, but other words are not from the same family of word meanings even though they may resemble other words in spelling or sound. I want you to listen carefully and after I say each pair of words, circle YES on your worksheet if you think the first word comes from the second one and circle NO if you do not think it does. After that, we will discuss any of your answers on which not everyone has agreed.

Halloween	hall
subscription	subscribe
satisfied	sat
description	describe
Hercules	her
prescription	prescribe
civilization	civilize
electricity	elect
number	numb
typewritten	typewrite

Sorting by Word Part Features

The rules children write are discussed to make sure that all have grasped the underlying principle for sorting the words into categories.

Instructions: Once Word Detectives get clues they have to make sense of them. They have to do a special kind of thinking in which they draw conclusions from the evidence, just as Sherlock Holmes and Dr. Watson did. In this activity you will sort words into categories, each of which has a word label and capital letter. Write the capital letter that shows the category to which each word belongs. When you complete the sort, you will be asked to write the rule you used in sorting words into categories. Then we will discuss the rules to make sure that everyone agrees.

Generalization: Suffix cannot be identified just on basis of sound or spelling, and the same suffix can be used for different meanings.

Labels for cards: Suffix Means *One Who* = A, Suffix Means Compare 2 Items = B, No Suffix, C

teacher, finger, smaller, corner, helper, baker, dollar, tougher, runner, bigger, ginger, slower, dancer, cuter, collar, editor, luckier

Sorting by Sentence Context

The purpose of this activity is to help children see the importance of analyzing words fully. The words in the Word Pool from which a word is chosen for the blank in the sentence are in the Student Record Form. Record for each lesson the number correct.

Instructions: Another way that Word Detectives have to make sense of their clues is by examining them for *context*—the place in which they occur and all the surrounding clues. Each of the three sentences you will see has a blank. Each of the Word Pools you will see has one word in the box that fits sensibly into the blank but mostly words that would not fit into the blank. To figure out which words would or would not fit into the blank—that is, into the context of the sentence—you need to pay close attention to all the spelling, sound, and meaning clues of the words in the pool and in the words in the sentence. You have to fully analyze all the evidence you have at hand! As soon as you think you know a word that would fit into the sentence, raise your hand. As a Word Detective, it is important that you examine all the evidence—consider all the words—before you make your decision about which word fits. If someone disagrees with you, we will discuss why or why not that word might work in that sentence.

He ripped his math paper on purpose, but then he said the tear was
_____.

(useful, accidental, laziness, magical, dreadful)

Mr. and Mrs. Lee are expecting their first baby, so they are new to _____.
(boyhood, peacefulness, parenthood, friendliness)

He paid a _____ bill for cable television services.
(careless, enjoyable, monthly, friendly)

The television comedy show was a great source of _____.
(enjoyment, enjoyable, treatment, humorous)

He asked his friend to drive because he was worried about his _____.
(silliness, movement, leadership, sleepiness)

LESSON **22** Morphological Awareness Treatment

Adding Word Parts for Meaning to Decoding

Student Response Booklet

Note: All lessons start with a warm-up, just as athletes warm up before a sports game. (See *More Talking Letters.*)

ACTIVITIES

Word Building

Instructions: Word Detectives solve cases by combining clues. We will start by building words from word part clues. I will show you word parts. As soon as you know the word that can be formed by these parts, raise your hand. When we agree, I will write it on the board and you can copy it in your Student Response Booklet. You will build the words from a base and fixes (*prefixes* before the base, or *suffixes* after the base).

element + ary = _____

sick + ness = _____

lead + er + ship = _____

will + ful = _____

nation + al = _____

sign + al = _____

beauty + ful = _____

sense + tion = _____

friend + ly = _____

friend + ly + ness = _____

Total correct = _____

Word Generating

Instructions: Word Detectives sometimes get their clues from generating and reasoning about similar cases. Readers can do the same—use what they know about words to generate new words in their minds. For 5 minutes, for each of the following word parts, think of a word that has that word part. Write the word in your Student Response Booklet. Go to the next word part and do the same, and so on. After 5 minutes, students share words generated for each word part. I will write one correct example for each word part on the board.

ity _____

ist _____

y _____

er _____

en _____

tion _____

able _____

ent _____

ish _____

ous _____

Total new correct words generated in 5 minutes = _____

Unit Finding

Instructions: Word Detectives solve mysteries by paying attention to details. The details you need to pay attention to in decoding are the base and the beginning and end "fixes" if there are any. Underline the base—the main meaning part of the word—and circle any fixes at the beginning or end that might modify or qualify that meaning. After 2 minutes, we will share with each other the word clues we found. I will write one shared correct example for each word part on the board.

possibility	runner	lovable	tallish
artist	lengthen	persistent	famous
foggy	affection		

Total number of words in which bases and fixes were correctly identified = _____

Word Transferring

Instructions: Once Word Detectives figure out the code, they can apply it to new words or cases. Here are some words that have the same parts that we have practiced. I will record how many you pronounce correctly and how long it took. We will graph your accuracy and time so you can see your progress.

possibility

artist

foggy

runner

lengthen

affection

lovable

persistent

tallish

famous

Correct words = _____   **Correct affixes = _____**

Total time = _____

Are They Relatives?

Instructions: To solve puzzles, Word Detectives need to pay attention not only to clues in a single word but also to how the clues in a word may signal that words are related in meaning to other words they know. Just as a child comes from her or his parents, some words come from—that is, they are made from—meaning of other words and thus belong to the same family of word meanings, but other words are not from the same family of word meanings even though they may resemble other words in spelling or sound. I want you to listen carefully and after I say each pair of words, circle YES on your worksheet if you think the first word comes from the second one and circle NO if you do not think it does. After that, we will discuss any of your answers on which not everyone has agreed.

Directions: Circle YES or NO beside the word pair.

Halloween	hall	YES	NO
subscription	subscribe	YES	NO
satisfied	sat	YES	NO
description	describe	YES	NO

Hercules	her	YES	NO
prescription	prescribe	YES	NO
civilization	civilize	YES	NO
electricity	elect	YES	NO
number	numb	YES	NO
typewritten	typewrite	YES	NO

Total correct in 2 minutes = _____

Sorting by Word Part Features

Instructions: Once Word Detectives get clues they have to make sense of them. They have to do a special kind of thinking in which they draw conclusions from the evidence, just as Sherlock Holmes and Dr. Watson did. In this activity you will sort words into categories, each of which has a word label and capital letter. Write the capital letter that shows the category to which each word belongs. When you complete the sort, you will be asked to write the rule you used in sorting words into categories. Then we will discuss the rules to make sure that everyone agrees.

Labels for categories: Suffix Means *One Who* = A, Suffix Means Compare 2 Items = B, No Suffix = C

teacher
finger
smaller
corner
helper
baker
dollar
tougher
runner
bigger
ginger
slower
dancer
cuter
collar
editor
luckier

Explain the rule you used to sort: _____

_____

_____

_____

Number sorted correctly = _____

Sorting by Sentence Context

Instructions: Another way that Word Detectives have to make sense of their clues is by examining them for *context*—the place in which they occur and all the surrounding clues. Each of the three sentences you will see has a blank. Each of the Word Pools you will see has one word that fits sensibly into the blank but mostly words that would not fit into the blank. To figure out which words would or would not fit into the blank—that is, into the context of the sentence—you need to pay close attention to all the spelling, sound, and meaning clues of the words in the pool and in the words in the sentence. You have to fully analyze all the evidence you have at hand! As soon as you think you know a word that would fit into the sentence, raise your hand. As a Word Detective, it is important that you examine all the evidence—consider all the words—before you make your decision about which word fits. If someone disagrees with you, we will discuss why or why not that word might work in that sentence.

He ripped his math paper on purpose, but then he said the tear was

_____.

(useful, accidental, laziness, magical, dreadful)

Mr. and Mrs. Lee are expecting their first baby, so they are new to

_____.

(boyhood, peacefulness, parenthood, friendliness)

He paid a _____ bill for cable television services.
(careless, enjoyable, monthly, friendly)

The television comedy show was a great source of

_____.

(enjoyment, enjoyable, treatment, humorous)

He asked his friend to drive because he was worried about his

_____.

(silliness, movement, leadership, sleepiness)

UNIT I
LESSON
23

Teacher
Material

LESSON 23 Morphological Awareness Treatment

Teacher Material

The following grapheme–phoneme correspondences are taught using *Talking Letters:*	Materials needed:
• Single-letter consonants • Short vowels in closed syllables • Long vowels in open syllables	• *Talking Letters* for automatic alphabetic principles • Work folders

WARM-UP (FOR THE TEACHER)

For the warm-up, name the letter or letter group on the *Talking Letters* card, say the pictured word containing a target phoneme, and then produce the target phoneme. Next, the students take a turn and repeat what is named or said by you. This approach develops orthographic awareness of spelling units; phonological awareness of corresponding phonemes in and out of word context; and, through close timing, the automaticity of spelling–phoneme correspondence. If Lessons 1–14 have been completed, just name the letter or letter group and produce the target phoneme, and then the students take a turn and repeat what you have said. Monitor whether children are coordinating looking at the relevant letters and pictured words with naming of the letters and words and producing phonemes.

LESSON OVERVIEW (READ TO STUDENTS)

It is normal to come across words you do not know. One way to figure out unknown words is to use their word parts that signal or "fix" their meaning. We will call these parts at the beginning of words *prefixes* because they come before the rest of the word, and those parts at the end of the word *postfixes* because they come after the rest of the word. (Another term for the parts at the end of word is *suffixes.*) Words also have base parts that signal their meaning. Some words only have bases; some have prefixes and bases; some have bases and postfixes; and some have prefixes, bases, and postfixes. We will do seven different kinds of activities in each session to teach you to be Word Detectives who use these word parts to decode words: *Word Building, Word Generating, Unit Finding, Word Transferring, Are They Relatives? Sorting by Word Part Features,* and *Sorting by Sentence Context.* These activities should give you lots of strategies for using word parts to figure out words. We will use our electronic timer for the second through fourth activities but not for the others. Let's begin.

203

ACTIVITIES

Word Building

From this list of 30 words with highly frequent prefixes and derivational suffixes, 10 are presented in each lesson (1–14) and are presented three times altogether; but these will be randomized across the three presentations to avoid list learning effects. For the last two sessions (13 and 14), half of the list (15) is presented for a final review of the whole set. See the Student Response Booklet kept in your Word Detectives Work Folder. This set of affixes was generated by examining words in the McGraw-Hill Specific Skills *Working within Words Series* for Grades 3–6 and by reviewing morphological units in selected reading passages in *Read Naturally*. From these, Bill Nagy identified 30 suffixes that occur most frequently and thus are highly useful for struggling readers. Given limited instructional time, these are the ones on which to focus. Capital letters indicate these high-utility affixes, which were practiced in various lessons. The prefixes, bases, and postfixes are kept on 3 × 5 cards (or 5 × 8 cards or larger, depending on how large the word parts must be for all children in group to see them) in large envelopes—marked *prefixes, bases, and suffixes*—for the teacher to use in presenting the word parts and used as needed for a specific lesson (see Student Response Booklet for word parts). Then for each lesson, the teacher draws from the large envelopes the large cards with the word parts needed for each word in a lesson and holds them up high for all students to see. After one student correctly synthesizes the word parts to pronounce the word, each child writes the complete word built from its parts in the row on a worksheet.

Instructions: Word Detectives solve cases by combining clues. We will start by building words from word part clues. I will show you word parts. As soon as you know the word that can be formed by these parts, raise your hand. When we agree, I will write it on the board and you can copy it in your Student Response Booklet. You will build the words from a base and fixes (*prefixes* before the base, or *suffixes* after the base).

> remember, unclear, invisible, dislike, important, harmless, mouthful, sickness, expensive, toward

Word Generating

Instructions: Word Detectives sometimes get their clues from generating and reasoning about similar cases. Readers can do the same—use what they know about words to generate new words in their minds. For 5 minutes, for each of the following word parts, think of a word that has that word part. Write the word in your Student Response Booklet. Go to the next word part and do the same, and so on. After 5 minutes, students share words generated for each word part. I will write one correct example for each word part on the board.

Note: Children do this independently for 5 minutes. Every 30 seconds, the teacher can prompt the children to try to think of a word for the next word part.

> re, un, in, dis, ant, less, ful, ness, ive, ward

Unit Finding

Children are directed to the Student Response Booklet with lists of words and asked to underline the base word and circle the affixes. Children receive R-File points if all word part items are completed correctly within 2 minutes.

Instructions: Word Detectives solve mysteries by paying attention to details. The details you need to pay attention to in decoding are the base and the beginning and end "fixes" if there are any. Underline the base—the main meaning part of the word—and circle any fixes at the beginning or end that might modify or qualify that meaning. After 2 minutes, we will share with each other the word clues we found. I will write one shared correct example for each word part on the board.

> repeat, undo, inadequate, disagree, distant, hopeless, graceful, meanness, secretive, backward

Word Transferring

For each lesson, children read a list with 10 words containing the same affixes practiced under Word Building. They read the list to a teacher who times them, records the time on their R-File record, and indicates whether 1) the affix part was pronounced correctly and 2) the whole word was pronounced correctly.

Instructions: Once Word Detectives figure out the code, they can apply it to new words or cases. Here are some words that have the same parts that we have practiced. I will record how many you pronounce correctly and how long it took. We will graph your accuracy and time so you can see your progress.

> repeat, undo, inadequate, disagree, distant, hopeless, graceful, meanness, secretive, backward

Are They Relatives?

Does the first word come from the second word? The purpose of this task is to describe whether word parts at the end of a base word signal a semantic relationship with a base word. Children can record the total number they got correct.

Instructions: To solve puzzles, Word Detectives need to pay attention not only to clues in a single word but also to how the clues in a word may signal that words are related in meaning to other words they know. Just as a child comes from her or his parents, some words come from—that is, they are made from—meaning of other words and thus belong to the same family of word meanings, but other words are not from the same family of word meanings even though they may resemble other words in spelling or sound. I want you to listen carefully and after I say each pair of words, circle YES on your worksheet if you think the first word comes from the second one and circle NO if you do not think it does. After that, we will discuss any of your answers on which not everyone has agreed.

animal	an
limit	lime
connection	connect
combination	combine
separation	separate
forget	forge
riddle	ride
pumpkin	pump
directions	direct
similarity	similar

Sorting by Word Part Features

The rules children write are discussed to make sure that all have grasped the underlying principle for sorting the words into categories.

Instructions: Once Word Detectives get clues they have to make sense of them. They have to do a special kind of thinking in which they draw conclusions from the evidence, just as Sherlock Holmes and Dr. Watson did. In this activity you will sort words into categories, each of which has a word label and capital letter. Write the capital letter that shows the category to which each word belongs. When you complete the sort, you will be asked to write the rule you used in sorting words into categories. Then we will discuss the rules to make sure that everyone agrees.

Generalization: The suffix for plurals has three different sounds associated with it.

Labels for cards: Suffix Pronounced /s/ = A, Suffix Pronounced /z/ = B, Suffix Pronounced /es/ = C

bees, buses, beds, chickens, fleas, foxes, legs, spines, inches, birds, snakes, hatches

Sorting by Sentence Context

The purpose of this activity is to help children see the importance of analyzing words fully. The words in the Word Pool from which a word is chosen for the blank in the sentence are in the Student Record Form. Record for each lesson the number correct.

Instructions: Another way that Word Detectives have to make sense of their clues is by examining them for *context*—the place in which they occur and all the surrounding clues. Each of the three sentences you will see has a blank. Each of the Word Pools you will see has one word in the box that fits sensibly into the blank but mostly words that would not fit into the blank. To figure out which words would or would not fit into the blank—that is, into the context of the sentence—you need to pay close attention to all the spelling, sound, and meaning clues of the words in the pool and in the words in the sentence. You have to fully analyze all the evidence you have at hand! As soon as you think you know a word that would fit into the sentence, raise your hand. As a Word Detective, it is important that you examine all the evidence—consider all the words—before you make your decision about which word fits. If someone disagrees with you, we will discuss why or why not that word might work in that sentence.

When my little sister wants a cookie, she smiles _____ at me.
(sourly, sleepily, sweetly, cuter, guilty)

Cleaning out the garbage can was a _____ job.
(thankful, lifeless, thankless, friendly)

He didn't like to walk home at night because the _____ scared him.
(invention, usefulness, darkness, darker)

LESSON **23** Morphological Awareness Treatment
Adding Word Parts for Meaning to Decoding

Student Response Booklet

Note: All lessons start with a warm-up, just as athletes warm up before a sports game. (See *Talking Letters* card.)

ACTIVITIES

Word Building

Instructions: Word Detectives solve cases by combining clues. We will start by building words from word part clues. I will show you word parts. As soon as you know the word that can be formed by these parts, raise your hand. When we agree, I will write it on the board and you can copy it in your Student Response Booklet. You will build the words from a base and fixes (*prefixes* before the base, or *suffixes* after the base).

re + memory = _____

un + clear = _____

in + vision + able = _____

dis + like = _____

import + ant = _____

harm + less = _____

mouth + ful = _____

sick + ness = _____

expense + ive = _____

to + ward = _____

Total correct = _____

Word Generating

Instructions: Word Detectives sometimes get their clues from generating and reasoning about similar cases. Readers can do the same—use what they know about words to generate new words in their minds. For 5 minutes, for each of the following word parts, think of a word that has that word part. Write the word in your Student Response Booklet. Go to the next word part and do the same, and so on. After 5 minutes, students share words generated for each word part. I will write one correct example for each word part on the board.

re _____

un _____

in _____

dis _____

ant _____

less _____

full _____

ness _____

ive _____

ward _____

Total new correct words generated in 5 minutes = _____

Unit Finding

Instructions: Word Detectives solve mysteries by paying attention to details. The details you need to pay attention to in decoding are the base and the beginning and end "fixes" if there are any. Underline the base—the main meaning part of the word—and circle any fixes at the beginning or end that might modify or qualify that meaning. After 2 minutes, we will share with each other the word clues we found. I will write one shared correct example for each word part on the board.

repeat	distant	secretive
undo	hopeless	backward
inadequate	graceful	
disagree	meanness	

Total number of words in which bases and fixes were correctly identified = _____

Helping Students with Dyslexia and Dysgraphia Make Connections: Differentiated Instruction Lesson Plans in Reading and Writing by V.W. Berninger and B.J. Wolf. Copyright © 2009 Paul H. Brookes Publishing Co. All Rights Reserved.

209

Word Transferring

Instructions: Once Word Detectives figure out the code, they can apply it to new words or cases. Here are some words that have the same parts that we have practiced. I will record how many you pronounce correctly and how long it took. We will graph your accuracy and time so you can see your progress.

repeat

undo

inadequate

disagree

distant

hopeless

graceful

meanness

secretive

backward

Correct words = _____   **Correct affixes** = _____

Total time = _____

Are They Relatives?

Instructions: To solve puzzles, Word Detectives need to pay attention not only to clues in a single word but also to how the clues in a word may signal that words are related in meaning to other words they know. Just as a child comes from her or his parents, some words come from—that is, they are made from—meaning of other words and thus belong to the same family of word meanings, but other words are not from the same family of word meanings even though they may resemble other words in spelling or sound. I want you to listen carefully and after I say each pair of words, circle YES on your work-sheet if you think the first word comes from the second one and circle NO if you do not think it does. After that, we will discuss any of your answers on which not everyone has agreed.

Directions: Circle YES or NO beside the word pair.

animal	an	YES	NO
limit	lime	YES	NO
connection	connect	YES	NO
combination	combine	YES	NO
separation	separate	YES	NO
forget	forge	YES	NO

riddle	ride	YES	NO
pumpkin	pump	YES	NO
directions	direct	YES	NO
similarity	similar	YES	NO

Total correct in 2 minutes = _____

Sorting by Word Part Features

Instructions: Once Word Detectives get clues they have to make sense of them. They have to do a special kind of thinking in which they draw conclusions from the evidence, just as Sherlock Holmes and Dr. Watson did. In this activity you will sort words into categories, each of which has a word label and capital letter. Write the capital letter that shows the category to which each word belongs. When you complete the sort, you will be asked to write the rule you used in sorting words into categories. Then we will discuss the rules to make sure that everyone agrees.

Labels for categories: Suffix Pronounced /s/ = A, Suffix Pronounced /z/ = B, Suffix Pronounced /es/ = C

bees

buses

beds

chickens

fleas

foxes

legs

spines

inches

birds

snakes

hatches

Explain the rule you used to sort: _____

_____

_____

_____

_____

Number sorted correctly = _____

Sorting by Sentence Context

Instructions: Another way that Word Detectives have to make sense of their clues is by examining them for *context*—the place in which they occur and all the surrounding clues. Each of the three sentences you will see has a blank. Each of the Word Pools you will see has one word that fits sensibly into the blank but mostly words that would not fit into the blank. To figure out which words would or would not fit into the blank—that is, into the context of the sentence—you need to pay close attention to all the spelling, sound, and meaning clues of the words in the pool and in the words in the sentence. You have to fully analyze all the evidence you have at hand! As soon as you think you know a word that would fit into the sentence, raise your hand. As a Word Detective, it is important that you examine all the evidence—consider all the words—before you make your decision about which word fits. If someone disagrees with you, we will discuss why or why not that word might work in that sentence.

When my little sister wants a cookie, she smiles _____ at me.
(sourly, sleepily, sweetly, cuter, guilty)

Cleaning out the garbage can was a _____ job.
(thankful, lifeless, thankless, friendly)

He didn't like to walk home at night because the

_____ scared him.
(invention, usefulness, darkness, darker)

LESSON 24 Morphological Awareness Treatment

Teacher Material

The following grapheme–phoneme correspondences are taught using *Talking Letters:* • Consonant blends and vowel teams	Materials needed: • *Talking Letters* for automatic alphabetic principles • Work folders

WARM-UP (FOR THE TEACHER)

For the warm-up, name the letter or letter group on the *Talking Letters* card, say the pictured word containing a target phoneme, and then produce the target phoneme. Next, the students take a turn and repeat what is named or said by you. This approach develops orthographic awareness of spelling units; phonological awareness of corresponding phonemes in and out of word context; and, through close timing, the automaticity of spelling–phoneme correspondence. If Lessons 1–14 have been completed, just name the letter or letter group and produce the target phoneme, and then the students take a turn and repeat what you have said. Monitor whether children are coordinating looking at the relevant letters and pictured words with naming of the letters and words and producing phonemes.

LESSON OVERVIEW (READ TO STUDENTS)

It is normal to come across words you do not know. One way to figure out unknown words is to use their word parts that signal or "fix" their meaning. We will call these parts at the beginning of words *prefixes* because they come before the rest of the word, and those parts at the end of the word *postfixes* because they come after the rest of the word. (Another term for the parts at the end of word is *suffixes.*) Words also have base parts that signal their meaning. Some words only have bases; some have prefixes and bases; some have bases and postfixes; and some have prefixes, bases, and postfixes. We will do seven different kinds of activities in each session to teach you to be Word Detectives who use these word parts to decode words: *Word Building, Word Generating, Unit Finding, Word Transferring, Are They Relatives? Sorting by Word Part Features,* and *Sorting by Sentence Context.* These activities should give you lots of strategies for using word parts to figure out words. We will use our electronic timer for the second through fourth activities but not for the others. Let's begin.

ACTIVITIES

Word Building

From this list of 30 words with highly frequent prefixes and derivational suffixes, 10 are presented in each lesson (1–14) and are presented three times altogether; but these will be randomized across the three presentations to avoid list learning effects. For the last two sessions (13 and 14), half of the list (15) is presented for a final review of the whole set. See the Student Response Booklet kept in your Word Detectives Work Folder. This set of affixes was generated by examining words in the McGraw-Hill Specific Skills *Working within Words Series* for Grades 3–6 and by reviewing morphological units in selected reading passages in *Read Naturally.* From these, Bill Nagy identified 30 suffixes that occur most frequently and thus are highly useful for struggling readers. Given limited instructional time, these are the ones on which to focus. Capital letters indicate these high-utility affixes, which were practiced in various lessons. The prefixes, bases, and postfixes are kept on 3 × 5 cards (or 5 × 8 cards or larger, depending on how large the word parts must be for all children in group to see them) in large envelopes—marked *prefixes, bases, and suffixes*—for the teacher to use in presenting the word parts and used as needed for a specific lesson (see Student Response Booklet for word parts). Then for each lesson, the teacher draws from the large envelopes the large cards with the word parts needed for each word in a lesson and holds them up high for all students to see. After one student correctly synthesizes the word parts to pronounce the word, each child writes the complete word built from its parts in the row on a worksheet.

Instructions: Word Detectives solve cases by combining clues. We will start by building words from word part clues. I will show you word parts. As soon as you know the word that can be formed by these parts, raise your hand. When we agree, I will write it on the board and you can copy it in your Student Response Booklet. You will build the words from a base and fixes (*prefixes* before the base, or *suffixes* after the base).

important, northern, leadership, golden, washable, dislike, elementary, projector, completely, addition

Word Generating

Instructions: Word Detectives sometimes get their clues from generating and reasoning about similar cases. Readers can do the same—use what they know about words to generate new words in their minds. For 5 minutes, for each of the following word parts, think of a word that has that word part. Write the word in your Student Response Booklet. Go to the next word part and do the same, and so on. After 5 minutes, students share words generated for each word part. I will write one correct example for each word part on the board.

Note: Children do this independently for 5 minutes. Every 30 seconds, the teacher can prompt the children to try to think of a word for the next word part.

ant, ary, ship, en, able, dis, ary, or, ly, tion

Unit Finding

Children are directed to the Student Response Booklet with lists of words and asked to underline the base word and circle the affixes. Children receive R-File points if all word part items are completed correctly within 2 minutes.

Instructions: Word Detectives solve mysteries by paying attention to details. The details you need to pay attention to in decoding are the base and the beginning and end "fixes" if there are any. Underline the base—the main meaning part of the word—and circle any fixes at the beginning or end that might modify or qualify that meaning. After 2 minutes, we will share with each other the word clues we found. I will write one shared correct example for each word part on the board.

> fragrant, dictionary, citizenship, shrunken, lovable, discount, secondary, tractor, happily, multiplication

Word Transferring

For each lesson, children read a list with 10 words containing the same affixes practiced under Word Building. They read the list to a teacher who times them, records the time on their R-File record, and indicates whether 1) the affix part was pronounced correctly and 2) the whole word was pronounced correctly

Instructions: Once Word Detectives figure out the code, they can apply it to new words or cases. Here are some words that have the same parts that we have practiced. I will record how many you pronounce correctly and how long it took. We will graph your accuracy and time so you can see your progress.

> fragrant, dictionary, citizenship, shrunken, lovable, discount, secondary, tractor, happily, multiplication

Are They Relatives?

Does the first word come from the second word? The purpose of this task is to describe whether word parts at the end of a base word signal a semantic relationship with a base word. Children can record the total number they got correct.

Instructions: To solve puzzles, Word Detectives need to pay attention not only to clues in a single word but also to how the clues in a word may signal that words are related in meaning to other words they know. Just as a child comes from her or his parents, some words come from—that is, they are made from—meaning of other words and thus belong to the same family of word meanings, but other words are not from the same family of word meanings even though they may resemble other words in spelling or sound. I want you to listen carefully and after I say each pair of words, circle YES on your worksheet if you think the first word comes from the second one and circle NO if you do not think it does. After that, we will discuss any of your answers on which not everyone has agreed.

allow	low
establishment	establish
hippopotamus	hip
readily	read
resemblance	resemble
comparison	compare
delight	deli
appearance	appear
perspiration	perspire
robot	rob

Sorting by Word Part Features

The rules children write are discussed to make sure that all have grasped the underlying principle for sorting the words into categories.

Instructions: Once Word Detectives get clues they have to make sense of them. They have to do a special kind of thinking in which they draw conclusions from the evidence, just as Sherlock Holmes and Dr. Watson did. In this activity you will sort words into categories, each of which has a word label and capital letter. Write the capital letter that shows the category to which each word belongs. When you complete the sort, you will be asked to write the rule you used in sorting words into categories. Then we will discuss the rules to make sure that everyone agrees.

Generalization: The suffix for past tense has three different sounds associated with it.

Labels for cards: Suffix Pronounced /d/ = A, Suffix Pronounced /ed/ = B, Suffix Pronounced /t/ = C

hopped, pushed, reported, exploded, splashed, jumped, wished, loaded, padded, cried, tripped, learned

Sorting by Sentence Context

The purpose of this activity is to help children see the importance of analyzing words fully. The words in the Word Pool from which a word is chosen for the blank in the sentence are in the Student Record Form. Record for each lesson the number correct.

Instructions: Another way that Word Detectives have to make sense of their clues is by examining them for *context*—the place in which they occur and all the surrounding clues. Each of the three sentences you will see has a blank. Each of the Word Pools you will see has one word in the box that fits sensibly into the blank but mostly words that would not fit into the blank. To figure out which words would or would not fit into the blank—that is, into the context of the sentence—you need to pay close attention to all the spelling, sound, and meaning clues of the words in the pool and in the words in the sentence. You have to fully analyze all the evidence you have at hand! As soon as you think you know a word that would fit into the sentence, raise your hand. As a Word Detective, it is important that you examine all the evidence—consider all the words—before you make your decision about which word fits. If someone disagrees with you, we will discuss why or why not that word might work in that sentence.

Don caught the man trying to steal his car, and the man had a _____ look to his face.
(guilty, warmish, energetic, wormy)

When he moved to a new state, he had to take a test for _____ of his driver's license.
(removal, renewal, movement, lengthen)

He signed up for lessons on the violin and he sang in the choir. He was a very

_____ boy.
(mechanical, musical, friendly, wonderful)

LESSON **24** Morphological Awareness Treatment

Adding Word Parts for Meaning to Decoding

Student Response Booklet

Note: All lessons start with a warm-up, just as athletes warm up before a sports game. (See *Talking Letters* card.)

ACTIVITIES

Word Building

Instructions: Word Detectives solve cases by combining clues. We will start by building words from word part clues. I will show you word parts. As soon as you know the word that can be formed by these parts, raise your hand. When we agree, I will write it on the board and you can copy it in your Student Response Booklet. You will build the words from a base and fixes (*prefixes* before the base, or *suffixes* after the base).

import + ance = _____

north + ern = _____

lead + er + ship = _____

gold + en = _____

wash + able = _____

dis + like = _____

element + ary = _____

project + or = _____

complete + ly = _____

add + tion = _____

Total correct = _____

Word Generating

Instructions: Word Detectives sometimes get their clues from generating and reasoning about similar cases. Readers can do the same—use what they know about words to generate new words in their minds. For 5 minutes, for each of the following word parts, think of a word that has that word part. Write the word in your Student Response Booklet. Go to the next word part and do the same, and so on. After 5 minutes, students share words generated for each word part. I will write one correct example for each word part on the board.

ant _____

ary _____

ship _____

en _____

able _____

dis _____

ary _____

or _____

ly _____

tion _____

Total new correct words generated in 5 minutes = _____

Unit Finding

Instructions: Word Detectives solve mysteries by paying attention to details. The details you need to pay attention to in decoding are the base and the beginning and end "fixes" if there are any. Underline the base—the main meaning part of the word—and circle any fixes at the beginning or end that might modify or qualify that meaning. After 2 minutes, we will share with each other the word clues we found. I will write one shared correct example for each word part on the board.

fragrant	lovable	happily
dictionary	discount	multiplication
citizenship	secondary	
shrunken	tractor	

Total number of words in which bases and fixes were correctly identified = _____

Word Transferring

Instructions: Once Word Detectives figure out the code, they can apply it to new words or cases. Here are some words that have the same parts that we have practiced. I will record how many you pronounce correctly and how long it took. We will graph your accuracy and time so you can see your progress.

> fragrant
>
> dictionary
>
> citizenship
>
> shrunken
>
> lovable
>
> discount
>
> secondary
>
> tractor
>
> happily
>
> multiplication
>
> **Correct words** = _____   **Correct affixes** = _____
>
> **Total time** = _____

Are They Relatives?

Instructions: To solve puzzles, Word Detectives need to pay attention not only to clues in a single word but also to how the clues in a word may signal that words are related in meaning to other words they know. Just as a child comes from her or his parents, some words come from—that is, they are made from—meaning of other words and thus belong to the same family of word meanings, but other words are not from the same family of word meanings even though they may resemble other words in spelling or sound. I want you to listen carefully and after I say each pair of words, circle YES on your worksheet if you think the first word comes from the second one and circle NO if you do not think it does. After that, we will discuss any of your answers on which not everyone has agreed.

Directions: Circle YES or NO beside the word pair.

allow	low	YES	NO
establishment	establish	YES	NO
hippopotamus	hip	YES	NO
readily	read	YES	NO
resemblance	resemble	YES	NO
comparison	compare	YES	NO

delight	deli	YES	NO
appearance	appear	YES	NO
perspiration	perspire	YES	NO
robot	rob	YES	NO

Total correct in 2 minutes = _____

Sorting by Word Part Features

Instructions: Once Word Detectives get clues they have to make sense of them. They have to do a special kind of thinking in which they draw conclusions from the evidence, just as Sherlock Holmes and Dr. Watson did. In this activity you will sort words into categories, each of which has a word label and capital letter. Write the capital letter that shows the category to which each word belongs. When you complete the sort, you will be asked to write the rule you used in sorting words into categories. Then we will discuss the rules to make sure that everyone agrees.

Labels for categories: Suffix Pronounced /d/ = A, Suffix Pronounced /ed/ = B, Suffix Pronounced /t/ = C

hopped

pushed

reported

exploded

splashed

jumped

wished

loaded

padded

cried

tripped

learned

Explain the rule you used to sort: _____

_____

_____

_____

_____

Number sorted correctly = _____

Sorting by Sentence Context

Instructions: Another way that Word Detectives have to make sense of their clues is by examining them for *context*—the place in which they occur and all the surrounding clues. Each of the three sentences you will see has a blank. Each of the Word Pools you will see has one word that fits sensibly into the blank but mostly words that would not fit into the blank. To figure out which words would or would not fit into the blank—that is, into the context of the sentence—you need to pay close attention to all the spelling, sound, and meaning clues of the words in the pool and in the words in the sentence. You have to fully analyze all the evidence you have at hand! As soon as you think you know a word that would fit into the sentence, raise your hand. As a Word Detective, it is important that you examine all the evidence—consider all the words—before you make your decision about which word fits. If someone disagrees with you, we will discuss why or why not that word might work in that sentence.

Don caught the man trying to steal his car, and the man had a

_____ look to his face.
(guilty, warmish, energetic, wormy)

When he moved to a new state, he had to take a test for

_____ of his driver's license.
(removal, renewal, movement, lengthen)

He signed up for lessons on the violin and he sang in the choir. He

was a very _____ boy.
(mechanical, musical, friendly, wonderful)

LESSON 25 | Morphological Awareness Treatment

Teacher Material

The following grapheme–phoneme correspondences are taught using *Talking Letters:*
- Other consonant combinations
- r- and l-controlled vowels

Materials needed:
- *Talking Letters* for automatic alphabetic principles
- Work folders

WARM-UP (FOR THE TEACHER)

For the warm-up, name the letter or letter group on the *Talking Letters* card, say the pictured word containing a target phoneme, and then produce the target phoneme. Next, the students take a turn and repeat what is named or said by you. This approach develops orthographic awareness of spelling units; phonological awareness of corresponding phonemes in and out of word context; and, through close timing, the automaticity of spelling–phoneme correspondence. If Lessons 1–14 have been completed, just name the letter or letter group and produce the target phoneme, and then the students take a turn and repeat what you have said. Monitor whether children are coordinating looking at the relevant letters and pictured words with naming of the letters and words and producing phonemes.

LESSON OVERVIEW (READ TO STUDENTS)

It is normal to come across words you do not know. One way to figure out unknown words is to use their word parts that signal or "fix" their meaning. We will call these parts at the beginning of words *prefixes* because they come before the rest of the word, and those parts at the end of the word *postfixes* because they come after the rest of the word. (Another term for the parts at the end of word is *suffixes*.) Words also have base parts that signal their meaning. Some words only have bases; some have prefixes and bases; some have bases and postfixes; and some have prefixes, bases, and postfixes. We will do seven different kinds of activities in each session to teach you to be Word Detectives who use these word parts to decode words: *Word Building, Word Generating, Unit Finding, Word Transferring, Are They Relatives? Sorting by Word Part Features,* and *Sorting by Sentence Context.* These activities should give you lots of strategies for using word parts to figure out words. We will use our electronic timer for the second through fourth activities but not for the others. Let's begin.

ACTIVITIES

Word Building

From this list of 30 words with highly frequent prefixes and derivational suffixes, 10 are presented in each lesson (1–14) and are presented three times altogether; but these will be randomized across the three presentations to avoid list learning effects. For the last two sessions (13 and 14), half of the list (15) is presented for a final review of the whole set. See the Student Response Booklet kept in your Word Detectives Work Folder. This set of affixes was generated by examining words in the McGraw-Hill Specific Skills *Working within Words Series* for Grades 3–6 and by reviewing morphological units in selected reading passages in *Read Naturally*. From these, Bill Nagy identified 30 suffixes that occur most frequently and thus are highly useful for struggling readers. Given limited instructional time, these are the ones on which to focus. Capital letters indicate these high-utility affixes, which were practiced in various lessons. The prefixes, bases, and postfixes are kept on 3 × 5 cards (or 5 × 8 cards or larger, depending on how large the word parts must be for all children in group to see them) in large envelopes—marked *prefixes, bases, and suffixes*—for the teacher to use in presenting the word parts and used as needed for a specific lesson (see Student Response Booklet for word parts). Then for each lesson, the teacher draws from the large envelopes the large cards with the word parts needed for each word in a lesson and holds them up high for all students to see. After one student correctly synthesizes the word parts to pronounce the word, each child writes the complete word built from its parts in the row on a worksheet.

Instructions: Word Detectives solve cases by combining clues. We will start by building words from word part clues. I will show you word parts. As soon as you know the word that can be formed by these parts, raise your hand. When we agree, I will write it on the board and you can copy it in your Student Response Booklet. You will build the words from a base and fixes (*prefixes* before the base, or *suffixes* after the base).

> different, unclear, remember, magical, invisible, harmless, scientist, brownish, nervous, creativity

Word Generating

Instructions: Word Detectives sometimes get their clues from generating and reasoning about similar cases. Readers can do the same—use what they know about words to generate new words in their minds. For 5 minutes, for each of the following word parts, think of a word that has that word part. Write the word in your Student Response Booklet. Go to the next word part and do the same, and so on. After 5 minutes, students share words generated for each word part. I will write one correct example for each word part on the board.

Note: Children do this independently for 5 minutes. Every 30 seconds, the teacher can prompt the children to try to think of a word for the next word part.

> ent, un, re, al, in, less, ist, ish, ous, ity

Unit Finding

Children are directed to the Student Response Booklet with lists of words and asked to underline the base word and circle the affixes. Children receive R-File points if all word part items are completed correctly within 2 minutes.

Instructions: Word Detectives solve mysteries by paying attention to details. The details you need to pay attention to in decoding are the base and the beginning and end "fixes" if there are any. Underline the base—the main meaning part of the word—and circle any fixes at the beginning or end that might modify or qualify that meaning. After 2 minutes, we will share with each other the word clues we found. I will write one shared correct example for each word part on the board.

> dependent, unpaid, review, accidental, income, careless, dentist, tallish, famous, electricity

Word Transferring

For each lesson, children read a list with 10 words containing the same affixes practiced under Word Building. They read the list to a teacher who times them, records the time on their R-File record, and indicates whether 1) the affix part was pronounced correctly and 2) the whole word was pronounced correctly.

Instructions: Once Word Detectives figure out the code, they can apply it to new words or cases. Here are some words that have the same parts that we have practiced. I will record how many you pronounce correctly and how long it took. We will graph your accuracy and time so you can see your progress.

> dependent, unpaid, review, accidental, income, careless, dentist, tallish, famous, electricity

Are They Relatives?

Does the first word come from the second word? The purpose of this task is to describe whether word parts at the end of a base word signal a semantic relationship with a base word. Children can record the total number they got correct.

Instructions: To solve puzzles, Word Detectives need to pay attention not only to clues in a single word but also to how the clues in a word may signal that words are related in meaning to other words they know. Just as a child comes from her or his parents, some words come from—that is, they are made from—meaning of other words and thus belong to the same family of word meanings, but other words are not from the same family of word meanings even though they may resemble other words in spelling or sound. I want you to listen carefully and after I say each pair of words, circle YES on your worksheet if you think the first word comes from the second one and circle NO if you do not think it does. After that, we will discuss any of your answers on which not everyone has agreed.

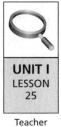
judgment	judge
architecture	architect
saddle	sad
carnival	car
fortune	fort
creation	create
cute	cut
progressive	progress
graduation	graduate
island	is

Sorting by Word Part Features

The rules children write are discussed to make sure that all have grasped the underlying principle for sorting the words into categories.

Instructions: Once Word Detectives get clues they have to make sense of them. They have to do a special kind of thinking in which they draw conclusions from the evidence, just as Sherlock Holmes and Dr. Watson did. In this activity you will sort words into categories, each of which has a word label and capital letter. Write the capital letter that shows the category to which each word belongs. When you complete the sort, you will be asked to write the rule you used in sorting words into categories. Then we will discuss the rules to make sure that everyone agrees.

Generalization: Suffix may mark part of speech.

Labels for cards: Suffix Creates Noun (person, place, thing) = A, Suffix Creates Verb (action) = B

(randomize) explorer, explores, argument, argues, multiplication, subtract, discussion, discussed, learner, learns, violinist, slept, musician, performed, governor, known, realization, realize

Sorting by Sentence Context

The purpose of this activity is to help children see the importance of analyzing words fully. The words in the Word Pool from which a word is chosen for the blank in the sentence are in the Student Record Form. Record for each lesson the number correct.

Instructions: Another way that Word Detectives have to make sense of their clues is by examining them for *context*—the place in which they occur and all the surrounding clues. Each of the three sentences you will see has a blank. Each of the Word Pools you will see has one word in the box that fits sensibly into the blank but mostly words that would not fit into the blank. To figure out which words would or would not fit into the blank—that is, into the context of the sentence—you need to pay close attention to all the spelling, sound, and meaning clues of the words in the pool and in the words in the sentence. You have to fully analyze all the evidence you have at hand! As soon as you think you know a word that would fit into the sentence, raise your hand. As a Word Detective, it is important that you examine all the evidence—consider all the words—before you make your decision about which word fits. If someone disagrees with you, we will discuss why or why not that word might work in that sentence.

When he made the coin disappear and then suddenly show up on the table, his mother

was proud he had learned a _____ trick.
(damaging, circular, magical, accidental)

Before using his father's tools, Sam had to get his father's _____.
(looseness, amazement, reversal, approval)

He bought tickets to all of his son's _____ events.
(lateness, historic, athletic, angelic, respectful)

LESSON **25** Morphological Awareness Treatment

Adding Word Parts for Meaning to Decoding

Student Response Booklet

Note: All lessons start with a warm-up, just as athletes warm up before a sports game. (See *Talking Letters* card.)

ACTIVITIES

Word Building

Instructions: Word Detectives solve cases by combining clues. We will start by building words from word part clues. I will show you word parts. As soon as you know the word that can be formed by these parts, raise your hand. When we agree, I will write it on the board and you can copy it in your Student Response Booklet. You will build the words from a base and fixes (*prefixes* before the base, or *suffixes* after the base).

differ + ent = _____

un + clear = _____

re + memory = _____

magic + al = _____

in + vision + able = _____

harm + less = _____

science + ist = _____

brown + ish = _____

nerve + ous = _____

create + ive + y = _____

Total correct = _____

Word Generating

Instructions: Word Detectives sometimes get their clues from generating and reasoning about similar cases. Readers can do the same—use what they know about words to generate new words in their minds. For 5 minutes, for each of the following word parts, think of a word that has that word part. Write the word in your Student Response Booklet. Go to the next word part and do the same, and so on. After 5 minutes, students share words generated for each word part. I will write one correct example for each word part on the board.

ent _____

un _____

re _____

al _____

in _____

less _____

ist _____

ish _____

ous _____

ity _____

Total new correct words generated in 5 minutes = _____

Unit Finding

Instructions: Word Detectives solve mysteries by paying attention to details. The details you need to pay attention to in decoding are the base and the beginning and end "fixes" if there are any. Underline the base—the main meaning part of the word—and circle any fixes at the beginning or end that might modify or qualify that meaning. After 2 minutes, we will share with each other the word clues we found. I will write one shared correct example for each word part on the board.

dependent	income	famous
unpaid	careless	electricity
review	dentist	
accidental	tallish	

Total number of words in which bases and fixes were correctly identified = _____

Word Transferring

Instructions: Once Word Detectives figure out the code, they can apply it to new words or cases. Here are some words that have the same parts that we have practiced. I will record how many you pronounce correctly and how long it took. We will graph your accuracy and time so you can see your progress.

dependent

unpaid

review

accidental

income

careless

dentist

tallish

famous

electricity

Correct words = _____   Correct affixes = _____

Total time = _____

Are They Relatives?

Instructions: To solve puzzles, Word Detectives need to pay attention not only to clues in a single word but also to how the clues in a word may signal that words are related in meaning to other words they know. Just as a child comes from her or his parents, some words come from—that is, they are made from—meaning of other words and thus belong to the same family of word meanings, but other words are not from the same family of word meanings even though they may resemble other words in spelling or sound. I want you to listen carefully and after I say each pair of words, circle YES on your worksheet if you think the first word comes from the second one and circle NO if you do not think it does. After that, we will discuss any of your answers on which not everyone has agreed.

Directions: Circle YES or NO beside the word pair.

judgment	judge	YES	NO
architecture	architect	YES	NO
saddle	sad	YES	NO
carnival	car	YES	NO
fortune	fort	YES	NO
creation	create	YES	NO

cute	cut	YES	NO
progressive	progress	YES	NO
graduation	graduate	YES	NO
island	is	YES	NO

Total correct in 2 minutes = _____

Sorting by Word Part Features

Instructions: Once Word Detectives get clues they have to make sense of them. They have to do a special kind of thinking in which they draw conclusions from the evidence, just as Sherlock Holmes and Dr. Watson did. In this activity you will sort words into categories, each of which has a word label and capital letter. Write the capital letter that shows the category to which each word belongs. When you complete the sort, you will be asked to write the rule you used in sorting words into categories. Then we will discuss the rules to make sure that everyone agrees.

Labels for categories: Suffix Creates Noun (person, place, thing) = A, Suffix Creates Verb (action) = B

explorer

explores

argument

argues

multiplication

subtract

discussion

discussed

learner

learns

violinist

slept

musician

performed

governor

known

realization

realize

Explain the rule you used to sort: _____

_____

_____

_____

_____

Number sorted correctly = _____

Sorting by Sentence Context

Instructions: Another way that Word Detectives have to make sense of their clues is by examining them for *context*—the place in which they occur and all the surrounding clues. Each of the three sentences you will see has a blank. Each of the Word Pools you will see has one word that fits sensibly into the blank but mostly words that would not fit into the blank. To figure out which words would or would not fit into the blank—that is, into the context of the sentence—you need to pay close attention to all the spelling, sound, and meaning clues of the words in the pool and in the words in the sentence. You have to fully analyze all the evidence you have at hand! As soon as you think you know a word that would fit into the sentence, raise your hand. As a Word Detective, it is important that you examine all the evidence—consider all the words—before you make your decision about which word fits. If someone disagrees with you, we will discuss why or why not that word might work in that sentence.

When he made the coin disappear and then suddenly show up on the

table, his mother was proud he had learned a _____ trick.
(damaging, circular, magical, accidental)

Before using his father's tools, Sam had to get his father's

_____.
(looseness, amazement, reversal, approval)

He bought tickets to all of his son's _____ events.
(lateness, historic, athletic, angelic, respectful)

LESSON 26 Morphological Awareness Treatment

Teacher Material

The following grapheme–phoneme correspondences are taught using *More Talking Letters:* • Consonant blends and vowel teams • Latinate and Greek	Materials needed: • *More Talking Letters* (see Table 1) for automatic alphabetic principles • Work folders

WARM-UP (FOR THE TEACHER)

For the warm-up, name the letter or letter group in *More Talking Letters* (see Table 1), say the pictured word containing a target phoneme, and then produce the target phoneme. Next, the students take a turn and repeat what is named or said by you. This approach develops orthographic awareness of spelling units; phonological awareness of corresponding phonemes in and out of word context; and, through close timing, the automaticity of spelling–phoneme correspondence. If Lessons 1–14 have been completed, just name the letter or letter group and produce the target phoneme, and then the students take a turn and repeat what you have said. Monitor whether children are coordinating looking at the relevant letters and pictured words with naming of the letters and words and producing phonemes.

LESSON OVERVIEW (READ TO STUDENTS)

It is normal to come across words you do not know. One way to figure out unknown words is to use their word parts that signal or "fix" their meaning. We will call these parts at the beginning of words *prefixes* because they come before the rest of the word, and those parts at the end of the word *postfixes* because they come after the rest of the word. (Another term for the parts at the end of word is *suffixes.*) Words also have base parts that signal their meaning. Some words only have bases; some have prefixes and bases; some have bases and postfixes; and some have prefixes, bases, and postfixes. We will do seven different kinds of activities in each session to teach you to be Word Detectives who use these word parts to decode words: *Word Building, Word Generating, Unit Finding, Word Transferring, Are They Relatives? Sorting by Word Part Features,* and *Sorting by Sentence Context.* These activities should give you lots of strategies for using word parts to figure out words. We will use our electronic timer for the second through fourth activities but not for the others. Let's begin.

ACTIVITIES

Word Building

From this list of 30 words with highly frequent prefixes and derivational suffixes, 10 are presented in each lesson (1–14) and are presented three times altogether; but these will be randomized across the three presentations to avoid list learning effects. For the last two sessions (13 and 14), half of the list (15) is presented for a final review of the whole set. See the Student Response Booklet kept in your Word Detectives Work Folder. This set of affixes was generated by examining words in the McGraw-Hill Specific Skills *Working within Words Series* for Grades 3–6 and by reviewing morphological units in selected reading passages in *Read Naturally.* From these, Bill Nagy identified 30 suffixes that occur most frequently and thus are highly useful for struggling readers. Given limited instructional time, these are the ones on which to focus. Capital letters indicate these high-utility affixes, which were practiced in various lessons. The prefixes, bases, and postfixes are kept on 3 × 5 cards (or 5 × 8 cards or larger, depending on how large the word parts must be for all children in group to see them) in large envelopes—marked *prefixes, bases, and suffixes*—for the teacher to use in presenting the word parts and used as needed for a specific lesson (see Student Response Booklet for word parts). Then for each lesson, the teacher draws from the large envelopes the large cards with the word parts needed for each word in a lesson and holds them up high for all students to see. After one student correctly synthesizes the word parts to pronounce the word, each child writes the complete word built from its parts in the row on a worksheet.

Instructions: Word Detectives solve cases by combining clues. We will start by building words from word part clues. I will show you word parts. As soon as you know the word that can be formed by these parts, raise your hand. When we agree, I will write it on the board and you can copy it in your Student Response Booklet. You will build the words from a base and fixes (*prefixes* before the base, or *suffixes* after the base).

> impolite, salty, reporter, announcement, mouthful, sickness, expensive, electric, amazing, toward

Word Generating

Instructions: Word Detectives sometimes get their clues from generating and reasoning about similar cases. Readers can do the same—use what they know about words to generate new words in their minds. For 5 minutes, for each of the following word parts, think of a word that has that word part. Write the word in your Student Response Booklet. Go to the next word part and do the same, and so on. After 5 minutes, students share words generated for each word part. I will write one correct example for each word part on the board.

Note: Children do this independently for 5 minutes. Every 30 seconds, the teacher can prompt the children to try to think of a word for the next word part.

> re, y, able, ent, ful, ness, ive, ic, ing, ward

Unit Finding

Children are directed to the Student Response Booklet with lists of words and asked to underline the base word and circle the affixes. Children receive R-File points if all word part items are completed correctly within 2 minutes.

Instructions: Word Detectives solve mysteries by paying attention to details. The details you need to pay attention to in decoding are the base and the beginning and end "fixes" if there are any. Underline the base—the main meaning part of the word—and circle any fixes at the beginning or end that might modify or qualify that meaning. After 2 minutes, we will share with each other the word clues we found. I will write one shared correct example for each word part on the board.

> replay, icy, laughable, excellent, colorful, loudness, talkative, angelic, thinking, sideward

Word Transferring

For each lesson, children read a list with 10 words containing the same affixes practiced under Word Building. They read the list to a teacher who times them, records the time on their R-File record, and indicates whether 1) the affix part was pronounced correctly and 2) the whole word was pronounced correctly.

Instructions: Once Word Detectives figure out the code, they can apply it to new words or cases. Here are some words that have the same parts that we have practiced. I will record how many you pronounce correctly and how long it took. We will graph your accuracy and time so you can see your progress.

> replay, icy, laughable, excellent, colorful, loudness, talkative, angelic, thinking, sideward

Sorting by Word Part Features

The rules children write are discussed to make sure that all have grasped the underlying principle for sorting the words into categories.

Instructions: Once Word Detectives get clues they have to make sense of them. They have to do a special kind of thinking in which they draw conclusions from the evidence, just as Sherlock Holmes and Dr. Watson did. In this activity you will sort words into categories, each of which has a word label and capital letter. Write the capital letter that shows the category to which each word belongs. When you complete the sort, you will be asked to write the rule you used in sorting words into categories. Then we will discuss the rules to make sure that everyone agrees.

difficult	cult
injury	jury

gradual	grade
exploratory	explore
spectator	special
powerful	power
catepillar	pillar
measurement	measure
movement	move
kidnap	nap

Sorting by Word Part Features

The rules children write are discussed to make sure that all have grasped the underlying principle for sorting the words into categories.

Instructions: Once Word Detectives get clues they have to make sense of them. They have to do a special kind of thinking in which they draw conclusions from the evidence, just as Sherlock Holmes and Dr. Watson did. In this activity you will sort words into categories, each of which has a word label and capital letter. Write the capital letter that shows the category to which each word belongs. When you complete the sort, you will be asked to write the rule you used in sorting words into categories. Then we will discuss the rules to make sure that everyone agrees.

Generalization: Suffix may mark part of speech.

Labels for cards: Suffix Creates Noun (person, place, thing) = A, Suffix Creates Adjective (characteristics of noun) = B

magician, magical, imagination, imaginary, reality, unrealistic, information, informative, informality, informal, cheerfulness, cheerful, expression, expressive

Sorting by Sentence Context

The purpose of this activity is to help children see the importance of analyzing words fully. The words in the Word Pool from which a word is chosen for the blank in the sentence are in the Student Record Form. Record for each lesson the number correct.

Instructions: Another way that Word Detectives have to make sense of their clues is by examining them for *context*—the place in which they occur and all the surrounding clues. Each of the three sentences you will see has a blank. Each of the Word Pools you will see has one word in the box that fits sensibly into the blank but mostly words that would not fit into the blank. To figure out which words would or would not fit into the blank—that is, into the context of the sentence—you need to pay close attention to all the spelling, sound, and meaning clues of the words in the pool and in the words in the sentence. You have to fully analyze all the evidence you have at hand! As soon as you think you know a word that would fit into the sentence, raise your hand. As a Word Detective, it is important that you examine all the evidence—consider all the words—before you make your decision about which word fits. If someone disagrees with you, we will discuss why or why not that word might work in that sentence.

Sometimes he ate a big breakfast, but _____ he ate just a banana.
(usually, heavily, luckily, busily, playfully)

He ripped his math paper on purpose, but then he said the tear was

_____.
(useful, accidental, laziness, magical, dreadful)

Mr. and Mrs. Lee are expecting their first baby, so they are new to _____.
(boyhood, peacefulness, parenthood, friendliness)

LESSON **26** Morphological Awareness Treatment
Adding Word Parts for Meaning to Decoding

Student Response Booklet

Note: All lessons start with a warm-up, just as athletes warm up before a sports game. (See *More Talking Letters*.)

ACTIVITIES

Word Building

Instructions: Word Detectives solve cases by combining clues. We will start by building words from word part clues. I will show you word parts. As soon as you know the word that can be formed by these parts, raise your hand. When we agree, I will write it on the board and you can copy it in your Student Response Booklet. You will build the words from a base and fixes (*prefixes* before the base, or *suffixes* after the base).

im + polite = _____

salt + y = _____

report + er = _____

announce + ment = _____

mouth + ful = _____

sick + ness = _____

expense + ive = _____

electric + y = _____

amaze + ment = _____

to + ward = _____

Total correct = _____

Word Generating

Instructions: Word Detectives sometimes get their clues from generating and reasoning about similar cases. Readers can do the same—use what they know about words to generate new words in their minds. For 5 minutes, for each of the following word parts, think of a word that has that word part. Write the word in your Student Response Booklet. Go to the next word part and do the same, and so on. After 5 minutes, students share words generated for each word part. I will write one correct example for each word part on the board.

re _____

y _____

able _____

ent _____

ful _____

ness _____

ive _____

ic _____

ing _____

ward _____

Total new correct words generated in 5 minutes = _____

Unit Finding

Instructions: Word Detectives solve mysteries by paying attention to details. The details you need to pay attention to in decoding are the base and the beginning and end "fixes" if there are any. Underline the base—the main meaning part of the word—and circle any fixes at the beginning or end that might modify or qualify that meaning. After 2 minutes, we will share with each other the word clues we found. I will write one shared correct example for each word part on the board.

replay	colorful	thinking
icy	loudness	sideward
laughable	talkative	
excellent	angelic	

Total number of words in which bases and fixes were correctly

identified = _____

Word Transferring

Instructions: Once Word Detectives figure out the code, they can apply it to new words or cases. Here are some words that have the same parts that we have practiced. I will record how many you pronounce correctly and how long it took. We will graph your accuracy and time so you can see your progress.

replay

icy

laughable

excellent

colorful

loudness

talkative

angelic

thinking

sideward

Correct words = _____   **Correct affixes = _____**

Total time = _____

Are They Relatives?

Instructions: To solve puzzles, Word Detectives need to pay attention not only to clues in a single word but also to how the clues in a word may signal that words are related in meaning to other words they know. Just as a child comes from her or his parents, some words come from—that is, they are made from—meaning of other words and thus belong to the same family of word meanings, but other words are not from the same family of word meanings even though they may resemble other words in spelling or sound. I want you to listen carefully and after I say each pair of words, circle YES on your worksheet if you think the first word comes from the second one and circle NO if you do not think it does. After that, we will discuss any of your answers on which not everyone has agreed.

Directions: Circle YES or NO beside the word pair.

difficult	cult	YES	NO
injury	jury	YES	NO
gradual	grade	YES	NO
exploratory	explore	YES	NO
spectator	special	YES	NO
powerful	power	YES	NO
caterpillar	pillar	YES	NO
measurement	measure	YES	NO

| movement | move | YES | NO |
| kidnap | nap | YES | NO |

Total correct in 2 minutes = _____

Sorting by Word Part Features

Instructions: Once Word Detectives get clues they have to make sense of them. They have to do a special kind of thinking in which they draw conclusions from the evidence, just as Sherlock Holmes and Dr. Watson did. In this activity you will sort words into categories, each of which has a word label and capital letter. Write the capital letter that shows the category to which each word belongs. When you complete the sort, you will be asked to write the rule you used in sorting words into categories. Then we will discuss the rules to make sure that everyone agrees.

Labels for categories: Suffix Creates Noun (person, place, thing) = A, Suffix Creates Adjective (characteristics of noun) = B

magician

magical

imagination

imaginary

reality

unrealistic

information

informative

informality

informal

cheerfulness

cheerful

expression

expressive

Explain the rule you used to sort: _____

_____

_____

_____

_____

Number sorted correctly = _____

Sorting by Sentence Context

Instructions: Another way that Word Detectives have to make sense of their clues is by examining them for *context*—the place in which they occur and all the surrounding clues. Each of the three sentences you will see has a blank. Each of the Word Pools you will see has one word that fits sensibly into the blank but mostly words that would not fit into the blank. To figure out which words would or would not fit into the blank—that is, into the context of the sentence—you need to pay close attention to all the spelling, sound, and meaning clues of the words in the pool and in the words in the sentence. You have to fully analyze all the evidence you have at hand! As soon as you think you know a word that would fit into the sentence, raise your hand. As a Word Detective, it is important that you examine all the evidence—consider all the words—before you make your decision about which word fits. If someone disagrees with you, we will discuss why or why not that word might work in that sentence.

Sometimes he ate a big breakfast, but _____ he ate just a banana.
(usually, heavily, luckily, busily, playfully)

He ripped his math paper on purpose, but then he said the tear was

_____.
(useful, accidental, laziness, magical, dreadful)

Mr. and Mrs. Lee are expecting their first baby, so they are new to

_____.
(boyhood, peacefulness, parenthood, friendliness)

LESSON 27 Morphological Awareness Treatment

Teacher Material

The following grapheme–phoneme correspondences are taught using *Talking Letters:*
- Single-letter consonants
- Short vowels in closed syllables
- Long vowels in open syllables

Materials needed:
- *Talking Letters* for automatic alphabetic principles
- Work folders

WARM-UP (FOR THE TEACHER)

For the warm-up, name the letter or letter group on the *Talking Letters* card, say the pictured word containing a target phoneme, and then produce the target phoneme. Next, the students take a turn and repeat what is named or said by you. This approach develops orthographic awareness of spelling units; phonological awareness of corresponding phonemes in and out of word context; and, through close timing, the automaticity of spelling–phoneme correspondence. If Lessons 1–14 have been completed, just name the letter or letter group and produce the target phoneme, and then the students take a turn and repeat what you have said. Monitor whether children are coordinating looking at the relevant letters and pictured words with naming of the letters and words and producing phonemes.

LESSON OVERVIEW (READ TO STUDENTS)

It is normal to come across words you do not know. One way to figure out unknown words is to use their word parts that signal or "fix" their meaning. We will call these parts at the beginning of words *prefixes* because they come before the rest of the word, and those parts at the end of the word *postfixes* because they come after the rest of the word. (Another term for the parts at the end of word is *suffixes.*) Words also have base parts that signal their meaning. Some words only have bases; some have prefixes and bases; some have bases and postfixes; and some have prefixes, bases, and postfixes. We will do seven different kinds of activities in each session to teach you to be Word Detectives who use these word parts to decode words: *Word Building, Word Generating, Unit Finding, Word Transferring, Are They Relatives? Sorting by Word Part Features,* and *Sorting by Sentence Context.* These activities should give you lots of strategies for using word parts to figure out words. We will use our electronic timer for the second through fourth activities but not for the others. Let's begin.

ACTIVITIES

Word Building

From this list of 30 words with highly frequent prefixes and derivational suffixes, 10 are presented in each lesson (1–14) and are presented three times altogether; but these will be randomized across the three presentations to avoid list learning effects. For the last two sessions (13 and 14), half of the list (15) is presented for a final review of the whole set. See the Student Response Booklet kept in your Word Detectives Work Folder. This set of affixes was generated by examining words in the McGraw-Hill Specific Skills *Working within Words Series* for Grades 3–6 and by reviewing morphological units in selected reading passages in *Read Naturally*. From these, Bill Nagy identified 30 suffixes that occur most frequently and thus are highly useful for struggling readers. Given limited instructional time, these are the ones on which to focus. Capital letters indicate these high-utility affixes, which were practiced in various lessons. The prefixes, bases, and postfixes are kept on 3 × 5 cards (or 5 × 8 cards or larger, depending on how large the word parts must be for all children in group to see them) in large envelopes—marked *prefixes, bases, and suffixes*—for the teacher to use in presenting the word parts and used as needed for a specific lesson (see Student Response Booklet for word parts). Then for each lesson, the teacher draws from the large envelopes the large cards with the word parts needed for each word in a lesson and holds them up high for all students to see. After one student correctly synthesizes the word parts to pronounce the word, each child writes the complete word built from its parts in the row on a worksheet.

Instructions: Word Detectives solve cases by combining clues. We will start by building words from word part clues. I will show you word parts. As soon as you know the word that can be formed by these parts, raise your hand. When we agree, I will write it on the board and you can copy it in your Student Response Booklet. You will build the words from a base and fixes (*prefixes* before the base, or *suffixes* after the base).

> washable, magical, dislike, important, leadership, nervous, announcement, sickness, impolite

Word Generating

Instructions: Word Detectives sometimes get their clues from generating and reasoning about similar cases. Readers can do the same—use what they know about words to generate new words in their minds. For 5 minutes, for each of the following word parts, think of a word that has that word part. Write the word in your Student Response Booklet. Go to the next word part and do the same, and so on. After 5 minutes, students share words generated for each word part. I will write one correct example for each word part on the board.

Note: Children do this independently for 5 minutes. Every 30 seconds, the teacher can prompt the children to try to think of a word for the next word part.

> able, al, dis, ant, ship, ous, ment, ness, im, er, y, en, tion, ish, ic

Unit Finding

Children are directed to the Student Response Booklet with lists of words and asked to underline the base word and circle the affixes. Children receive R-File points if all word part items are completed correctly within 2 minutes.

Instructions: Word Detectives solve mysteries by paying attention to details. The details you need to pay attention to in decoding are the base and the beginning and end "fixes" if there are any. Underline the base—the main meaning part of the word—and circle any fixes at the beginning or end that might modify or qualify that meaning. After 2 minutes, we will share with each other the word clues we found. I will write one shared correct example for each word part on the board.

> lovable, musical, disagree, distant, friendship, courageous, enjoyment, loudness, important, teacher, sunny, brighten, attention, selfish, athletic

Word Transferring

For each lesson, children read a list with 10 words containing the same affixes practiced under Word Building. They read the list to a teacher who times them, records the time on their R-File record, and indicates whether 1) the affix part was pronounced correctly and 2) the whole word was pronounced correctly.

Instructions: Once Word Detectives figure out the code, they can apply it to new words or cases. Here are some words that have the same parts that we have practiced. I will record how many you pronounce correctly and how long it took. We will graph your accuracy and time so you can see your progress.

> lovable, musical, disagree, distant, friendship, courageous, enjoyment, loudness, important, teacher, sunny, brighten, attention, selfish, athletic

Are They Relatives?

Does the first word come from the second word? The purpose of this task is to describe whether word parts at the end of a base word signal a semantic relationship with a base word. Children can record the total number they got correct.

Instructions: To solve puzzles, Word Detectives need to pay attention not only to clues in a single word but also to how the clues in a word may signal that words are related in meaning to other words they know. Just as a child comes from her or his parents, some words come from—that is, they are made from—meaning of other words and thus belong to the same family of word meanings, but other words are not from the same family of word meanings even though they may resemble other words in spelling or sound. I want you to listen carefully and after I say each pair of words, circle YES on your worksheet if you think the first word comes from the second one and circle NO if you do not think it does. After that, we will discuss any of your answers on which not everyone has agreed.

unreasonable	reason
attention	tent
psychologist	psychology
attendance	dance
interest	rest
biologist	biology
scientist	science
appendicitis	appendix
promise	prom
subscribe	crib

Sorting by Word Part Features

The rules children write are discussed to make sure that all have grasped the underlying principle for sorting the words into categories.

Instructions: Once Word Detectives get clues they have to make sense of them. They have to do a special kind of thinking in which they draw conclusions from the evidence, just as Sherlock Holmes and Dr. Watson did. In this activity you will sort words into categories, each of which has a word label and capital letter. Write the capital letter that shows the category to which each word belongs. When you complete the sort, you will be asked to write the rule you used in sorting words into categories. Then we will discuss the rules to make sure that everyone agrees.

Generalization: Some words have more than one suffix.

Labels for cards: One Prefix = A, One Suffix = B, Two Suffixes = C

(randomize) return, remember, pretend, cooperate, transmit, invite, dislike, displays, misspell, extend, slowly, quickly, happily, sadly, quietly, successfully, respectfully, factually, officially, sensitively

Sorting by Sentence Context

The purpose of this activity is to help children see the importance of analyzing words fully. The words in the Word Pool from which a word is chosen for the blank in the sentence are in the Student Record Form. Record for each lesson the number correct.

Instructions: Another way that Word Detectives have to make sense of their clues is by examining them for *context*—the place in which they occur and all the surrounding clues. Each of the three sentences you will see has a blank. Each of the Word Pools you will see has one word in the box that fits sensibly into the blank but mostly words that would not fit into the blank. To figure out which words would or would not fit into the blank—that is, into the context of the sentence—you need to pay close attention to all the spelling, sound, and meaning clues of the words in the pool and in the words in the sentence. You have to fully analyze all the evidence you have at hand! As soon as you think you know a word that would fit into the sentence, raise your hand. As a Word Detective, it is important that you examine all the evidence—consider all the words—before you make your decision about which word fits. If someone disagrees with you, we will discuss why or why not that word might work in that sentence.

He paid a _____ bill for cable television services.
(careless, enjoyable, monthly, friendly)

The television comedy show was a great source of _____.
(enjoyment, enjoyable, treatment, humorous)

He asked his friend to drive because he was worried about his _____.
(silliness, movement, leadership, sleepiness)

LESSON **27** Morphological Awareness Treatment
Adding Word Parts for Meaning to Decoding

Student Response Booklet

Note: All lessons start with a warm-up, just as athletes warm up before a sports game. (See *Talking Letters* card.)

ACTIVITIES

Word Building

Instructions: Word Detectives solve cases by combining clues. We will start by building words from word part clues. I will show you word parts. As soon as you know the word that can be formed by these parts, raise your hand. When we agree, I will write it on the board and you can copy it in your Student Response Booklet. You will build the words from a base and fixes (*prefixes* before the base, or *suffixes* after the base).

wash + able = _____

magic + al = _____

dis + like = _____

un + import + ant = _____

lead + er + ship = _____

nerve + ous = _____

announce + ment = _____

sick + ness = _____

im + polite = _____

Total correct = _____

Word Generating

Instructions: Word Detectives sometimes get their clues from generating and reasoning about similar cases. Readers can do the same—use what they know about words to generate new words in their minds. For 5 minutes, for each of the following word parts, think of a word that has that word part. Write the word in your Student Response Booklet. Go to the next word part and do the same, and so on. After 5 minutes, students share words generated for each word part. I will write one correct example for each word part on the board.

able _____

al _____

dis _____

ant _____

ship _____

ous _____

ment _____

ness _____

im _____

er _____

y _____

en _____

tion _____

ish _____

ic _____

Total new correct words generated in 5 minutes = _____

Unit Finding

Instructions: Word Detectives solve mysteries by paying attention to details. The details you need to pay attention to in decoding are the base and the beginning and end "fixes" if there are any. Underline the base—the main meaning part of the word—and circle any fixes at the beginning or end that

might modify or qualify that meaning. After 2 minutes, we will share with each other the word clues we found. I will write one shared correct example for each word part on the board.

lovable	friendship	important	attention
musical	courageous	teacher	selfish
disagree	enjoyment	sunny	athletic
distant	loudness	brighten	

Total number of words in which bases and fixes were correctly identified = _____

Word Transferring

Instructions: Once Word Detectives figure out the code, they can apply it to new words or cases. Here are some words that have the same parts that we have practiced. I will record how many you pronounce correctly and how long it took. We will graph your accuracy and time so you can see your progress.

lovable

musical

disagree

distant

friendship

courageous

enjoyment

loudness

important

teacher

sunny

brighten

attention

selfish

athletic

Correct words = _____   **Correct affixes =** _____

Total time = _____

Are They Relatives?

Instructions: To solve puzzles, Word Detectives need to pay attention not only to clues in a single word but also to how the clues in a word may signal that words are related in meaning to other words they know. Just as a child comes from her or his parents, some words come from—that is, they are made from—meaning of other words and thus belong to the same family of word meanings, but other words are not from the same family of word meanings even though they may resemble other words in spelling or sound. I want you to listen carefully and after I say each pair of words, circle YES on your worksheet if you think the first word comes from the second one and circle NO if you do not think it does. After that, we will discuss any of your answers on which not everyone has agreed.

Directions: Circle YES or NO beside the word pair.

unreasonable	reason	YES	NO
attention	tent	YES	NO
psychologist	psychology	YES	NO
attendance	dance	YES	NO
interest	rest	YES	NO
biologist	biology	YES	NO
scientist	science	YES	NO
appendicitis	appendix	YES	NO
promise	prom	YES	NO
subscribe	crib	YES	NO

Total correct in 2 minutes = _____

Sorting by Word Part Features

Instructions: Once Word Detectives get clues they have to make sense of them. They have to do a special kind of thinking in which they draw conclusions from the evidence, just as Sherlock Holmes and Dr. Watson did. In this activity you will sort words into categories, each of which has a word label and capital letter. Write the capital letter that shows the category to which each word belongs. When you complete the sort, you will be asked to write the rule you used in sorting words into categories. Then we will discuss the rules to make sure that everyone agrees.

Labels for categories: Prefix = A, One Suffix = B,
Two Suffixes = C

return

remember

pretend

cooperate

transmit

invite

dislike

displays

misspell

extend

slowly

quickly

happily

sadly

quietly

successfully

respectfully

factually

officially

sensitively

Explain the rule you used to sort: _____

_____

_____

_____

_____

Number sorted correctly = _____

Sorting by Sentence Context

Instructions: Another way that Word Detectives have to make sense of their clues is by examining them for *context*—the place in which they occur and all the surrounding clues. Each of the three sentences you will see has a blank. Each of the Word Pools you will see has one word that fits sensibly into the blank but mostly words that would not fit into the blank. To figure out which words would or would not fit into the blank—that is, into the context of the sentence—you need to pay close attention to all the spelling, sound, and meaning clues of the words in the pool and in the words in the sentence. You have to fully analyze all the evidence you have at hand! As soon as you think you know a word that would fit into the sentence, raise your hand. As a Word Detective, it is important that you examine all the evidence—consider all the words—before you make your decision about which word fits. If someone disagrees with you, we will discuss why or why not that word might work in that sentence.

He paid a _____ bill for cable television services.
(careless, enjoyable, monthly, friendly)

The television comedy show was a great source of

_____.

(enjoyment, enjoyable, treatment, humorous)

He asked his friend to drive because he was worried about his

_____.

(silliness, movement, leadership, sleepiness)

LESSON 28 Morphological Awareness Treatment

Teacher Material

The following grapheme–phoneme correspondences are taught using *Talking Letters:*
• Consonant blends and vowel teams

Materials needed:
• *Talking Letters* for automatic alphabetic principles
• Work folders

WARM-UP (FOR THE TEACHER)

For the warm-up, name the letter or letter group on the *Talking Letters* card, say the pictured word containing a target phoneme, and then produce the target phoneme. Next, the students take a turn and repeat what is named or said by you. This approach develops orthographic awareness of spelling units; phonological awareness of corresponding phonemes in and out of word context; and, through close timing, the automaticity of spelling–phoneme correspondence. If Lessons 1–14 have been completed, just name the letter or letter group and produce the target phoneme, and then the students take a turn and repeat what you have said. Monitor whether children are coordinating looking at the relevant letters and pictured words with naming of the letters and words and producing phonemes.

LESSON OVERVIEW (READ TO STUDENTS)

It is normal to come across words you do not know. One way to figure out unknown words is to use their word parts that signal or "fix" their meaning. We will call these parts at the beginning of words *prefixes* because they come before the rest of the word, and those parts at the end of the word *postfixes* because they come after the rest of the word. (Another term for the parts at the end of word is *suffixes.*) Words also have base parts that signal their meaning. Some words only have bases; some have prefixes and bases; some have bases and postfixes; and some have prefixes, bases, and postfixes. We will do seven different kinds of activities in each session to teach you to be Word Detectives who use these word parts to decode words: *Word Building, Word Generating, Unit Finding, Word Transferring, Are They Relatives? Sorting by Word Part Features,* and *Sorting by Sentence Context.* These activities should give you lots of strategies for using word parts to figure out words. We will use our electronic timer for the second through fourth activities but not for the others. Let's begin.

ACTIVITIES

Word Building

From this list of 30 words with highly frequent prefixes and derivational suffixes, 10 are presented in each lesson (1–14) and are presented three times altogether; but these will be randomized across the three presentations to avoid list learning effects. For the last two sessions (13 and 14), half of the list (15) is presented for a final review of the whole set. See the Student Response Booklet kept in your Word Detectives Work Folder. This set of affixes was generated by examining words in the McGraw-Hill Specific Skills *Working within Words Series* for Grades 3–6 and by reviewing morphological units in selected reading passages in *Read Naturally*. From these, Bill Nagy identified 30 suffixes that occur most frequently and thus are highly useful for struggling readers. Given limited instructional time, these are the ones on which to focus. Capital letters indicate these high-utility affixes, which were practiced in various lessons. The prefixes, bases, and postfixes are kept on 3 × 5 cards (or 5 × 8 cards or larger, depending on how large the word parts must be for all children in group to see them) in large envelopes—marked *prefixes, bases, and suffixes*—for the teacher to use in presenting the word parts and used as needed for a specific lesson (see Student Response Booklet for word parts). Then for each lesson, the teacher draws from the large envelopes the large cards with the word parts needed for each word in a lesson and holds them up high for all students to see. After one student correctly synthesizes the word parts to pronounce the word, each child writes the complete word built from its parts in the row on a worksheet.

Instructions: Word Detectives solve cases by combining clues. We will start by building words from word part clues. I will show you word parts. As soon as you know the word that can be formed by these parts, raise your hand. When we agree, I will write it on the board and you can copy it in your Student Response Booklet. You will build the words from a base and fixes (*prefixes* before the base, or *suffixes* after the base).

> unclear, completely, harmless, mouthful, scientist, elementary, northern, different, amazing, projector

Word Generating

Instructions: Word Detectives sometimes get their clues from generating and reasoning about similar cases. Readers can do the same—use what they know about words to generate new words in their minds. For 5 minutes, for each of the following word parts, think of a word that has that word part. Write the word in your Student Response Booklet. Go to the next word part and do the same, and so on. After 5 minutes, students share words generated for each word part. I will write one correct example for each word part on the board.

Note: Children do this independently for 5 minutes. Every 30 seconds, the teacher can prompt the children to try to think of a word for the next word part.

> re, un, in, ly, less, ful, ist, ive, ary, ern, ward, ent, ing, or, ity

Unit Finding

Children are directed to the Student Response Booklet with lists of words and asked to underline the base word and circle the affixes. Children receive R-File points if all word part items are completed correctly within 2 minutes.

Instructions: Word Detectives solve mysteries by paying attention to details. The details you need to pay attention to in decoding are the base and the beginning and end "fixes" if there are any. Underline the base—the main meaning part of the word—and circle any fixes at the beginning or end that might modify or qualify that meaning. After 2 minutes, we will share with each other the word clues we found. I will write one shared correct example for each word part on the board.

> repeat, unfair, income, happily, hopeless, helpful, artist, talkative, dictionary, eastern, backward, excellent, thinking, senator, electricity

Word Transferring

For each lesson, children read a list with 10 words containing the same affixes practiced under Word Building. They read the list to a teacher who times them, records the time on their R-File record, and indicates whether 1) the affix part was pronounced correctly and 2) the whole word was pronounced correctly.

Instructions: Once Word Detectives figure out the code, they can apply it to new words or cases. Here are some words that have the same parts that we have practiced. I will record how many you pronounce correctly and how long it took. We will graph your accuracy and time so you can see your progress.

> repeat, unfair, income, happily, hopeless, helpful, artist, talkative, dictionary, eastern, backward, excellent, thinking, senator, electricity

Are They Relatives?

Does the first word come from the second word? The purpose of this task is to describe whether word parts at the end of a base word signal a semantic relationship with a base word. Children can record the total number they got correct.

Instructions: To solve puzzles, Word Detectives need to pay attention not only to clues in a single word but also to how the clues in a word may signal that words are related in meaning to other words they know. Just as a child comes from her or his parents, some words come from—that is, they are made from—meaning of other words and thus belong to the same family of word meanings, but other words are not from the same family of word meanings even though they may resemble other words in spelling or sound. I want you to listen carefully and after I say each pair of words, circle YES on your worksheet if you think the first word comes from the second one and circle NO if you do not think it does. After that, we will discuss any of your answers on which not everyone has agreed.

pleasure	sure
happen	pen
great	eat
insecticide	insect
microscopic	microscope
flower	flow
democratic	democracy
interrupt	up
geographical	geography
comparison	compare

Sorting by Word Part Features

The rules children write are discussed to make sure that all have grasped the underlying principle for sorting the words into categories.

Instructions: Once Word Detectives get clues they have to make sense of them. They have to do a special kind of thinking in which they draw conclusions from the evidence, just as Sherlock Holmes and Dr. Watson did. In this activity you will sort words into categories, each of which has a word label and capital letter. Write the capital letter that shows the category to which each word belongs. When you complete the sort, you will be asked to write the rule you used in sorting words into categories. Then we will discuss the rules to make sure that everyone agrees.

Generalization: Sometimes words have two suffixes.

Labels for cards: Suffix Creates Adjective (qualities of nouns) = A, Suffix Creates Adverb (qualities of verbs) = B

(randomize) generous, humorous, serious, courageous, attentive, attractive, successful, joyful, persistently, independently, increasingly, collectively, correctly, brilliantly, friendly, shyly

Sorting by Sentence Context

The purpose of this activity is to help children see the importance of analyzing words fully. The words in the Word Pool from which a word is chosen for the blank in the sentence are in the Student Record Form. Record for each lesson the number correct.

Instructions: Another way that Word Detectives have to make sense of their clues is by examining them for *context*—the place in which they occur and all the surrounding clues. Each of the three sentences you will see has a blank. Each of the Word Pools you will see has one word in the box that fits sensibly into the blank but mostly words that would not fit into the blank. To figure out which words would or would not fit into the blank—that is, into the context of the sentence—you need to pay close attention to all the spelling, sound, and meaning clues of the words in the pool and in the words in the sentence. You have to fully analyze all the evidence you have at hand! As soon as you think you know a word that would fit into the sentence, raise your hand. As a Word Detective, it is important that you examine all the evidence—consider all the words—before you make your decision about which word fits. If someone disagrees with you, we will discuss why or why not that word might work in that sentence.

The damaged airplane was not _____.
(courageous, allowable, dangerous, flyable)

Word Detectives analyze each word _____.
(fuller, quickly, fullest, fully)

Once the student became a Word Detective, reading was _____.
(easily, enjoyment, easier, enjoying)

LESSON **28** | Morphological Awareness Treatment
Adding Word Parts for Meaning to Decoding

Student Response Booklet

Note: All lessons start with a warm-up, just as athletes warm up before a sports game. (See *Talking Letters* card.)

ACTIVITIES

Word Building

Instructions: Word Detectives solve cases by combining clues. We will start by building words from word part clues. I will show you word parts. As soon as you know the word that can be formed by these parts, raise your hand. When we agree, I will write it on the board and you can copy it in your Student Response Booklet. You will build the words from a base and fixes (*prefixes* before the base, or *suffixes* after the base).

un + clear = _____

complete + ly = _____

harm + less = _____

mouth + ful = _____

science + ist = _____

element + ary = _____

north + ern = _____

differ + ent = _____

amaze + ing = _____

project + or = _____

Total correct + _____

Word Generating

Instructions: Word Detectives sometimes get their clues from generating and reasoning about similar cases. Readers can do the same—use what they know about words to generate new words in their minds. For 5 minutes, for each of the following word parts, think of a word that has that word part. Write the word in your Student Response Booklet. Go to the next word part and do the same, and so on. After 5 minutes, students share words generated for each word part. I will write one correct example for each word part on the board.

re _____

un _____

in _____

ly _____

less _____

ful _____

ist _____

ive _____

ary _____

ern _____

ward _____

ent _____

ing _____

ity _____

Total new correct words generated in 5 minutes = _____

Unit Finding

Instructions: Word Detectives solve mysteries by paying attention to details. The details you need to pay attention to in decoding are the base and the beginning and end "fixes" if there are any. Underline the base—the main meaning part of the word—and circle any fixes at the beginning or end that might modify or qualify that meaning. After 2 minutes, we will share with each other the word clues we found. I will write one shared correct example for each word part on the board.

repeat	hopeless	dictionary	thinking
unfair	helpful	eastern	senator
income	artist	backward	electricity
happily	talkative	excellent	

Total number of words in which bases and fixes were correctly identified = _____

Word Transferring

Instructions: Once Word Detectives figure out the code, they can apply it to new words or cases. Here are some words that have the same parts that we have practiced. I will record how many you pronounce correctly and how long it took. We will graph your accuracy and time so you can see your progress.

repeat

unfair

income

happily

hopeless

helpful

artist

talkative

dictionary

eastern

backward

excellent

thinking

senator

electricity

Correct words = _____   **Correct affixes** = _____

Total time = _____

Are They Relatives?

Instructions: To solve puzzles, Word Detectives need to pay attention not only to clues in a single word but also to how the clues in a word may signal that words are related in meaning to other words they know. Just as a child comes from her or his parents, some words come from—that is, they are made

from—meaning of other words and thus belong to the same family of word meanings, but other words are not from the same family of word meanings even though they may resemble other words in spelling or sound. I want you to listen carefully and after I say each pair of words, circle YES on your worksheet if you think the first word comes from the second one and circle NO if you do not think it does. After that, we will discuss any of your answers on which not everyone has agreed.

Directions: Circle YES or NO beside the word pair.

pleasure	sure	YES	NO
happen	pen	YES	NO
great	eat	YES	NO
insecticide	insect	YES	NO
microscopic	microscope	YES	NO
flower	flow	YES	NO
democratic	democracy	YES	NO
interrupt	up	YES	NO
geographical	geography	YES	NO
comparison	compare	YES	NO

Total correct in 2 minutes = _____

Sorting by Word Part Features

Instructions: Once Word Detectives get clues they have to make sense of them. They have to do a special kind of thinking in which they draw conclusions from the evidence, just as Sherlock Holmes and Dr. Watson did. In this activity you will sort words into categories, each of which has a word label and capital letter. Write the capital letter that shows the category to which each word belongs. When you complete the sort, you will be asked to write the rule you used in sorting words into categories. Then we will discuss the rules to make sure that everyone agrees.

Labels for categories: Suffix for Adjective (describes noun) = A, Suffix for Adverb (describes verb) = B, Two Suffixes = C

generous

humorous

serious

courageous

attentive

attractive

successful

joyful

persistently

independently
increasingly
collectively
correctly
brilliantly
friendly
shyly

Explain the rule you used to sort: _____

_____

_____

_____

Number sorted correctly = _____

Sorting by Sentence Context

Instructions: Another way that Word Detectives have to make sense of their clues is by examining them for *context*—the place in which they occur and all the surrounding clues. Each of the three sentences you will see has a blank. Each of the Word Pools you will see has one word that fits sensibly into the blank but mostly words that would not fit into the blank. To figure out which words would or would not fit into the blank—that is, into the context of the sentence—you need to pay close attention to all the spelling, sound, and meaning clues of the words in the pool and in the words in the sentence. You have to fully analyze all the evidence you have at hand! As soon as you think you know a word that would fit into the sentence, raise your hand. As a Word Detective, it is important that you examine all the evidence—consider all the words—before you make your decision about which word fits. If someone disagrees with you, we will discuss why or why not that word might work in that sentence.

The damaged airplane was not _____.
(courageous, allowable, dangerous, flyable)

Word Detectives analyze each word _____.
(fuller, quickly, fullest, fully)

Once the student became a Word Detective, reading was

_____.

(easily, enjoyment, easier, enjoying)

REFERENCES

Aylward, E., Richards, T., Berninger, V.W., Nagy, W., Field, K., Grimme, A., et al. (2003). Instructional treatment associated with changes in brain activation in children with dyslexia. *Neurology, 61,* 212–219.

Bear, D., Invernizzi, M., Templeton, S., & Johnston, F. (2000). *Words their way: Word study for phonics, vocabulary, and spelling instruction* (2nd ed.). Upper Saddle River, NJ: Merrill Prentice Hall.

Berninger, V.W. (1994). *Reading and writing acquisition: A developmental neuropsychological perspective.* Madison, WI: WCB Brown & Benchmark Publishing. Reprinted 1996, Westview Press, Boulder, CO.

Berninger, V.W. (1998). *PAL Intervention Kit: Talking Letters cards.* San Antonio, TX: Pearson Assessment.

Berninger, V.W. (2007). *Process Assessment of the Learner, Second Edition (PAL-II): Diagnostic for reading and writing* (PAL-II Reading and Writing). San Antonio, TX: Pearson Assessment.

Berninger, V.W., Abbott, R.D., Abbott, S.P., Graham, S., & Richards, T. (2002). Writing and reading: Connections between language by hand and language by eye. *Journal of Learning Disabilities, 35,* 39–56.

Berninger, V.W., & Abbott, S.P. (2003). *PAL research-supported reading and writing lessons.* San Antonio, TX: Pearson Assessment. Also PAL Reproducibles for the Lessons.

Berninger, V.W., Nagy, W., Carlisle, J.F., Thomson, J., Hoffer, D., Abbott, S.P., et al. (2003). Effective treatment for dyslexics in grades 4 to 6. In B. Foorman (Ed.), *Preventing and remediating reading difficulties: Bringing science to scale* (pp. 382–417). Timonium, MD: York Press.

Berninger, V.W., Raskind, W., Richards, T., Abbott, R.D., & Stock, P. (2008). A multidisciplinary approach to understanding developmental dyslexia within working-memory architecture: Genotypes, phenotypes, brain, and instruction. *Developmental Neuropsychology, 33,* 707–744.

Berninger, V.W., & Richards, T. (2002). *Brain literacy for educators and psychologists.* New York: Academic Press.

Chenault, B., Thomson, J., Abbott, R., & Berninger, V.W. (2006). Effects of prior attention training on child dyslexics' response to composition instruction. *Developmental Neuropsychology, 29,* 243–260.

Doyle, A.C. (1986). *The adventures of Sherlock Holmes.* New York: Penguin Group.

Duffy, G. (2002). The case for direct explanation of strategies. In M. Pressley & C. Block (Eds.), *Comprehension instruction: Research-based best practices* (pp. 28–41). New York: Guilford Press.

Fuchs, L., & Fuchs, D. (1999). Monitoring student progress toward the development of reading competence: A review of three forms of classroom-based assessment. *School Psychology Review, 28,* 659–671.

Fuchs, L., Fuchs, D., Hamlet, C., Phillips, N., & Bentz, J. (1994). Classwide curriculum-based measurement: Helping general educators meet the challenge of student diversity. *Exceptional Children, 60,* 518–537.

Henry, M. (1990). *Words integrated: Integrated decoding and spelling instruction based on word origin and word structure.* Austin, TX: PRO-ED.

Ihnot, C. (1997). *Read naturally.* St. Paul, MN: Turman Publishing.

Kaufman, A.S., & Kaufman, N.L. (2004). *Kaufman Test of Educational Achievement, Second Edition.* San Antonio, TX: Pearson Assessment.

Kintsch, W. (1998). *Comprehension: A paradigm for cognition.* Cambridge, England: Cambridge University Press.

Nagy, W., Berninger, V.W., & Abbott, R.D. (2006). Contributions of morphology beyond phonology to literacy outcomes of upper elementary and middle school students. *Journal of Educational Psychology, 98,* 134–147.

Nagy, W., Berninger, V.W., Abbott, R.D., Vaughan, K., & Vermeulen, K. (2003). Relationship of morphology and other language skills to literacy skills in at-risk second graders and at-risk fourth grade writers. *Journal of Educational Psychology, 95,* 730–742.

National Reading Panel. (2000). *Teaching children to read: An evidence-based assessment of the scientific research literature on reading and its applications for reading instruction.* Washington, DC: National Institute of Child Health and Human Development.

Richards, T., Aylward, E., Raskind, W., Abbott, R.D., Field, K., Parsons, A., et al. (2006). Converging evidence for triple word form theory in children with dyslexia. *Developmental Neuropsychology, 30,* 547–589.

Richards, T., Berninger, V.W., Aylward, E., Richards, A., Thomson, J., Nagy, W., et al. (2002). Reproducibility of proton MR spectroscopic imaging (PEPSI): Comparison of dyslexic and normal reading children and effects of treatment on brain lactate levels during language tasks. *American Journal of Neuroradiology, 23,* 1678–1685.

Thomson, J., Chenault, B., Abbott, R.D., Raskind, W., Richards, T., Aylward, E., et al. (2005). Converging evidence for attentional influences on the orthographic word form in child dyslexics. *Journal of Neurolinguistics, 18,* 93–126.

Torgesen, J., Wagner, R., & Rashotte, C. (1999). *Test of Word Reading Efficiency.* Austin, TX: PRO-ED.

Venezky, R. (1970). *The structure of English orthography.* The Hague: Mouton.

Venezky, R. (1999). *The American way of spelling.* New York: Guilford Press.

Wechsler, D. (2001). *Wechsler Individual Achievement Test–Second Edition (WIAT-II).* San Antonio, TX: Pearson Assessment.

Woodcock, R.W. (1987). *Woodcock Reading Mastery Test–Revised.* Circle Pines, MN: American Guidance Service.

Woodcock, R.W., McGrew, K.S., & Mather, N. (2000). *Woodcock-Johnson III: Tests of Achievement.* Itasca, IL: Riverside.

Mark Twain Writers Workshop

Why It Is Important to Teach Writing Explicitly to Students with Dyslexia or Dysgraphia

Dyslexia is not only a reading disorder but also a writing disorder; typically, spelling is impaired at some stage during or throughout writing development (Berninger, Nielsen, Abbott, Wijsman, & Raskind, 2008b). Although both boys and girls with dyslexia may have persisting writing problems, boys with dyslexia are more impaired in their writing than are girls (Berninger, Nielsen, Abbott, Wijsman, & Raskind, 2008a).

This Writers Workshop for children with dyslexia in grades 4–9 (Berninger & Hidi, 2004; Berninger, Winn, Stock, Abbott, Eschen, Lin, et al., 2008) is grounded in the Writers Workshop Model, which has been pioneered, developed, and validated by Bernice Wong, Professor Emeritus of Special Education at Simon Frasier University (Vancouver, BC), for preadolescent and adolescent students who are low achieving, have learning disabilities, and learn English as a Second Language (see Wong & Berninger, 2004; Wong, Butler, Ficzere, & Kuperis, 1996, 1997; Wong, Butler, Ficzere, Kuperis, Corden, & Zelmer, 1994). This Writers Workshop provides in each lesson explicit instruction in spelling words and in composing.

Implemented in fourteen 2- to 2½-hour sessions plus pretest and posttest, or twenty-eight 1- to 1½-hour sessions.

UNIT II
Intro-
duction

Motivation May Be the Consequence, Not Cause, of Writing Problems

Motivation is not necessarily the first link in the causal chain in learning. Motivation can also be the outcome of success in learning. Therefore, for a student who is writing avoidant, it cannot be assumed that the problem is lack of motivation; it may be that the student avoids what he or she cannot do. Thus, one effective way for increasing motivation to write is to teach the student the skills needed to be a successful writer. The more successful a student is in learning to write, the more engaged and the less avoidant the student becomes in future writing activities. Motivation is a variable that emerges from—as well as contributes to—a dynamic, interacting system that includes the teacher and student(s) in the instructional environment. When both learning and teaching are really difficult, both students and teachers often need to be more motivated than normal in order to learn and teach, respectively. For further discussion of these issues, see Berninger and Hidi (2006).

Role of Hope in Motivating Struggling Writers

Students with chronic school failure may lose faith that they can learn successfully. Thus, we always begin our instructional interventions for students with dyslexia in the upper grades with a story created to instill hope that 1) they can learn and 2) teachers can teach them. This "hope story," which is told the first day, is repeated and elaborated in greater depth throughout the intervention. Often this hope story revolves around a hero such as a famous figure in the culture who illustrates with his or her life that initial lack of success can be transformed into success. For example, we used the life of Albert Einstein for this purpose in an earlier intervention for students with dyslexia (Berninger, 2000). The general public thinks of Einstein as a hugely successful adult, but when he was beginning formal schooling that success was not self-evident to young Albert or his family. As we explained to the children, he had begun to talk later than other preschool children, had many behavioral problems early in his schooling, was almost required to repeat first grade, and did not begin to like school until he was transferred to another school with a different teaching style. Although Einstein did not have dyslexia (specific to problems in reading and spelling words), he probably had a form of language learning disability (using language to learn) and was able to do his best thinking in nonverbal format, which he then translated into verbal expression (e.g., see Overbye, 2001; Paterni, 2000). In this Writers Workshop, the life of Mark Twain is used to tell the hope story that continues from the first to the last day of the Writers Workshop. On the first day of the workshop, the teacher tells the students the life story of Mark Twain (based on Ward, Duncan, & Burns, 2001):

> Samuel Clemens was born in a two-room shack in Missouri on a day when Halley's Comet was approaching Earth. He was 2 months premature and was a thin, sickly infant. His mother did not think he had any promise but clung to the ray of hope that Halley's Comet lit up the sky the night he was born—which might mean that there was hope for young Sam. Sometimes the family had money but sometimes it did not. Sam attended three private schools because there were no public schools in those days. He was not a very good student and often played hooky.

268

When he was in sixth grade, his father died. Sam had to drop out of school to help support the family. That's when he left home to work on river boats on the Mississippi. He wrote about those experiences in his novel, *Huckleberry Finn.* In his writing he used a new name, Mark Twain, which is a pen name.

When the Civil War between the North and South began, Mark Twain went West where he worked as a printer, miner, and newspaperman. A news editor reportedly complained that Mark Twain had spelled the same word ten different ways in one story. Mark Twain responded, as the story goes, that he felt sorry for anyone who could not think of ten different ways to spell the same word!

Eventually Mark Twain moved East to marry and settle down in New York, where he wrote the first novel ever written on a typewriter—*Tom Sawyer.* Because of financial troubles, he turned to the lecture circuit and traveled all over the United States and the world giving humorous talks. In his lifetime he was known as a storyteller, rather than a writer, and entertainer and became the most famous American of his day and an Ambassador for America around the world.

Halley's Comet was leaving earth on the Christmas day when he died. Mark Twain's mother was right—Halley's Comet was a ray of good hope for his life which turned out very successful.

To instill in the children identification with Mark Twain, the story theme of *hope* is developed throughout the 3-week workshop. Children wear name tags with a picture of Mark Twain. In the University of Washington Multidisciplinary Learning Disabilities Center (UWLDC) Mark Twain Writers Workshop, the name tags had a humorous cartoon of Mark Twain standing on a world globe. Students keep their work in a folder with pictures of Mark Twain as a writer at various stages of his life. Periodically, the teacher reads excerpts from *Tom Sawyer* or *Huckleberry Finn* that illustrate Twain's knack for writing the way people talk. The teacher leads a discussion about how some writing is based on how people speak.

In addition to the compositions children write at school, students work at home on a long-term writing project, called *Mark Twain in Stars War/Star Peace 3001,* for which students are encouraged to travel in time to the future, in contrast to the main character who traveled to the past in *A Connecticut Yankee in King Arthur's Court.* They are asked to travel in their imagination to the next millennium and use their imagination to describe life at that time. They are to choose a *Star Wars* or a *Star Peace* theme—whichever they think describes the world at that time. They are asked to use Mark Twain's style and tell a story that reflects how people think, talk, and behave 1,000 years from now. They bring drafts of their stories to class at designated times to show their teacher, who provides feedback. On the last day of the workshop, each student chooses either to read his or her *Star Wars* or *Star Peace* story to the class or to have a teacher read it to the class.

Reengaging Reluctant Writers

Students with chronic school failure may become disengaged from school learning and need to be reengaged in school learning. One way to accomplish this goal of reengagement is through interest in an intellectually engaging activity—for example, science workshops, drama (reading and acting play parts), solving mysteries, play with language and humor, and virtual reality problem solving activities—all of which we have used in specific treatment studies for students with dyslexia (see Berninger & Hidi, 2004). To engage students in the writing process in this Writers Workshop, we used

computer-assisted writing instruction in a social context with goal setting and daily teacher feedback coupled with writing about topics such as autobiography before, during, and after school and the future world in the next millennium.

Celebrating Writing Success

At the end of the Mark Twain Writers Workshop, a Writers Fest should be held to celebrate the children's writing accomplishments. Explain that professional writers share their writing with others through public readings as well as in book or other written form. Each child chooses his or her favorite piece of writing produced during the workshop by reading it to the group. Awards are presented to each child that acknowledge some accomplishment; awards can be customized for individual accomplishments. These are captured in the line in the center of the Mark Twain Writers Workshop Award (see p. 316). The teacher hand-writes the child's name and writing accomplishment on the award. Examples of awards in the Mark Twain Writers Workshop include

1. Most humorous story about a computer

2. Most imaginative story about a robot

3. Best science fiction for *Star Wars/Star Peace 3001*

4. Most inspiring personal narrative

5. Outstanding compare-and-contrast essay

6. Most improvement in word choice

7. Most improvement in sentence construction

8. Most improvement in text organization

9. Met daily goals for improvement

Awards can be given for any aspect of writing that children perceive as an authentic accomplishment. In the University of Washington study, the reward for the teachers was watching one adolescent receive an award for writing the way kids talk, and the whole group stood up and spontaneously cheered and applauded. The writer knew he had really communicated with his audience!

Evidence of the Effectiveness of Mark Twain Writers Workshop

Children who have participated in the Mark Twain Writers Workshop improved not only in spelling and composition skills but also in their self-efficacy as writers (Berninger & Hidi, 2006). For a comparison of how the younger students in grades 4–6 responded to the writing instruction compared with the older students in grades 7–9, see Berninger, Winn, et al. (2008). Not only did students improve in their spelling and composing, but also in their brain activation; good readers/spellers and students with dyslexia differed before treatment in specific brain regions, which normalized after the specialized orthographic spelling treatment in the Mark Twain Writers Workshop (Richards et al., 2006).

References

Berninger, V. (2000). Dyslexia: An invisible, treatable disorder. The story of Einstein's Ninja Turtles. *Learning Disability Quarterly, 23*, 175–195.

Berninger, V., Abbott, R., Whitaker, D., Sylvester, L., & Nolen, S. (1995). Integrating low-level skills and high-level skills in treatment protocols for writing disabilities. *Learning Disability Quarterly, 18*, 293–309. Validation of PWRR strategy and alphabet retrieval games.

Berninger, V., & Hidi, S. (2006). Mark Twain's writers' workshop: A nature–nurture perspective in motivating students with learning disabilities to compose. In S. Hidi, & P. Boscolo (Eds), *Motivation in writing* (pp. 159–179). Amsterdam: Elsevier.

Berninger, V.W., Nielsen, K.H., Abbott, R.D., Wijsman, E., & Raskind, W. (2008a). Gender differences in severity of writing and reading disabilities. *Journal of School Psychology, 46*, 151–172.

Berninger, V.W., Nielsen, K.H., Abbott, R.D., Wijsman, E., & Raskind, W. (2008b). Writing problems in developmental dyslexia: Under-recognized and under-treated. *Journal of School Psychology, 46*(1), 1–21.

Berninger, V.W., Winn, W.D., Stock, P., Abbott, R.D., Eschen, K., Lin, S-J., et al. (2008). Tier 3 specialized writing instruction for students with dyslexia. *Reading and Writing: An Interdisciplinary Journal, 21*(1–2), 95–129.

Overbye, D. (2000). *Einstein in love: A scientific romance.* New York: Penguin Books.

Paterniti, M. (2000). *Driving Mr. Albert: A trip across America with Einstein's brain.* New York: Delta.

Richards, T., Aylward, E., Berninger, V., Field, K., Parsons, A., Richards, A., et al. (2006). Individual fMRI activation in orthographic mapping and morpheme mapping after orthographic or morphological spelling treatment in child dyslexics. *Journal of Neurolinguistics, 19*, 56–86.

Ward, G., Duncan, D., & Burns, K. (2001). *Mark Twain.* New York: Alfred A. Knopf.

Wong, B., & Berninger, V. (2004). Cognitive processes of teachers in implementing composition research in elementary, middle, and high school classrooms. In B. Shulman, K. Apel, B. Ehren, E. Silliman, & A. Stone (Eds.), *Handbook of language and literacy development and disorders* (pp. 600–624). New York: Guilford Press.

Wong, B., Butler, D., Ficzere, S., & Kuperis, S. (1996). Teaching low achievers and students with learning disabilities to plan, write, and revise opinion essays. *Journal of Learning Disabilities, 29*, 197–212.

Wong, B., Butler, D., Ficzere, S., & Kuperis, S. (1997). Teaching adolescents with learning disabilities and low achievers to plan, write, and revise compare-and-contrast essays. *Learning Disabilities Research & Practice, 12*, 2–15.

Wong, B., Butler, D., Ficzere, S., Kuperis, S., Corden, M., & Zelmer, J. (1994). Teaching problem learners revision skills and sensitivity to audience through two instructional modes: Student–teacher versus student–student interactive dialogues. *Learning Disabilities Research & Practice, 9*, 78–90.

Overview of Writers Workshop

Each workshop has three parts. Part 1 is the warm-up (with *Talking Letters*) in which alphabetic principle is practiced in a way to make it automatic and strategic for spelling. Part 2 teaches word spelling strategies (with either photographic leprechauns or mor-

phological strategies). Part 3 engages students in the composing processes of planning, translating, and reviewing/revising for three genres: essays, narratives, and reports. The effectiveness of this approach to writing is related to the integration of transcription (handwriting and spelling) and composition instruction across levels of language (sub-word letter, letter, and text) close in time.

The *PAL-II User Guide* (Berninger, 2007b), which is included in the PAL-II Diagnostic for Reading and Writing (PAL-II RW; Berninger, 2007a), contains the following instructional tools that teachers can print out for the lesson plans: Talking Letters, Nickname Cards, Substitute Cards, PAL Reading and Writing Lessons (Lesson Sets 1–15), Lists 12a and 12b (Sets 1–4) and Graphic Organizers in the Reproducibles for the PAL Reading and Writing Lessons, and Letter Retrieval Before and After Games. The PAL-II RW web site will have a teacher portal in the near future containing other published sources for these instructional materials.

ORTHOGRAPHIC SPELLING STRATEGIES (7 LESSONS)

Talking Letters and substitute spelling units in alphabetic principle (Berninger & Abbott, 2003, Reproducibles)

Photographic Leprechaun Spelling Strategy described in Orthographic Spelling Treatment (see p. 277)

Proofreaders' Secret Trick Described in Orthographic Spelling Treatment (see p. 278)

SRA word searches, anagrams (see p. 278), proofreading (Dixon & Englemann, 2001)

Fry's Selective Reminding of Instant Words (Level 3) (Fry, 1996) for constructing word lists to learn and practice the orthographic spelling strategies

Crossword Puzzles (Dixon & Englemann, 2001)

Homework—Collect anagrams and reversible words (Dixon & Englemann, 2001) (see p. 308)

MORPHOLOGICAL SPELLING STRATEGIES (7 LESSONS)

Talking Letters and substitute spelling units in alphabetic principle (Berninger & Abbott, 2003, Reproducibles)

Word Building Strategy Described in Morphological Spelling Treatment (see p. 289)

Word Dissecting Strategy Described in Morphological Spelling Treatment (see p. 289)

SRA word building, word dissecting, word contracting, and morphological spelling rules

Fry's Word Variants (Level 3) (Fry, 1996)

Crossword Puzzles (Dixon & Englemann, 2001)

Homework—Collect Mommy Longwords with word meaning parts. See MommyLongwords Searches (p. 310).

Instructional Resources for Writers Workshop

Berninger, V., & Abbott, S. (2003). *PAL Research-Supported Reading and Writing Lessons,* San Antonio, TX: Pearson Assessment. (Lesson Sets 5 and 7 and Reproducibles.)

Fry, E. (1996). *Spelling book: Level 1–6. Words most needed plus phonics.* Westminster, CA: Teacher Created Materials.

Dixon, R., & Englemann, S. (2001). *Spelling through morphographs.* DeSoto, TX: SRA/ McGraw-Hill. (Excellent program once students have mastered Fry program.)

Overview of Writing Skills and Instruction

Canter, A.S., Paige, L.Z., Roth, M.D., Romero, I., & Carroll, S.A. (Eds.). (2009). *Helping children at home and school. II: Handouts for families and educators.* Bethesda, MD: National Association of School Psychologists.

See handout for parents and teachers by Berninger and Dunn for Writing in Intermediate and Secondary Grades. Available in hard copy and on CD.

Handwriting and Keyboarding

Benbow, M. (1990). *Loops and groups: A kinesthetic writing system.* San Antonio, TX: Therapy Skill Builders.

Fry, E. (1993) *Computer keyboarding for beginners.* Westminster, CA: Teacher Created Resources.

Olsen, J. (2004). *Handwriting Without Tears: A complete handwriting curriculum for all children.* Cabin John, MD: Handwriting Without Tears.

Rubel, B. (1995). *Big strokes for little folks.* Tucson, AZ: Therapy Skill Builders.

Spelling

Bear, D., Ivernezzi, M., Templeton, S., & Johnston, F. (2000). *Words their way: Word study for phonics, vocabulary, and spelling instruction* (2nd ed.). Upper Saddle River, NJ: Merrill Prentice Hall.

Berninger, V.W., & Abbott, S.P. (2003). *PAL research-supported reading and writing lessons.* San Antonio, TX: Pearson Assessment. Lesson sets 4, 5, and 7

Dixon, R., & Englemann, S. (2001). *Spelling through morphographs.* DeSoto, TX: SRA/McGraw-Hill.

Excellent program for students who have completed the Fry program to consider development of morphological aspects of spelling.

Fry, E. (1996). *Spelling book: Words most needed plus phonics (grades 1–6).* Westminster, CA: Teacher Created Resources.
Contains lessons with words and strategies for teaching children to spell high-frequency words alone and in dictated sentences and apply phonics knowledge to spelling and morpheme variants. Provides placement test for placing children at their instructional level. http://www.teachercreated.com

Gentry, J. (2004). *The science of spelling: The explicit specifics that make great readers and writers (and spellers!).* New York: Heinemann. www.heinemann.com

Henry, M.K. (2003). *Unlocking literacy: Effective decoding and spelling instruction.* Baltimore: Paul H. Brookes Publishing Co.
Explains how to teach decoding of words of Anglo Saxon, Latinate, and Greek origin based on the phonological, orthographic, and morphological units in words.

Masterson, J., Apel, K., & Wasowicz, J. (2002). *SPELL-2 spelling performance evaluation for language & literacy* (2nd ed.). Evanston, IL: Learning By Design.
Spelling assessment software for Grade 2 through adult.

Wasowicz, J., Apel, K., Masterson, J., & Whitney, A. (2004). *SPELL-Links to reading & writing: A word study program for K–adult.* Evanston, IL: Learning By Design.
Assessment linked to instruction. http://www.learningbydesign.com

Sentence Construction

Farbman, E. (1989). *Sentence sense: A writers' guide.* Boston: Houghton Mifflin.

Composition (Discourse Level)

Auman, M. (2003). *Step up to writing* (2nd ed.). Longmont, CO: Sopris West.

Berninger, V.W., & Abbott, S.P. (2003). *PAL research-supported reading and writing lessons.* San Antonio, TX: Pearson Assessment.
Lesson sets 8, 9, and 10 for composition strategies. Lesson sets 4 and 5 for spelling and composing. Lesson set 3 for handwriting and composing. Lesson sets 13 and 14 for integrating reading and writing and speaking in content areas.

Carlisle, J.F. (1996). *Models for writing, levels A, B, and C.* Novato, CA: Academic Therapy Publications. Also www.highnoonbooks.com, reproducibles for classroom use.

Graham, S., & Harris, K.R. (2005). *Writing better: Effective strategies for teaching students with learning difficulties.* Baltimore: Paul H. Brookes Publishing Co.

Nelson, N.W., Bahr, C., & Van Meter, A. (2004). *The Writing Lab approach to language instruction and intervention.* Baltimore: Paul H. Brookes Publishing Co.
Offers practical suggestions for teachers to use in scaffolding instruction for students with language learning disability and for using software to support the composing.

Teacher Created Resources. *Traits of good writing* (grades 1–2, 3–4, or 5–6). Westminster, CA: Author.

Wong, B.Y.L., & Berninger, V.W. (2005). Cognitive processes of teachers in implementing composition research in elementary, middle, and high school classrooms. In B. Shulman, K. Apel, B. Ehren, E. Silliman, & A. Stone (Eds.), *Handbook of language and literacy: Development and disorders* (pp. 600–626). New York: Guilford Press. This chapter

shows teachers how to apply the cognitive processes model of writing to teaching composing explicitly—making instructional plans, implementing them in practice, reviewing student progress on a regular basis, and revising instructional approach when necessary. It also illustrates Wong's model for integrated lessons for using the computer in the instructional program in writing with middle school and high school students. It calls attention to the importance of teaching students explicit strategies for managing time in completing assignments outside class.

Teaching Students with Dyslexia to Pay Attention to Written Language

Chenault, B., Thomson, J., Abbott, R.D., & Berninger, V.W. (2006). Effects of prior attention training on child dyslexics' response to composition instruction. *Developmental Neuropsychology, 29,* 243–260.

Kerns, K.A., Eso, K., & Thomson, J. (1999). Investigation of a direct intervention for improving attention in young children. *Developmental Neuropsychology, 16*(2), 273–295.

Web Site with Resources for Students Learning Written English

Web address for the software, English Discoveries. Once you reach the web site, you can navigate it by clicking on one of the menu items on the left-hand side of the page. http://techno-ware-esl.com/engdisc.html

Instructional Resources for Sustaining Writers Workshop

Part I of Each Spelling Lesson

ALPHABETIC PRINCIPLE IN THE PHONEME TO GRAPHEME(S) DIRECTION

Given the importance of alphabetic principle in spelling, all lessons begin with warm-up in which the correspondences (alternative one- to two-letter spelling units for representing each phoneme) are practiced using *Talking Letters* cards and students write all the possible spelling units for a specific phoneme, which is illustrated in a set of pictured words called a *substitute chart*. Students use that chart to self-check (Berninger & Abbott, 2003, Lesson Set 5 [and *Talking Letters* Cards] and Lesson Set 7, substitute chart in Reproducibles, pp. 43–44). The warm-up consists of the teacher naming a pictured word, saying the target phoneme in it, and naming the letter or letters in the corresponding spelling unit. Children then imitate saying the word, making the phoneme, and naming

the letters. The teacher and students alternate turns in this modeling–imitating process for a set of phoneme–spelling unit correspondences in each lesson. Following the modeling, children are given pictured words with target phonemes and are asked to write all the possible spelling units (alternations) that might go with the target phoneme. These are referred to as *substitutions*—just as the coach may substitute players, different letters may substitute for (stand for) the same phoneme. They check their work against the substitute chart on pages 43 and 44 of the Reproducibles (Berninger & Abbott, 2003).

Talking Letters (TL) Followed by Substitutes (Sub)

Lesson 1

TL: first four rows of consonant side and second row, *-le* syllable and schwa on vowel side

Sub: consonants

Lesson 2

TL: first four rows and first two items on fifth row of consonant side and first rows and silent 3 on vowel side

Sub: vowels

Lesson 3

TL: last two rows of consonant side; fifth, sixth, and seventh rows of vowel side

Sub: consonants

Lesson 4

TL: first four rows and first two items on fifth row of consonant side; first two rows of vowel side

Sub: vowels

Lesson 5

TL: third, fourth, and seventh rows of vowel side

Sub: consonants

Lesson 6

TL: fifth and sixth rows of consonant side; fifth and sixth rows of vowel side

Sub: vowels

Lesson 7

TL: first four rows and first two items on fifth row of consonant side; first two rows of vowels

Sub: consonants

Lesson 8

TL: third, fourth, and seventh rows of vowel side

Sub: vowels

Lesson 9

    TL: fifth and sixth rows of consonants; fifth and sixth rows of vowels

    Sub: consonants

Lesson 10

    TL: first four rows and first two items on fifth row of consonant side; first two rows of vowels

    Sub: vowels

Lesson 11

    TL: third, fourth, and seventh rows of vowels

    Sub: consonants

Lesson 12

    TL: fifth and sixth rows of consonants and fifth and sixth rows of vowels

    Sub: vowels

Lesson 13

    TL: first four rows and first two items on fifth row of consonant side; first two rows of vowels

    Sub: consonants

Lesson 14

    TL: third, fourth, and seventh rows of vowels

    Sub: vowels

Part II of Each Spelling Lesson:
Go to Orthographic or Morphological Treatment

Complete all of orthographic before beginning morphological.

ORTHOGRAPHIC SPELLING TREATMENT

Background

Two orthographic strategies were taught using Instant Words from Dr. Fry's Spelling Program (Fry, 1996): *Photographic Leprechaun* and *Proofreader's Trick*. In each lesson, a word set (16 words) is used—once for each of the two spelling strategies that are taught and practiced. The list with each word set is annotated and shows (underscore and bold) the designated position(s) in which students should name the letter(s) for the Photographic Leprechaun strategy.

    Overall, each word set is practiced two times—once with the strategy for looking for spelling units that are not phonologically encodable with any or full certainty and once with the reverse spelling strategy used by proofreaders. After each spelling lesson is com-

pleted, collect probes (writing 16 taught words in that lesson from dictation; see p. 288). Students spell words in writing from dictation in the word set practiced in the session.

In addition, children completed *visual word search* (circle letters that spell a real word), *anagrams* (rearrange the letters to spell a real word), and *proofreading* (correct the spelling errors) activities in the *SRA Morphograph Spelling Program* (Dixon & Englemann, 2001):

For developing and reinforcing *orthographic skills:*

1. *Word searches* (top p. 25, bottom p. 26, top p. 29, bottom p. 33, bottom 39, top p. 45, bottom p. 53, top p. 76, top p. 89, top p. 116, middle p. 128, top p. 147, bottom p. 163, and top p. 209)

2. *Anagrams* (p. 9 Part D, p. 10 Part D, p. 12 Part E, p. 15 Part D, p. 35 Part E, and p. 54 Part E)

3. *Proofreading* (p. 42 Part C, p. 51 Part E, p. 91 Part D, p. 105 Part E, p. 110 Part D, p. 110 Part D, p. 122 Part E, p. 125 Part D, p. 129 Part D, p. 136 Part E, p. 142 Part D, p. 146 Part D, p. 151 Part D, p. 159 Part E, p. 177 Part D, p. 183 Part D, p. 190 Part D, p. 192 Part D, p. 197 Part D, p. 204 Part C, p. 207 Part B, p. 215 Part E, p. 217 Part D, p. 223 Part D, and p. 230 Part B)

For developing and refining *morphological skills:*

Crossword puzzles (pp. 176–190)

Directions Given by the Teacher

The teacher should take probes (asking each child to spell each taught word; see p. 306) at the end of each lesson to record on growth graph for percent correct. This will be a record of short-term retention of the spellings that is kept for assessing response to instruction.

Photographic Leprechaun Strategy

Say: Take out the word set (designate) and the two 3 × 5 cards from your work folder. Use the cards to cover up the words above and below the target word. Look at (name the target word). Look carefully at each letter in the word as you name each letter moving in left to right direction. Now close your eyes and look at the word that is now coded in your mind's eye by the photographic leprechaun who took a photograph of it. Most of the spelling units have a small sound called a *phoneme* that goes with it, as we discussed when we worked with the substitute chart for alphabetic principle. However, some letters do not (they are silent), or they have a very vague (reduced) sound that does not correspond in predictable way, or they are one of the predictable substitutions—but those letters must be memorized for a specific word. I will call those letters to your attention by asking you to name the letter or letters in specific word positions. As soon as you know the answer, raise your hand. Remember to keep your eyes closed until I say we are working on a new target word.

The lists that follow for Photographic Leprechauns show the position(s) (via underlining or bolding) in which students should name the letter(s).

Proofreader's Trick *(recommended by Kenn Apel, Florida State University, for spelling remediation)*

Say: Now we will learn a second strategy for creating a precise representation of a word's spelling in long-term memory. Proofreaders use this strategy so we will call it the *proofreader's secret trick.* Open your eyes and take a good look at the target word and name all the letters in it. Now close your eyes again and look at the word in your mind's eye where the photographic leprechaun put the snapshot of it. While holding that word in memory, I want you to spell it backward, quietly naming each letter in reverse order,

starting with the last letter and ending with the first letter. Open your eyes only when you name the first letter. Then check your reverse spelling against the target word in the word in the word set in front of you. Then we will try the next one.

Probes

Later in the session, ask students to spell words in writing from each of the word sets practiced in the session. Have student partners exchange their papers and mark the words that are and are not correct against the model word set. Make sure students pay attention to the correct spelling. Check correctness of scoring and keep as probe measures.

PHOTOGRAPHIC LEPRECHAUN

Teacher instructions: Before the lesson, find the word sets in the Photographic Leprechaun and Proofreader's Trick Worksheet (which start on p. 281); make enough copies for the number of children completing the lesson. Use this word list to teach each of the orthographic strategies (Photographic Leprechaun and Proofreader's Trick). When teaching the Photographic Leprechaun strategy, one word at a time, ask the children to identify each of the letters indicated in parentheses in the Word Sets that follow. Use the worksheets for Spelling Probes for Photographic Leprechaun and Proofreader's Trick (p. 288) at the end of the lesson to evaluate the response to spelling instruction.

Word Set 1

eleven (5th)
example (2nd, last 2)
several (4th and 5th)
table (last 2)
enough (3rd and 4th, last 2)
notice (last 2)
people (3rd, last 2)
doctor (5th)
family (4th)
voice (2nd and 3rd, last 2)
sign (3rd)
color (4th)
town (2nd and 3rd)
sentence (5th, last 2)
questions (5th and 6th, 7th)
certain (5th and 6th)

Word Set 2

different (7th)
picture (4th and 5th, last 2)
usually (2nd and 3rd, 4th and 5th)
travel (5th)
answer (4th)
order (4th)
upon (1st)
between (5th and 6th)
during (first 3)
person (5th)
night (2nd, 3rd, and 4th)
measure (4th and 5th, last 2)
minutes (4th, 6th)
often (3rd, 4th)
listen (4th, 5th)
course (2nd and 3rd, last 2)

Word Set 3

gard<u>e</u>n (5th)
capt<u>ai</u>n (5th and 6th)
auth<u>o</u>r (5th)
fr<u>o</u>nt (3rd)
surf<u>a</u>ce (5th, last 2)
b<u>ui</u>lding (2nd and 3rd)
h<u>ea</u>vy (2nd and 3rd)
reas<u>o</u>n (2nd and 3rd, 5th)
o<u>ce</u>an (2nd and 3rd, 4th)
b<u>ui</u>lt (2nd and 3rd)
int<u>e</u>rest (4th and 5th, 6th)
i<u>s</u>land (2nd)
sudd<u>e</u>nly (5th)
b<u>ea</u>utiful (2nd, 3rd, 4th)
ma<u>chi</u>ne (3rd and 4th, 5th and 7th)
r<u>e</u>ady (2nd and 3rd)

Word Set 4

milli<u>o</u>n (5th, 6th)
s<u>y</u>stem (2nd and 5th)
gen<u>e</u>ral (4th and 6th)
instrum<u>e</u>nts (8th)
t<u>ea</u>cher (2nd and 3rd, 6th)
br<u>ough</u>t (3rd to 7th)
re<u>gi</u>on (3rd, 4th and 5th)
sp<u>ea</u>k (3rd and 4th)
lang<u>ua</u>ge (5th and 6th, 7th and 8th)
bel<u>ie</u>ve (4th, 5th, and 7th)
re<u>s</u>ult (3rd)
thous<u>a</u>nd (6th)
simp<u>le</u> (last 2)
cen<u>tu</u>ry (4th and 5th)
governm<u>e</u>nt (8th)
inst<u>ea</u>d (5th and 6th)

Word Set 5

am<u>o</u>ng (3rd)
dista<u>nce</u> (5th, last 2)
la<u>ugh</u>ed (3rd, 4th, and 5th)
materi<u>a</u>l (6th, 7th)
for<u>e</u>st (4th)
<u>ci</u>r<u>c</u>le (1st, 4th, 2nd and 3rd, last 2)
dic<u>ti</u>onary (4th and 5th, 6th, 8th and 9th)
poss<u>i</u>ble (5th, last 2)
nat<u>u</u>ral (3rd and 4th, 6th)
<u>e</u>xactly (2nd)
mel<u>o</u>dy (4th)
ca<u>tch</u> (last 3)
bott<u>o</u>m (5th)
climb<u>e</u>d (5th)
va<u>ll</u>ey (2nd and 3rd, 5th)
pres<u>i</u>dent (5th, 7th)

Word Set 6

tr<u>ou</u>ble (3rd and 4th, last 2)
en<u>gi</u>ne (3rd, 4th and 6th)
contr<u>o</u>l (last 2)
practi<u>ce</u> (last 2)
hist<u>o</u>ry (5th)
do<u>ll</u>ars (5th)
sepa<u>ra</u>te (4th, 6th, and last)
rh<u>y</u>th<u>m</u> (3rd, last)
<u>co</u>r<u>n</u>er (2nd and 3rd, last 2)
nece<u>ss</u>ary (4th, 7th and 8th)
li<u>qui</u>d (3rd and 4th)
elem<u>e</u>nts (3rd and 5th)
<u>pa</u>rti<u>cu</u>lar (2nd and 3rd, last 2)
ki<u>tch</u>en (3rd to 5th, 6th)
indi<u>c</u>ate (4th)
<u>wr</u>ong (first 2)

Word Set 7

wag<u>o</u>n (4th)
pr<u>e</u>tty (3rd)
sign<u>a</u>l (5th)
fam<u>ou</u>s (4th and 5th)
simi<u>la</u>r (4th, last 2)
promi<u>s</u>e (5th, last 2)
tot<u>a</u>l (4th)
ima<u>gi</u>ne (4th, 5th and 7th)
me<u>ssa</u>ge (last 3)
posi<u>ti</u>on (5th and 6th, 7th)
cott<u>o</u>n (5th)
aver<u>a</u>ge (last 3)
tit<u>le</u> (last 2)
fr<u>ui</u>t (3rd and 4th)
h<u>eigh</u>t (2nd to 5th)
pen<u>ci</u>l (4th, 5th)

PHOTOGRAPHIC LEPRECHAUN AND PROOFREADER'S TRICK WORKSHEET

WORD SET 1

1. eleven

2. example

3. several

4. table

5. enough

6. notice

7. people

8. doctor

9. family

10. voice

11. sign

12. color

13. town

14. sentence

15. questions

16. certain

PHOTOGRAPHIC LEPRECHAUN AND PROOFREADER'S TRICK WORKSHEET

WORD SET 2

1. different _____

2. picture _____

3. usually _____

4. travel _____

5. answer _____

6. order _____

7. upon _____

8. between _____

9. during _____

10. person _____

11. night _____

12. measure _____

13. minutes _____

14. often _____

15. listen _____

16. course _____

PHOTOGRAPHIC LEPRECHAUN AND PROOFREADER'S TRICK WORKSHEET

WORD SET 3

1. garden

2. captain

3. author

4. front

5. surface

6. building

7. heavy

8. reason

9. ocean

10. built

11. interest

12. island

13. suddenly

14. beautiful

15. machine

16. ready

PHOTOGRAPHIC LEPRECHAUN AND PROOFREADER'S TRICK WORKSHEET

WORD SET 4

1. million _____

2. system _____

3. general _____

4. instruments _____

5. teacher _____

6. brought _____

7. region _____

8. speak _____

9. language _____

10. believe _____

11. result _____

12. thousand _____

13. simple _____

14. century _____

15. government _____

16. instead _____

PHOTOGRAPHIC LEPRECHAUN AND PROOFREADER'S TRICK WORKSHEET

WORD SET 5

1. among

2. distance

3. laughed

4. material

5. forest

6. circle

7. dictionary

8. possible

9. natural

10. exactly

11. melody

12. catch

13. bottom

14. climbed

15. valley

16. president

PHOTOGRAPHIC LEPRECHAUN AND PROOFREADER'S TRICK WORKSHEET

WORD SET 6

1. trouble

2. engine

3. control

4. practice

5. history

6. dollars

7. separate

8. rhythm

9. corner

10. necessary

11. liquid

12. elements

13. particular

14. kitchen

15. indicate

16. wrong

PHOTOGRAPHIC LEPRECHAUN AND PROOFREADER'S TRICK WORKSHEET

WORD SET 7

1. wagon

2. pretty

3. signal

4. famous

5. similar

6. promise

7. total

8. imagine

9. message

10. position

11. cotton

12. average

13. title

14. fruit

15. height

16. pencil

SPELLING PROBE FOR PHOTOGRAPHIC LEPRECHAUN AND PROOFREADER'S TRICK

Name _____   Date _____   Number correct _____

1. _____

2. _____

3. _____

4. _____

5. _____

6. _____

7. _____

8. _____

9. _____

10. _____

11. _____

12. _____

13. _____

14. _____

15. _____

16. _____

MORPHOLOGICAL SPELLING TREATMENT

Background

This treatment uses the word sets that contain high-frequency words with high-frequency morphemes. A set of 16 words is practiced twice in each lesson, once with each of two different strategies: Word Building and Word Dissecting. The first strategy is building a word from its meaning parts and the second strategy is breaking a word down into its meaning parts. The lists of Meaning Detective word sets used in each lesson for learning and practicing each of the morphology strategies are included.

Near the end of each session, collect probes for the taught words by asking children to spell them in writing from dictation. Check correctness of these probe measures and graph them for a visible record of response to instruction. In addition, children complete word building, word dissecting, word contracting, and spelling-rule activities from *SRA Spelling Morphographs* (Dixon & Englemann, 2001).

Directions Given by the Teacher

Morphological Word Building Strategy

Say: Listen while I say a word part by part, and look at the parts on your worksheet. These parts are *morphemes* or meaning units in words. They have spellings, sounds, and meaning. Some are *root words* or *bases*. Some are *prefixes* that go at the beginning of words, and some are *suffixes* that go at the end of words. I want you to use these word parts to build and spell a whole word. Please write the word, which you built from the parts you see and heard me say, on the worksheet for this lesson in your folder. Later, we will share and discuss these.

Morphological Dissecting Strategy

Say: This time I will say a word and you may look at the written word while I say it. I want you to break the written words down into their component meaning parts. These parts are morphemes or meaning parts in words. They have spellings, sounds, and meaning. Some are root words or bases. Some are prefixes that go at the beginning of words, and some are suffixes that go at the end of words. I want you to rewrite each word on the list for the lesson part by part. See a blank for base, a blank for prefix, and three blanks for suffixes. You will not need all of these for every word, but use the ones you do need for each word. Later, we will discuss how you dissected each of these words.

Probes

The teacher should take probes (asking each child to spell each taught word; see p. 306) at the end of each lesson to record on growth graph for percent correct. This will be a record of short-term retention of the spellings that is kept for assessing response to instruction.

Meaning Detectives Word Sets

Word Set 1

atypically = a type ic al ly
activists = act ive ist s
breathlessness = breath less ness
breathtaking = breath take ing
boyishness = boy ish ness
beloved = be love ed

convention = convene tion
conversation = converse (a) tion
classically = class ic al ly
conversion = convert ion
compartment = com part ment
carelessly = care less ly
carelessness = care less ness
critically = critic al ly
conceptual = concept (u) al
constructively = construct ive ly

Word Set 2

dangerously = danger ous ly
decomposable = de compose able
deduced = deduce ed
departure = depart ure
defining = define ing
destruction = destruct ion
dictatorship = dictate or ship
deplaned = de plane ed
detective = detect ive
deceptive = deceive ive
discovered = dis cover ed
disproves = dis prove s
disquieting = dis quiet ing
discontented = dis content ed
displeasure = dis please ure
dislikes = dis like s

Word Set 3

emotionless = emote ion less
exports = ex port s
extracting = extract ing
expressions = express ion s
factually = fact (u) al ly
forcefully = force ful ly
gloriously = glory ous ly
friendliness = friend ly ness
helplessness = help less ness
heroically = hero ic al ly
hopelessly = hope less ly
inattentively = in attend ive ly
inexpensive = in expense ive ly
inspirational = inspire (a) tion al
indirectly = in direct ly
inhalation = inhale (a) tion

Word Set 4

insecurity = in secure ity
incurable = in cure able
intensively = intense ive ly
injection = inject ion
induced = induce ed
instruction = instruct ion
joyously = joy ous ly
likelihood = like ly hood
likeliest = like ly est
lifelessness = life less ness
lovelier = love ly er

loveliest = love ly est
lonelier = lone ly er
loneliest = lone ly est
magically = magic al ly
misbehaved = mis behave ed

Word Set 5

mismatched = mis match ed
mistaken = mis take en
misspelling = mis spell ing
musically = music al ly
misquoting = mis quote ing
passages = pass age s
nervousness = nerve ous ness
packaging = pack age ing
painfulness = pain ful ness
progression = progress ion
protection = protect tion
prewashed = pre wash ed
prestretched = pre stretch ed
overreacted = over re act ed
overcoats = over coat s
questionable = quest ion able

Word Set 6

shakiness = shaky ness
renamed = re name ed
reformed = re form ed
refreshing = re fresh ing
recovering = recover ing
restructure = re struct ure
retention = retain tion
revision = revise ion
receptionist = receive tion ist
restlessness = rest less ness
restfully = rest ful ly
rightfully = right ful ly
shiniest = shiny est
straightened = straight en ed
thoughtfully = thought ful ly
transplanted = trans plant ed

Word Set 7

transportation = trans port (a) tion
transfusion = trans fuse ion
transformation = trans form (a) tion
unshakable = un shake able
uninformed = un inform ed
unproven = un prove en
unrefillable = un re fill able
unmistakable = un mis take able
unstructured = un struct ure ed
unathletic = un athlete ic
unfriendly = un friend ly
ungraded = un grade ed
unnerving = un nerve ing
uselessness = use less ness
widening = wide en ing
medically = med ic al ly

WORD BUILDING: MORPHOLOGICAL SPELLING

WORD SET 1

Listen to and look at the word parts the teacher says and write a whole word from those parts on a line below.

Word Parts	Whole Word
1. a type ic al ly	
2. act ive ist s	
3. breath less ness	
4. breath take ing	
5. boy ish ness	
6. be love ed	
7. convene tion	
8. converse (a) tion	
9. class ic al ly	
10. convert ion	
11. com part ment	
12. care less ly	
13. care less ness	
14. critic al ly	
15. concept (u) al	
16. construct ive ly	

UNIT II
FORMS

WORD BUILDING: MORPHOLOGICAL SPELLING

WORD SET 2

Listen to and look at the word parts the teacher says and write a whole word from those parts on a line below.

Word Parts	*Whole Word*
1. danger ous ly	
2. de compose able	
3. deduce ed	
4. depart ure	
5. define ing	
6. destruct ion	
7. dictate or ship	
8. de plane ed	
9. detect ive	
10. deceive ive	
11. dis cover ed	
12. dis prove s	
13. dis quiet ing	
14. dis content ed	
15. dis please ure	
16. dis like s	

WORD BUILDING: MORPHOLOGICAL SPELLING

WORD SET 3

Listen to and look at the word parts the teacher says and write a whole word from those parts on a line below.

Word Parts	Whole Word
1. emote ion less	
2. ex port s	
3. extract ing	
4. express ion s	
5. fact (u) al ly	
6. force ful ly	
7. glory ous ly	
8. friend ly ness	
9. help less ness	
10. hero ic al ly	
11. hope less ly	
12. in attend ive ly	
13. in expense ive ly	
14. inspire (a) tion al	
15. in direct ly	
16. inhale (a) tion	

WORD BUILDING: MORPHOLOGICAL SPELLING

WORD SET 4

Listen to and look at the word parts the teacher says and write a whole word from those parts on a line below.

Word Parts	*Whole Word*
1. in secure ity	
2. in cure able	
3. intense ive ly	
4. inject ion	
5. induce ed	
6. instruct ion	
7. joy ous ly	
8. like ly hood	
9. like ly est	
10. life less ness	
11. love ly er	
12. love ly est	
13. lone ly er	
14. lone ly est	
15. magic al ly	
16. mis behave ed	

WORD BUILDING: MORPHOLOGICAL SPELLING

WORD SET 5

Listen to and look at the word parts the teacher says and write a whole word from those parts on a line below.

Word Parts	*Whole Word*
1. mis match ed	
2. mis take en	
3. mis spell ing	
4. music al ly	
5. mis quote ing	
6. pass age s	
7. nerve ous ness	
8. pack age ing	
9. pain ful ness	
10. progress ion	
11. protect tion	
12. pre wash ed	
13. pre stretch ed	
14. over re act ed	
15. over coat s	
16. quest ion able	

WORD BUILDING: MORPHOLOGICAL SPELLING

WORD SET 6

Listen to and look at the word parts the teacher says and write a whole word from those parts on a line below.

Word Parts	*Whole Word*
1. shaky ness	
2. re name ed	
3. re form ed	
4. re fresh ing	
5. recover ing	
6. re struct ure	
7. retain tion	
8. revise ion	
9. receive tion ist	
10. rest less ness	
11. rest ful ly	
12. right ful ly	
13. shiny est	
14. straight en ed	
15. thought ful ly	
16. trans plant ed	

WORD BUILDING: MORPHOLOGICAL SPELLING

WORD SET 7

Listen to and look at the word parts the teacher says and write a whole word from those parts on a line below.

Word Parts	Whole Word
1. trans port (a) tion	
2. trans fuse ion	
3. trans form (a) tion	
4. un shake able	
5. un inform ed	
6. un prove en	
7. un re fill able	
8. un mis take able	
9. un struct ure ed	
10. un athlete ic	
11. un friend ly	
12. un grade ed	
13. un nerve ing	
14. use less ness	
15. wide en ing	
16. med ic al ly	

WORD DISSECTING: MORPHOLOGICAL SPELLING

WORD SET 1

Listen to and look at the word on the left and write each of its meaning parts in the appropriate category.

word	prefix	base word	suffix	suffix	suffix
1. atypically					
2. activists					
3. breathlessness					
4. breathtaking					
5. boyishness					
6. beloved					
7. convention					
8. conversation					
9. classically					
10. conversion					
11. compartment					
12. carelessly					
13. carelessness					
14. critically					
15. conceptual					
16. constructively					

WORD DISSECTING: MORPHOLOGICAL SPELLING

WORD SET 2

Listen to and look at the word on the left and write each of its meaning parts in the appropriate category.

word	prefix	base word	suffix	suffix	suffix
1. dangerously					
2. decomposable					
3. deduced					
4. departure					
5. defining					
6. destruction					
7. dictatorship					
8. deplaned					
9. detective					
10. deceptive					
11. discovered					
12. disproves					
13. disquieting					
14. discontented					
15. displeasure					
16. dislikes					

WORD DISSECTING: MORPHOLOGICAL SPELLING

WORD SET 3

Listen to and look at the word on the left and write each of its meaning parts in the appropriate category.

word	prefix	base word	suffix	suffix	suffix
1. emotionless					
2. exports					
3. extracting					
4. expressions					
5. factually					
6. forcefully					
7. gloriously					
8. friendliness					
9. helplessness					
10. heroically					
11. hopelessly					
12. inattentively					
13. inexpensive					
14. inspirational					
15. indirectly					
16. inhalation					

WORD DISSECTING: MORPHOLOGICAL SPELLING

WORD SET 4

Listen to and look at the word on the left and write each of its meaning parts in the appropriate category.

word	prefix	base word	suffix	suffix	suffix
1. insecurity	_____	_____	_____	_____	_____
2. incurable	_____	_____	_____	_____	_____
3. intensively	_____	_____	_____	_____	_____
4. injection	_____	_____	_____	_____	_____
5. induced	_____	_____	_____	_____	_____
6. instruction	_____	_____	_____	_____	_____
7. joyously	_____	_____	_____	_____	_____
8. likelihood	_____	_____	_____	_____	_____
9. likeliest	_____	_____	_____	_____	_____
10. lifelessness	_____	_____	_____	_____	_____
11. lovelier	_____	_____	_____	_____	_____
12. loveliest	_____	_____	_____	_____	_____
13. lonelier	_____	_____	_____	_____	_____
14. loneliest	_____	_____	_____	_____	_____
15. magically	_____	_____	_____	_____	_____
16. misbehaved	_____	_____	_____	_____	_____

WORD DISSECTING: MORPHOLOGICAL SPELLING

WORD SET 5

Listen to and look at the word on the left and write each of its meaning parts in the appropriate category.

word	prefix	base word	suffix	suffix	suffix
1. mismatched					
2. mistaken					
3. misspelling					
4. musically					
5. misquoting					
6. passages					
7. nervousness					
8. packaging					
9. painfulness					
10. progression					
11. protection					
12. prewashed					
13. prestretched					
14. overreacted					
15. overcoats					
16. questionable					

WORD DISSECTING: MORPHOLOGICAL SPELLING

WORD SET 6

Listen to and look at the word on the left and write each of its meaning parts in the appropriate category.

word	prefix	base word	suffix	suffix	suffix
1. shakiness					
2. renamed					
3. reformed					
4. refreshing					
5. recovering					
6. restructure					
7. retention					
8. revision					
9. receptionist					
10. restlessness					
11. restfully					
12. rightfully					
13. shiniest					
14. straightened					
15. thoughtfully					
16. transplanted					

WORD DISSECTING: MORPHOLOGICAL SPELLING

WORD SET 7

Listen to and look at the word on the left and write each of its meaning parts in the appropriate category.

word	prefix	base word	suffix	suffix	suffix
1. transportation					
2. transfusion					
3. transformation					
4. unshakable					
5. uninformed					
6. unproven					
7. unrefillable					
8. unmistakable					
9. unstructured					
10. unathletic					
11. unfriendly					
12. ungraded					
13. unnerving					
14. uselessness					
15. widening					
16. medically					

SPELLING PROBES FOR MORPHOLOGICAL SPELLING

Name _____   Date _____   Number correct _____

1. _____

2. _____

3. _____

4. _____

5. _____

6. _____

7. _____

8. _____

9. _____

10. _____

11. _____

12. _____

13. _____

14. _____

15. _____

16. _____

FEEDBACK FORM

Name_____ Lesson_____ Circle one: Draft 1 or Revision

FOR ALL LESSONS:

Sentence formation

1	2	3	4	5
poor	fair	good	very good	outstanding

Meaningful organization of sentences in text

1	2	3	4	5
poor	fair	good	very good	outstanding

Word choice

1	2	3	4	5
poor	fair	good	very good	outstanding

My Writing Goal for my next writing assignment is _____

_____

_____

FOR LESSONS 11–14 ONLY:

Relevance of notes to report topic

1	2	3	4	5
poor	fair	good	very good	outstanding

Organization of notes in outline

1	2	3	4	5
poor	fair	good	very good	outstanding

Report content

1	2	3	4	5
poor	fair	good	very good	outstanding

Clarity of report writing

1	2	3	4	5
poor	fair	good	very good	outstanding

Paragraph structure (main idea and supporting details)

1	2	3	4	5
poor	fair	good	very good	outstanding

HOMEWORK FOR
MARK TWAIN WRITERS WORKSHOP

Dear Parent,

We are giving students some activities to do at home in order to maximize how much they learn from participation in the Mark Twain Writers Workshop. Every year we find that many children have writing talent in creating and expressing their ideas in writing despite their reading and spelling problems. We want to encourage their writing talent as much as possible. This year we are encouraging children to write a story titled, "Mark Twain in Star Wars or Star Peace (choose one) 3001." Instead of traveling back into the past as Twain did in *A Connecticut Yankee in King Arthur's Court,* we want students to travel into the future and exercise their imagination. We will be doing a lot of writing this year and learning strategies for essay, story, and report writing. Children will spend about an hour per day on activities related to composing. This assignment is an opportunity to have more time to think, explore ideas, and express their imagination. We are asking that the students bring their drafts in progress to us on _____(date) for teacher feedback. The final versions are due _____. The drafts and final versions may be handwritten or in an electronic file.

We hope to publish these stories during the school year. Your child can choose to publish under his or her own name or under a pen name as Mark Twain did. The winner of the Wong Award for best Mark Twain story will be announced at the party to celebrate completion of the Mark Twain Writers Workshop. Other awards will also be given at this party.

Children also will be encouraged to complete activities related to spelling written words. Until the expected completion of the Mark Twain Writers Workshop on _____(date), your child has been asked to look for anagrams (scrambled letters that can be rearranged to spell a word) in the newspaper, magazines they read, or other sources. They also have been asked to look for words that spell a real word no matter in which direction they are spelled (a *palindrome*). We encourage them to bring the anagrams and reversible words to the workshop to share when they find them. They do not have to bring them in every day.

Your child has been asked to search for long words that contain designated word parts. Attached is the Mommy Longwords list of kinds of words we want students to listen and look for and bring examples to class.

All these activities are optional, and we understand if your child is not able to do them because of other commitments. However, parents often ask what they can do to help their child. These are activities that can be done at home to benefit your child's writing.

Sincerely,

PHOTOGRAPHIC LEPRECHAUNS HOMEWORK
(attach to Homework letter)

Find as many words as you can that are real words, whether the word is spelled forward or backward (a *palindrome*). Bring them each day as you find them.

Collect as many anagrams (scrambled letters that spell a real word) that you can solve and bring them in to share with the other students. Bring them each day as you find them.

MOMMY LONGWORDS HOMEWORK
(attach to Homework letter)

Mommy Longwords Contest: Find the longest words you can in which the past tense (happened in the past) marker –ed rhymes with *red*, is pronounced as the first sound in *dog*, or is pronounced as the first sound in *ten*.

Mommy Longwords Contest: Find the longest word you can that ends in *er* and compares only two things, and the longest word you can that ends in <u>est</u> and compares two or more things.

Mommy Longwords Contest: Find the longest words you can in which the plural (more than one thing) marker ends with the same syllable as *buses*, ends with the same sound as at the beginning of *sun*, or ends with the last sound in *bees*.

Mommy Longwords Contest: Find the longest words you can that begins with *pre* (that means *before*).

Mommy Longwords Contest: Find the longest word you can that begins with *un* that means *not*, that begins with *im* that means *not*, that begins with *in* (that means *not*), or that begins with *dis* (that means *not*).

Mommy Longwords Contest: Find the longest word you can that begins with *re* (that means *to do again*).

Mommy Longwords Contest: Find the longest word you can that ends with *able* and changes a noun (a thing) into an adjective (a word that describes).

Mommy Longwords Contest: Find the longest word you can that ends in *al* and changes another word into an adjective (a word that describes).

Mommy Longwords Contest: Find the largest word you can that ends in *tion.*

Mommy Longwords Contest: Find the longest word you can that ends in *sion.*

Mommy Longwords Contest: Find the longest word you can that ends in *ist.*

Mommy Longwords Contest: Find the longest word you can that ends in *ant* or *ent.*

Mommy Longwords Contest: Find the longest word you can that ends in *ance* or *ence.*

Mommy Longwords Contest: Find the longest word you can that ends in *ful* or *less.*

EVENT/PLOT PLAN

List events.

Then number them in the order in which they occurred.

Decide whether you will tell the story in the order in which it occurred or some other order (and if so, why?).

Is there a conflict or problem to be solved? If so, how does it conclude?

Is the story an adventure, mystery, romance, biography, or other? (describe)

Who is the narrator who tells the story? The author? Someone else? Is the story written in first person ("I") or third person (someone other than the characters in it)?

CHARACTER PLAN

List all the people in the story. Describe what each looks like. Describe what kind of person each one is, what each likes and does not like, how each typically behaves, and how he or she behaved in a particular situation. Are there any nonhuman characters in the story? If so, list and describe them, too.

Character   **Description**

SETTING PLAN

Where does the story take place? Does it take place in more than one setting? List all the places and describe each one.

When does the story take place? Does it take place in more than one time? List all the times and indicate whether the story will be told in exactly the same order as it happened in real time.

PROBES

Name _____ Lesson _____

Spelling

Number of correctly spelled dictated words: _____ (maximum is 16)

Word set: (circle one)   1   2   3   4   5   6   7

Taught spelling strategy: (circle one)   Orthographic   Morphological

Keyboarding

Number of correctly located letters on keys: _____ (maximum is 26)

Composing

(circle one)   First draft   Revised draft

Amount of time spent on first draft: _____ (minutes)

Amount written: (number of words) _____

Compositional fluency or rate: (words per minute) _____

Percent of correctly spelled words in composition: _____ %

NOTE-TAKING STRATEGIES

1. Read for the "big picture."

2. Read again and write notes.

3. Write the main ideas first.

4. Then write points to support each main idea.

Mark Twain Writers Workshop Award

Awarded to

_____

for

_____
_____
_____

Composing Lessons for Mark Twain Writers Workshop

1. During the first half hour, the teacher models planning activities using graphic organizers and reflective discussions and the children write their first drafts.

2. During the second half hour, student pairs work with computers. First, they do warm-up activities finding letters on the keyboard.

3. Students then enter the first drafts into the computer so the compositions can be revised.

4. Then the teacher uses prompts (see p. 318) to help students revise their compositions at the word, sentence, and text levels.

5. Use the feedback form (see p. 307) to give feedback for the relevant writing activities in the current lesson.

6. At the end of the session, the teacher provides feedback about whether the students met goals set at the end of the previous session. Whether or not goals were met can be used to assess response to instruction. Then students set new goals for improving their compositions at the word, sentence, and text levels in the next session.

The composing activities span creative writing to report writing. Many of the composing lessons have been published for teachers to use in the context of other lesson sets based on controlled, randomized, or instructional design experiments (Berninger & Abbott, 2003, Lesson Sets 4, 5, 7, 8, 10, 13, and 14, each of which has the references for the published peer-reviewed instructional research).

Instructional Resources for Composing

Berninger, V.W., & Abbott, S. (2003). *PAL Research-Supported Reading and Writing Lessons*. San Antonio, TX: Pearson Assessment.

Educational Development Corporation (EDC) offers an extensive selection of science paperbacks including *Planet Earth* by Philip Clark available from http://www.edcpub.com

Protecting Trees & Forests by Felicity Brooks is an Usborne book available from www.DiscoverUsborneBooks.com and a Scholastic book available from www.scholastic.com. Or, choose an alternative title at either web site or other comparable book, and adapt the last five lessons as necessary.

LESSON **1** Informative Essay—Descriptive

Essay Writing (Lessons 1–5)
Narrative Writing (Lessons 6–10)
Report Writing (Lessons 11–14)

"Describe a computer to a child who cannot see."

PLANNING

Teacher-Led Reflective Discussion

Encourage students to talk about the following questions: What does a computer look like? What can a computer be used for? What parts does a computer have? How does a computer work? What things must be considered in describing a computer to a child who is blind? Ask students to discuss what would be easy and what would be difficult for a child who is blind to understand about a computer. How do you think Mark Twain would describe a computer?

Ask students for examples of dull words and more interesting words. Discuss the importance of writing in complete, grammatical sentences (sentence construction). Ask students for examples of complete, grammatical sentences. Discuss the importance of writing text that has a clear organizational scheme. Ask students for examples of words that can signal text organization in giving written directions. If students cannot come up with examples, provide some of your own, but still encourage them to come up with their own examples.

Graphic Organizers for Student Partners to Use in Planning

Use the Web Plan (Berninger & Abbott, 2003, Reproducibles, top p. 141) to generate ideas about computers, but use the Grouping Plan (Berninger & Abbott, Reproducibles, p. 141) to organize the ideas about computers into four subtopics: Its Looks, Its Uses, Its Parts, and/or Its Inner Workings.

WRITING FIRST DRAFT

Writing Prompts

Say: You are to write an essay explaining what a computer looks like to a child who cannot see. You may use your written plans, but you should also add other sentences to make your informative essay as complete and as interesting as possible. Remember you can keep planning and you do not have to stick to your written plans exactly. As you write, think about the words you use, the sentences you build, and the organization you create in your essay. It is important that you write for 10 minutes. Your pencil does not have an eraser, but you can make changes by crossing out and rewriting. Remember that the first draft does not have to be perfect. Concentrate on generating your ideas and filling in the details in your plans.

If any student stops writing before 10 minutes, *say:* What else can you think of? Reread what you have written already and think of something else to say.

Feedback (see Feedback Form, p. 307)

Teachers should score each composition on three criteria along a scale from 1 (poor) to 2 (fair) to 3 (good) to 4 (very good) to 5 (outstanding): whether sentences are complete and well structured (sentence formation), whether sentences are organized in a meaningful way (text organization), and whether word choice is interesting (word choice). This scoring should be done before the next lesson when students are given the scores on each criterion during the feedback at the end of the revision session to use in planning their goals for the next lesson.

LESSON 2 Informative Essay—Compare and Contrast

"In what ways are pencils and computers alike and different?"

PLANNING

Teacher-Led Reflective Discussion

Encourage children to talk about the following questions: How expensive are pencils and computers? How many people have pencils and computers? How easy is it to take pencils and computers wherever you go? What can pencils do that computers cannot do, and what can computers do that pencils cannot do? Ask children to discuss the advantages and disadvantages of pencils and computers. Encourage children to come up with their own questions for comparing pencils and computers. Discuss whether Mark Twain would think pencils and computers are more alike or more different.

Discuss the importance of using interesting words (word choice). Ask students for examples of dull words and more interesting words. Discuss the importance of writing in complete, grammatical sentences (sentence construction). Ask students for examples of complete, grammatical sentences. Discuss the importance of writing text that has a clear organizational scheme. Ask students for examples of words that can signal text organization in giving written directions. If children cannot come up with examples, provide some, but still encourage them to come up with their own examples.

Graphic Organizers for Student Partners to Use in Planning

Use the Weave Structure Plan (a matrix in Berninger & Abbott, 2003, Reproducibles, p. 144). Have children fill in the two topics that are being compared—pencils and computers—in the matrix. First, in the Alike section of the Weaving Plan, ask children to fill in the categories on which the topics can be compared besides the heading "on what?" Under the heading "how," write the specific evidence for how pencils and computers are alike on each category of comparison. Then, in the Different section of the Weaving Plan, ask children to fill in categories on which topics can be compared besides the heading "on what?" Under the heading "how," write the specific evidence for how pencils and computers are different on each category of comparison.

WRITING FIRST DRAFT

Writing Prompts

Say: You are to write an essay explaining how pencils and computers are alike and different. You may use your written plans, but you should also add other sentences to make your informative essay as complete and as interesting as possible. Remember you can keep planning and you do not have to stick to your written plans exactly. As you write, think about

320

the words you use, the sentences you build, and the organization you create in your essay. It is important that you write for 10 minutes. Your pencil does not have an eraser, but you can make changes by crossing out and rewriting. Remember that the first draft does not have to be perfect. Concentrate on generating your ideas and filling in the details in your plans.

If any student stops writing before 10 minutes, *say:* What else can you think of? Reread what you have written already and think of something else to say.

Feedback

Teachers should score each composition on three criteria along a scale from 1 (poor) to 2 (fair) to 3 (good) to 4 (very good) to 5 (outstanding): whether sentences are complete and well structured, whether sentences are organized in a meaningful way, and whether word choice is interesting. This scoring should be done before the next lesson when students are given the scores on each criterion during the feedback at the end of the session to use in planning their goals for the next lesson.

REVIEWING AND REVISING (REFLECTING/EXTENDING) FOR LESSON 1 COMPOSITION

Teacher-Led Reflective Discussion

The teacher reads each composition aloud, hums or sighs where writing is unclear, and leads a discussion of how clarity can be improved. Students and teacher suggest how each composition could be improved in terms of whether word choice is interesting, whether sentences are complete, and whether the essay is organized meaningfully (order of sentences). Children make notes in colored marker on their original draft to use when they compose later at the computer. If necessary, the teacher models how to add ideas, rewrite sentences, and change words.

Computer-Keyboard Warm-Up

The teacher dictates one of 26 random alphabet letters. The student finds and touches the letter on the laminated keyboard. The teacher records the number of correct touches on the probe sheet (see p. 321). Use this order: q, r, f, z, y, g, b, a, i, e, u, d, m, c, s, h, j, n, w, t, p, k, x, l, o, v.

Using Keyboard and Word Processing Program to Enter Revised Draft

The teacher assists students in entering the draft to revise. The teacher shows them how to use relevant features of the word processing program, which will have the spell-check feature turned off, for text entry. Students can refer to their notes on the first draft and make additional revisions. Students also receive feedback on their revised drafts using the same criteria and teacher rating scale as for the feedback on their first drafts.

Feedback

Teachers give children scores on sentence construction, sentence organization, and word choice from Lesson 1 composition. Teachers and students set realistic writing goals for improving one of these in the next composition.

LESSON **3** Persuasive Essay Writing—Opinions

"Is it easier to write with a pencil or a computer?"

PLANNING

Teacher-Led Reflective Discussion

Encourage children to talk about the following questions: What are the advantages of a pencil? What are the disadvantages of a pencil? What are the advantages of computers? What are the disadvantages of computers? Ask children to have a "pretend argument." One child should take one position and the other child should take an opposite position. (Ask them to pretend play if both have the same point of view.) Ask them to present all the evidence they can think of to support their point of view. Discuss which writing tool Mark Twain would probably prefer.

Graphic Organizers for Student Partners to Use in Planning

Use Sides of Argument Plan and Argument Plan (Berninger & Abbott, 2003, Reproducibles, p. 152). On the one side of the Sides of Argument Plan sheet write one side of the argument (opinion) and list all the evidence supporting that opinion. On the other side write the contrasting side of the argument (opinion) and list all the evidence supporting that opinion. Use the Argument Plan to decide what you believe, reasons (evidence) for your opinion, and conclusion.

WRITING FIRST DRAFT

Writing Prompts

Say: You are to write an essay on whether it is easier to write with a pencil or computer. Describe the advantages and disadvantages for both pencils and computers. Tell your concluding opinion and support it with evidence. You may use your written plans, but you should also add other sentences to make your informative essay as complete and as interesting as possible. Remember you can keep planning and you do not have to stick to your written plans exactly. As you write, think about the words you use, the sentences you build, and the organization you create in your essay. It is important that you write for 10 minutes. Your pencil does not have an eraser, but you can make changes by crossing out and rewriting. Remember that the first draft does not have to be perfect. Concentrate on generating your ideas and filling in the details in your plans."

If any student stops writing before 10 minutes, *say:* What else can you think of? Reread what you have written already and think of something else to say.

Feedback

Teachers should score each composition on three criteria along a scale from 1 (poor) to 2 (fair) to 3 (good) to 4 (very good) to 5 (outstanding): whether sentences are complete and well structured, whether sentences are organized in a meaningful way, and whether word choice is interesting. This scoring should be done before the next lesson when students are given the scores on each criterion during the feedback at the beginning of the revision session.

REVIEWING AND REVISING (REFLECTING/EXTENDING) FOR LESSON 2 COMPOSITION

Feedback

Teachers give children scores on sentence construction, sentence organization, and word choice from Lesson 2 composition. Teachers and students set realistic writing goals for improving one of these in the next composition.

Teacher-Led Reflective Discussion

The teacher reads each partner's composition aloud, hums or sighs where writing is unclear, and leads discussion of how clarity can be improved. Students and teacher suggest how each composition could be improved in terms of whether word choice is interesting, whether sentences are complete, and whether the essay is organized meaningfully (order of sentences). Children make notes in colored marker on their original draft to use when they compose later at the computer. If necessary, the teacher models how to add ideas, rewrite sentences, and change words.

Computer-Keyboard Warm-Up

The teacher dictates one of 26 random alphabet letters. The student finds and touches the letter on the laminated keyboard. The teacher records the number of correct touches on the probe sheet. Use this order: a, y, m, r, c, t, q, d, p, h, y, e, i, b, j, k, n, k, w, g, f, u, x, z, l, o.

Using Keyboard and Word Processing Program to Enter Revised Draft

The teacher assists students in entering the revised drafts. The teacher shows them how to use relevant features of the word processing program, which will have the spell-check feature turned off, for text entry. Students can refer to their notes on the first draft and make additional revisions. Students also receive feedback on their revised drafts using the same criteria and teacher rating scale as for the feedback on their first drafts.

LESSON **4** Persuasive Essay—Argument

"Should children be able to watch TV whenever they want and choose the shows they watch?"

Take a position and convince others that you are right.

PLANNING

Teacher-Led Reflective Discussion

Encourage children to talk about the following questions: What is your opinion about whether children should be able to watch television (TV) whenever they want? What is your opinion about whether children should choose the shows they watch? What are some of the arguments (evidence + persuasion) that support your position on each question? What kinds of evidence can you provide to support each of your arguments? Ask children to have a "pretend argument." One child should take one position and the other child should take an opposite position. (Ask them to pretend play if both have the same point of view.) Discuss what Mark Twain might think about TV.

Graphic Organizers for Student Partners to Use in Planning

Use the Boxing Match and Taking Sides Plans (Berninger & Abbott, 2003, Reproducibles, pp. 152 and 155). Remind them of "boxing match" in Lesson 3 and ask them to try to "throw punches" in each other's arguments.

Ask students to state their opinion in the form of a general statement at the top of the Taking Sides Plan sheet. Then ask them to come up with reasons or facts that support their opinion. Ask them to list as many reasons or facts as they can to reject the opposing opinion. Then have them summarize by integrating the opinion with the reasons for it and end with a conclusion and reasons for it.

WRITING FIRST DRAFT

Writing Prompts

Say: You are to write an essay on whether children should be able to watch TV whenever they want and choose the shows they watch. Tell the advantages and disadvantages for children deciding which shows to watch and when. Give your opinion and then arguments to support your opinion and then evidence to support your arguments. You may use your written plans, but you should also add other sentences to make your informative essay as complete and as interesting as possible. Remember you can keep planning and do not have to stick to your written plans exactly. As you write, think about the words you use, the sentences you build, and the organization you create in your essay. It is important that you

write for 10 minutes. Your pencil does not have an eraser, but you can make changes by crossing out and rewriting. Remember that the first draft does not have to be perfect. Concentrate on generating your ideas and filling in the details in your plans.

If any student stops writing before 10 minutes, *say:* What else can you think of? Reread what you have written already and think of something else to say.

Feedback

Teachers should score each composition on three criteria along a scale from 1 (poor) to 2 (fair) to 3 (good) to 4 (very good) to 5 (outstanding): whether sentences are complete and well structured, whether sentences are organized in a meaningful way, and whether word choice is interesting. This scoring should be done before the next lesson when students are given the scores on each criterion during the feedback at the end of the session to use in planning their goals for the next lesson.

REVIEWING AND REVISING (REFLECTING/EXTENDING) FOR LESSON 3 COMPOSITION

Teacher-Led Reflective Discussion

The teacher reads each composition aloud, hums or sighs where writing is unclear, and leads discussion of how clarity can be improved. Students and teacher suggest how each composition could be improved in terms of whether word choice is interesting, whether sentences are complete, and whether the essay is organized meaningfully (order of sentences). Children make notes in colored marker on their original draft to use when they compose later at the computer. If necessary, the teacher models how to add ideas, rewrite sentences, and change words.

Computer Keyboard Warm-Up

The teacher dictates one of 26 random alphabet letters. The student finds and touches the letter on the laminated keyboard. The teacher records the number of correct touches on the probe sheet. Use this order: c, w, z, b, k, o, r, p, y, n, e, i, t, u, x, d, v, l, a, q, f, m, h, g, s, j.

Using Keyboard and Word Processing Program to Enter Revised Draft

The teacher assists students in entering the draft to revise. The teacher shows them how to use relevant features of the word processing program, which will have the spell-check feature turned off, for text entry. Students can refer to their notes on the first draft and make additional revisions. Students also receive feedback on their revised drafts using the same criteria and teacher rating scale as for the feedback on their first drafts.

Feedback

Teachers give children scores on sentence construction, sentence organization, and word choice from Lesson 3 composition. Teachers and students set realistic writing goals for improving one of these in the next composition.

LESSON **5** Planning, Writing, Reviewing, and Revising
PWRR Strategy and Narrative Writing

Homework: First review of progress on *Mark Twain in Star Wars/Star Peace 3001* story is due.

If I Ran the School or *Class Clown*

TEACHER MODELING

Say: I'm going to teach you the *Plan, Write, Review/Revise (PWRR) strategy* for Composing by modeling it for you (Berninger, Abbott et al., 1995; Berninger & Abbott, 2003, p. 223). First, I am going to model planning for you. I will think aloud about what I am going to write about in my story on daydreaming. Listen as I think aloud. I will write about when I daydream. I will write about why I daydream. I will write about what I daydream about. Now it is your turn to plan. When do you daydream? (allow time for children to think and share) Why do you daydream? (allow time for children to think and share) What do you daydream about? (allow time for children to think and share).

Say: Now I am going to model writing my story about daydreaming. Watch me as I write this on the board. (*Write:* I daydream when I have to sit still for a long while. I daydream becaus [sic] I get board [sic]. I daydream about what I would be doing if I were not here.)

Say: Now I am going to model reviewing and revising. First I will read my story aloud. Now I will revise it to make it better. I am thinking of sentences that I can add to it to make it better. I think I will give two examples for the last sentence. Watch while I add those sentences to what I have already written on the board. (*Write:* For example, I would rather be sailing. Or, I would prefer to see a movie). Now I am going to revise a sentence to make it better. I think that the first one is too wordy. I am going to strike out *have to.* The sentence will still make sense. Now I am going to think about my word choice. I think I am going to substitute *time* for *while* in the first sentence. Now I will check my spelling. Oops, I misspelled *because.* I forgot the *e* on the end. Oops, I misspelled *board.* The spelling I used is for another meaning. I am changing it to *bored.* Now I will check my capitalization and punctuation. Oops, I forgot to put a period at the end of the last sentence.

INTRODUCING TOPIC, TEXT STRUCTURE, AND IDEA GENERATING IN PLANNING TO WRITE NARRATIVES

Say: Please use the PWRR strategy to write a story about a topic you choose. All stories need a topic—something to write about. You may choose a topic for your story—either *Class Clown* or *If I Ran the School.* The topic can also be the title.

Stories also need a specific kind of structure or organization. We call this organization *narrative structure* because it is like the one that good storytellers or narrators use. This structure has a *plot,* which is a sequence of events. Cartoons are like written stories because each picture stands for something that happened in order. The first picture took place before the second picture, which took place before the third picture. This order is a *sequence.*

326

Stories have sequence, too. We call the sequence of events the *plot.* Stories also need *characters*—the people that cause the events to take place. They are like the actors in a play. Stories also need a *setting.* The events occur in a specific place and time. Readers liked Mark Twain's stories because they are humorous. Think how you can inject humor into your story.

Graphic Organizers for Student Partners to Use in Planning

Say: So the first thing I want you to do is to daydream and think of the events that will take place in your story. List them in the Event/Plot Plan (p. 311). As you imagine the events, also think of the characters who will cause the events. List them in the Character Plan (p. 312). Finally, think of all the settings (place and time) where the events will take place and list them in the Setting Plan (p. 313). These plans are at the end of the Mark Twain Composing Lessons.

WRITING FIRST DRAFT

Say: Now write the story using the topic (title) you chose and the plot, character, and setting plans you wrote. It is important that you write for 10 minutes. Your pencil does not have an eraser, but you can make changes by crossing out and rewriting. Remember that the first draft does not have to be perfect. Concentrate on generating your ideas and filling in the details in your plans.

If any student stops writing before 10 minutes, *say:* What else can you think of? Reread what you have written already and think of something else to say.

Feedback

Teachers should score each composition on three criteria along a scale from 1 (poor) to 2 (fair) to 3 (good) to 4 (very good) to 5 (outstanding): whether sentences are complete and well structured, whether sentences are organized in a meaningful way, and whether word choice is interesting. This scoring should be done before the next lesson when students are given the scores on each criterion during the feedback at the end of the session to use in planning their goals for the next lesson.

REVIEWING AND REVISING FOR LESSON 4 COMPOSITION

Teacher-Led Reflective Discussion

The teacher reads each composition aloud, hums or sighs where writing is unclear, and leads a discussion of how clarity can be improved. Students and teacher suggest how each composition could be improved in terms of whether word choice is interesting, whether sentences are complete, and whether the essay is organized meaningfully (order of sentences). Children make notes in colored marker on their original drafts to use when they compose later at the computer. If necessary, the teacher models how to add ideas, rewrite sentences, and change words.

Computer Keyboard Warm-Up

The teacher dictates one of 26 random alphabet letters. The student finds and touches the letter on the laminated keyboard. The teacher records the number of correct touches on the probe sheet. Use this order: c, r, m, v, a, i, b, g, z, h, u, x, e, j, l, q, y, w, p, s, f, t, d, k, n, o.

Using Keyboard and Word Processing Program to Enter Revised Draft

The teacher assists students in entering the draft to revise. Teachers show them how to use relevant features of the word processing program, which will have the spell-check feature turned off, for text entry. Students can refer to their notes on the first draft and make additional revisions. Students also receive feedback on their revised drafts using the same criteria and teacher rating scale as for the feedback on their first drafts.

Feedback

Teachers give children scores on sentence construction, sentence organization, and word choice from Lesson 4 composition. Teachers and students set realistic writing goals for improving one of these in the next composition.

Illustrating

Say: Pictures add to good stories. With these colored markers I want you to illustrate your story. Use art to express the ideas in another way.

Getting Ready to Publish

Students show the teacher what has been written so far on *Mark Twain in Star Wars/Star Peace 3001.* The teacher provides feedback and suggestions for revision and further development of the story.

LESSON **6** Narrative Writing

My Personal Robot

Text PWRR Strategy. *Say:* Today you are going to use the PWRR strategy to write a story, *My Personal Robot.*

PLANNING

Say: Sometimes writing can be used to play and to pretend about what does not exist. We call this kind of pretending *imagination.* Let your imagination go wild. Brainstorm all the features of your personal robot. What does it look like? What does it sound like? What does it feel like if you touch it? What does it smell like? What does it do for you? Do you like it? Why or why not? How would it be like other robots? How would it be different from other robots? What would be special about this robot? What do you think Mark Twain would think about robots?

Allow children time to talk about each of these ideas.

Graphic Organizers for Student Partners to Use in Planning

Say: Now complete the Event/Plot, Character, and Setting Plans (see pp. 311–313) for the story about your personal robot.

WRITING FIRST DRAFT

Say: Now write the story, *My Personal Robot.* It is important that you write for 10 minutes. Your pencil does not have an eraser, but you can make changes by crossing out and rewriting. Remember that the first draft does not have to be perfect. Concentrate on generating your ideas and filling in the details in your plans.

If any student stops writing before 10 minutes, *say:* What else can you think of? Reread what you have written already and think of something else to say.

Feedback

Teachers should score each composition on three criteria along a scale from 1 (poor) to 2 (fair) to 3 (good) to 4 (very good) to 5 (outstanding): whether sentences are complete and well structured, whether sentences are organized in a meaningful way, and whether word choice is interesting. This scoring should be done before the next lesson when students are given the scores on each criterion during the feedback at the end of the session to use in planning their goals for the next lesson.

Teacher-Led Reflective Discussion

Say: Now we will read our stories silently, and I will cue you with one prompt at a time to think about how you might change the story to make it better.

Ask each of these questions in this order and allow children time to make the relevant revisions before proceeding to the next question. Children make notes in colored marker on their original drafts to use when they compose later at the computer. If necessary, the teacher models how to add ideas, rewrite sentences, and change words.

1. Can you think of sentences to add to make it better?

2. Can you think of ways to improve the sentences; for example, by adding or subtracting words or replacing words?

3. Can you think of a better choice for specific words you have used?

4. Did you misspell any words? Circle each word you misspelled or are uncertain of the spelling. We will fix those if necessary.

5. Is the capitalization and punctuation correct for each sentence?

Computer Keyboard Warm-Up

The teacher dictates one of 26 random alphabet letters. The student finds and touches the letter on the laminated keyboard on which the letter key is covered with masking tape. The student lifts tape for immediate feedback as to whether the letter touch is correct. If it is not correct, the student consults the model keyboard that shows where the letter is and then touches the correct letter key. The teacher records the number of correct touches on the probe sheet. Use this order: l, f, a, w, i, q, r, t, x, c, u, e, s, k, o, j, m, g, y, b, p, d, h, z, v, n.

Using Keyboard and Word Processing Program to Enter Revised Draft

The teacher assists students in entering the draft to revise. The teacher shows them how to use relevant features of the word processing program, which will have the spell-check feature turned off, for text entry. Students can refer to their notes on the first draft and make additional revisions. Students also receive feedback on their revised drafts using the same criteria and teacher rating scale as for the feedback on their first drafts.

Feedback

Teachers give children scores on sentence construction, sentence organization, and word choice from Lesson 5 composition. Teachers and students set realistic writing goals for improving one of these in the next composition.

Illustrating

Select the picture that most resembles your robot, or draw your own picture.

LESSON **7** First Part of a Three-Part Autobiography

My Life Before I Started School

Text PWRR Strategy. *Say:* Today you are going to use the PWRR strategy to write part one of a three-part autobiography (the story of your life written by you). Sometimes you have to write over longer stretches of time than one session. Today you will write about your life before you went to school.

PLANNING

Say: Try to remember as many events as you can before you went to school. Think of events you remember and ones your family has told you about. Good writing draws on information in your memory as well as your imagination.

Graphic Organizer for Individual Students

Say: Use the Event Plan in the Plot Plan (p. 311) at the end of Mark Twain Composing Lessons to write down as many things as you can remember. Think more about each of these events and details you might add about them. Then think about what else you would like to share about your life before you went to school. Make some notes about those ideas.

WRITING FIRST DRAFT

Say: Now write a story titled *My Life Before I Started School.* It is important that you write for 15 minutes. Your pencil does not have an eraser, but you can make changes by crossing out and rewriting. Remember that the first draft does not have to be perfect. Concentrate on generating your ideas and filling in the details in your plans.

If any student stops writing before 15 minutes, *say:* What else can you think of? Reread what you have written already and think of something else to say.

Feedback

Teachers should score each composition on three criteria along a scale from 1 (poor) to 2 (fair) to 3 (good) to 4 (very good) to 5 (outstanding): whether sentences are complete and well structured, whether sentences are organized in a meaningful way, and whether word choice is interesting. This scoring should be done before the next lesson when students are given the scores on each criterion during the feedback at the end of the session to use in planning their goals for the next lesson.

REVIEWING AND REVISING FOR LESSON 6 COMPOSITION

Teacher-Led Reflective Discussion

Say: Now we will read our stories silently, and then I will cue you with one prompt at a time to think about how you might change the story to make it better.

Ask each of these questions in this order and allow children time to make the relevant revisions before proceeding to the next question. Children make notes in colored marker on their original drafts to use when they compose later at the computer. If necessary, teacher models how to add ideas, rewrite sentences, and change words.

1. Can you think of sentences to add to make it better?

2. Can you think of ways to improve the sentences; for example, by adding or subtracting words or replacing words?

3. Can you think of a better choice for specific words you have used?

4. Did you misspell any words? Circle each word you misspelled or are uncertain of the spelling. We will fix those if necessary.

5. Is the capitalization and punctuation correct for each sentence?

Computer Keyboard Warm-Up

The teacher dictates one of 26 random alphabet letters. The student finds and touches the letter on the laminated keyboard on which the letter key is covered with masking tape. The student lifts the tape for immediate feedback as to whether the letter touch is correct. If it is not correct, the student consults the model keyboard that shows where the letter is and then touches the correct letter key. The teacher records the number of correct touches on the probe sheet. Use this order: d, s, w, m, t, f, q, j, z, n, u, b, h, c, y, v, e, i, p, k, a, r, x, l, g, o.

Using Keyboard and Word Processing Program to Enter Revised Draft

The teacher assists students in entering the draft to revise. The teacher shows them how to use relevant features of the word processing program, which will have the spell-check feature turned off, for text entry. Students can refer to their notes on the first draft and make additional revisions. Students also receive feedback on their revised drafts using the same criteria and teacher rating scale as for the feedback on their first drafts.

Feedback

Teachers give children scores on sentence construction, sentence organization, and word choice from Lesson 6 composition. Teachers and students set realistic writing goals for improving one of these in the next composition.

Illustrating

Say: Draw a picture of yourself before you came to school. Make a caption to tell how old you were and what you were doing.

LESSON **8** Second Part of a Three-Part Autobiography

My Life Since I Started School

Text PWRR Strategy. *Say:* Today you will use the PWRR strategy (Berninger & Abbott, 2003, p. 223) to continue telling your life story. Today we will write about your life since your started school.

PLANNING

Say: Try to remember as many events as you can since you started school.

Graphic Organizer for Individual Students

Say: Use the Event Plan (p. 311) to write down as many things as you can. Search your memory; good writing draws from your memory banks. Then think more about each of these events and details you might add about them. Then think about what else you would like to share about your life since you started school. Make some notes about those ideas. Are there similarities between your life and Mark Twain's? Are there differences between your life and Mark Twain's?

WRITING FIRST DRAFT

Say: Now write a story titled, *My Life Since I Started School.* It is important that you write for 15 minutes. Your pencil does not have an eraser, but you can make changes by crossing out and rewriting. Remember that the first draft does not have to be perfect. Concentrate on generating your ideas and filling in the details in your plans.

If any student stops writing before 15 minutes, *say:* What else can you think of? Reread what you have written already and think of something else to say.

Feedback

Teachers should score each composition on three criteria along a scale from 1 (poor) to 2 (fair) to 3 (good) to 4 (very good) to 5 (outstanding): whether sentences are complete and well structured, whether sentences are organized in a meaningful way, and whether word choice is interesting. This scoring should be done before the next lesson when students are given the scores on each criterion during the feedback at the end of the session to use in planning their goals for the next lesson.

REVIEWING AND REVISING FOR LESSON 7

Teacher-Led Reflective Discussion

Say: Now we will read our stories aloud, and then I will cue you with one prompt at a time to think about how you might change the story to make it better.

Ask each of these questions in this order and allow children time to make the relevant revisions before proceeding to the next question.

1. Can you think of sentences to add to make it better?

2. Can you think of ways to improve the sentences; for example, by adding or subtracting words or replacing words?

3. Can you think of a better choice for specific words you have used?

4. Did you misspell any words? Circle each word you misspelled or are uncertain of the spelling. We will fix those if necessary.

5. Is the capitalization and punctuation correct for each sentence?

Computer Keyboard Warm-Up

The teacher dictates one of 26 random alphabet letters. The student finds and touches the letter on the laminated keyboard on which the letter key is covered with masking tape. The student lifts the tape for immediate feedback as to whether the letter touch is correct. If it is not correct, the student consults the model keyboard that shows where the letter is and then touches the correct letter key. The teacher records the number of correct touches on the probe sheet. Use this order: u, r, t, a, l, i, z, s, w, g, m, o, h, x, q, e, n, k, o, f, v, y, d, j, b, c.

Using Keyboard and Word Processing Program to Enter Revised Draft

The teacher assists students in entering the draft to revise. Teachers show them how to use relevant features of the word processing program, which will have the spell-check feature turned off, for text entry. Students can refer to their notes on the first draft and make additional revisions. Students also receive feedback on their revised drafts using the same criteria and teacher rating scale as for the feedback on their first drafts.

Feedback

Teachers give children scores on sentence construction, sentence organization, and word choice from Lesson 7 composition. Teachers and students set realistic writing goals for improving one of these in the next composition.

Illustrating

Say: Draw a picture of yourself after you started school. Make a caption to tell how old you were and what you were doing.

 LESSON **9** | Third Part of a Three-Part Autobiography

My Life in the Future

Text PWRR Strategy. *Say:* Today you are going to use the PWRR plan to write about you future after school, as you imagine it.

PLANNING

Say: Try to imagine life after school.

Graphic Organizer for Individual Students

Say: Use the Web Plan (Berninger & Abbott, 2003, p. 141) to write down as many things as you can about what life might be like. Then think more about each of the possibilities and details about them that you might add. Make some notes about those ideas.

WRITING FIRST DRAFT

Say: Write your autobiography, *My Life After School.* It is important that you write for 15 minutes. Draw on your memory and your imagination; good writing depends on both. Your pencil does not have an eraser, but you can make changes by crossing out and rewriting. Remember that the first draft does not have to be perfect. Concentrate on generating your ideas and filling in the details in your plans.

If any student stops writing before 15 minutes, *say:* What else can you think of? Reread what you have written already and think of something else to say.

Feedback

Teachers should score each composition on three criteria along a scale from 1 (poor) to 2 (fair) to 3 (good) to 4 (very good) to 5 (outstanding): whether sentences are complete and well structured, whether sentences are organized in a meaningful way, and whether word choice is interesting. This scoring should be done before the next lesson when students are given the scores on each criterion during the feedback at the end of the session to use in planning their goals for the next lesson.

REVIEWING AND REVISING FOR LESSON 8 COMPOSITION

Teacher-Led Reflective Discussion

Say: Now we will read our stories silently, and then I will cue you with one prompt at a time to think about how you might change the story to make it better.

Ask each of these questions in this order and allow children time to make the relevant revisions before proceeding to the next question.

1. Can you think of sentences to add to make it better?

2. Can you think of ways to improve the sentences; for example, by adding or subtracting words or replacing words?

3. Can you think of a better choice for specific words you have used?

4. Did you misspell any words? Circle each word you misspelled or are uncertain of the spelling. We will fix those if necessary.

5. Is the capitalization and punctuation correct for each sentence?

Computer Keyboard Warm-Up

The teacher dictates one of 26 random alphabet letters. The student finds and touches the letter on the laminated keyboard on which the letter key is covered with masking tape. The student lifts the tape for immediate feedback as to whether the letter touch is correct. If it is not correct, the student consults the model keyboard that shows where the letter is and then touches the correct letter key. The teacher records the number of correct touches on the probe sheet. Use this order: q, t, l, f, x, k, c, n, m, o, u, g, e, y, w, h, z, a, v, b, j, p, s, r, i, d.

Using Keyboard and Word Processing Program to Enter Revised Draft

The teacher assists students in entering the draft to revise. The teacher shows them how to use relevant features of the word processing program, which will have the spell-check feature turned off, for text entry. Students can refer to their notes on the first draft and make additional revisions. Students also receive feedback on their revised drafts using the same criteria and teacher rating scale as for the feedback on their first drafts.

Feedback

Teachers give children scores on sentence construction, sentence organization, and word choice from Lesson 8 composition. Teachers and students set realistic writing goals for improving one of these in the next composition.

Illustrating

Say: Draw a picture of yourself in the future after you are no longer in school. Make a caption to tell how old you are and what you are doing.

LESSON **10** | Synthesizing Chapters and
Getting Ready to Publish in Book Format

(Top right box) UNIT II LESSON 10

My Autobiography

REVIEWING AND REVISING FOR LESSON 9 COMPOSITION

Teacher-Led Reflective Discussion

Say: Now we will read our autobiographies silently, and then I will cue you with one prompt at a time to think about how you might change the story to make it better.

Ask each of these questions in this order and allow children time to make the relevant revisions before proceeding to the next question. Children make notes in colored marker on their original drafts to use when they compose later at the computer. If necessary, teacher models how to add ideas, rewrite sentences, and change words.

1. Can you think of sentences to add to make it better?

2. Can you think of ways to improve the sentences; for example, by adding or subtracting words or replacing words?

3. Can you think of a better choice for specific words you have used?

4. Did you misspell any words? Circle each word you misspelled or are uncertain of the spelling. We will fix those if necessary.

5. Is the capitalization and punctuation correct for each sentence?

Computer Keyboard Warm-Up

The teacher dictates one of 26 random alphabet letters. The student finds and touches the letter on the laminated keyboard on which the letter key is covered with masking tape. The student lifts the tape for immediate feedback as to whether the letter touch is correct. If it is not correct, the student consults the model keyboard that shows where the letter is and then touches the correct letter key. The teacher records the number of correct touches on the probe sheet. Use this order: i, t, q, b, c, r, y, m, a, e, g, f, u, z, d, x, j, k, n, s, h, w, l, p, o, v.

Using Keyboard and Word Processing Program to Enter Revised Draft

The teacher assists students in entering the draft to revise. The teacher shows them how to use relevant features of the word processing program, which will have the spell-check feature turned off, for text entry. Students can refer to their notes on the first draft and make additional revisions. Students also receive feedback on their revised drafts using the same criteria and teacher rating scale as for the feedback on their first drafts.

Getting Ready to Publish

Say: Today we are going to put together the three chapters in your autobiography to tell your whole life story. Good writers learn to put together what they have written over time. Sometimes they publish their work to share with others.

PLANNING

Say: Think about how you are going to piece together each of the three chapters. Can you write some sentences to help the reader go from what you have written in the last chapter to what will be in the next chapter?

DRAFTING

Say: Add those sentences to help glue together the three chapters.

REVIEWING AND REVISING

Say: You can print out all three parts of your autobiography. Carefully read and review each part and the connections between them and make any final revisions you wish. At this stage, you may want to share your life's story with one of the other participants in the Mark Twain's Writers Workshop. However, some students like to keep their stories personal. It is your choice whether or not you share your autobiography with the partner(s) with whom you are working.

Feedback

Teachers give children scores on sentence construction, sentence organization, and word choice from Lesson 9 composition. Teachers and students set realistic writing goals for improving one of these in the next composition.

Illustrating

You may wish to add some photographs your family has taken of you in addition to your hand-drawn illustrations for your completed autobiography.

Getting Ready to Publish

Students show the teachers what has been written so far on *Mark Twain in Star Wars/Star Peace 3001*. Teachers provide feedback and suggestions for revision and further development of the story. Students choose their pen names, just like Mark Twain was a pen name for Samuel Clemens.

LESSON **11** Taking Notes from Source Material for Report

Homework: Second draft of *Mark Twain Star Wars/Star Peace 3001* story is due. Teacher reviews progress with each student.

Why Plants and Trees Are Necessary for Survival of Planet Earth

Read and take notes in *Planet Earth* and in *Protecting Trees & Forests.*

Teacher-Led Reflective Discussion on Note-Taking Strategies at End of Mark Twain Composing Lessons (see p. 315)

1. Look for book features that aid in finding relevant information; for example, table of contents, glossary, pictures, information that is highlighted in boxes, index.

2. Search for key words and pictures related to topic of your report.

3. Write the information in note form: legible handwriting, complete and accurate but not verbatim (word for word)—paraphrase (same ideas but not exactly the same wording).

4. Begin to organize the information—think of key phrases or sentences that might group or summarize information that goes together to support a main idea.

Reading and Taking Notes

Students work with partners to read source material and discuss what to record in note form—however, each student makes his or her own set of notes. Teachers circulate and assist students as necessary and appropriate.

Computer Keyboard Warm-Up

The teacher dictates one of 26 random alphabet letters. The student finds and touches the letter on the real keyboard and looks at the monitor for feedback. The teacher records the number of correct touches on the probe sheet. Use this order: g, n, p, l, u, v, y, s, i, d, z, k, t, q, j, f, x, o, b, c, m, e, w, h, a, r.

Using Keyboard and Word Processing Program to Enter Notes

The teacher assists students in entering their first set of notes. The teacher shows them how to use relevant features of the word processing program, which will have the spell-check feature turned off, for text entry. Students can refer to their notes and make additional revisions. Students also receive feedback on their notes as to their relevance to the topic of the report (on a scale of 1 to 5).

Feedback

Use part of form for note taking and report writing.

LESSON **12** | Taking Notes from Source Material for Report

Why Plants and Trees Are Necessary for Survival of Planet Earth

Read and take notes in *Planet Earth* and *Protecting Trees & Forests.*

Teacher-Led Reflective Discussion on Note-Taking Strategies

1. Look for book features that aid in finding relevant information; for example, table of contents, glossary, pictures, information that is highlighted in boxes, index.

2. Search for key words and pictures related to topic of your report.

3. Write the information in note form: legible handwriting, complete and accurate but not verbatim (word for word)—paraphrase (same ideas but not exactly the same wording).

4. Begin to organize the information—think of key phrases or sentences that might group or summarize information that goes together to support a main idea.

Reading and Taking Notes

Students work with partners to read source material and discuss what to record in note form—however, each student makes his or her own set of notes. Teachers circulate and assist students as necessary and appropriate.

Computer Keyboard Warm-Up

The teacher dictates one of 26 random alphabet letters. The student finds and touches the letter on the real keyboard and looks at the monitor for feedback. The teacher records the number of correct touches on the probe sheet. Use this order: g, v, c, x, o, b, m, j, p, f, z, s, a, q, l, w, u, y, e, h, r, i, t, d, k, n.

Using Keyboard and Word Processing Program to Enter Second Set of Notes

The teacher assists students in entering their notes. The teacher shows them how to use relevant features of the word processing program, which will have the spell-check feature turned off, for notes entry. Students can refer to their notes for the first draft and make additional revisions. Students also receive feedback on their notes as to their relevance to the topic of the report.

Feedback

Use part of form for note taking and report writing.

 Integrating Notes from
Multiple Sources for Report—
Outlines and Paragraph Structure

Why Plants and Trees Are Necessary for Survival of Planet Earth

Teacher-Led Reflective Discussion

The teacher models for students and discusses with them how they first need to figure out three or four main points they want to address in their reports to answer the question of why plants and trees are necessary. These are entered as the main headings in the outline with Roman numerals. Then they need to decide which information in their notes supports each of these main points (main ideas) and list that information with capital letters under the main points. Point out that some of the information has details that elaborate on the supporting information and can be listed with Arabic numerals under the information upon which it elaborates. Show children samples of model outlines. The teacher also models how to go from sample outline to generation of a written paragraph with a main idea, supporting evidence, and elaborated information about the supported evidence.

Student-Generated Outlines

Students are given hard copy of both sets of notes that were previously entered into the computer. They first write their outlines with pencils. Later in the session they will enter them into the computer. Students exchange their outlines and give each other feedback. Students also generate a first draft of the first paragraph of the report based on the outline.

Computer Keyboard Warm-Up

The teacher dictates one of 26 random alphabet letters. The student finds and touches the letter on the real keyboard and looks at the monitor for feedback. The teacher records the number of correct touches on the probe sheet. Use this order: y, n, b, s, h, m, e, w, z, j, g, d, c, i, f, u, r, t, a, l, p, q, o, v.

Using Keyboard and Word Processing Program to Enter Outline and Introductory Paragraph

The teacher assists students in entering the outlines and paragraphs. The teacher shows them how to use relevant features of the word processing program, which will have the spell-check feature turned off, for text entry. Students can refer to their outlines and written paragraphs and make additional revisions. Students receive feedback on the organization of their outlines and paragraph structure.

Feedback

Use part of form for note taking and report writing.

LESSON **14** Report Writing

Homework: Final draft of *Mark Twain Star Wars/Star Peace 3001* story is due.

Why Plants and Trees Are Necessary for Survival of Planet Earth

Teacher-Led Reflective Discussion

The teacher models the process of translating an outline into three well-constructed paragraphs.

Student-Generated Reports

Students work independently to write, with a pencil, the first draft of their reports based on the hard copy of the outlines and paragraph from the Lesson 13 session. Once written, they share the paragraphs with their partners and teacher for feedback.

Computer Keyboard Warm-Up

The teacher dictates one of 26 random alphabet letters. The student finds and touches the letter on the real keyboard and looks at the monitor for feedback. The teacher records the number of correct touches on the probe sheet. Use this order: x, j, e, k, y, n, b, s, h, m, w, z, g, d, c, i, f, u, r, t, a, l, p, q, o, v.

Using Keyboard and Word Processing Program to Enter Report

The teacher assists students in entering the report. The teacher shows them how to use relevant features of the word processing program, which will have the spell-check feature turned off, for text entry. Students can refer to their outlines and notes and make additional revisions. Students receive feedback on the final report using the same criteria and teacher rating scale as for the feedback throughout the workshop and feedback on the relevance of the main points to the question posed in the title of the report.

Feedback

Use part of form for note taking and report writing.

Culminating Writers Workshop Celebration

Each student reads aloud to the group his or her favorite piece of writing composed during the workshop. The teacher reads selections from *Mark Twain in Star Wars/Star Peace 3001*.

The teacher gives out awards for different accomplishments in writing, using the forms provided (see p. 316).

John Muir Writing-Readers in Science

This curriculum is based on the life of John Muir, an immigrant to the United States from Scotland. His life provides the *hope* theme. He overcame an early industrial accident to achieve his dream that led to the establishment of the U.S. National Parks and the environmental conservation movement. John Muir, who was a scientist and writer, recorded his observations of nature in his journal. Thus, he is a scientist-writer who is also a role model for integrating science and writing. The goal of these lessons is to teach children to integrate writing with the other language systems—oral (listening) and reading—because skilled writing requires listening and reading-writers.

This curriculum was implemented in eight 3-hour sessions in the research study that showed it improved reading and writing skills (Berninger et al., 2008) and normalized brain regions associated with phonological processing and hand sensation (Richards et al., 2007). However, it could also be implemented in twenty-four 1-hour sessions spaced over 5 or 6 weeks: Complete all four components in the same day or do two components of a lesson on 2 days, but complete all four components of one lesson before moving on to the next lesson in the sequence. Students keep work in a work folder with John Muir in nature on the front and in his scribble room on the back (Cornell, 2000). Students will need access to desktops and/or laptops with Kurzweil (Kurzweil Educational Systems, Inc., Bedford, MA) or comparable software. The *PAL-II User Guide* (Berninger, 2007b), which is included in the PAL-II Diagnostic for Reading and Writing (PAL-II RW; Berninger, 2007a), contains the following instructional tools that teachers can print out for the lesson plans: Talking Letters, Nickname Cards, Substitute Cards, PAL Reading and Writing Lessons

(Lesson Sets 1–15), Lists 12a and 12b (Sets 1–4) and Graphic Organizers in the Reproducibles for the PAL Reading and Writing Lessons, and Letter Retrieval Before and After Games. The PAL-II RW web site will have a teacher portal in the near future containing other published sources for these instructional materials.

For progress monitoring, teachers can partner with school psychologists who can administer and interpret norm-referenced measures of reading fluency, handwriting, spelling, and written composition at pretest and posttest. The school psychologist should also be able to assist in preparing visual displays and interpretation of the "Jabberwocky" decoding and reading fluency probes collected in each lesson, as well as writing samples collected in each lesson that can be analyzed for legibility of handwriting, number of words, and number of correctly spelled words.

John Muir Curriculum for Developing Phonological Decoding/ Spelling and Science Report Writing

Pretesting

a. Individual pretesting with TOWRE sight word and pseudoword efficiency while the rest of the group is introduced to the words for Monopoly for National Parks (see Unit III Resources, p. 366)

b. Group pretesting for WJ III Spell Sounds

c. Individual Pretesting for Reading Writers (PAL-II Expository Note Taking): Read the text about three new animals that is displayed on the computer monitor and take notes with pen and paper on a clipboard; and Writing Readers (PAL-II Expository Report Writing): Write a report based on the notes with pen and paper on a clipboard.

d. Group pretesting with PAL-II Alphabet Writing, Copy A, and Copy B

ORGANIZATION OF INSTRUCTION

Part 1. Developing Phonological and Phonological–Orthographic Awareness (Begin with Spelling)

1-1. Listening to Develop Phonological Awareness in Spoken Words (Using Bird Names)

a. Listen to bird names and clap number of syllables in each and then count with colored tokens the number of phonemes in each syllable.

1-2. Applying Multiple Phonological-Orthographic Connections (Using Bird Names)

a. Practice with Substitute Cards to show how the pictured sound can be spelled in multiple ways (the alternations in alphabetic principle; Venetzky, 1970, 1999). Use Substitute Cards to spell bird names. Sound the electronic bird call for that bird name when it is spelled correctly.

Part 2. Developing Connections between Listening to Aural Language and Writing Written Language (Use Spelling to Translate Oral Language into Written Language)

a. Listen to the CD of John Muir's life story and adventures (Gilchrist, 2000) and take notes 1) while listening to the newest part of the ongoing story, and 2) while listening to the replay (using audio recorder) of a few sentences from the last session. Apply spelling to integrate listening and writing.

b. Review and revise the spelling in the notes. Keep revisions in a personal dictionary.

Part 3. Applying Multiple Orthographic–Phonological Connections While Reading Paperback about John Muir's Life (So Children Can Develop Writing–Reading Connections)

a. Children take turns reading sentences on designated pages orally. When they come to words they cannot pronounce, use the Nickname Cards to decode it and group discusses strategies to use in decoding unknown words.

Part 4. Reading–Writing Connections in Note Taking

a. Listen to the story about John Muir's life (Cornell, 2000), which was scanned into the computer (read by Kurzweil); follow along as text appears on the monitor; and learn strategies for note taking (teachers should display these strategies; see p. 368). Strategies help students deal with executive function problems (Altemeier, Jones, Abbott, & Berninger, 2006; Hooper, Swartz, Wakely, deKruif, & Montgomery, 2002).

b. Listen to Source 1 for the writing topic of the day (read by Kurzweil), follow along on the monitor, and take notes on a clipboard with a pen.

c. Listen to Source 2 for writing the topic of the day (read by Kurzweil), follow along on the monitor, and take notes on a clipboard with a pen.

Part 5. Writing–Reading Connections in Using Notes to Write Reports

a. Use the *computer keyboard warm-up* to develop automaticity in finding letters on the keyboard. (Transcription is important in composition [e.g., Graham, Berninger, Abbott, Abbott, & Whitaker, 1997]; alphabet writing by keyboarding is related to composition [Berninger, Abbott, Jones, et al., 2006].)

b. Learn strategies for planning, drafting, reviewing, and revising science reports.

c. Plan for today's composition (e.g., Troia, Graham, & Harris, 1999).

d. Translate to produce today's composition draft (e.g., Troia & Graham, 2002).

e. Review and revise yesterday's composition (e.g., MacArthur, Schwartz, & Graham, 1991).

LESSON **1** John Muir's Workshop Lessons

Part 1. Developing Phonological and Phonological–Orthographic Awareness

    a. Listening to Jabberwocky words (bird names), clapping their syllables, counting their phonemes

       Rock dove, black-capped chickadee, mourning dove, white-breasted nuthatch, downy woodpecker, house wren

    b. Spelling bird names from dictation (using Substitute Card). Electronic Bird Call feedback for plausible spelling

       Rock dove, black-capped chickadee, mourning dove, white-breasted nuthatch, downy woodpecker, house wren

Part 2. Developing Listening (Oral Language) and Writing Connections

    a. Listening to John Muir's CD of his life story and adventures and 1) taking notes while listening to the newest part of the ongoing story and 2) summarizing from listening memory and written notes the new information about his life. (Apply spelling to writing and integrate listening and writing.)

       To locate the part to play on the CD, the title of the selection is listed along with the first two sentences and last two sentences of the oral text.

       1. "Dreaming in the Wind"

         "Ah! You're here already. I wasn't expecting you so soon."

         "Oh, I'll tell you some of those when we get to that part of the story, but we're not there yet. I was busy having my own adventures as a boy, right there in Scotland."

       2. "Climbing Castle Walls"

         "Oh, how we boys loved adventure! My friends and I had a game we called 'Scoochers.'"

         "My father's strap was waiting for me. No punishment could drive out the love of wild nature and adventure that seemed to flow through my veins like blood."

    b. Reviewing the notes and written summaries for spelling (individual progress monitoring)—highlighting correctly spelled words while the group does *Mad Libs for Summer Camp–Introduction* (generating and spelling words that fit the sentence context and grammar cues—parts of speech)

Part 3. Developing Orthographic–Phonological Connections

a. Applying Nicknames to reading Jabberwocky words (PAL List 12a, Set 1)

b. Reading John Muir's autobiography (using Nickname Card for decoding unknown words). Teacher reads p. 4, introduction to John Muir, father of America's National Parks and a scientist-writer who described nature in the wilderness and his scientific explorations of nature. Students in small groups read aloud Chapter 1, "Free as the Wind," pp. 5–10 (Cornell, 2000), switching turns when punctuation signals the end of a sentence.

c. Olympic races (individual progress monitoring with transfer Jabberwocky words; PAL List 12b, Set 1 in Reproducibles) while the group plays Monopoly for National Parks. (Decode names of nature on the game board and playing cards.)

Part 4. Reading–Writing for Note Taking

a. Introduce procedures to use next time for Kurzweil presentation of source material 1 and 2. That is, download sample reading text that has been scanned into the system. Show how student can choose a voice that reads the text orally while the student reads it silently as individual words coinciding to the spoken words are highlighted on the screen to focus his or her attention during note taking.

Part 5. Writing–Reading for Report Writing

a. Explain that beginning in Lesson 1, using notes taken while reading text, students will write a report by pen and then enter it into the computer.

LESSON **2** John Muir's Workshop Lessons

Part 1. Developing Phonological and Phonological–Orthographic Awareness

    a.   Listening to Jabberwocky words (bird names), clapping their syllables, counting their phonemes

        Northern flicker, American robin, American crow, northern mockingbird, broad-winged hawk, great crested flycatcher

    b.   Spelling bird names from dictation (using Substitute Card). Electronic Bird Call feedback for plausible spelling

        Northern flicker, American robin, American crow, northern mockingbird, broad-winged hawk, great crested flycatcher

Part 2. Developing Listening (Oral Language) and Writing Connections

    a.   Listening to John Muir's CD of his life story and adventures and 1) taking notes while listening to the newest part of the ongoing story, and 2) summarizing from listening memory and written notes the new information about his life. (Apply spelling to writing and integrate listening and writing.)

        To locate the part to play on the CD, the title of the selection is listed along with the first two sentences and last two sentences of the oral text.

        3. "To America!"

            "There was a book in school about a faraway land called, *America.* In those days, America was brand new country and it was still wild and open."

            "Free to roam through the woods, explore the shores of the lakes and wander up the streams. It was a paradise."

    b.   Reviewing the notes and written summaries for spelling (individual progress monitoring); highlighting correctly spelled words while the group does *Mad Libs for Summer Camp—Our Favorite Counselor* (spelling words that fit the sentence context)

Part 3. Developing Orthographic–Phonological Connections

    a.   Reading Jabberwocky words (applying Nicknames; PAL List 12a, Set 2)

    b.   Reading John Muir's autobiography (using Nickname Card for decoding unknown words)

Students read, taking turns when punctuation indicates the end of a sentence (to create sentence awareness): Chapter 2, "Backwoods Genius" (pp. 11–15); and Chapter 3, "Only Wild Beauty" (pp. 16–21).

c. Olympic races (individual progress monitoring with transfer Jabberwocky words; PAL List 12b, Set 2) while the group plays Monopoly for National Parks. (Decode names of nature on the game board and playing cards.)

Part 4. Reading–Writing for Note Taking

a. Teacher modeling of strategies for note taking

b. Listening to and reading text for *Mt. St. Helens, the Glacier Covered Volcano That Blew Its Top,* which is presented by the Kurzweil program; and taking notes on a clipboard with a pen

Part 5. Writing–Reading for Report Writing

a. Computer keyboard warm-up (Letter Retrieval Games, 5 before and 5 after in Lesson 1 in *PAL-II User Guide* [Berninger, 2007b or 1998])

b. Teacher modeling strategies for planning, drafting, reviewing, and revising science reports. Graphic organizer for Events + Details. (See Unit 2, Mark Twain Writers Workshop.)

c. Planning informational essay: Descriptive report with sequential events on *Mt. St. Helens, the Glacier Covered Volcano That Blew Its Top* (by integrating two sources of information and graphic organizers)

d. Drafting by pen an informational essay: Descriptive report with sequential events on *Mt. St. Helens, the Glacier Covered Volcano That Blew Its Top*

e. Entering the draft by keyboarding into a word processing program

LESSON **3** John Muir's Workshop Lessons

Part 1. Developing Phonological and Phonological–Orthographic Awareness

a. Listening to Jabberwocky words (bird names), clapping their syllables, counting their phonemes

   Ruffed grouse, red-eyed vireo, great horned owl, hermit thrush, pileated woodpecker, ovenbird

b. Spelling bird names from dictation (using Substitute Card). Electronic bird call feedback for plausible spelling

   Ruffed grouse, red-eyed vireo, great horned owl, hermit thrush, pileated woodpecker, ovenbird

Part 2. Developing Listening (Oral Language) and Writing Connections

a. Listening to John Muir's CD of his life story and adventures and 1) taking notes while listening to the newest part of the ongoing story, and 2) summarizing from listening memory and written notes the new information about his life. (Apply spelling to writing and integrate listening and writing.)

   To locate the part to play on the CD, the title of the selection is listed along with the first two sentences and last two sentences of the oral text.

   4. "Woods, Lakes, Boys, and Birds"

      "The woods where we lived were filled with the songs of a hundred species of feathery singers. And as fall came on, the lakes filled up with hundreds of brightly colored ducks and geese."

      "Every wild lesson a love lesson, not thrashed, but charmed into us. Oh! That glorious Wisconsin wilderness!"

   5. "Life on a Wisconsin Farm"

      "Very soon though the hard work of running a farm began. I was up at dawn or before each morning to do my chores."

      "Fly far away from that farm, far from all that hard, hard work. But I had no wings, just feet and I was stuck to the ground, to that farm, and that work for years to come yet."

b. Reviewing the notes and written summaries for spelling (individual progress monitoring)—highlighting correctly spelled words while the group does *Mad Libs for Summer Camp: Safety Precautions for Campers* (spelling words that fit the sentence context)

Part 3. Developing Orthographic–Phonological Connections

a. Reading Jabberwocky words (applying Nicknames; PAL List 12a, Set 3)

b. Reading John Muir's autobiography (using Nickname Card for decoding unknown words)

Chapter 4, "Favorite Animals," pp. 22–26; and Chapter 5, "Forever a Mountaineer," pp. 27–35

c. Olympic races (individual progress monitoring with transfer Jabberwocky words; PAL List 12b, Set 3) while the group plays Monopoly for National Parks. (Decode names of nature on the game board and playing cards.)

Part 4. Reading–Writing for Note Taking

a. Teacher modeling of strategies for note taking

b. Listening to and reading Source 1 for *Mt. Ranier: Mountain of Many Seasons,* which is presented by the Kurzweil program; and taking notes on a clipboard with a pen

Part 5. Writing–Reading for Report Writing

a. Computer keyboard warm-up (Letter Retrieval Games, 5 before and 5 after in Lesson 1 in *PAL-II User Guide* [Berninger, 2007b or 1998])

b. Teacher modeling of strategies for planning, drafting, reviewing, and revising science reports based on multiple sources of information

c. Planning informational essay: Descriptive report with sequential events on *Mt. Ranier: Mountain of Many Seasons.* Graphic organizer Events + Details

d. Drafting by pen an informational essay: Descriptive report with sequential events on *Mt. Ranier: Mountain of Many Seasons*

e. Entering the draft by keyboarding into a word processing program

f. Reviewing and revising on computer *Mt. St. Helens: The Glacier Covered Volcano That Blew Its Top*

LESSON **4** John Muir's Workshop Lessons

Part 1. Developing Phonological and Phonological–Orthographic Awareness

    a.   Listening to Jabberwocky words (bird names), clapping their syllables, counting their phonemes

         Eastern wood-pewee, scarlet tanager, pied-billed grebe, common moorhen, American bittern, American coot

    b.   Spelling bird names from dictation (using Substitute Card). Electronic Bird Call feedback for plausible spelling

         Eastern wood-pewee, scarlet tanager, pied-billed grebe, common moorhen, American bittern, American coot

Part 2. Developing Listening (Oral Language) and Writing Connections

    a.   Listening to John Muir's CD of his life story and adventures and 1) taking notes while listening to the newest part of the ongoing story, and 2) summarizing from listening memory and written notes the new information about his life. (Apply spelling to writing and integrate listening and writing.)

         To locate the part to play on the CD, the title of the selection is listed along with the first two sentences and last two sentences of the oral text.

         7.   "My Amazing Machines"

              "We worked everyday but Sunday, and Sunday was church. In the afternoon, after church I had my only free time and I'd walk for miles to borrow books from neighbors."

              "I could help people. Maybe I could really make a difference in the world!"

    b.   Reviewing the notes and written summaries for spelling (individual progress monitoring)—highlighting correctly spelled words while the group does *Mad Libs for Summer Camp: Campfire Stories* (spelling words that fit the sentence context).

Part 3. Developing Orthographic–Phonological Connections

    a.   Reading Jabberwocky words (applying Nicknames; PAL List 12a, Set 4)

    b.   Reading John Muir's autobiography (using Nickname Card for decoding unknown words) (Chapter 6, "Snow Flowers, Ice Rivers, and a Dog," pp. 36–44)

c. Olympic races (individual progress monitoring with transfer Jabberwocky words; PAL List 12b, Set 4) while the group plays Monopoly for National Parks. (Decode names of nature on the game board and playing cards.)

Part 4. Reading–Writing for Note Taking

a. Teacher modeling of strategies for note taking

b. Listening to and re-reading and reviewing Source 1 about Mt. St. Helens, and Source 2 about Mt. Ranier from Lessons 1 and 2, which are presented by Kurzweil program, and taking notes on a clipboard with a pen

Part 5. Writing–Reading for Report Writing

a. Computer keyboard warm-up (Letter Retrieval Games, 5 before and 5 after in Lesson 1 in *PAL-II User Guide* [Berninger, 2007b or 1998])

b. Teacher modeling of strategies for planning, drafting, reviewing, and revising science reports based on multiple sources of information. Graphic organizer: Weave for compare and contrast

c. Planning compare and contrast essay on Mt. St. Helens and Mt. Ranier

d. Drafting by pen a compare and contrast essay on Mt. St. Helens and Mt. Ranier

e. Entering the draft by keyboarding into a word processing program

f. Reviewing and revising on computer *Mt. Ranier: Mountain of Many Seasons*

LESSON **5** John Muir's Workshop Lessons

Part 1. Developing Phonological and Phonological–Orthographic Awareness

    a.   Listening to Jabberwocky words (bird names), clapping their syllables, counting their phonemes

        Green heron, spotted sandpiper, wood duck, marsh wren, Virginia rail, swamp sparrow

    b.   Spelling bird names from dictation (using Substitute Card). Electronic Bird Call feedback for plausible spelling

        Green heron, spotted sandpiper, wood duck, marsh wren, Virginia rail, swamp sparrow

Part 2. Developing Listening (Oral Language) and Writing Connections

    a.   Listening to John Muir's CD of his life story and adventures and 1) taking notes while listening to the newest part of the ongoing story, and 2) summarizing from listening memory and written notes the new information about his life. (Apply spelling to writing and integrate listening and writing.)

        To locate the part to play on the CD, the title of the selection is listed along with the first two sentences and last two sentences of the oral text.

    8.   "Blind! — and a Vision"

        "The next year, I came back to Madison, this time to attend the university. I studied all kinds of things: botany and geology, and chemistry."

        "As my eyes adjusted to the light, I approached the window and looked out at the sun streaming through the trees and the wind playing on the branches. I decided right then and there that I would dedicate my life, not to machines, but to nature, to wild and growing things, to the beauty of mountains and trees, wild animals and birds."

    9.   "Home in the Mountains"

        "To celebrate, I set off walking on a thousand mile walk, from Indiana to the Gulf of Mexico, taking the wildest, leafiest, least-trodden way that I could find, zigzagging like a butterfly. I wrote in my journal my new address: John Muir, Earth planet, Universe."

        "The beautiful clean granite walls, almost a mile high, set straight up into the sky. And over the top of those huge walls come falling waterfalls, tumbling and roaring and streaming and singing their mountain songs."

10. "At the Top of Yosemite Falls"

"One summer morning I was up walking along the high rim of the valley, along the edges of the cliffs, looking three thousand feet down into the Great Yosemite. The trouble is, the cliffs are rounded off at the edges, so I had trouble finding a place with a sharp edge where I could walk out and look straight down the face of the cliff to the bottom."

"From here, with the waterfall booming all around me, I could get a clear view down into the very heart of the slowly chanting throng of silvery streamers. I got back to camp about dark, excited, exhilarated, triumphant, determined to have as many mountain adventures as I could find."

b. Reviewing the notes and written summaries for spelling (individual progress monitoring)—highlighting correctly spelled words while the group does *Mad Libs for Summer Camp—Fourth of July* (spelling words that fit the sentence context)

Part 3. Developing Orthographic–Phonological Connections

a. Reading Jabberwocky words (applying Nicknames; PAL List 12a, Set 1)

b. Reading John Muir's autobiography (using Nickname Card for decoding unknown words) (Chapter 7, "Make the Mountains Glad," pp. 45–51; and "Fellow Mortals," pp. 52–56)

c. Olympic races (individual progress monitoring with transfer Jabberwocky words; PAL List 12b, Set 1) while the group plays Monopoly for National Parks. (Decode names of nature on the game board and playing cards.)

Part 4. Reading–Writing for Note Taking

a. Teacher modeling of strategies for note taking

b. Listening to and reading text about Controversies about the Mountains, which is presented by the Kurzweil program, and taking notes on a clipboard with a pen

Part 5. Writing–Reading for Report Writing

a. Computer keyboard warm-up (Letter Retrieval Games, 5 before and 5 after in Lesson 1 in *PAL-II User Guide* [Berninger, 2007b or 1998])

b. Teacher modeling of strategies for planning, drafting, reviewing, and revising science reports. Graphic organizers are *Sides of an Argument, Knocking Out–Counter-Argument,* and *Taking Sides.*

c. Planning a persuasive essay on controversies about Mt. St. Helens and Mt. Ranier (by integrating two sources of information and graphic organizers)

d. Drafting by pen a persuasive essay on controversies about Mt. St. Helens and Mt. Ranier

e. Entering the draft by keyboarding into a word processing program

f. Reviewing and revising on computer comparing and contrasting Mt. St. Helens and Mt. Ranier

LESSON 6 | John Muir's Workshop Lessons

Part 1. Developing Phonological and Phonological–Orthographic Awareness

    a.   Listening to Jabberwocky words (bird names), clapping their syllables, counting their phonemes

        Black-bellied plover, laughing gull, American oystercatcher, herring gull, greater yellowlegs, royal tern

    b.   Spelling bird names from dictation (using Substitute Card). Electronic Bird Call feedback for plausible spelling

        Black-bellied plover, laughing gull, American oystercatcher, herring gull, greater yellowlegs, royal tern

Part 2. Developing Listening (Oral Language) and Writing Connections

    a.   Listening to John Muir's CD of his life story and adventures and 1) taking notes while listening to the newest part of the ongoing story, and 2) summarizing from listening memory and written notes the new information about his life. (Apply spelling to writing and integrate listening and writing.)

        To locate the part to play on the CD, the title of the selection is listed along with the first two sentences and last two sentences of the oral text.

    11.   "An Avalanche Ride"

        "One of my most exciting Yosemite adventures took place on a fine winter morning after a big snowstorm. I was eager to see avalanches, snow rivers that slide down the mountains after big storms."

        "In all my mountaineering, I've enjoyed only this one avalanche ride, and the start was so sudden and the end came so soon, I had but little time to think what was happening. Though at such times, one thinks fast."

    12.   "A Meeting with a Bear"

        "I was out walking one day with a dog friend of mine called Carlo. Now, Carlo was a St. Bernard, a sheep dog."

        "Their days are warmed by the same sun and they live under the same blue sky, and their lives turn and ebb with the same heart pulsings as our own. And we're poured from the same first fountain."

b. Reviewing the notes and written summaries for spelling (individual progress monitoring)—highlighting correctly spelled words while the group does *Mad Libs for Summer Camp—Swimming and Scuba Diving* (spelling words that fit the sentence context)

Part 3. Developing Orthographic–Phonological Connections

a. Reading Jabberwocky words (applying Nicknames; PAL List 12a, Set 2)

b. Reading John Muir's autobiography (using Nickname Card for decoding unknown words; Chapter 9, "Nature's Goodness," pp. 57–61)

c. Olympic races (individual progress monitoring with transfer Jabberwocky words; PAL List 12b, Set 2) while the group plays Monopoly for National Parks. (Decode names of nature on the game board and playing cards.)

Part 4. Reading–Writing for Note Taking

For text, use *Protecting Trees and Forests* by Felicity Brooks (available from Usborne Publishing and Scholastic, Inc.).

a. Teacher modeling of strategies for note taking

b. Listening to and reading text, "Our Forests Are Endangered," which is presented by the Kurzweil program, and taking notes on a clipboard with a pen

Part 5. Writing–Reading for Report Writing

a. Computer keyboard warm-up (Letter Retrieval Games, 5 before and 5 after in Lesson 1 in *PAL-II User Guide* [Berninger, 2007b or 1998])

b. Teacher modeling of strategies for planning, drafting, reviewing, and revising science reports

c. Planning an informative essay, "Our Endangered Forests"

d. Drafting by pen an informative essay, "Our Endangered Forests"

e. Entering the draft by keyboarding into a word processing program

f. Reviewing and revising on computer controversies about Mt. St. Helens and Mt. Ranier

LESSON **7** | John Muir's Workshop Lessons

Part 1. Developing Phonological and Phonological–Orthographic Awareness

    a.   Listening to Jabberwocky words (bird names), clapping their syllables, counting their phonemes

         Willett, common tern, sanderling, black skimmer, European starling, brown-headed cowbird

    b.   Spelling bird names from dictation (using Substitute Card). Electronic Bird Call feedback for plausible spelling

         Willett, common tern, sanderling, black skimmer, European starling, brown-headed cowbird

Part 2. Developing Listening (Oral Language) and Writing Connections

    a.   Listening to John Muir's CD of his life story and adventures and 1) taking notes while listening to the newest part of the ongoing story, and 2) summarizing from listening memory and written notes the new information about his life. (Apply spelling to writing and integrate listening and writing.)

         To locate the part to play on the CD, the title of the selection is listed along with the first two sentences and last two sentences of the oral text.

       14.   "A Fight for the Sequoias"

           "Oh, not everyone appreciates the great harmony of nature. There are thousands of people coming to California, and the more people that came, the more destruction they brought with them."

      "You can take your children and your grand children, when you have them. Those trees will outlive all of us."

    b.   Reviewing the notes and written summaries for spelling (individual progress monitoring)—highlighting correctly spelled words while the group does *Mad Libs for Summer Camp: Canoeing and Hiking* (spelling words that fit the sentence context)

Part 3. Developing Orthographic–Phonological Connections

    a.   Reading Jabberwocky words (applying Nicknames; PAL List 12a, Set 3)

    b.   Reading John Muir's autobiography (using Nickname Card for decoding unknown words; (Explore More, Be True to Yourself, One Large Family, Joy in the Midst of Hardship, This Whole Wide World, pp. 62–67)

c.   Olympic races (individual progress monitoring with transfer Jabberwocky words; PAL List 12b, Set 3) while the group plays Monopoly for National Parks. (Decode names of nature on the game board and playing cards.)

Part 4. Reading–Writing for Note Taking

a.   Teacher modeling of strategies for note taking

b.   Listening to and re reading text about Saving Our Endangered Forests, which is presented by the Kurzweil program, and taking notes on a clipboard with a pen

Part 5. Writing–Reading for Report Writing

a.   Computer keyboard warm-up (Letter Retrieval Games, 5 before and 5 after in Lesson 1 in *PAL-II User Guide* [Berninger, 2007b or 1998])

b.   Teacher modeling of strategies for planning, drafting, reviewing, and revising science reports based on multiple sources of information

c.   Planning a persuasive essay, "Saving Our Endangered Forests" (by integrating two sources of information and graphic organizers)

d.   Reviewing and revising on computer "Saving Our Endangered Forests" for the second and final time

LESSON **8** John Muir's Workshop Lessons

Part 1. Developing Phonological and Phonological–Orthographic Awareness

a. Listening to Jabberwocky words (bird names), clapping their syllables, counting their phonemes

Common yellowthroat, Baltimore oriole, northern cardinal, house finch, song sparrow, American goldfinch

b. Spelling bird names from dictation (using Substitute Card). Electronic Bird Call feedback for plausible spelling

Common yellowthroat, Baltimore oriole, northern cardinal, house finch, song sparrow, American goldfinch

Part 2. Developing Listening (Oral Language) and Writing Connections

a. Listening to John Muir's CD of his life story and adventures and 1) taking notes while listening to the newest part of the ongoing story, and 2) summarizing from listening memory and written notes the new information about his life. (Apply spelling to writing and integrate listening and writing.)

To locate the part to play on the CD, the title of the selection is listed along with the first two sentences and last two sentences of the oral text.

15. "Presidents, Parks, and Preservation"

"One of the men who read my words was Teddy Roosevelt. The president was a very enthusiastic man and he was excited about my ideas of protecting wild land."

"Nearly two million acres of wild forestland. That's the kind of effect a night in the mountains can have on a person."

16. "Go to the Mountains"

"Go to the mountains or out into nature anywhere and see for yourself. Nature will stream into you like sunshine flows into trees."

"Really, I only went out for a walk, but I decided to stay out till sundown. For going out to nature, I found, was really going home."

b. Reviewing the notes and written summaries for spelling (individual progress monitoring)—highlighting correctly spelled words while the group does *Mad Libs for Summer Camp—Plants* (spelling words that fit the sentence context)

Part 3. Developing Orthographic–Phonological Connections

    a.   Reading Jabberwocky words (applying Nicknames; PAL List 12a, Set 4)

    b.   Olympic races (individual progress monitoring with transfer Jabberwocky words; PAL List 12b, Set 4) while the group plays Monopoly for National Parks. (Decode names of nature on the game board and playing cards.)

    c.   Individual posttesting TOWRE sight word efficiency and phonemic reading efficiency

Part 4. Reading–Writing for Note Taking

    a.   Individual posttesting for reading writers and writing readers

    b.   Group posttesting for WIAT-II Spelling

    c.   Group posttesting for WJ III Spelling Sounds

Part 5. Writing–Reading for Report Writing

    a.   Group posttesting for PAL Copy A and Copy B

    b.   Individual posttesting for PAL-II Expository Note Taking and Report Writing

    c.   Revising "Saving Our Endangered Forests"

REFERENCES

UNIT III
REFER-
ENCES

Altemeier, L., Jones, J., Abbott, R.D., & Berninger, V.W. (2006). Executive factors in becoming writing readers and reading writers: Note taking and report writing in third and fifth graders. *Developmental Neuropsychology, 29*(1), 161–173.

Berninger, V.W., Abbott, R.D., Jones, J., Wolf, B.J., Gould, L., Anderson-Youngstrom, M., et al. (2006). Early development of language by hand: Composing, reading, listening, and speaking connections; three letter-writing modes; and fast mapping in spelling. *Developmental Neuropsychology, 29*(1), 61–92.

Berninger, V.W., Winn, W., Stock, P., Abbott, R.D., Eschen, K., Lin, C., et al. (2008). Tier 3 specialized writing instruction for students with dyslexia. *Reading and Writing: An Interdisciplinary Journal, 21*(1), 95–130.

Cornell, J. (2000). *John Muir: My life with nature.* Nevada City, CA: Dawn Publications.

Gilchrist, G. (2000). *John Muir: My life of adventures* [CD recording]. Nevada City, CA: Dawn Publications.

Graham, S., Berninger, V.W., Abbott, R.D., Abbott, S.P., & Whitaker, D. (1997). The role of mechanics in composing of elementary school students: A new methodological approach. *Journal of Educational Psychology, 89*(1), 170–182.

Hooper, S., Swartz, C., Wakely, M., deKruif, R., & Montgomery, J. (2002). Executive functions in elementary school children with and without problems in written expression. *Journal of Learning Disabilities, 35,* 57–68.

MacArthur, C.A., Schwartz, S.S., & Graham, S. (1991). Effects of a reciprocal peer revision strategy in special education classrooms. *Learning Disability Research and Practice, 6,* 201–210.

Richards, T., Berninger, V.W., Winn, W., Stock, S., Wagner, R., Muse, A., et al. (2007). Functional MRI activation in children with dyslexia during pseudoword aural repeat and visual decode: Before and after treatment. *Neuropsychology, 21*(6), 732–747.

Troia, G.A., & Graham, S. (2002). The effectiveness of a highly explicit, teacher-directed strategy instruction routine: Changing the writing performance of students with learning disabilities. *Journal of Learning Disabilities, 35*(4), 290–305.

Troia, G.A., Graham, S., & Harris, K.R. (1999). Teaching students with learning disabilities to mindfully plan when writing. *Exceptional Children, 65,* 235–252.

Venezky, R.L. (1970). *The structure of English orthography.* The Hague: Mouton.

Venezky, R.L. (1999). *The American way of spelling.* New York: Guilford Press.

Wijsman, E.M., Peterson, D., Leutenegger, A.L., Thomson, J.B., Goddard, K.A., Hsu, L., et al. (2000). Segregation analysis of phenotypic components of learning disabilities: I. Nonword memory and digit span. *American Journal of Human Genetics, 67*(3), 631–646.

INSTRUCTIONAL RESOURCES

Berninger, V.W. (1998). *PAL guides for reading and writing intervention.* San Antonio, TX: Pearson Assessment. This whole instructional guide can also be accessed through Berninger (2007b).

Alphabet Retrieval Game (24 lessons) on p. 193

Berninger, V.W., & Abbott, S. (2003). *PAL research-supported reading and writing lessons.* San Antonio, TX: Pearson Assessment. This set of 15 lesson plans can also be accessed through Berninger (2007b).

Phonological awareness (PAL Lesson Sets 5, 11, and 12)

Jabberwocky words for teaching and probes (Lesson Set 10; Lists 12a Sets 1–4, pp. 166–170; Lists 12b Sets 1–4, pp. 182, 184, 186, and 188)

Nicknames in alphabetic principle (graphemes to phonemes, Lesson Set 6; and Reproducibles, pp. 41–42)

Substitutions (phonemes to spelling units, Lesson Set 7; and Reproducibles, pp. 43–44), Report writing (Lesson Sets 8, 10, 13, and 14)

Brooks, F. (1994). *Protecting trees and forests.* London: Usborne Publishing.

An Usborne Conservation Guide available from www.DiscoverUsborneBooks.com and a Scholastic book available from www.scholastic.com. The designated pages for this source material in Unit III lessons should be scanned via Kurzweil into the computer.

Corcoran, T. (1985). *Mt. St. Helens: The story behind the scenery.* Las Vegas, NV: KC Publications. The designated pages for this source material in Unit III lessons should be scanned via Kurzweil into the computer.

Cornell, J. (2000). *John Muir: My life with nature.* Nevada City, CA: Dawn Publications.

Dengler, W. (1992). *Mount Rainier: The continuing story.* Las Vegas, NV: KC Publications. The designated pages for this source material in Unit III lessons should be scanned via Kurzweil into the computer.

For The Birds. (2000). *LLC Birdsong Identiflyer, audio bird song dictionary.* P.O. Box 1731; Seneca, SC 29679-1731.

1. Rock dove, black-capped chickadee, mourning dove, white-breasted nuthatch, downy woodpecker, house wren
2. Northern flicker, American robin, American crow, northern mockingbird, broad-winged hawk, great crested flycatcher
3. Ruffed grouse, red-eyed vireo, great horned owl, hermit thrush, pileated woodpecker, ovenbird
4. Eastern wood-pewee, scarlet tanager, piled-billed grebe, common moorhen, American bittern, American coot
5. Green heron, spotted sandpiper, wood duck, marsh wren, Virginia rail, swamp sparrow
6. Black-bellied plover, laughing gull, American oystercatcher, herring gull, greater yellowlegs, royal tern
7. Willett, common tern, sanderling, black skimmer, European starling, brown-headed cowbird
8. Common yellowthroat, Baltimore oriole, northern cardinal, house finch, song sparrow, American goldfinch
9. Red-winged blackbird, house sparrow, rock dove, black-capped chickadee, mourning dove, white-breasted nuthatch

10. Downy woodpecker, house wren, northern flicker, American robin, American crow, northern mockingbird.

Gilchrist, G. (2000). *John Muir: My life of adventures.* CD recording by storyteller Garth Gilchrist. Nevada City, CA: Dawn Publications.

National Parks Monopoly. The National Parks Edition of Monopoly (r) is produced by USAopoly Inc. of Encinitas, California, a privately held corporation and the licensee of Hasbro Inc.'s Monopoly game, founded in 1994 to create, manufacture and market specialty editions. Sole sponsorship is provided by Pacific Trail Inc., a leading manufacturer of recreational outerwear based in Seattle, Washington. A portion of the proceeds from game sales will be used by the National Park Foundation to benefit our nation's parks.

National Park Series: The Story Behind the Scenery covers more than 75 parks and Indian culture. Catalogue available by calling 800-626-9673 or writing to KC Publications, 3245 E. Patrick Lane, Suite A, Las Vegas, NV 89120. For these lessons we used the books for Mount Ranier and Mount St. Helens in Washington State. Depending on where a school is located, other titles may be of more interest and can be adapted for the curriculum. The designated pages for this source material in Unit III lessons should be scanned via Kurzweil into the computer.

Osborne, M., & Boyce, N. (2004). *Ancient Greece and the Olympics.* New York: Random House.

Price, R., & Stern, L. (1990, 2001). *Mad Libs: World's greatest word game.* New York: Price, Stern, Sloan.

Snow, R. (1984). *Mount Rainier: The story behind the scenery.* Las Vegas, NV: KC Publications. The designated pages for this source material in Unit III lessons should be scanned via Kurzweil into the computer.

NOTE TAKING STRATEGIES

1. Look for book features that aid in finding relevant information; for example, table of contents, glossary, pictures, information that is highlighted in boxes, and index.

2. Search for key words and pictures related to the topic of your report.

3. Write the information in note form: legible handwriting; complete and accurate but not verbatim (word for word); paraphrase (same ideas but not exactly the same wording).

4. Begin to organize the information. Think of key phrases or sentences that might group or summarize information that goes together to support a main idea.

Sequoyah Writing Reader Club

CWY
ᎤᎦ
GᏪᏪ
ᎣᏓ

This lesson set builds on the Word Detectives lessons (Unit I) taught initially to improve the reading of students with dyslexia; the Mark Twain Workshop lessons (Unit II) taught subsequently to improve the writing skills of students with dyslexia; and then the John Muir Science Writing Workshop (Unit III) taught to teach writing-reading skills in the science content area—including planning, drafting, and reviewing and revising essays—to students with dyslexia. The hope theme for this unit is built on the contributions of Sequoyah, a Cherokee Indian who was injured in a hunting accident and disabled but by age 50 had devised an alphabet for writing down the oral Cherokee language. As a result, Cherokee is one of the few native languages with a written version to preserve the culture. To honor his contribution, the giant redwoods of California are named *Sequoia*.

In the first set of five lessons, the warm-up emphasizes the integration of writing and reading skills. Students start with warm-ups designed to review and provide practice in creating automatic knowledge of spelling–sound correspondences in alphabetic principle and phonological awareness of sounds in spoken words and transfer of both kinds of knowledge to oral reading of unfamiliar words ("Jabberwocky" words [as in *Through the Looking-Glass*], or pseudowords in reading assessments) and spelling. In the next set of seven lessons, the warm-up emphasizes orthographic spelling strategies from the Mark Twain lessons (Unit II) and morphological awareness from the Word Detective lessons (Unit I). Collectively, these warm-up activities provide continuing review and practice in developing phonological, orthographic, and morphological awareness, all of which are critical to developing the ability to read unfamiliar words orally when sentence context clues are not available or the ability to spell written words.

CWY
ᏚᏳᎻ
ᎦᏪᎩ
ᎤᎳ

UNIT IV
Intro-
duction

In the first five lessons, children also continue to develop their comprehension of written language. To begin, students answer teacher-directed questions about the designated parts of the written text they read. The question-asking and question-answering sessions are guided by the teacher, who engages the students in reflective discussion that is guided by students' oral responses to the questions. That is, quality reading comprehension instruction cannot be purely scripted—teachers should adapt their comments and further questions in response to children's answers, comments, or questions. (*Note:* Answers are provided only when the facts are stated explicitly in text, not when answers may draw on children's background knowledge, inferential thinking, personal views, and so forth.) In addition, students learn a summarization strategy for explaining the main idea and supporting details of the text they have written. To strengthen the link between reading comprehension and written composition about the written text just read, children then write summaries of the text that was read in the lesson.

In the next seven lessons, children develop their oral reading fluency through 1) oral choral reading and 2) individual practice with passages geared to their own reading rate. The purpose of the choral reading led by the teacher, in which each child reads orally at the pace set by the teacher, is not only to practice decoding without fear of making a mistake but also to provide a "no-tech" approach to giving students access to the content of reading material they may not be able to read independently. In these seven lessons, students also practice three kinds of writing skills: 1) written summarization of main ideas and supporting details; 2) essay writing on a topic related to the topic of the passage selection for the day used for choral reading; and 3) journal writing in which the summary is extended by students writing their opinions, thoughts, and questions that came to mind as they read.

The Writing Readers Workshop ends with three culminating activities: 1) writing the book report based on review of all journal entries during the last seven lessons; 2) writing a compare-and-contrast essay about the Iroquois culture and contemporary U.S. culture; and 3) authors sharing their book reports and compare-and-contrast essays, with award certificates given by the teacher (see p. 404).

FIRST READING SELECTION

Sequoyah: The Cherokee Man Who Gave His People Writing (first five lessons focused on linguistics)

SECOND READING SELECTION

If You Lived with the Iroquois (seven lessons focused on cultural anthropology, three culminating sessions)

Evidence for Unit IV Lessons

During the 2006–2007 school year, an after-school tutorial used lessons in Unit IV. A complete report on the study is in preparation, but initial findings presented in a symposium at the annual meeting of the Society of Scientific Study of Reading (Berninger, Stock, Lee, Abbott, & Breznitz, 2007) showed that reading and writing gains were observed when orthographic and morphological awareness were added (Lessons 6–12 in Unit IV) to phonological awareness and orthographic–phonological correspondences in alphabetic principle (Lessons 1–5 in Unit IV).

CWY
ᎤᏙᎯ
ᏗᏠᎯ
ᎤᏓ

UNIT IV
Intro-
duction

These findings provided additional evidence that struggling readers and writers benefit from three kinds of linguistic awareness for word forms and their parts: phonological (P), orthographic (O), and morphological (M). For other evidence for the instructional value of POM, see the Introduction to Unit I and the textbook, *Teaching Students with Dyslexia and Dysgraphia: Lessons from Teaching and Science* (Berninger & Wolf, 2009), that accompanies this workbook. Not only do students who successfully complete the Sequoyah Writing Reader Workshop receive a certificate of merit, but also the teachers who successfully teach Units I–IV receive two certificates of merit. The first is for teaching students who struggle in reading and writing that English is not hopelessly irregular (the Spell and Phone Certificate; see p. 405). The second is for their membership in the POM POM society (see p. 406)—open only to those who recognize the importance of teaching students how phonology, orthography, and morphology have to be integrated to learn to read and spell written English.

References

Berninger, V.W., Stock, P., Lee, Y., Abbott, R., & Breznitz, Z. (2007, July). *Working memory enhancement through accelerated reading training.* Presentation in symposium on "Can the dyslexic brain do better? Enhancement of reading fluency" (Z. Breznitz, organizer and chair). Society for the Scientific Study of Reading, Prague, Czechoslovakia.

Berninger, V.W., & Wolf, B. (2009). *Teaching students with dyslexia and dysgraphia: Lessons from teaching and science.* Baltimore: Paul H. Brookes Publishing Co.

Levine, E. (1999). *If you lived with the Iroquois.* New York: Scholastic Paperbacks.

Rumford, J. (2004). *Sequoyah: The Cherokee man who gave his people writing* (A.S. Huckaby, Trans.). Boston: Houghton Mifflin.

LESSON **1** Sequoyah Writing Reader Club

WARM-UP

Say: Welcome to the Sequoyah Writing Reader Club! Just like athletes warm up before the game, we are going to do warm-up activities. Today we are going to program our brains so that the correspondences between spelling and sound become automatic. I will point to and name a letter, name a word with the associated sound, and make that sound by itself. Then you will take a turn and do the same thing. Today we will do only vowels. For each row I will name the kind of syllable in which the vowel occurs and then we will do all the vowels that go with that syllable type. To warm up our brains, we will do this quickly and we will time how long it takes the group to do these warm-ups. Each time, we will see if we can beat our time last time.

On the posted growth graph, write the time that it took to do all the rows (except the schwa). Stop at the vowel.dot for consonant silent *e* (*x* over it).

BIRD NAMES: PHONOLOGICAL AWARENESS AND ELECTRONIC BIRD NAME FEEDBACK (10 MINUTES)

Listening to Bird Names

Say: Now we are going to listen for and count the sounds in spoken words.

1. Count the number of syllables—hold up fingers (eyes closed). If all agree, move to the next bird name, If they do not all agree, then clap syllables and reach group consensus.

2. Count the number of phonemes in the pronounced syllable—do one syllable at a time in the bird's name. Using a clipboard as a desktop, put out one colored token (from the envelope) for each phoneme in the syllable. Check across group members. If all agree, move on. If they do not agree, then the teacher says the syllable one phoneme at a time, exaggerating the phoneme segments (modeling).

   common yellowthroat, Baltimore oriole, northern cardinal, house finch, song sparrow, American goldfinch

3. Electronic Bird Call each time the whole group gets it right the first time or after group reaches consensus.

Sounding Out Jabberwocky Words (Teacher-Guided Reading)

Say: Now we are going to put these automatic correspondences and awareness of sounds in spoken words to work to sound out Jabberwocky words, which are words you can pronounce but which have no meaning. Each of the spelling units that has a sound that goes with it is either underlined or is not underlined. The spelling units alternate between not underlined and underlined. However, note that the silent e spelling unit is one spelling unit with both the vowel and final e underlined. The consonant in between them is another spelling unit. Look at the spelling units and make the sound that goes with each one.

Then blend all the sounds together and pronounce the word. We will take turns. If anyone gets stuck, anyone in the group can help out. We will do Set 1 today.

Set 1	sm<u>ew</u>bry	tr<u>a</u>be	h<u>ai</u>fr<u>aff</u>
	pl<u>uce</u>	h<u>e</u>b<u>t</u>rou	s<u>oa</u>t<u>y</u>az
	pr<u>ite</u>	bl<u>e</u>sp	
	kn<u>elph</u>	n<u>i</u>m<u>oi</u>n	

Today we are going to start reading the book *Sequoyah: The Cherokee Man Who Gave His People Writing*. As we read and discuss this book, you will learn about Native Americans and about *linguistics*—the science of language. There is a picture of Sequoyah and a child on the front cover.

Who is the author? (pause for an answer.) *James Rumford*

Say: I will ask you to read certain pages silently for information or your thoughts about the text. Sometimes I will ask you to read a sentence or two out loud. Turn to the title page of the book.

Who is pictured here? (pause for the answer) *Sequoyah*

Find the title in English. Find the title in Cherokee.

Turn the page. Who translated this book into Cherokee? (pause for the answer) *Anna Sixkiller Huckaby*

Turn to the next page. To whom is the book dedicated? (pause for the answer) *Rumford's father*

Tell two interesting facts about this man. *He stopped to read every historic marker. He would have told this story.*

Turn to the next page. What is the setting for the story? Where did it take place? (pause for the answer) *California*

When did it take place? (pause for the answer) *1958*

About how long ago was that? (pause for the answer) *about 50 years*

Look at the illustration on the next page. What are the tall trees? *redwoods*

How old are they? *thousands of years*

What are they called? *giant Sequoias*

Where did the name come from? *Cherokee Indian man who lived when the United States was new*

Do you think Sequoia trees are named after the main character in the book we are reading? *yes*

How is the spelling of the trees and man different? *i versus y, and no ending h for the trees*

Why do you think the words are pronounced the same but spelled differently? Discuss how linguists (language scientists) discovered that there are many symbols of writing (spellings) that can stand for the same sounds in our speech. This is normal and not to be feared. Writing is talk written down.

Look at the story written in English. Look at the story written in Cherokee. How many languages can you speak? How many languages can you write?

Turn the page. Was Sequoyah famous? *yes*

But how is this qualified? Not in the way you might think. Try to explain what the author means. There are many different ways to be famous, not just Hollywood famous. Sequoyah was famous for having the redwood trees named after him. As we read more of the story we will learn more about why he was famous.

What does it mean that he "led his people" and was "tall and strong as the trees"? Does it mean he was a very tall man physically? What does it mean to use language figuratively? We call this *metaphor.* Can you think of different ways to lead and be strong?

Look at the next page. What do you think the Cherokee word at the top left of the page means? *It might mean Sequoia tree.*

Turn the page and look at the picture. Then read the text on the page beside it. Who do you think the man in the picture is? (pause) *Sequoyah*

What is he doing? *He is a metal worker.*

Where was he born? *Eastern Tennessee*

Find the first sentence that shows Sequoyah did not have an easy life. I will ask someone to read it out loud. This man Sequoyah was injured in an accident and disabled. Is there another sentence that explains other challenges? You can infer (make an educated guess) from the second sentence that he never knew his father. Students may also raise the issue of being biracial.

Find the sentence that tells some of the things Sequoyah built out of metal. *turned iron into chisels and drills and silver into forks and spoons*

(Ask someone to read the last sentence out loud.)

Turn the page. What do you think Sequoyah is thinking in the picture on this page? (Pause and take suggestions from different students.) *He is selling spoons and forks he made but he is looking at the man who is reading and writing English. He may be thinking that he could figure out a writing system for his spoken language, Cherokee.*

What do you think the Cherokee word at the top left hand of the picture might be? *It might mean forks or writing.*

Read the text on the next page. How was Sequoyah like a chief? (Ask someone to read that sentence out loud.) *He loved his people.*

Tell one thing Sequoyah wanted for his people. (Ask someone to read that sentence out loud.) *He wanted them to stand tall as any people.*

What does the metaphor *stand tall* mean on this page? *be proud*

Tell another thing that Sequoyah wanted for his people. (Ask someone to read that sentence out loud.) *He did not want them to disappear in the white man's world.*

Why do you suppose he thought the Cherokee might disappear? *Conflicts were occurring between Europeans and Indians as the Europeans spread west and took over their land.*

Tell yet another thing that Sequoyah wanted for his people. (Ask someone to read the sentence out loud.) *He did not want their Cherokee voices to fade away.*

What is one way to keep a voice from fading away? *convert voice to writing*

Compare the English and Cherokee writing systems on this page. Encourage students to discuss how the letters are alike and how they are different. Encourage students to explain that English speakers really cannot read Cherokee—not because they cannot look at the letters but because they do not know spoken Cherokee and how the letters stand for Cherokee speech. Help students to conclude that writing is talk written down in symbols. Reading requires translating the written symbols into speech. This is what linguistic science has taught us.

WRITTEN SUMMARIZATION AND JABBERWOCKY PROBES

Say: Now I would like you to take out the lined paper and write a summary of what we have just read and discussed about Sequoyah and the Cherokee language. In your summary include the main ideas of the story so far—the main points the author is making. Also include supporting details. While you are writing, the helpers will take you individually one at a time and ask you to read a list of Jabberwocky words. You will graph how many you can pronounce.

When you finish your written summary and have graphed how many Jabberwocky words in Set 1 you can pronounce, our first Sequoyah Writing Reader Club will be completed.

LESSON **2** | Sequoyah Writing Reader Club

WARM-UP

Say: Just like last time, we will start with our writing readers warm-up. Take out your *Talking Letters* card. This time we will do the consonant side of the card. Remember, we will program our brains by pointing to and naming a letter, naming the pictured word, and making the sound in it that goes with it. Usually the sound comes at the beginning, but sometimes in the middle, and is marked with one dot below or at the end and with two dots below. An *x* over a letter means the letter is silent. Again, we will time how long it takes us to do this and see if we can beat our time from last time. We are timing so that the correspondences between letters and sounds become automatic in your brain/mind.

Record the time on the posted growth graph and compare it with the time last time.

Say: Did you notice how many letters were in most of the letter units you named? (Pause and help the students discover that most were two-letter groups.) Explain that in English most of the predictability between talk and writing involves two-letter spelling units but sometimes involves one-letter spelling units.

Listening to Bird Names (Teacher-Guided Reading)

1. Count the number of syllables—hold up fingers (eyes closed). If all agree, move to the next bird name. If they do not all agree, then clap syllables and reach group consensus.

2. Count the number of phonemes in the pronounced syllable—do one syllable at a time in the bird's name. Using a clipboard as a desktop, put out one colored token (from the envelope) for each phoneme in the syllable. Check across group members. If all agree, move on. If they do not agree, then the teacher says the syllable one phoneme at a time, exaggerating the phoneme segments (modeling).

   red-winged blackbird, house sparrow, rock dove, black-capped chickadee, mourning dove, white-breasted nuthatch

3. Electronic Bird Call each time the whole group gets it right the first time or after the group reaches consensus.

Sounding Out Jabberwocky Words (Teacher-Guided Reading)

Say: Now we are going to put these automatic correspondences and awareness of sounds in spoken words to work to sound out Jabberwocky words, which are words you can pronounce but which have no meaning. Each of the spelling units that has a sound that goes with it is either underlined or is not underlined. The spelling units alternate between not underlined and underlined. However, note that the silent e spelling unit is one spelling unit with both the vowel and final e underlined. The consonant in between them is another spelling unit. Look at the spelling units and make the sound that goes with each one. Then blend all the sounds together and pronounce the word. We will take turns. If anyone gets stuck, anyone in the group can help out. We will do Set 2 today.

Set 2   y<u>ig</u>fr<u>ue</u>   qu<u>oo</u>pdr<u>o</u>   j<u>e</u>k<u>s</u>ie
             l<u>u</u>t<u>k</u>aw   gl<u>o</u>f<u>e</u>   sw<u>e</u>j<u>ee</u>ty
             cl<u>o</u>s<u>trills</u>   v<u>o</u>p<u>f</u>ow
             z<u>ull</u>cr<u>u</u>sk   gr<u>a</u>x

Say: Now we will read more in the book, *Sequoyah: The Cherokee Man Who Gave His People Writing*. Sometimes I will ask you to read a sentence or two out loud.

Look at the picture of Sequoyah and two men. What do you think this illustration shows? *human communication often involves talking*

Read the text on the next page. What did Sequoyah decide to do at 50? (Ask someone to read out loud the sentence that answers this question.) *capture the people's voice in writing*

Did Sequoyah speak English or read any language? (Ask someone to read the sentence out loud that answers these questions.) *no*

What did Sequoyah propose to do? Did the people believe him? (Ask someone to read the sentences out loud that answer these questions.) *write the language; no*

Compare the story on this page in English and in Cherokee. Do you think you as an English speaker could figure out how to create a writing system for Cherokee? Why or why not? Encourage students to share their opinions on these issues. Help them to understand that to develop a writing system one first needs to have knowledge of the spoken language.

Look at the top of the next page. What is Sequoyah doing in this picture? *trying to write the Cherokee spoken language in written symbols*

What do you think the words in Cherokee at the top left might mean? *they might mean Sequoyah drawing or writing*

Look at the next page. What did Sequoyah start writing? (Ask someone to read out loud the sentence that answers this question.) *one symbol for each word*

What did Sequoyah write on? (Ask someone to read the sentence out loud that answers this question.) *cabin shingles*

Turn the page. What do you think is happening in the picture? *People were talking about what Sequoyah was doing.*

Look at the text on the next page. What did the people think about what Sequoyah was doing? (Ask someone to read out loud a sentence that answers the question. Note that the first four sentences can be read out loud, each by a different student.)

What did the people decide to do to stop Sequoyah from writing down their spoken language? (Ask someone to read out loud a sentence that answers the question. Note that the last two sentences on the page can be read out loud.)

Look at the illustration on the next page. What is happening in the picture? Read the next page. What did the people do? (Ask someone to read out loud the sentence that answers this question.) *the people burned down his cabin*

Did Sequoyah learn the lesson that the people meant to teach him? What lesson did he learn? (Ask someone to read sentences out loud that answer these questions.) *Sequoyah learned a different lesson—disaster sometimes happens for a reason and sometimes it says follow a different path.*

What is the plot of a story? What does it mean that most plots in stories lead to some sort of conflict that needs to be resolved? What is the conflict in this story?

WRITTEN SUMMARIZATION AND JABBERWOCKY PROBES

Now I would like you to take out the lined paper and write a summary of what we have just read and discussed about Sequoyah and the Cherokee language. In your summary include the main ideas of the story so far—the main points the author is making. Also include supporting details. While you are writing, the helpers will take you individually one at a time and ask you to read a list of Jabberwocky words. You will graph how many you can pronounce.

When you finish your written summary and have graphed how many Jabberwocky words in Set 2 you can pronounce, our second Sequoyah Writing Reader Club will be completed.

LESSON **3** Sequoyah Writing Reader Club

Say: Just like last time, we will start with our writing readers' warm-up. Take out your *Talking Letters* card. This time we will do the vowel side of the card. I will say the kind of syllable the vowel letter is in (short, long, vowel team, *l*-controlled, *r*-controlled, or silent e). Remember, we will program our brains by pointing to and naming a letter, naming the pictured word, and making the sound in it that goes with it. Usually the sound comes at the beginning, but sometimes in the middle, and is marked with one dot below or at the end and with two dots below. An *x* over a letter means the letter is silent. Again we will time how long it takes us to do this and see if we can beat our time from last time. We are timing so that the correspondences between letters and sounds become automatic.

Record the time on the posted growth graph and compare it with the time last time and with the first time vowels were practiced.

Say: Did you notice how many letters were in most of the letter units you named? (Pause and help the students discover that most were two-letter groups.) Explain that in English most of the predictability between talk and writing involves two-letter spelling units but sometimes involves one-letter spelling units.

Listening to Bird Names (Teacher-Guided Reading)

1. Count the number of syllables—hold up fingers (eyes closed). If all agree, move to the next bird name. If they do not all agree, then clap syllables and reach group consensus.

2. Count the number of phonemes in the pronounced syllable—do one syllable at a time in the bird's name. Using a clipboard as a desktop, put out one colored token (from the envelope) for each phoneme in the syllable. Check across group members. If all agree, move on. If they do not agree, then the teacher says the syllable one phoneme at a time, exaggerating the phoneme segments (modeling).

   downy woodpecker, house wren, northern flicker, American robin, American crow, northern mockingbird

3. Electronic Bird Call each time the whole group gets it right the first time or after the group reaches consensus.

Sounding Out Jabberwocky Words (Teacher-Guided Reading)

Say: Now we are going to put these automatic correspondences and awareness of sounds in spoken words to work to sound out Jabberwocky words, which are words you can pronounce but which have no meaning. Each of the spelling units that has a sound that goes with it is either underlined or is not underlined. The spelling units alternate between not underlined and underlined. However, note that the silent e spelling unit is one spelling unit with both the vowel and final e underlined. The consonant in between them is another spelling unit. Look at the spelling units and make the sound that goes with each one. Then blend all the sounds together and pronounce the word. We will take turns. If anyone gets stuck, anyone in the group can help out. We will do Set 3 today.

Set 3	chunglewums	fladorudge	sceanruz
	whulls	wraltway	snubarth
	thermb	cimdaut	
	sligursheck	sognoy	

Say: Now we will read more in the book, *Sequoyah: The Cherokee Man Who Gave His People Writing*. Sometimes I will ask you to read a sentence or two out loud.

Look at the picture on the next page. Where else did you see this picture? *front cover*

Who do you think the girl is? We will learn this as we read the story today.

What do you think the words at the top mean? *They might mean* Girl reading to Sequoyah.

Read the next page. For each question I will ask one of you to read out loud sentences that answer the questions. How did Sequoyah change his approach after his cabin burned down? *He stopped writing a different symbol for every word.*

Why did he make this change? *too many marks and squiggles to remember*

What was his new plan? *invented letters to spell out the sounds of the language*

How many letters did he use altogether? *84*

When did the people stop laughing at him? *When his 6-year-old daughter Ayoka (in the picture) learned to read. See how her name was spelled.*

When did the people stop jeering at Sequoyah? What does *jeering* mean? Can you make up a sentence using the word *jeering*?

What are *warriors*? Can you make up a sentence using the word *warriors*?

Look at the picture on the next page. What do you think this picture illustrates?

What do you think the letters at the top of the page represent? *They might stand for Sequoyah's Syllabary.*

Read the text on the next page. How do you know that Sequoyah's writing system was a good one? *The people learned the Cherokee letters quickly. They started using them to read and write. They wrote notes to each other.*

Why do you think the spelling given for Sequoyah's name at the bottom of this page is different from the one on the back cover and some of the illustrations in the book?

How did the Cherokee people honor Sequoyah? *They gave him a silver medal in 1824.*

Explain how the conflict resolution occurred in the plot in this true story. What do we call true stories? *nonfiction*

What do we call made-up stories? *fiction*

WRITTEN SUMMARIZATION AND JABBERWOCKY PROBES

Now I would like you to take out the lined paper and write a summary of what we have just read and discussed about Sequoyah and the Cherokee language. In your summary, include the main ideas of the story so far—the main points the author is making. Also include supporting details. While you are writing, the helpers will take you individually one at a time and ask you to read a list of Jabberwocky words. You will graph how many you can pronounce.

When you finish your written summary and have graphed how many Jabberwocky words in Set 3 you can pronounce, our third Sequoyah Writing Reader Club will be completed.

LESSON **4** Sequoyah Writing Reader Club

WARM-UP

Say: Just like last time, we will start with our writing readers' warm-up. Take out your *Talking Letters* card. This time we will do the consonant side of the card. Remember, we will program our brains by pointing to and naming a letter, naming the pictured word, and making the sound in it that goes with it. Usually the sound comes at the beginning, but sometimes in the middle and is marked with one dot below or at the end and with two dots below. An *x* over a letter means the letter is silent. Again, we will time how long it takes us to do this and see if we can beat our time from last time. We are timing so that the correspondences between letters and sounds become automatic.

Record the time on the posted growth graph and compare it with the time last time and with the first time consonants were practiced.

Say: Did you notice how many letters were in most of the letter units you named? (Pause and help the students discover that most were two-letter groups.) Explain that in English most of the predictability between talk and writing involves two-letter spelling units but sometimes involves one-letter spelling units.

Listening to Bird Names (Teacher-Guided Reading)

Say: Now we are going to listen for and count the sounds in spoken words.

1. Count the number of syllables—hold up fingers (eyes closed). If all agree, move to next bird name. If they do not all agree, then clap syllables and reach group consensus.

2. Count the number of phonemes in the pronounced syllable—do one syllable at a time in the bird's name. Using a clipboard as a desktop, put out one colored token (from the envelope) for each phoneme in the syllable. Check across group members. If all agree, move on. If they do not agree, then the teacher says the syllable one phoneme at a time, exaggerating the phoneme segments (modeling).

   rock dove, black-capped chickadee, mourning dove, white-breasted nuthatch, downy woodpecker, house wren

3. Electronic Bird Call each time the whole group gets it right the first time or after the group reaches consensus.

Sounding Out Jabberwocky Words (Teacher-Guided Reading)

Say: Now we are going to put these automatic correspondences and awareness of sounds in spoken words to work to sound out Jabberwocky words, which are words you can pronounce but which have no meaning. Each of the spelling units that has a sound that goes with it is either underlined or is not underlined. The spelling units alternate between not underlined and underlined. However, note that the silent e spelling unit is one spelling unit with both the vowel and final e underlined. The consonant in between them is another spelling unit. Look at the spelling units and make the sound that goes with each one. Then blend all the sounds together and pronounce the word. We will take turns. If anyone gets stuck, anyone in the group can help out. We will do Set 4 today.

Set 4	kn<u>e</u>lph	bl<u>e</u>sp	swej<u>ee</u>ty
	qu<u>oo</u>pdro	clos<u>tri</u>ll<u>s</u>	pr<u>i</u>t<u>e</u>
	so<u>gn</u>oy	wh<u>ull</u>s	
	v<u>o</u>p<u>f</u>ow	ch<u>u</u>ng<u>lewu</u>ms	

Say: Now we will read more in the book, *Sequoyah: The Cherokee Man Who Gave His People Writing*. Sometimes I will ask you to read a sentence or two out loud.

Look at the illustration. What is shown in this picture? *printing press*

Read the next page. Who was Worcester? *a missionary*

What is a missionary? How did he help Sequoyah? *showed him how to use lead type to print the Cherokee writing*

Tell two outcomes of being able to print the Cherokee language? *1. They could print newspapers and books. 2. They could make sure that their words never faded away.*

Try pronouncing the four Cherokee words at the bottom of the page. The left shows how to pronounce the words written by the words themselves, and the right shows how to pronounce them with the Cherokee writing system by their syllables. Pause and then *say:* Congratulations! You have now learned to read Cherokee because you can translate those written syllables into spoken Cherokee!

Which way is the most efficient way to use written language as cues to spoken words? Help students see that phonemes are more efficient because fewer visual symbols are needed to write down all the words by syllables than by whole words.

Do you find it interesting that Sequoyah, with no formal education, used the same two ways to develop a writing system and in the same order as human civilizations over the past few thousand years? The progression was from words (pictographs or logographs) to syllabaries. Explain how each of these kinds of writing systems works.

Look at the illustration and then read the text on the next page that summarizes three kinds of disasters the Cherokee had to survive. What were the three disasters?

1. Soldiers (government) forced them from their lands. Where did they move to? *reservations*

    What are reservations?

2. Sickness. Explain how the Indians did not have immunity to viruses the Europeans introduced. What is *immunity*?

3. Children had to give up their native languages and move from their families' homes and attend boarding schools where only English was spoken.

    Which disaster do you think is illustrated in the picture to the left?

What survived all these disasters? *the Cherokee writing and their books did not fade away*

Discuss some of the advantages of spoken language. What are some of the disadvantages of spoken language?

Discuss some of the advantages of written language. What are some of the disadvantages of written language?

Find the pages with the giant sequoia trees and the text that begins with the question, "Who was this Sequoyah?" Tell the three answers to this question that the author gives.

1. He was a famous man. Why? *invented Cherokee alphabet*

2. He was a brave man. Why? *never gave up*

3. He was a leader. Why? *showed his people how to survive and be proud (stand tall)*

Look at the summary of the Cherokee alphabet. How many symbols are there? *77 pictured but apparently 84, according to the next page*

What is unique about the Cherokee writing system? *It is really a* syllabary—*a written symbol stands for a spoken syllable.*

How is this writing system different from written English? *We use an alphabetic writing system, in which 26 letters stand for about 44 sounds* (like we practice with Jabberwocky words).

WRITTEN SUMMARIZATION AND JABBERWOCKY PROBES

Now I would like you to take out the lined paper and write a summary of what we have just read and discussed about Sequoyah and the Cherokee language. In your summary, include the main ideas of the story so far—the main points the author is making. Also include supporting details. While you are writing, the helpers will take you individually one at a time and ask you to read a list of Jabberwocky words. You will graph how many you can pronounce.

When you finish your written summary and have graphed how many Jabberwocky words in Set 4 you can pronounce, our fourth Sequoyah Writing Reader Club will be completed.

| LESSON **5** | Sequoyah Writing Reader Club |

WARM-UP

Talking Letters Warm-Up: vowel side; time on wall chart

Listening to Bird Names

Say: Now we are going to listen for and count the sounds in spoken words.

1. Count the number of syllables—hold up fingers (eyes closed). If all agree, move to the next bird name. If they do not all agree, then clap syllables and reach group consensus.

2. Count the number of phonemes in the pronounced syllable—do one syllable at a time in the bird's name. Using a clipboard as a desktop, put out one colored token (from the envelope) for each phoneme in the syllable. Check across group members. If all agree, move on. If they do not agree, then the teacher says the syllable one phoneme at a time, exaggerating the phoneme segments (modeling).

   Willett, common tern, sanderling, black skimmer, European starling, brown-headed cowbird

3. Electronic Bird Call each time the whole group gets it right the first time or after the group reaches consensus.

Sounding Out Jabberwocky Words (Teacher-Guided Reading)

Say: Now we are going to put these automatic correspondences and awareness of sounds in spoken words to work to sound out Jabberwocky words, which are words you can pronounce but which have no meaning. Each of the spelling units that has a sound that goes with it is either underlined or is not underlined. The spelling units alternate between not underlined and underlined. However, note that the silent e spelling unit is one spelling unit with both the vowel and final e underlined. The consonant in between them is another spelling unit. Look at the spelling units and make the sound that goes with each one. Then blend all the sounds together and pronounce the word. We will take turns. If anyone gets stuck, anyone in the group can help out. We will do Set 5 today.

Set 5	he<u>rm</u>b	glo<u>fe</u>	plu<u>ce</u>
	ha<u>if</u>raff	tra<u>be</u>	sli<u>gu</u>rsh<u>ek</u>
	je<u>ks</u>ie	sme<u>wb</u>ry	
	so<u>at</u>yaz	fla<u>do</u>rudge	

Say: Now we will read more in the book, *Sequoyah: The Cherokee Man Who Gave His People Writing.* We will read to answer questions and discuss what a summary is.

What is a *summary*? Where does it usually appear? Read the summary of the story about Sequoyah on the next page.

What is a genius? Why was Sequoyah a genius?

Is Sequoyah a hero only among the Cherokee? For whom else is he a hero? *also all Americans*

Who was the first to describe the giant redwood trees now named *Sequoias?* *Endlicher*

What country was Endlicher from? *Austria in Europe*

What was he interested in? *language and writing systems*

Why do you think Endlicher named the giant redwoods *Sequoias*?

What is a legend? How do you separate fact and fiction?

Look at the next page. What were six facts about Sequoyah the man?

Look at the inside cover on the front, the inside cover of the back of the book, and the back cover of the book. What other information did you learn from the inside front cover that you could add to the summary of Sequoyah's life? How can a summary at the beginning aid the reader in understanding a story?

What did you learn about the author and translator from the inside back cover? Can you write Sequoyah's name the way it is on the back cover?

WRITTEN SUMMARIZATION AND JABBERWOCKY PROBES

Now I would like you to take out the lined paper and write a summary of what we have just read and discussed about Sequoyah and the Cherokee language. In your summary, include the main ideas of the story so far—the main points the author is making. Also include supporting details. While you are writing, the helpers will take you individually one at a time and ask you to read a list of Jabberwocky words. You will graph how many you can pronounce.

When you finish your written summary and have graphed how many Jabberwocky words in all eight sets you can pronounce, our fifth Sequoyah Writing Reader Club will be completed.

Culminating Activities

1. Read the following Cherokee Blessing together at the end of the Sequoyah unit and send it home with students:

> **Cherokee Prayer Blessing**
>
> May the Warm Winds of Heaven
> Blow softly upon your house.
> May the Great Spirit
> Bless all who enter there.
> May your Moccasins
> Make happy tracks
> in many snows,
> and may the Rainbow
> Always touch your shoulder.

2. Discuss what the students have learned about linguistics—the science of language—from Sequoyah and the story of the Cherokee written language.

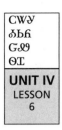

LESSON **6** Sequoyah Writing Reader Club

Photographic Leprechaun and Proofreaders' Trick—Lesson 1 in Unit II (Mark Twain's Spelling Lessons); and Relating Units and Sorts—Lesson 15 in Unit I (Word Detectives)

If You Lived with the Iroquois

Today we are going to begin to read a nonfiction book that provides an introduction to anthropology—the science of comparing cultures. You will have an opportunity to compare the culture of the Iroquois Indians in North America in the past with current culture of the diverse population living in North America at the beginning of the 21st century.

Say: Choral reading is a way a community can enjoy reading together. For each page we will begin with choral reading. The teacher will be like the choir director who takes the lead. The others will read along, keeping the pace and saying all the words aloud. Then, for each page we will summarize each of the pages orally. Please recall the strategy for summarizing: State the main ideas and all the supporting details.

Pages for choral reading and oral summarization: 80, 6–13

Summaries and Writing in Journals

First think of your Indian name. That will be your pen name. First, write a summary. Then start writing your thoughts about what you have just read.

At the end of each Club we will first write a summary of what was read that day. Here is a strategy for writing a summary:

1. Write the main idea.

2. Write all the details that support that main idea.

3. Use those notes to write an essay on the Language and Government of the Iroquois.

4. Write your opinions, thoughts, and questions that come to mind as you read in your journal.

Next, we will write in our journals. When we wrote summaries, you wrote about the main idea and supporting details for what the author wrote. When you write journals, you write your opinions, questions, and thoughts that come to mind as you read. In other words, it is like a conversation in which you take your turn and respond to what the author has written.

Later in the clubs we will use our journals to write a book report titled, *If You Lived with the Iroquois* to explain to others what the book is about and to share your opinions and thoughts about the book.

ORTHOGRAPHIC SPELLING PROBES FROM LESSON 1 IN MARK TWAIN'S SPELLING LESSONS (UNIT II)

Read Naturally

At the student's instructional level determined by oral reading speed, each student does a cold read, practices oral reading of the selection to a reading buddy, and does a hot read and graphs the reading rate.

LESSON **7** Sequoyah Writing Reader Club

WARM-UP

Photographic Leprechaun and Proofreaders' Trick—Lesson 2 in Mark Twain's Spelling Lessons (Unit II); and Relating Units and Sorts—Lesson 16 in Word Detectives (Unit I)

If You Lived with the Iroquois

Today we will continue reading a nonfiction book that provides an introduction to anthropology—the science of comparing cultures. You will have an opportunity to compare the culture of the Iroquois Indians in North America in the past with the current culture of the diverse population living in North America at the beginning of the 21st century.

Say: Choral reading is a way a community can enjoy reading together. For each page, we will begin with choral reading. The teacher will be like the choir director who takes the lead. The others will read along, keeping the pace and saying all the words aloud. Then, for each page, we will summarize each of the pages orally. Please recall the strategy for summarizing—state the main ideas and all the supporting details.

Pages for choral reading and oral summarization: 14–22

Summaries and Writing in Journals

Use your Indian name, which is your pen name for what you author in your journal. First, write a summary. Then start writing your thoughts about what you have just read.

At the end of each Club we will first write a summary of what was read that day. Here is a strategy for writing a summary:

1. Write the main idea.

2. Write all the details that support that main idea.

3. Use those notes to write an essay on Iroquois longhouses.

4. Write your opinions, thoughts, and questions that came to mind as you read in your journal.

Next, we will write in our journals. When we wrote summaries, you wrote about the main idea and supporting details for what the author wrote. When you write journals, you write your opinions, questions, and thoughts that come to mind as you read. In other words, it is like a conversation in which you take your turn and respond to what the author has written.

Later in the clubs we will use our journals to write book reports to share with others what the book is about and our opinions about it.

ORTHOGRAPHIC SPELLING PROBES FROM LESSON 1 IN MARK TWAIN'S SPELLING LESSONS (UNIT II)

Read Naturally

At the student's instructional level determined by oral reading speed, each student does a cold read, practices oral reading the selection to a reading buddy, and does a hot read and graphs the reading rate.

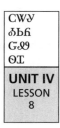

LESSON 8 Sequoyah Writing Reader Club

WARM-UP

Photographic Leprechaun and Proofreaders' Trick—Lesson 3 in Mark Twain's Spelling Lessons (Unit II) and Relating Units and Sorts in Lesson 17 in Unit I (Word Detectives)

If You Lived with the Iroquois

Today we will continue reading a nonfiction book that provides an introduction to anthropology—the science of comparing cultures. You will have an opportunity to compare the culture of the Iroquois Indians in North America in the past with the current culture of the diverse population living in North America at the beginning of the 21st century.

Say: Choral reading is a way a community can enjoy reading together. For each page, we will begin with choral reading. The teacher will be like the choir director who takes the lead. The others will read along, keeping the pace and saying all the words aloud. Then, for each page, we will summarize each of the pages orally. Please recall the strategy for summarizing—state the main ideas and all the supporting details.

Pages for choral reading and oral summarization: 23–31

Summaries and Writing in Journals

Use your Indian name, which is your pen name for what you author in your journal. First, write a summary. Then start writing your thoughts about what you have just read.

At the end of each Club we will first write a summary of what was read that day. Here is a strategy for writing a summary:

1. Write the main idea.

2. Write all the details that support that main idea.

3. Use those notes to write an essay on Iroquois longhouses.

4. Write your opinions, thoughts, and questions that came to mind as you read in your journal.

Next, we will write in our journals. When we wrote summaries, you wrote about the main idea and supporting details for what the author wrote. When you write journals, you write your opinions, questions, and thoughts that come to mind as you read. In other words, it is like a conversation in which you take your turn and respond to what the author has written.

Later in the clubs we will use our journals to write book reports to share with others what the book is about and our opinions about it.

ORTHOGRAPHIC SPELLING PROBES FROM LESSON 1 IN MARK TWAIN'S SPELLING LESSONS (UNIT II)

Read Naturally

At the student's instructional level determined by oral reading speed, each student does a cold read, practices oral reading the selection to a reading buddy, and does a hot read and graphs the reading rate.

EVALUATE RESPONSE TO INSTRUCTION

Did number of words in summaries increase from Lesson 1 to Lesson 8?

Did quality of summary (main idea + supporting details) improve from Lesson 1 to Lesson 8?

LESSON **9** Sequoyah Writing Reader Club

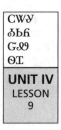

Photographic Leprechaun and Proofreaders' Trick—Lesson 4 in Mark Twain's Spelling Lessons (Unit II); and Relating Units and Sorts—Lesson 18 in Word Detectives (Unit I)

If You Lived with the Iroquois

Today we will continue reading a nonfiction book that provides an introduction to anthropology—the science of comparing cultures. You will have an opportunity to compare the culture of the Iroquois Indians in North America in the past with the current culture of the diverse population living in North America at the beginning of the 21st century.

Say: Choral reading is a way a community can enjoy reading together. For each page, we will begin with choral reading. The teacher will be like the choir director who takes the lead. The others will read along, keeping the pace and saying all the words aloud. Then, for each page, we will summarize each of the pages orally. Please recall the strategy for summarizing—state the main ideas and all the supporting details.

Pages for choral reading and oral summarization: 32–40

Summaries and Writing in Journals

Use your Indian name, which is your pen name for what you author in your journal. First, write a summary. Then start writing your thoughts about what you have just read.

At the end of each Club we will first write a summary of what was read that day. Here is a strategy for writing a summary:

1. Write the main idea.

2. Write all the details that support that main idea.

3. Use those notes to write an essay on Iroquois longhouses.

4. Write your opinions, thoughts, and questions that came to mind as you read in your journal.

Next, we will write in our journals. When we wrote summaries, you wrote about the main idea and supporting details for what the author wrote. When you write journals, you write your opinions, questions, and thoughts that come to mind as you read. In other words, it is like a conversation in which you take your turn and respond to what the author has written.

Later in the clubs we will use our journals to write book reports to share with others what the book is about and our opinions about it.

ORTHOGRAPHIC SPELLING PROBES FROM LESSON 1 IN MARK TWAIN'S SPELLING LESSONS (UNIT II)

Read Naturally

At the student's instructional level determined by oral reading speed, each student does a cold read, practices oral reading the selection to a reading buddy, and does a hot read and graphs the reading rate.

LESSON **10** Sequoyah Writing Reader Club

Photographic Leprechaun and Proofreaders' Trick—Lesson 5 in Mark Twain's Spelling Lessons (Unit II); and Relating Units and Sorts—Lesson 19 in Word Detectives (Unit I)

If You Lived with the Iroquois

Today we will continue reading a nonfiction book that provides an introduction to anthropology—the science of comparing cultures. You will have an opportunity to compare the culture of the Iroquois Indians in North America in the past with the current culture of the diverse population living in North America at the beginning of the 21st century.

Say: Choral reading is a way a community can enjoy reading together. For each page, we will begin with choral reading. The teacher will be like the choir director who takes the lead. The others will read along, keeping the pace and saying all the words aloud. Then, for each page, we will summarize each of the pages orally. Please recall the strategy for summarizing—state the main ideas and all the supporting details.

Pages for choral reading and oral summarization: 41–50

Summaries and Writing in Journals

Use your Indian name, which is your pen name for what you author in your journal. First, write a summary. Then start writing your thoughts about what you have just read.

At the end of each Club we will first write a summary of what was read that day. Here is a strategy for writing a summary:

1. Write the main idea.

2. Write all the details that support that main idea.

3. Use those notes to write an essay on Iroquois longhouses.

4. Write your opinions, thoughts, and questions that came to mind as you read in your journal.

Next, we will write in our journals. When we wrote summaries, you wrote about the main idea and supporting details for what the author wrote. When you write journals, you write your opinions, questions, and thoughts that come to mind as you read. In other words, it is like a conversation in which you take your turn and respond to what the author has written.

Later in the clubs we will use our journals to write book reports to share with others what the book is about and our opinions about it.

ORTHOGRAPHIC SPELLING PROBES FROM LESSON 1 IN MARK TWAIN'S SPELLING LESSONS (UNIT II)

Read Naturally

At the student's instructional level determined by oral reading speed, each student does a cold read, practices oral reading the selection to a reading buddy, and does a hot read and graphs the reading rate.

LESSON **11** Sequoyah Writing Reader Club

Photographic Leprechaun and Proofreaders' Trick—Lesson 6 in Mark Twain's Spelling Lessons (Unit II); and Relating Units and Sorts—Lesson 20 in Word Detectives (Unit I)

If You Lived with the Iroquois

Today we will continue reading a nonfiction book that provides an introduction to anthropology—the science of comparing cultures. You will have an opportunity to compare the culture of the Iroquois Indians in North America in the past with the current culture of the diverse population living in North America at the beginning of the 21st century.

Say: Choral reading is a way a community can enjoy reading together. For each page, we will begin with choral reading. The teacher will be like the choir director who takes the lead. The others will read along, keeping the pace and saying all the words aloud. Then, for each page, we will summarize each of the pages orally. Please recall the strategy for summarizing—state the main ideas and all the supporting details.

Pages for choral reading and oral summarization: 51–59

Summaries and Writing in Journals

Use your Indian name, which is your pen name for what you author in your journal. First, write a summary. Then start writing your thoughts about what you have just read.

At the end of each Club we will first write a summary of what was read that day. Here is a strategy for writing a summary:

1.   Write the main idea.

2.   Write all the details that support that main idea.

3.   Use those notes to write an essay on Iroquois longhouses.

4.   Write your opinions, thoughts, and questions that came to mind as you read in your journal.

Next, we will write in our journals. When we wrote summaries, you wrote about the main idea and supporting details for what the author wrote. When you write journals, you write your opinions, questions, and thoughts that come to mind as you read. In other words, it is like a conversation in which you take your turn and respond to what the author has written.

Later in the clubs we will use our journals to write book reports to share with others what the book is about and our opinions about it.

ORTHOGRAPHIC SPELLING PROBES FROM
LESSON 1 IN MARK TWAIN'S SPELLING LESSONS (UNIT II)

Read Naturally

At the student's instructional level determined by oral reading speed, each student does a cold read, practices oral reading the selection to a reading buddy, and does a hot read and graphs the reading rate.

LESSON **12** Sequoyah Writing Reader Club

Photographic Leprechaun and Proofreaders' Trick—Lesson 7 in Mark Twain's Spelling Lessons (Unit II); and Relating Units and Sorts—Lesson 21 in Word Detectives (Unit I)

If You Lived with the Iroquois

Today we will continue reading a nonfiction book that provides an introduction to anthropology—the science of comparing cultures. You will have an opportunity to compare the culture of the Iroquois Indians in North America in the past with the current culture of the diverse population living in North America at the beginning of the 21st century.

Say: Choral reading is a way a community can enjoy reading together. For each page, we will begin with choral reading. The teacher will be like the choir director who takes the lead. The others will read along, keeping the pace and saying all the words aloud. Then, for each page, we will summarize each of the pages orally. Please recall the strategy for summarizing—state the main ideas and all the supporting details.

Pages for choral reading and oral summarization: 60–70, 79

Summaries and Writing in Journals

Use your Indian name, which is your pen name for what you author in your journal. First, write a summary. Then start writing your thoughts about what you have just read.

At the end of each Club we will first write a summary of what was read that day. Here is a strategy for writing a summary:

1. Write the main idea.

2. Write all the details that support that main idea.

3. Use those notes to write an essay on Iroquois longhouses.

4. Write your opinions, thoughts, and questions that came to mind as you read in your journal.

Next, we will write in our journals. When we wrote summaries, you wrote about the main idea and supporting details for what the author wrote. When you write journals, you write your opinions, questions, and thoughts that come to mind as you read. In other words, it is like a conversation in which you take your turn and respond to what the author has written.

Later in the clubs we will use our journals to write book reports to share with others what the book is about and our opinions about it.

ORTHOGRAPHIC SPELLING PROBES FROM
LESSON 1 IN MARK TWAIN'S SPELLING LESSONS (UNIT II)

Read Naturally

At the student's instructional level determined by oral reading speed, each student does a cold read, practices oral reading the selection to a reading buddy, and does a hot read and graphs the reading rate.

LESSON **13**

Sequoyah Writing Reader Club

Culminating Session 1: Authors Writing a Book Report

This time, you have an opportunity to write a summary of your summaries—a book report about *If You Lived with the Iroquois.* Express your opinion and evaluation of the book. You may review all the journal entries you have made about the book in writing this report.

LESSON **14** Sequoyah Writing Reader Club

Culminating Session 2:
Authors Writing a Compare-and-Contrast Essay

Write a compare-and-contrast essay about life in an Iroquois village and life in your city in the year (current year).

LESSON **15** Sequoyah Writing Reader Club

Culminating Session 3: Authors Sharing Their Writing

Authors take turns reading their book reports and compare-and-contrast essays.

The teacher gives out Sequoyah Writing Reader certificates to each author for different aspects of reading, writing, and/or reading-writing in which each student has shown improvement during the course of the Sequoyah Writing Reader Workshop.

Also, the teacher might purchase one dream catcher kit from a web site (e.g., http://www .the7thfire.com/dream_catchers/dream_catcher_Kits.html). Students can learn about the Native American symbolism underlying dream catchers and construct their own.

MONITORING RESPONSE TO INSTRUCTIONAL INTERVENTION

Teachers can use a variety of data collected during the course of the writing-readers workshop to evaluate the effectiveness of the intervention for each individual student. Data that can be used for evidence of effectiveness include

1. Jabberwocky probes from Lesson 1 to Lesson 5: Does accuracy increase and time decrease?

2. Orthographic spelling probes from Lessons 6–12: Does accuracy increase?

3. *Reading Naturally* cold and hot readings: Are more words read in 1 minute?

4. Number of words in journal entries and essays: Does number increase?

5. Quality of writing in journal entries and essays: Does it improve? Is it grade-appropriate?

6. Quality of writing in the book report based on journal entries: Is it grade-appropriate?

7. Quality of writing in the compare-and-contrast essay in Lesson 14: Does it improve? Is it grade-appropriate?

INSTRUCTIONAL RESOURCES

BOOKS

Ihnot, C. (1997). *Read naturally*. St. Paul, MN: Turman Publishing.

Levine, E. (1999). *If you lived with the Iroquois* (80 pages). New York: Scholastic Paperbacks.

Rumford, J. (2004). *Sequoyah: The Cherokee man who gave his people writing* (32 pages). Boston: Houghton Mifflin's Children's Books. Translator: Anna Sixkiller Huckaby.

PAL *TALKING LETTERS* CARDS

Berninger, V.W. (1998). *Talking letters*. San Antonio, TX: Pearson Assessment.

PAL JABBERWOCKY WORD LISTS FOR PROBES

Berninger, V.W., & Abbott, S. (2003). *Reproducibles for PAL reading and writing lessons*. San Antonio, TX: Pearson Assessment.
List 12a, Sets 1–4, pp. 166–17; List 12b, Sets 1–4, pp. 182, 184, 186, and 188

BIRD NAMES (FIVE ELECTRONIC CARDS AND PLAYER)

For The Birds, Inc. (2000). *Birdsong Identiflyer audio birdsong dictionary,* P.O. Box 1731; Salem, SC 29676. http://www.identiflyer.com

Sequoyah Writing Reader Club Award

Awarded to

_____

for

_____

_____

_____

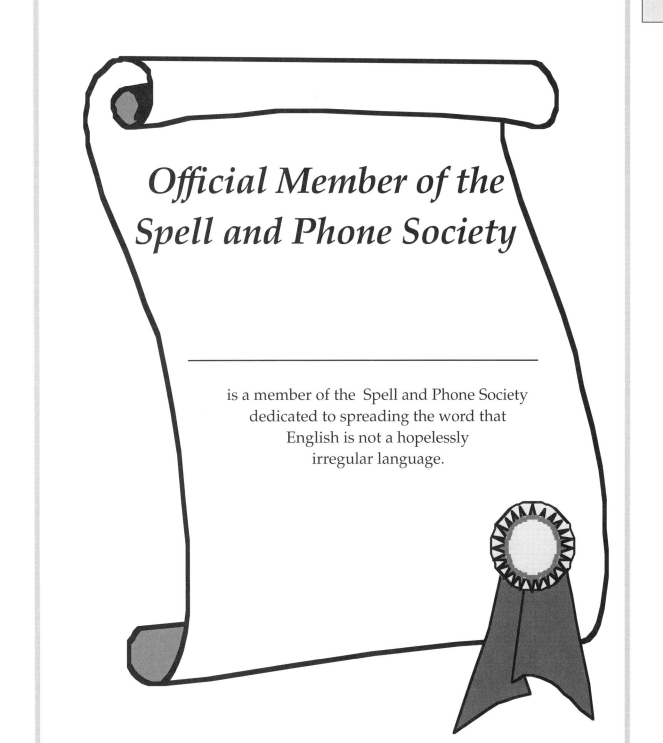

Official Member of the
Spell and Phone Society

_____

is a member of the Spell and Phone Society
dedicated to spreading the word that
English is not a hopelessly
irregular language.

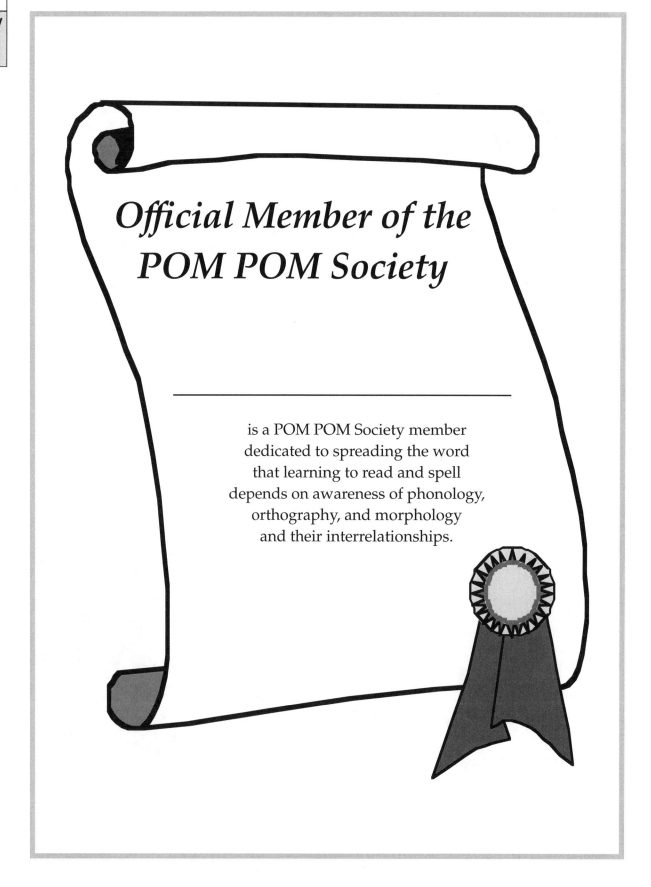

Official Member of the
POM POM Society

_____

is a POM POM Society member
dedicated to spreading the word
that learning to read and spell
depends on awareness of phonology,
orthography, and morphology
and their interrelationships.

DATE DUE

NOV 1 5 2012	
NOV. 0 8 2013	